ROBERT LOUIS STEVENSON, only child of Thomas
Stevenson, engineer and lighthouse-keeper, and Margaret
Balfour, daughter of a Scots minister, was born in Edinburgh in 1850. In 1871 he exchanged the study of
engineering for the law. From 1876 he pursued a full-
time literary career, beginning as an essayist and travel
writer with the publication of *An Inland Voyage* (1878),
Edinburgh: Picturesque Notes (1879), *Travels with a
Donkey in the Cévennes* (1879) and *Virginibus Puerisque*
(1881). He is probably best known for *Treasure Island*
(1883), *Kidnapped* (1886), and *The Strange Case of Dr.
Jekyll and Mr. Hyde* (1886). Stevenson travelled widely
on the Continent and in the South Seas, where he settled
in 1889–90 (*Catriona* was written at Vailima in Samoa)
until his death on 3 December 1894.

EMMA LETLEY has spent several years teaching litera-
ture at the University of Hong Kong and is currently
Visiting Lecturer at the Roehampton Institute in London.
She has edited R. L. Stevenson's *The Master of Ballantrae*
and *Treasure Island* for The World's Classics (1983,
1985).

THE WORLD'S CLASSICS

ROBERT LOUIS STEVENSON

Kidnapped

AND

Catriona

Edited with an Introduction by

EMMA LETLEY

Oxford   New York

OXFORD UNIVERSITY PRESS

Oxford University Press, Walton Street, Oxford OX2 6DP

Oxford New York
Athens Auckland Bangkok Bombay
Calcutta Cape Town Dar es Salaam Delhi
Florence Hong Kong Istanbul Karachi
Kuala Lumpur Madras Madrid Melbourne
Mexico City Nairobi Paris Singapore
Taipei Tokyo Toronto

and associated companies in
Berlin Ibadan

Oxford is a trade mark of Oxford University Press

Kidnapped first published 1886
Catriona first published 1893
First issued in one volume as a World's Classics paperback 1986

British Library Cataloguing in Publication Data

Data available

Library of Congress Cataloging in Publication Data
Stevenson, Robert Louis, 1850-1894.
Kidnapped; and, Catriona.
(The World's classics)
Bibliography: p.
Summary. A sixteen-year-old orphan is kidnapped by his villainous
uncle, but later escapes and becomes involved in the struggle of the
Scottish highlanders against English rule.
1. Scotland—History—18th century—Fiction.
[1. Adventure and adventurers—Fiction. 2. Scotland—
History—18th century—Fiction]. I. Letley, Emma.
II. Title: Kidnapped. III. Title: Catriona.
PR5481 L48 1968 823'.8 [Fic] 85-29667
ISBN 0-19-281726-4 (pbk.)

7 9 10 8 6

Printed in Great Britain by
BPC Paperbacks Ltd
Aylesbury, Bucks

CONTENTS

INTRODUCTION

> Mr. Stevenson is the Defoe of our generation. Since the days when 'Robinson Crusoe' first delighted English readers, no book of adventure has appeared that can pretend to rivalry with the story of 'Treasure Island' . . . It is high praise, therefore, of this new volume to say that it is no unworthy companion of 'Treasure Island'.[1]

So wrote a reviewer in the *St. James's Gazette* on the publication of *Kidnapped* in July 1886. It was, on the whole, very well-received, not only as a worthy successor to *Treasure Island* but also as a romance with an interest for an adult as well as a juvenile audience. Both the novels presented here occupy an important place in Stevenson's literary career: *Kidnapped*, as the last novel published before he left Scotland for good; and *Catriona*, as the last complete novel to come out before his death.

Stevenson was born in Edinburgh, the son of Thomas Stevenson and Margaret Balfour. Thomas Stevenson was a well-to-do harbour and lighthouse engineer, based in Edinburgh, and his son was educated at the Edinburgh Academy and University. Echoes of his Scottish background are frequent in both novels, and the city of Edinburgh plays an important part, especially in *Catriona*. But Stevenson could not remain in Scotland: by temperament a traveller, he was also prompted by ill health to journey extensively in search of more suitable climates. Initially he had intended to follow his father's profession and study engineering, but then he decided to read for the Bar and was admitted in 1875. He did not, however, practise as an advocate but rather kept to his decision, made in 1871, to pursue a literary career. In spite of the widespread success of *Treasure Island* (1883) and *Dr. Jekyll and Mr. Hyde* (1886) Stevenson was not, as a full-time

1 *Robert Louis Stevenson: The Critical Heritage*, ed. Paul Maixner (1981), p. 233.

writer, financially independent until he received an inheritance on his father's death in 1887.

He started writing *Kidnapped* at Bournemouth in March 1885; it was begun, he told the critic, Watts-Dunton, 'partly as a lark, partly as a pot-boiler'.[2] In the same month, James Henderson, editor of the magazine *Young Folks*, accepted Stevenson's proposal for another serial. It is interesting that he did so, because *Treasure Island*, for all its strengths, had not appealed very strongly to the youthful readers of Henderson's magazine; *The Black Arrow* had, however, fared rather better. In March, too, Stevenson wrote to W. E. Henley that he 'must tackle *Kidnapped* seriously, or be content to have no bread, which you would scarcely recommend. It is all I shall be able to do to wait for the Young Folk money, on which I'll have to live as best I can till the book comes in.' Henley suggested that plays might make his friend some much-needed money; but Stevenson, at this point, could not agree. The stage, not in any case his true medium, was but a 'lottery': 'In other words, I must go on and drudge at *Kidnapped*, which I hate, and am unfit to do . . . These are my cold and blighting sentiments. It is bad enough to have to live by an art—but to think to live by an art combined with commercial speculation—that way madness lies.'[3]

Although Henderson had accepted the idea for Stevenson's next serial, sustained work on *Kidnapped* did not proceed at once. His letters make no further mention of the novel until January 1886 (*Dr. Jekyll and Mr. Hyde* and sickness having occupied his time in the intervening period). By 25 January 1886, however, he had completed sixteen chapters. Thomas Stevenson had, as often with his son's literary plans, taken an active interest; he had been the most enthusiastic of listeners to the early chapters of *Treasure Island*, offering suggestions as to content and characterization. In the earlier

2 Roger G. Swearingen, *The Prose Writings of Robert Louis Stevenson: A Guide* (1980), p. 104.

3 *Letters*, XXIV, 146, 147 (all references to Stevenson's letters and essays refer to the Swanston Edition of the *Works of Robert Louis Stevenson*).

novel he had proposed that a kind of religious tract should be inserted in the Ben Gunn parts, and in January 1886, he suggested that 'a scene of religion' be included in *Kidnapped*. Stevenson responded warmly, and the results of his father's suggestion are found in the Mr Henderland sections in Chapter XVI (p. 98f.).

All went well with *Kidnapped* for a short time, but by April 1886 Stevenson could not continue with the book; illness had got the better of him and he wrote to his father that he had finally decided to take up a suggestion made by his friend Sidney Colvin: 'I am to leave the door open for a sequel if the public take to it, and this will save me from butchering a lot of good material to no purpose.'[4] In the event, *Kidnapped* (1886) had to wait until 1893 for its sequel, *Catriona*. Between the publication of the two books important changes had taken place in the author's life: his father had died in 1887, and in that year, he, his mother, and his wife, Fanny, had gone to the United States. In 1888 and 1889 they had voyaged around the South Seas, and it was there, in 1889, that Stevenson bought the estate at Upolu in Samoa where he built Vailima and lived until his death in 1894.

As early as May 1887, Stevenson had agreed with his publisher, Cassell, to write and deliver a book of about the same length as *Kidnapped* to be entitled *David Balfour*. The new book retained this title in the United States, but there was some confusion in Britain, where readers tended to think that this was just another name for *Kidnapped* and not a completely new novel. In British editions, therefore, it was re-titled *Catriona*—although the two-volume edition of 1895 and the Edinburgh Edition are both called *The Adventures of David Balfour*, with *Kidnapped* as Part I and *Catriona* as Part II.

Little further is heard of *Catriona* until September 1890, when Stevenson remarks to Henry James that one chapter is written; but then there is another delay in progress until October 1891 when he reports, again to Henry James, that

4 *Letters*, XXIV, 190.

it is 'on the stocks at last'.[5] By February 1892, his enthusiasm
for his new novel has become obvious:

Really I think it is spirited; and there's a heroine that (up to now)
seems to have attractions: *absit omen!* David, on the whole, seems
excellent. Alan does not come in till the tenth chapter, and I am
only at the eighth, so I don't know if I can find him again; but
David is on his feet, and doing well, and very much in love, and
mixed up with the Lord Advocate and the (untitled) Lord Lovat,
and all manner of great folk. And the tale interferes with my
eating and sleeping. The join is bad; I have not thought to strain
too much for continuity; so this part be alive, I shall be content.
But there's no doubt David seems to have changed his style, de'il
ha'e him! And much I care, if the tale travel![6]

On 2 March, fifteen chapters had been drafted; on 8 March
he was about half-way; and on 30 September he wrote to
Sidney Colvin:

David Balfour done, and its author along with it, or nearly so.
Strange to think of even our doctor here repeating his nonsense
about debilitating climate. Why, the work I have been doing the
last twelve months, in one continuous spate, mostly with
annoying interruptions and without any collapse to mention,
would be incredible in Norway.

Tired out as he was, Stevenson was nevertheless very pleased
with *Catriona*; as he said to Colvin, 'in fact these labours
of the last year—I mean *Falesá* [*The Beach of Falesa*, a short
story of the South Seas] and D.B., not Samoa, of course—seem
to me to be nearer what I mean than anything I have ever
done; nearer what I mean by fiction; the nearest thing before
was *Kidnapped*.'[7]

Although he dismissed it in writing to Colvin, Samoa un-
doubtedly plays a very important part in Stevenson's life
during the period of writing *Catriona*. Indeed, Fanny Stevenson comments that never was a novel composed 'in more distracting circumstances', a time 'With the natives on the verge

  5 *Letters*, XXV, 108.   6 *Letters*, XXV, 158.   7 *Letters*, XXV, 250.

of war, and amid the most kaleidoscopic political changes, uncertain as to what moment his personal liberty might be restrained, his every action misconstrued and resented by the white inhabitants of the island . . .'[8] A word of explanation is necessary here: during the time that *Catriona* was 'on the stocks', Stevenson became very much involved in Samoan politics, and he was in fact working on his book on the subject, *A Footnote to History*, at the same time as writing *Catriona*. Under the Berlin Convention of 1889 the island was divided between Germany, England and the United States. The native ruler, Malietoa Laupepa, previously deposed by the Germans, was reinstated, and his very popular kinsman, Mataafa, was excluded from rule. After a time, fierce rivalry arose between the two. In 1891, two officials, one Swedish and one German, came to Samoa and antagonized both the white and the native populations. In this troubled situation, Stevenson not only made it his business to obtain as much as possible of the inside story from those involved but also wrote letters to *The Times* deploring the high-handed treatment of the Samoan problem.[9] It was thus in a very different atmosphere from that of Bournemouth in 1885–6 that *Catriona* was written and published, and the Samoan influence is reflected in various aspects of the novel, resulting in a rather more sombre atmosphere than in *Kidnapped*. The different circumstances of composition account in part for a certain disparity between the two novels.

In *Catriona*, David remarks that in the guise of brother and sister, he and Catriona 'made a most uneven pair' (p. 413). Are the two books themselves, we might ask, an 'uneven pair?' Stevenson himself was aware of a certain lack of continuity and a little worried by the joins, both between the two novels and within *Catriona* itself. *Kidnapped*, despite

8 'Prefatory Note by Mrs. R. L. Stevenson', *The Works of Robert Louis Stevenson*, Tusitala Edition, VII, xv.

9 For further information on Stevenson's involvement in Samoa see *Letters From Samoa* in *In The South Seas* and *Letters from Samoa*, Swanston Edition, XVIII.

its appeal for adults, was written primarily as a boys' adventure tale; *Catriona*, although rather oddly placed with the girls' magazine *Atalanta*, is not predominantly a juvenile story but a historical romance with a conventional romantic plot and carefully constructed female characters. An account of certain aspects of the two novels does, however, show important links.

Both *Kidnapped* and *Catriona* have their genesis in Scotland and Scottish history, both in their characterization and in their employment of Scottish historical fact. Henry James remarked of Stevenson, 'We know very little about a talent till we know where it grew up, and it would halt terribly at the start any account of the author of *Kidnapped* which should omit to insist promptly that he is a Scot of the Scots.'[10] Stevenson was fascinated by Scottish history throughout his life, and in October 1881 had become most involved with the Appin Murder; he had even suggested to his father that he could write 'The Murder of Red Colin, A Story of the Forfeited Estates' as part of his application for the Professorship of History and Constitutional Law at Edinburgh University (a somewhat unlikely scheme, given his reputation as a student, that, unsurprisingly, came to nothing). His interest continued, and the person of Alan Breck and the shooting of Colin Campbell are both based on fact, as is the trial of James of the Glens which forms the basis of Part I of *Catriona*.[11]

In considering the part that history plays in *Kidnapped* as a boys' story we can take note of David's own comments in the text. In Chapter XXV, after the singing contest between Alan Breck and Robin Oig, he writes:

10 *Henry James and Robert Louis Stevenson*, ed. J. Adam Smith (1948), p. 139.

11 For the historical background to both novels, see F. W. C. Hersey (ed.), *Robert Louis Stevenson's 'Kidnapped'. Followed by Who Killed the Red Fox?* (Boston, 1938), and David N. MacKay, *The Appin Murder: The Historical Basis of 'Kidnapped' and 'Catriona'* (Edinburgh, 1911). A recent critical discussion is found in Andrew Noble, 'Highland History and Narrative Form in Scott and Stevenson', in *Robert Louis Stevenson*, ed. Andrew Noble (1983), pp. 134–87.

It was the last I saw of him, for I was in the Low Countries at the University of Leyden, when he stood his trial, and was hanged in the Grassmarket. And I have told this at so great length, partly because it was the last incident of any note that befell me on the wrong side of the Highland Line, and partly because (as the man came to be hanged) it's in a manner history [pp. 172-3, and see note, p. 482 below].

'In a manner history' is an apt description of the way in which historical matter is used in the text. The details are there and carefully authenticated but they are almost always secondary to the adventure story itself. David tells the Robin Oig story mainly because it was the last of his personal adventures, and, almost as an afterthought, for its historical importance. His view of what makes history ('the man came to be hanged') is that of a boy recounting an adventure story not that of an historical commentator. Similarly, at Stirling Castle, he writes: 'I looked upon it, not only as a place famous in history, but as the very doors of salvation to Alan and myself' (p. 174). The focus is on the actions and events in David's life not on the movements of history.

Whilst the use of history in *Kidnapped* is but 'in a manner' historical, so too, we could say, the novel's setting is 'in a manner' geographical. The book is much more firmly located in the real world than is the imaginary isle of *Treasure Island*; and the Scottish places, some of them visited and explored by the young Stevenson, certainly live most vividly for the reader. Indeed, one of the book's great strengths is the immediacy of its physical descriptions in sections such as 'The Islet' (p. 82f.). This said, however, Scotland is as much a psychological as a geographical place. The way the Highland Line is used clarifies this. Crossing it, towards the end of the novel, David returns to his 'own land' (p. 174). In the text's careful plotting, David has to leave his enclosed, inland, Lowland environment to go to sea and be cast up on an alien, Highland coastline with people whose language (Gaelic) he does not know and whom he finds both strange and, at times, near-savage. The Highlands and the 'wrong side' of the Highland Line become the testing place for the hero of romance, and in psychological terms their precise location is not of primary importance.

The use of history and of setting both contribute to *Kidnapped*'s strength as an adventure story. Discussing romance with Henry James, Stevenson laid stress on two qualities vital to the 'elementary novel of adventure': 'Danger is the matter with which this class of novel deals; fear, the passion with which it idly trifles; and the characters are portrayed only so far as they realise the sense of danger and provoke the sympathy of fear.'[12] *Kidnapped*'s clear-cut structure is designed to give maximum scope to this 'matter' and this 'passion': it is this fact, above all, that makes the book a worthy successor to *Treasure Island*.

There is, first of all, an emphasis on the strange and the unknown in the build-up to David's arrival at the House of Shaws, found in the curses of Janet Clouston and in the disquieting responses of those from whom he asks directions. Then, the place itself is worryingly decayed and incomplete, constructed to provoke unease:

So I set forward by a little faint track in the grass that led in my direction. It was very faint indeed to be the only way to a place of habitation; yet I saw no other. Presently it brought me to stone uprights, with an unroofed lodge beside them, and coats of arms upon the top. A main entrance, it was plainly meant to be, but never finished; instead of gates of wrought iron, a pair of hurdles were tied across with a straw rope . . .

The nearer I got to that, the drearier it appeared. It seemed like the one wing of a house that had never been finished. What should have been the inner end stood open on the upper floors . . . [pp. 8–9].

'Was this the palace I had been coming to?' asks David in some bewilderment. The faint path and unfinished house look forward, with an acute sense of timing on Stevenson's part, to the moment of greatest danger for David when Ebenezer sends him to the top of the tower with its incomplete staircase. There is here real, physical danger; but, as in *Treasure Island*, this tends to be unobtrusively controlled. This is one

12 'A Humble Remonstrance', IX, 155.

very obvious function of having a first person narrator in a boys' story: the reader knows that the protagonist has, after all, lived to tell, write and indeed publish the tale; the form offers its own kind of reassurance. In *Treasure Island* moments of potentially intolerable fear are defused when the hero falls asleep or is knocked senseless; this also happens in *Kidnapped* when David is knocked unconscious on the *Covenant* (p. 36. This was another of Thomas Stevenson's suggestions). Also, like Jim Hawkins, David has 'many thoughts of far voyages and foreign places', and the excitement generated by them tends to counterbalance the danger inherent in the tale. Interestingly, for all the thoughts of foreign places, *Kidnapped* never actually leaves Scotland and Scotland's coastline. David muses about Carolina and of 'slaving alongside of negroes in the tobacco fields' (p. 48); but this is fantasy, and he remains, at this time, below deck off the Scottish shores.

The reader sees David's story in a definite context—that of the ballad, a popular form with a limited action or actions, much dialogue, an impersonality of attitude (in particular, of moral attitude), and, above all, a story. Ballad references are interspersed throughout the novel (cf. the use of songs in *Catriona*).[13] In Chapter IV, at the House of Shaws, David is reminded of 'a story like some ballad I had heard folk singing, of a poor lad that was a rightful heir and a wicked kinsman that tried to keep him from his own' (p. 19). Mr Riach pronounces David's story, 'like a ballad' (p. 43); and talking with Alan, after the murder of the Red Fox, David reflects:

Of all deaths, I would truly like least to die by the gallows; and the picture of that uncanny instrument came into my head with extraordinary clearness (as I had once seen it engraved at the top of a pedlar's ballad) and took away my appetite for courts of justice [p. 115].

Here, there is immediate fear of the gallows, but this is, almost at once, turned back into a story, into something

13 See W. W. Robson, 'On *Kidnapped*' in *Stevenson and Victorian Scotland* ed. Jenni Calder (1981) pp. 88–106.

which David has seen on a 'pedlar's ballad'; it is part of his memory not of his future. He is, in fact, rather fond of defining himself in these terms as, when stranded on the wrong side of the Firth of Forth, he comments: 'A moment back, and I had seen myself knocking at Mr. Rankeillor's door to claim my inheritance, like a hero in a ballad; and here was I back again, a wandering, hunted blackguard, on the wrong side of Forth' (p. 175). Right at the end of the novel, he sees himself as 'the beggar in the ballad | who | had come home' (p. 204).

David also likes to *re*-write his story; this has a double effect, seen in the following passage when, ill and frightened, he comments:

. . . and when I slept in my wet bed, with the rain beating above and the mud oozing below me, it was to live over again in fancy the worst part of my adventures—to see the tower of Shaws lit by lightning, Ransome carried below on the men's backs, Shuan dying on the round-house floor, or Colin Campbell grasping at the bosom of his coat [p. 160].

The reader here is reminded of the highlights of David's adventures; he is asked, too, to remember that this is a story, a self-consciously constructed narrative; and he sees David, like Stevenson himself, making the events and places into a tale: 'By what I have read in books, I think few that have held a pen were ever really wearied, or they would write of it more strongly' (p. 145).

The moral impersonality that is connected with the ballad form is also found in *Kidnapped*, especially in the treatment of Alan Breck. Like Jim in *Treasure Island*, David has to make a choice. Just as Jim has to decide between Silver and the Cabin Party so David has to choose between Alan and the Captain of the *Covenant*. He has to opt either for his Whiggish heritage or for Alan's 'lawless' Jacobitism. The issue of moral dilemma is crucial to Stevenson's ideas on adventure stories. In an essay on Dumas, he writes, 'There is no quite good book without a good morality; but the world is wide, and so are morals.'[14] David has to come to appreciate this

14 'A Gossip on Dumas's Novels', IX, 129.

breadth of morality. He begins his adventures with the principles of a good Kirk-going, Lowland Scot, with his Bible in his pocket, and strong ideas about loyalty to King George, the sin of deserting the Royalist Army, and the inherent wrong of card-playing. Much of his value system is challenged by Alan Breck, and it is he who puts the case most succinctly: '. . . you Low-country bodies have no clear idea of what's right and wrong' (p. 115). In the course of the story, David comes to understand something of the complexity of Alan's own morality, and this (in *Kidnapped*, although not in *Catriona*) effectively solves the dilemma for him.

Setting and history in *Kidnapped* are thus both clearly influenced by Stevenson's Scottish background; and he wanted, too, to make his novel decidedly Scots in style. Although James Henderson, editor of *Young Folks*, had warned him against too much broad Scots for a young audience, Stevenson felt that Scots language was vital to his book. He wrote to Charles Baxter:

What's mair, Sir, it's Scotch: no strong, for the sake o' they pork-puddens [pock-puddens?], but jist a kitchen o't, to leeven the wersh, sapless, fushionless, stotty, stytering South Scotch they think sae muckle o'. Its name is Kidnaaaapped; or Memoyers of the Adventyers of David Balfour in the Year Seeventeen Hunner and Fifty Wan.[15]

He also wrote to a French translator of his work, warning quite specifically about 'Scotticisms used deliberately' both in *The Master of Ballantrae* and in *Kidnapped*,[16] and he guarded them closely from such friends and editors as Sidney Colvin who were inclined to standardize his language. In the novel there are many significant uses of Lowland Scots: David maintains a consistent relationship with his Scots roots both in dialogue and in narrative touches (some of these are detailed

15 RLS: *Stevenson's Letters to Charles Baxter*, ed. De Lancey Ferguson and Marshall Waingrow (1956), pp. 165–6. I am indebted to Dr. Douglas Mack for suggesting the reading 'pock-puddens': a jocular or pejorative nickname for an Englishman (also a steamed pudding cooked in a muslin bag).

16 *Letters*, XXV, 52.

in the Notes to pp. 131, 269). In the fluctuations of their friendship, David and Alan are marked out by a Scots-English contrast which expresses distance or distaste. At other times, their shared Lowland Scots dialect stresses their good feelings for one another.[17] It is important that Stevenson did not give Alan 'Highland English' and David, Lowland Scots as he might, realistically, have done; this prevents his reader from making too simple, and simplistic, a differentiation between them, as does the writer's comment to J. M. Barrie that he intentionally gave David 'a Gaelic name'.[18]

Kidnapped is singled out from most boys' fiction of the period by its uses of Scots. The most usual practice in texts for a young audience is for the author to employ mainly Standard English, a habit designed to comply or collude with market pressures and to appease the sensibilities of the parent inevitably casting a watchful eye over the author's shoulder. Where non-Standard forms of language are used, these tend to be the mark of a villain or, at best, an unsympathetic character. Women or girl characters, unless they are servants, tend not to use dialectal forms; as the daughters of fictional heroines descended from Richardson's Clarissa, or Dickens's Lizzie Hexam, women distinguished alike for their linguistic and their moral purity, it would be very odd if they did. *Kidnapped* stands almost alone as a children's story which makes serious use of Scots; other contemporary Scots children's writers are much more circumspect—George Mac-Donald, William Black and S. R. Crockett are examples.

Catriona shares with *Kidnapped* a particular moment of Scottish history, a Scots setting, and Lowland Scots language; and, perhaps most importantly, it shares a hero, who, although he may have 'changed his style', is recognizably the 'Mr. Betwixt and Between' of the earlier novel. And yet, at the start of the novel, we find that David is in a rather different setting; he has quite clearly left behind him the place of his boyish excitements:

17 See Note to p. 163 and Mildred Wilsey, '*Kidnapped* in Manuscript', *The American Scholar*, New York, XVII (Spring 1948), 213–20.
18 *Letters*, XXV, 155.

My youth, as I have told you, was already inured to dangers; but such danger as I had seen the face of but that morning, in the midst of what they call the safety of a town, shook me beyond experience. Peril of slavery, peril of shipwreck, peril of sword and shot, I had stood all of these without discredit; but the peril there was in the sharp voice and the fat face of Simon, properly Lord Lovat, daunted me wholly [pp. 261–2].

Catriona is a much more political book than its predecessor; its use of history is both angrier and more analytic, its 'perils' of a much more complex kind than the 'fears and dangers' of *Kidnapped*. The stress in Part I has moved away from the stock-in-trade of adventure towards intrigue and corruption. Stevenson had a copy of the *Trial of James of the Glens*, the 'blessed little volume' bought for him by his father in 1881,[19] and he makes careful use of its details. David is gradually drawn into events which have far greater and more subtle reverberations in the political world than anything he encounters in *Kidnapped*. Prestongrange's reasons for not accepting David's evidence (p. 245f.), and David's deliberations as to his own motivation—a far more extended piece of self-searching than anything we find in *Kidnapped* (p. 232f.)—are indications of this. In order to placate the Campbells, James of the Glens must be made a scapegoat whatever the available evidence; the trial is thus merely a formal exercise with a predetermined outcome. For David, it is a process that 'had the externals of a sober process of law, [but] was in its essence a clan battle between savage clans' (p. 346).

In presenting this material, Stevenson's view is coloured not only by his knowledge of Scottish history but also by his Samoan experiences; *Catriona* is, in part, a different kind of novel from *Kidnapped* precisely because of *where* it was written. The concerns that inform *Catriona* are also crucial to *A Footnote to History*. Some examples from the latter suggest the connections. In 1885, the colonial powers ruling Samoa drew up a document giving a council of two Germans and two Samoans the power to make laws and to impose

19 *Letters*, XXV, 351.

taxes.[20] The Samoans were denied the opportunity of seeing the document. Compare this with the suppression of James More's evidence in *Catriona* (p. 358). A *Footnote*, too, is crucially concerned with the ways in which politics, rhetoric and biassed judges cloud the process of justice. The following passage, in particular, shows the cross-fertilization between *Catriona* and Stevenson's Samoan book:

On the evening of the Emperor's birthday, March 22nd, 1887, certain Germans were congregated in a public bar. The season and the place considered, it is scarce cynical to assume they had been drinking; nor, so much being granted, can it be thought exorbitant to suppose them possibly in fault for the squabble that took place. A squabble, I say; but I am willing to call it a riot. And this was the new fault of Laupepa; this it is that was described by a German commodore as 'the trampling upon by Malietoa of the German Emperor.' I pass the rhetoric by to examine the point of liability. Four natives were brought to trial for this horrid fact: not before a native judge, but before the German magistrate of the tripartite municipality of Apia.[21]

There is a comparison here between the kinds of events that Stevenson was witnessing in Samoa and those at James's trial in *Catriona*. James, too, is tried not by his own people of Appin, but by their hostile and long-time enemies, the Campbells; and he also is involved in a legal situation much distorted by public rhetoric. Whilst it would be naive to take these parallels too far (given the vast differences in social organization and government between eighteenth-century Scotland and nineteenth-century Samoa), it is clear that the matters that angered Stevenson in A *Footnote* find their way also into Part I of *Catriona*. The sober note of the opening chapters of the Scottish novel reflects something of Stevenson's disquiet at the colonial carve-up of the South Sea islands.

He was, whilst writing both A *Footnote* and *Catriona*, often haunted by Scotland, and this is a recurrent note in his

20 A *Footnote to History*, XVII, 30.
21 Ibid., p. 41.

correspondence during the period, as in this comment to
J. M. Barrie: 'It is a singular thing that I should live here
in the South Seas under conditions so new and so striking,
and yet my imagination so continually inhabit that cold old
huddle of grey hills from which we come.'[22] In *Catriona*, however, the 'cold old huddle of grey hills' has given way mainly
to the city and an exploration of city experience, an area
absent from the rugged terrain of *Kidnapped*. From Samoa,
Stevenson contrives to make Edinburgh come extraordinarily
alive from the first paragraphs of the novel: 'The tall, black
city, and the numbers and movement and noise of so many
folk made a new world for me, after the moorland braes, the
sea-sands and the still country-sides that I had frequented
up to then' (p. 215). It is for David a 'new world' of man-made
structures, and the manner in which the town is described
immediately makes it an appropriate setting for political
intrigue: it is 'for all the world like a rabbit-warren, not only
by the number of its indwellers, but the complication of its
passages and holes' (p. 216).

In *Catriona*, the main division found in *Kidnapped* between
Lowland and Highland is replaced by that between Scotland
and Holland, with Holland becoming the strange place of
romance for the protagonists and also the place of their
romantic fulfilment. In much Victorian fiction, sexual
passion is not realized on home ground; the place of passion
tends to be on the Continent, as in Charlotte Brontë's *Villette*
or Elizabeth Barrett's *Aurora Leigh*.[23] Although *Catriona* is
far from sexually explicit (it is barely even suggestive), there
is a sense that Stevenson (and certainly David Balfour) is more
assured in writing about passion once he has moved his
characters safely away from Scottish soil.

When the text leaves Scotland, its genre undergoes a
certain change: in one sense it reverts to the simpler forms
of romance, with Holland as the 'outlandish' place (found in
the Highlands of Scotland in *Kidnapped*); in another way, it

22 *Letters*, XXV, 264.
23 An interesting discussion of this is found in Elizabeth Barrett,
Aurora Leigh, and Other Poems (1978), introduction by Cora Kaplan.

becomes a more traditional love story than the reader tends to expect from the serious political import of Part I, and the historical issues raised in that section. In the 'Father and Daughter' chapters, we find a conventional romantic plot, with a series of difficulties and obstacles to be overcome before the characters can reach the predetermined goal of marriage. Alan makes only a brief appearance, primarily in the role of confidant to David rather than Jacobite adventurer, and the Appin Murder has largely receded into a far-distant background.

In this second part, there is little coincidence between *A Footnote* and *Catriona*; and, interestingly, there is much less stress on Scotland (even as a place in the imaginative sense). In my view the strongest parts of *Catriona* are those where there is the greatest similarity between the two books. Nowhere in *Catriona* is the writer's relationship with Scotland so clear as in the 'Tale of Tod Lapraik'; and there is here a vital point of parallel interest in *A Footnote*. In the section covering the years 1888-9, Stevenson describes the Samoans awaiting the arrival of the Berlin Convention's commissioners:

Months passed, these angel-deliverers still delayed to arrive, and the impatience of the natives became changed to an ominous irritation. They have had much experience of being deceived, and they began to think they were deceived again. *A sudden crop of superstitious stories buzzed about the islands.* Rivers had come down red; unknown fishes had been taken on the reef and found to be marked with menacing runes; a headless lizard crawled among chiefs in council . . . *And doubtless such fabrications are, in simple societies, a natural expression of discontent; and those who forge, and even those who spread them, work towards a conscious purpose.*[24]

Here the 'crop of superstitious stories' arises during a time of anxiety, waiting and discontent; the 'Tod Lapraik' tale, similarly, appears at a very appropriate moment in the narrative when David is waiting imprisoned on the Bass Rock, in

24 *A Footnote*, op. cit., p. 160 (my italics).

considerable anxiety, to see if he will be able to escape in time for James of the Glens's trial at Inverary. The tale of 'Tod Lapraik' allows the reader to share in this process of waiting (the references to Lady Grange [see Notes to pp. 285, 314, 347] highlight this also). In the case of Samoa, Stevenson suggested that those who made and perpetuated the superstitious stories 'work[ed] towards a conscious purpose'; so, too, is there a purpose behind Stevenson's inclusion of this tale in *Catriona*. Two comments made by David Balfour suggest what this may be. Shortly after the trial he remarks, 'It must be owned the view I had taken of the world in these last months was fit to cast a gloom upon my character' (p. 359). He has been much disillusioned, having seen intrigue and dissimulation at their worst. The tone of 'Tod Lapraik' is in keeping with the resulting 'gloom'. Later still, he looks back once more at the trial and comments that 'the villains of that horrid plot were decent, kind, respectable fathers of families, who went to kirk and took the sacrament!' (pp. 382–3).

Throughout his life Stevenson was fascinated by duality and doubleness; and, as we know from A *Footnote*, he was at the time of writing *Catriona* currently interested in the way that superstitious thinking tends to arise at certain moments in history—times especially of waiting and anxiety before the intervention of a controlling authority. In this sense, 'Tod Lapraik' is the equivalent of the red rivers, unknown fishes and headless lizard of Samoan folklore. It is a superstitious tale of duality par excellence, with a hero who is part weaver, part incubus; it is a very chilling story indeed, brilliantly conveying the atmosphere of the Bass Rock; it expresses the teller's (Black Andie's) combination of rationalism and superstition; it gives credibility to the fears of the Highlanders who guard the rock prison; and, on an imaginative level, it underlines David's fears at this crucial point in the narrative. The immediate power of the story does not derive from advancing the plot (any more than the Samoans' tales accelerate the arrival of the commissioners sent by the Berlin Convention) but from its psychological effects, and, in particular, from its exploration of the *unco*, the strange and uncanny. It both holds up the narrative (which is sound both in artistic and in psychological terms) and occasions a rift between Andie and the Highlanders which, in turn, prompts Andie to act on David's behalf.

The broader Scots of the tale gives 'Tod Lapraik' a vital place in the language plot of *Catriona* and, once more, Stevenson's contemporary preoccupations in *A Footnote* are not irrelevant:

I am asking what will be understood by a Samoan studying their literary work, the Berlin Act; I am asking what is the result of taking a word out of one state of society, and applying it to another, of which the writers know less than nothing, and no European knows much. Several interpreters and several days were employed last September in the fruitless attempt to convey to the mind of Laupepa the sense of the word 'resignation'. What can a Samoan gather from the words, *election? election of a king? election of a king according to the laws and customs of Samoa?*[25]

Here, Stevenson's concern is with a legal language that is inadequate to convey ideas to the Samoans—the written, formal words ('literary work') mean little to the people to whom they are addressed. The 'Tod Lapraik' tale, too, questions the adequacy of formal, written (and often anglicized) language. In *Catriona*, the Scots of the 'Tod Lapraik' tale takes up earlier uses of the language, such as Auld Merren's predictions (p. 234), and wins an imaginative victory over Standard, literary English. Scots becomes the register of an alternative morality and a different way of looking at the issues raised by the novel. Charles Stewart's excitement about the ignominious way the trial is conducted is thus expressed in Scots (pp. 283–4) but the judgement, effectively murder, is given in English—the English of the Chief of the Campbells (p. 357). This anglicized legal language has as little relevance to the true facts of the case as the Standard English of the Berlin Convention's documents have to the realities of Samoa.

'Tod Lapraik' is very much an oral piece (it gains much from being read aloud); so, too, are the songs which appear after the trial (pp. 357–8). Songs, of course, feature in *Kidnapped*; there are the generalized and reassuring ballad references discussed above, and Jacobite songs, such as 'Johnnie Cope' or 'Charlie is my darling'. However, these were used mainly to heighten the atmosphere of adventure or, in a literal sense, as signals between the characters in the story. In *Catriona*, the contemporary songs are used to stress not adventure but the misconduct of James's trial, and to make a further contrast with the anglicized, legal voice. The fact that a darker commentary, found both in the narrative and in the songs, follows on from the tale of the diabolic makes a strong imaginative link between the dualistic elements dramatized in 'Tod Lapraik' and the double-dealing and duplicity so strongly present in James's trial.

In contrast to the oral/aural power of 'Tod Lapraik' and the songs, written documents tend to come off poorly. James's Judgement is one such; David's 'Memorial' is an impotent document, destined to disappear and to achieve nothing whatsoever; the Biblical texts on God's laws are largely irrelevant at Inverary; the letter to James More when he has 'sold' Alan is part of a plot of extreme bad faith; and even Barbara's good-humoured note to David causes uncomfortable complications in the novel's romantic plot. Overall, the spoken forms and oral elements fare considerably better. Stevenson's contemporary South Seas story, *The Beach of Falesa*, makes a similar comment on the inadequacy of written documents in the marriage certificate (valid for one night) issued to bind Wiltshire to Uma. Stevenson's experiences with publishing this story, recently fully brought to light, could also have made him somewhat chary of printed papers.[26]

In the romantic plot of *Catriona*, Barbara and Catriona are important characters in Stevenson's oeuvre: hitherto he had

26 *The Beach of Falesa*, XVII, 202. R.L.S.'s publishers were uneasy about this marriage contract; Cassell, for example, insisted that it should be for 'one week'. For a full discussion of this text, see Barry Menikoff, *Robert Louis Stevenson and The Beach of Falesa: a Study in Victorian Publishing* (Edinburgh, 1985).

included no fully drawn female personae in his fiction. His best-remembered successes before 1893—*Treasure Island* (1883), *Kidnapped* (1886) and *Dr. Jekyll and Mr. Hyde* (1886)—proceed without any strongly developed female interest. Even *The Master of Ballantrae* (1889) concentrates on the Old Lord and the brothers at the expense of Alison.

In the later part of his life, Stevenson was determined to create memorable female characters—not only in *Catriona*, but also in the unfinished *Weir of Hermiston*. He also had plans afoot for *Sophia Scarlet*—'a regular novel; heroine and hero, and false accusation, and love, and marriage, and all the rest of it—all planted in a big South Sea plantation run by ex-English officers'. Fanny, too, quotes R.L.S. as saying, 'There was a time . . . when I didn't dare to really draw a woman; but I have no fear now. I shall show a little of what I can do in the two Kirstys [in *Weir*]; but in *Sophia Scarlet* the main interest shall be centred in the women.'[27]

Catriona obviously derives from a similar impulse to portray women characters successfully. Old Lady Allardyce is a memorable character in the Scottish tradition of John Galt and Scott, and both Barbara Grant (modelled on 'the beautiful and witty Mrs. Ferrier', daughter of Christopher North[28]) and Catriona herself are convincing and lively figures. There were, however, problems for Stevenson in writing about women in this novel: they tended to 'run away' with him. Originally he had intended the book to be only 200 pages or so; but, at only Chapter XXI, it had reached 150 pages. On 3 June 1892 he wrote to Sidney Colvin:

I am very curious to see what you will think of my two girls. My own opinion is quite clear; I am in love with both. I foresee a few pleasant years of spiritual flirtation. The creator (if I may name myself, for the sake of argument, by such a name) is essentially unfaithful. For the duration of the two chapters in which I dealt with Miss Grant, I totally forgot my heroine, and even—but this is a flat secret—tried to win away David.[29]

27 Swearingen, op. cit., p. 165.
28 'Prefatory Note by Mrs. R. L. Stevenson', op. cit., p. xvi.
29 *Letters*, XXV, 202.

Fanny comments that at this time, '. . . the family caught occasional glimpses of Catriona and Miss Grant . . . and it was with the greatest difficulty that he was able to keep her [Barbara] in the secondary position in the story'.[30]

In one way, the pull towards Barbara Grant is quite understandable; in her dealings with David, the 'gomeral' as she calls him, she is a much more spirited creation than Catriona. Jenni Calder has commented that, in Part II of the novel, Catriona 'becomes silly and truculent, endowed with numerous qualities which are often disparagingly considered pre-eminently feminine'.[31] To some extent, I would agree; the feminine wiles and continual playing with different clothes are a little tiresome, and there is a certain problem with Catriona's lack of a sense of humour. The tensions in her relationship with David, however, and in particular her lack of knowledge of social *mores*, are very well done; the differing social sensitivities of the 'uneven pair' are convincing; and Catriona's angry reaction to Barbara's note, for example, seems to me rather more a part of her social naïvety, and her difference from Barbara, than merely 'silly truculence'.

It is possible to find a certain unease on Stevenson's part in the treatment of his heroine; he is considerably more assured with Barbara in *Catriona*, and with his native Polynesian, Uma, and her sexuality, in *Falesa*, than he is with his Highland heroine. But, it is important to see the presentation of Catriona in terms of *David*'s character; his insistence on seeing her as a child is part of his 'stockishness', part of his Lowland caution, and, of course, part of his immaturity. Catriona herself suggests she should have been a 'man child', but it is David, trying to control his growing passion, who continues to see her in childish terms; for him she is, at least ostensibly, one who recounts 'childish tales' she has learned from Neil, and who exhibits occasional 'childish freak[s]' and 'bairnly whims'. The following example is particularly telling:

30 'Prefatory Note', op. cit., p. xvi.
31 *Catriona*, Chambers Centenary Edition (1980), Introduction by Jenni Calder, p. xix.

We had our walk daily. Out in the streets I felt more safe; I relaxed a little in my guardedness; and for one thing, there was no Heineccius. This made these periods not only a relief to myself, but a particular pleasure to my poor child [p. 420].

David is 'safer' outside, away from the indoors atmosphere of 'danger'; there is no Heineccius to help him distance himself from the heroine and from intimacy; but then, almost as soon as he has made this comment, he reverts to seeing her as 'my poor child'. Ultimately it is surely David, and not Stevenson, who feels more at ease with a child-Highlander, a child, or a 'sister', than with a grown woman?

Out of Scotland and Scots history came *Kidnapped*; from a combination of Scotland and Samoan politics came *Catriona*. At his death, Stevenson had other Scottish plans, perhaps also coloured by his experiences in the South Seas, well underway. *Heathercat*, a story of the Scottish Covenanters, had been started; so also had *The Young Chevalier*, a novel about the Young Pretender in France; and *Weir of Hermiston* was progressing well. To the end of his life, Stevenson was haunted by that 'cold old grey huddle of hills' from which he came; and it is this haunting, realized dramatically in the material and the texture of both *Kidnapped* and *Catriona*, that finally binds a potentially 'uneven pair' together.

NOTE ON THE TEXT

THE text of both novels is that of the first British book edition of each (*Kidnapped*: Cassell, 1886, and *Catriona*: Cassell, 1893). Stevenson made some revisions to *Kidnapped* for the combined volume of the two books entitled *The Adventures of David Balfour* (1895); these are contained in the Edinburgh Edition (1895; hereafter EE), and details of substantial divergences between the First Edition and EE are given in the Explanatory Notes. Those few occasions when there has been reason not to follow the First Edition are detailed in the notes to pp. 44, 106, 193, and 195.

Footnote glosses and comments, accompanied in the text by a superior number, are Stevenson's own; the Glossary of Scots words has been prepared for this edition.

The maps included at the front of each novel are reproduced from those in EE.

The existence of an explanatory note is indicated in the text with an asterisk.

SELECT BIBLIOGRAPHY

(Place of publication is London unless otherwise stated.)

BIBLIOGRAPHY

George H. Ford (ed.), *Victorian Fiction: A Second Guide to Research* (Cambridge, Mass., 1978) [includes a chapter on RLS by Robert Kiely].

George L. MacKay, *The Stevenson Library of Edwin J. Beinecke*, 6 vols. (New Haven, 1958).

W. F. Prideaux, *Bibliography of Robert Louis Stevenson* (1903; revised 1917).

Roger G. Swearingen, *The Prose Writings of Robert Louis Stevenson: A Guide* (1980).

EDITIONS

Collected editions of the works of R.L.S. include:

The Edinburgh Edition, ed. Sidney Colvin (1894–8).

The Pentland Edition, with Bibliographical Notes by Edmund Gosse (1906–7).

The Swanston Edition, with an Introduction by Andrew Lang (1911–12).

The Vailima Edition, ed. Lloyd Osbourne, with Prefatory Notes by Fanny van de Grift Stevenson (1922–3).

The Tusitala Edition (1923–4).

LETTERS

Vailima Letters (1895).

The Letters of Robert Louis Stevenson to His Family and Friends, ed. Sidney Colvin (1899; new edition, 1911).

Henry James and Robert Louis Stevenson: A Record of Friendship and Criticism, ed. Janet Adam Smith (1948).

RLS: Stevenson's Letters to Charles Baxter, ed. De Lancey Ferguson and Marshall Waingrow (New Haven, 1956).

BIOGRAPHY

Graham Balfour, *The Life of Robert Louis Stevenson* (1901).

Jenni Calder, *RLS: A Life Study* (1980).

Elsie Noble Caldwell, *Last Witness for Robert Louis Stevenson* (Norman, Oklahoma, 1960).
David Daiches, *Robert Louis Stevenson and His World* (1973).
J. C. Furnas, *Voyage to Windward* (1951).
J. A. Hammerton, *Stevensoniana: An Anecdotal Life and Appreciation of Robert Louis Stevenson* (Edinburgh, revised edition 1910).
James Pope Hennessy, *Robert Louis Stevenson* (1974).

CRITICISM

Jenni Calder (ed.), *Stevenson and Victorian Scotland* (Edinburgh, 1981). See especially W. W. Robson, 'On *Kidnapped*', pp. 88–106.
David Daiches, *Robert Louis Stevenson* (Glasgow, 1947).
Edwin M. Eigner, *Robert Louis Stevenson and Romantic Tradition* (Princeton, 1965).
Francis R. Hart, *The Scottish Novel: A Critical Survey* (1978).
Robert Kiely, *Robert Louis Stevenson and the Fiction of Adventure* (Cambridge, Mass., 1974).
Paul Maixner, *Robert Louis Stevenson: The Critical Heritage* (1981).
Andrew Noble (ed.), *Robert Louis Stevenson* (1983). See especially 'Highland History and Narrative Form in Scott and Stevenson', pp. 134–87.
Wilsey, Mildred, 'Kidnapped in Manuscript', *The American Scholar*, New York, XVII, 213–20 (Spring 1948).

HISTORICAL BACKGROUND
to *Kidnapped* and *Catriona*

F. W. C. Hersey (ed.), *Robert Louis Stevenson's 'Kidnapped'. Followed by 'Who Killed the Red Fox?'* (Boston, 1938).
Andrew Lang, *Historical Mysteries* (1904).
David N. Mackay, *The Appin Murder: The Historical basis of 'Kidnapped' and 'Catriona'* (Edinburgh, 1911).
—— *The Trial of James Stewart* (Edinburgh, 1907).

MISCELLANEOUS

George L. MacKay, *Some Notes on Robert Louis Stevenson, His Finances and His Agents and Publishers* (New Haven, 1958).

A CHRONOLOGY OF
ROBERT LOUIS STEVENSON

1850   Born in Edinburgh, 13 November.

1862–3   Excursions with his parents to Germany, the Riviera and Italy.

1867   Enters Edinburgh University to study engineering.

1871   Makes decision to abandon engineering and study law.

1872   Passes preliminary examinations for the Scottish Bar.

1873   Crisis with his father over his agnosticism; following this, and a bout of ill health, goes to Suffolk to stay with his Balfour cousins. Meets Frances Sitwell, one of the most important influences on his life until his marriage. Beginning of his friendship with Sidney Colvin. Further ill health sends R.L.S. south to France at the end of the year.

1874   At Menton in France. Returns to Edinburgh in May and resumes reading for the Bar. Contributes to *Cornhill Magazine*.

1875   Meets W. E. Henley in Edinburgh. Called to Scottish Bar but does not practise as an advocate. Visits France and joins his cousin, Bob Stevenson, at the artists' colony at Barbizon, Fontainebleau (1875–6); contributes to *Vanity Fair* and the *Academy*.

1876   Makes canoe trip around the canals of northern France, later to be recorded in *An Inland Voyage*. Meets Fanny Osbourne, a married woman with two children, from Indiana.

1877   Divides year between Edinburgh, London and Fontainebleau.

1878   Fanny returns to her husband in California and, eventually, divorce proceedings begin. R.L.S. goes on travels with his donkey, Modestine, in the Cévennes. Publication of *An Inland Voyage* and *Edinburgh: Picturesque Notes*.

1879   Divides time between Edinburgh, London and France. Very ill in March and April. Sets off on long and exhausting journey to join Fanny in America, later to be published in *The Amateur Emigrant*. *Travels with a Donkey* published.

1880   Marries Fanny in San Francisco in May. They stay in the Californian mountains (the visit is described in *The Silverado Squatters*). Publication of *Deacon Brodie*, R.L.S.'s first play, written in collaboration with W. E. Henley.

1881   At Braemar; writes 15 chapters of *Treasure Island*. Visits Davos in Switzerland where *Treasure Island* is completed (serialized in *Young Folks*, October 1881–January 1882). Publication of *Virginibus Puerisque*.

1882   At Davos, then R.L.S. and Fanny move to Hyères in France, their main home from March 1883 to July 1884. Publication of *Familiar Studies of Men and Books* and *New Arabian Nights*.

1883   Publication of *The Silverado Squatters* and *Treasure Island*. Serialization of *The Black Arrow* in *Young Folks* (June–October).

1884   Illness at Nice in January and further serious ill health in May. The Stevensons return to England at about the same time as an outbreak of cholera at Hyères. They go to Bournemouth, their home from September of this year until August 1887. Publication of *Austin Guinea* and *Beau Austin*, both in collaboration with W. E. Henley. Henry James publishes 'The Art of Fiction' in September; Stevenson's rejoinder, 'A Humble Remonstrance', is published in December.

1885   Moves to 'Skerryvore' in Bournemouth (the house was a wedding present from Thomas Stevenson to Fanny). Begins *Kidnapped* in spring of this year but then abandons it temporarily. Henry James pays a long visit to Bournemouth. Publication of *A Child's Garden of Verses*; *Prince Otto*; *More New Arabian Nights*; *The Dynamiter*, with Fanny Stevenson; and *Macaire*, with W. E. Henley.

1886   Publication of *The Strange Case of Dr. Jekyll and Mr.*

Hyde, Stevenson's first large-scale British and American success. In January, 16 chapters of *Kidnapped* completed; and the whole novel finished in April/May of this year. Serialized in *Young Folks*, 1 May–31 July 1886.

1887   Thomas Stevenson dies in May. In August, R.L.S. sails for America with his mother, Fanny, and his stepson, Lloyd. For reasons of health, stays at Saranac in the Adirondack Mountains. Publication of *The Merry Men and Other Tales and Fables*; *Memories and Portraits* (contains 'Memoirs of an Islet'; 'A Gossip on a Novel of Dumas's'; 'A Gossip on Romance' and 'A Humble Remonstrance'); and *A Memoir of Fleeming Jenkin*.

1888   Scribner's, Stevenson's American publishers, commission a volume on the South Seas. Voyages on the yacht *Casco* to the Marquesas, the Paumotus, Tahiti and then Hawaii. Publication of *The Black Arrow* and *The Misadventures of John Nicholson*.

1889   Mrs. Thomas Stevenson returns to Scotland. R.L.S., Fanny and Lloyd remain in Honolulu. Voyage on the trading schooner, *Equator*, to the Gilbert Islands and then to Samoa. Publication of *The Wrong Box*, with Lloyd; and *The Master of Ballantrae*. Buys an estate at Opulu, Samoa, where Vailima is later built.

1890   A third voyage, in the trading steamer *Janet Nicholl*, in the eastern and western Pacific. Further ill health, including a serious haemorrhage, leads the Stevensons to realize that R.L.S. can never again leave a tropical climate. In October they take up residence at Upolu. Publications of *In the South Seas* and *Ballads*. In September one chapter of *David Balfour* [*Catriona*] written, then abandoned until October of the following year.

1891   At Vailima; works on *The Wrecker*, with Lloyd, and on *A Footnote to History*. Returns briefly to *David Balfour* [*Catriona*] in October.

1892   Becomes further involved in Samoan politics. Publication of *Across the Plains*, *A Footnote to History* and *The Wrecker*. Begins to work seriously on *David Balfour* [*Catriona*] in February and completes the novel in September. Serialized in *Atalanta* (December 1892– September 1893).

1893   War breaks out in Samoa. Stevenson supports Mataafa.
        Visits Honolulu. Publication of *Island Nights Entertain-
        ments* and *Catriona*.

1894   The tribe of Mataafa build 'The Road of the Loving
        Hearts' in gratitude to R.L.S. for helping their cause.
        Publication of *The Ebb-Tide*. Dies on 3 December of a
        cerebral haemorrhage.

1896   Posthumous publication of *Weir of Hermiston*.

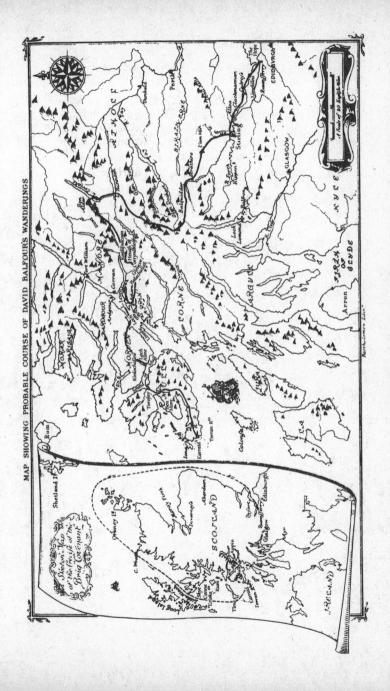

MAP SHOWING PROBABLE COURSE OF DAVID BALFOUR'S WANDERINGS

KIDNAPPED

Being the Adventures of David Balfour*; How he was Kidnapped and Cast away; his Sufferings in a Desert Isle; his Journey in the West Highlands; his Acquaintance with Alan Breck Stewart and other notorious Highland Jacobites; with all that he Suffered at the hands of his Uncle, Ebenezer Balfour of Shaws, falsely so-called: Written by Himself, and now set forth by

ROBERT LOUIS STEVENSON

DEDICATION

My dear Charles Baxter,

If you ever read this tale, you will likely ask yourself more questions than I should care to answer: as for instance how the Appin murder has come to fall in the year 1751, how the Torran rocks have crept so near to Earraid, or why the printed trial is silent as to all that touches David Balfour. These are nuts beyond my ability to crack. But if you tried me on the point of Alan's guilt or innocence, I think I could defend the reading of the text. To this day you will find the tradition of Appin clear in Alan's favour.* If you inquire, you may even hear that the descendants of 'the other man' who fired the shot are in the country to this day. But that other man's name, inquire as you please, you shall not hear; for the Highlander values a secret for itself and for the congenial exercise of keeping it. I might go on for long to justify one point and own another indefensible; it is more honest to confess at once how little I am touched by the desire of accuracy. This is no furniture for the scholar's library, but a book for the winter evening schoolroom when the tasks are over and the hour for bed draws near; and honest Alan, who was a grim old fire-eater in his day, has in this new avatar no more desperate purpose than to steal some young gentleman's attention from his Ovid, carry him awhile into the Highlands and the last century, and pack him to bed with some engaging images to mingle with his dreams.

As for you, my dear Charles, I do not even ask you to like this tale. But perhaps when he is older, your son will; he may then be pleased to find his father's name on the fly-leaf; and in the meanwhile it pleases me to set it there, in memory of many days that were happy and some (now perhaps as pleasant to remember) that were sad. If it is strange for me to look back from a distance both in time and space on those bygone adventures of our youth, it must be stranger for you

who tread the same streets—who may tomorrow open the door
of the old Speculative,* where we begin to rank with Scott
and Robert Emmet* and the beloved and inglorious Macbean*
—or may pass the corner of the close where that great society,
the L. J. R.,* held its meetings and drank its beer, sitting in
the seats of Burns and his companions. I think I see you,
moving there by plain daylight, beholding with your natural
eyes those places that have now become for your companion
a part of the scenery of dreams. How, in the intervals of
present business, the past must echo in your memory! Let
it not echo often without some kind thoughts of your friend,

R. L. S.

Skerryvore,
Bournemouth.

CONTENTS

xiv Contents

XX. THE FLIGHT IN THE HEATHER: THE ROCKS 127

XXI. THE FLIGHT IN THE HEATHER: THE HEUGH OF CORRYNAKIEGH 134

XXII. THE FLIGHT IN THE HEATHER: THE MOOR 141

XXIII. CLUNY'S CAGE 149

XXIV. THE FLIGHT IN THE HEATHER: THE QUARREL 156

XXV. IN BALQUHIDDER 166

XXVI. END OF THE FLIGHT: WE PASS THE FORTH 173

XXVII. I COME TO MR. RANKEILLOR 181

XXVIII. I GO IN QUEST OF MY INHERITANCE 190

XXIX. I COME INTO MY KINGDOM 196

XXX. GOOD-BYE 204

KIDNAPPED

BEING

MEMOIRS OF THE ADVENTURES OF DAVID BALFOUR IN THE YEAR 1751

CHAPTER I

I SET OFF UPON MY JOURNEY TO THE HOUSE OF SHAWS

I WILL begin the story of my adventures with a certain morning early in the month of June, the year of grace 1751, when I took the key for the last time out of the door of my father's house. The sun began to shine upon the summit of the hills as I went down the road; and by the time I had come as far as the manse, the blackbirds were whistling in the garden lilacs, and the mist that hung around the valley in the time of the dawn was beginning to arise and die away.

Mr. Campbell, the minister of Essendean, was waiting for me by the garden gate, good man! He asked me if I had breakfasted; and hearing that I lacked for nothing, he took my hand in both of his and clapped it kindly under his arm.

'Well, Davie, lad,' said he, 'I will go with you as far as the ford, to set you on the way.'

And we began to walk forward in silence.

'Are ye sorry to leave Essendean?' said he, after a while.

'Why, sir,' said I, 'if I knew where I was going, or what was likely to become of me, I would tell you candidly. Essendean is a good place indeed, and I have been very happy there; but then I have never been anywhere else. My father and mother, since they are both dead, I shall be no nearer to in Essendean than in the Kingdom of Hungary; and to speak truth, if I thought I had a chance to better myself where I was going, I would go with a good will.'

'Ay?' said Mr. Campbell. 'Very well, Davie. Then it behoves me to tell your fortune; or so far as I may. When your mother was gone, and your father (the worthy, Christian man) began to sicken for his end, he gave me in charge a certain letter, which he said was your inheritance. "So soon," says he, "as I am gone, and the house is redd up and the gear disposed of" (all which, Davie, hath been done), "give my boy this letter into his hand, and start him off to the house of Shaws, not far from Cramond. That is the place I came from," he said, "and it's where it befits that my boy should return. He is a steady lad," your father said, "and a canny goer; and I doubt not he will come safe, and be well liked where he goes." '

'The house of Shaws!' I cried. 'What had my poor father to do with the house of Shaws?'

'Nay,' said Mr. Campbell, 'who can tell that for a surety? But the name of that family, Davie boy, is the name you bear—Balfour of Shaws: an ancient, honest, reputable house, peradventure in these latter days decayed. Your father, too, was a man of learning as befitted his position; no man more plausibly conducted school; nor had he the manner or the speech of a common dominie; but (as ye will yourself remember) I took aye a pleasure to have him to the manse to meet the gentry; and those of my own house, Campbell of Kilrennet, Campbell of Dunswire, Campbell of Minch, and others, all well-kenned gentlemen, had pleasure in his society. Lastly, to put all the elements of this affair before you, here is the testamentary letter itself, superscrived by the own hand of our departed brother.'

He gave me the letter, which was addressed in these words: 'To the hands of Ebenezer Balfour, Esq., of Shaws, in his house of Shaws, these will be delivered by my son, David Balfour.' My heart was beating hard at this great prospect now suddenly opening before a lad of seventeen years of age, the son of a poor country dominie in the Forest of Ettrick.

'Mr. Campbell,' I stammered, 'and if you were in my shoes, would you go?'

'Of a surety,' said the minister, 'that would I, and without pause. A pretty lad like you should get to Cramond (which is near in by Edinburgh) in two days of walk. If the worst came to the worst, and your high relations (as I cannot but suppose them to be somewhat of your blood) should put you to the door, ye can but walk the two days back again and risp at the manse door. But I would rather hope that ye shall be well received, as your poor father forecast for you, and for anything that I ken, come to be a great man in time. And here, Davie, laddie,' he resumed, 'it lies near upon my conscience to improve this parting, and set you on the right guard against the dangers of the world.'

Here he cast about for a comfortable seat, lighted on a big boulder under a birch by the trackside, sate down upon it with a very long, serious upper lip, and the sun now shining in upon us between two peaks, put his pocket-handkerchief over his cocked hat to shelter him. There, then, with uplifted forefinger, he first put me on my guard against a considerable number of heresies, to which I had no temptation, and urged upon me to be instant in my prayers and reading of the Bible. That done, he drew a picture of the great house that I was bound to, and how I should conduct myself with its inhabitants.

'Be soople, Davie, in things immaterial,' said he. 'Bear ye this in mind, that, though gentle born, ye have had a country rearing. Dinnae shame us, Davie, dinnae shame us! In yon great, muckle house, with all these domestics, upper and under, show yourself as nice, as circumspect, as quick at the conception, and as slow of speech as any. As for the laird—remember he's the laird; I say no more: honour to whom honour. It's a pleasure to obey a laird; or should be, to the young.'

'Well, sir,' said I, 'it may be; and I'll promise you I'll try to make it so.'

'Why, very well said,' replied Mr. Campbell, heartily. 'And now to come to the material, or (to make a quibble) to the immaterial. I have here a little packet which contains four things.' He tugged it, as he spoke, with some difficulty, from the skirt pocket of his coat. 'Of these four things, the first is your legal due: the little pickle money for your father's books and plenishing, which I have bought (as I have explained from the first) in the design of re-selling at a profit to the incoming dominie. The other three are gifties that Mrs. Campbell and myself would be blithe of your acceptance. The first, which is round, will likely please ye best at the first off-go; but, O Davie, laddie, it's but a drop of water in the sea; it'll help you but a step, and vanish like the morning. The second, which is flat and square and written upon, will stand by you through life, like a good staff for the road, and a good pillow to your head in sickness. And as for the last, which is cubical, that'll see you, it's my prayerful wish, into a better land.'

With that he got upon his feet, took off his hat, and prayed a little while aloud, and in affecting terms, for a young man setting out into the world; then suddenly took me in his arms and embraced me very hard; then held me at arm's length, looking at me with his face all working with sorrow; and then whipped about, and crying good-bye to me, set off backward by the way that we had come at a sort of jogging run. It might have been laughable to another; but I was in no mind to laugh. I watched him as long as he was in sight; and he never stopped hurrying, nor once looked back. Then it came in upon my mind that this was all his sorrow at my departure; and my conscience smote me hard and fast, because I, for my part, was overjoyed to get away out of that quiet country-side, and go to a great, busy house, among rich and respected gentlefolk of my own name and blood.

'Davie, Davie,' I thought, 'was ever seen such black ingratitude? Can you forget old favours and old friends at the mere whistle of a name? Fie, fie; think shame!'

And I sat down on the boulder the good man had just left, and opened the parcel to see the nature of my gifts. That which he had called cubical, I had never had much doubt of; sure enough it was a little Bible, to carry in a plaidneuk. That which he had called round, I found to be a shilling piece; and the third, which was to help me so wonderfully both in health and sickness all the days of my life, was a little piece of coarse yellow paper, written upon thus in red ink:—

'TO MAKE LILLY OF THE VALLEY WATER.* Take the flowers of lilly of the valley and distil them in sack, and drink a spooneful or two as there is occasion. It restores speech to those that have the dumb palsey. It is good against the Gout; it comforts the heart and strengthens the memory; and the flowers, put into a Glasse, close stopt, and set into ane hill of ants for a month, then take it out, and you will find a liquor which comes from the flowers, which keep in a vial; it is good, ill or well, and whether man or woman.'

And then, in the minister's own hand, was added:

'Likewise for sprains, rub it in; and for the cholic, a great spooneful in the hour.'

To be sure, I laughed over this; but it was rather tremulous laughter; and I was glad to get my bundle on my staff's end and set out over the ford and up the hill upon the farther side; till, just as I came on the green drove-road running wide through the heather, I took my last look of Kirk Essendean, the trees about the manse, and the big rowans in the kirkyard where my father and my mother lay.

CHAPTER II

I COME TO MY JOURNEY'S END

ON the forenoon of the second day, coming to the top of a hill, I saw all the country fall away before me down to the sea; and in the midst of this descent, on a long ridge, the city of Edinburgh smoking like a kiln.* There was a flag upon the castle, and ships moving or lying anchored in the firth; both of which, for as far away as they were, I could distinguish clearly; and both brought my country heart into my mouth.

Presently after, I came by a house where a shepherd lived, and got a rough direction for the neighbourhood of Cramond;

and so, from one to another, worked my way to the westward of the capital by Colinton, till I came out upon the Glasgow road. And there, to my great pleasure and wonder, I beheld a regiment marching to the fifes, every foot in time; an old red-faced general on a grey horse at the one end, and at the other the company of Grenadiers, with their Pope's-hats. The pride of life seemed to mount into my brain at the sight of the red coats and the hearing of that merry music.

A little farther on, and I was told I was in Cramond parish, and began to substitute in my inquiries the name of the house of Shaws. It was a word that seemed to surprise those of whom I sought my way. At first I thought the plainness of my appearance, in my country habit, and that all dusty from the road, consorted ill with the greatness of the place to which I was bound. But after two, or maybe three, had given me the same look and the same answer, I began to take it in my head there was something strange about the Shaws itself.

The better to set this fear at rest, I changed the form of my inquiries, and spying an honest fellow coming along a lane on the shaft of his cart, I asked him if he had ever heard tell of a house they called the house of Shaws.

He stopped his cart and looked at me, like the others.

'Ay,' said he. 'What for?'

'It's a great house?' I asked.

'Doubtless,' says he. 'The house is a big, muckle house.'

'Ay,' said I, 'but the folk that are in it?'

'Folk?' cried he. 'Are ye daft? There's nae folk there—to call folk.'

'What?' says I; 'not Mr. Ebenezer?'

'Ou, ay,' says the man, 'there's the laird, to be sure, if it's him you're wanting. What'll like be your business, mannie?'

'I was led to think that I would get a situation,' I said, looking as modest as I could.

'What?' cries the carter, in so sharp a note that his very horse started; and then, 'Well, mannie,' he added, 'it's nane of my affairs; but ye seem a decent-spoken lad; and if ye'll take a word from me, ye'll keep clear of the Shaws.'

The next person I came across was a dapper little man in a beautiful white wig, whom I saw to be a barber on his rounds; and knowing well that barbers were great gossips, I asked him plainly what sort of a man was Mr Balfour of the Shaws.

'Hoot, hoot, hoot,' said the barber, 'nae kind of a man, nae kind of a man at all'; and began to ask me very shrewdly what my business was; but I was more than a match for him at that, and he went on to his next customer no wiser than he came.

I cannot well describe the blow this dealt to my illusions. The more indistinct the accusations were, the less I liked them, for they left the wider field to fancy. What kind of a great house was this, that all the parish should start and stare to be asked the way to it? or what sort of a gentleman, that his ill-fame should be thus current on the wayside? If an hour's walking would have brought me back to Essendean, I had left my adventure then and there, and returned to Mr. Campbell's. But when I had come so far a way already, mere shame would not suffer me to desist till I had put the matter to the touch of proof; I was bound, out of mere self-respect, to carry it through; and little as I liked the sound of what I heard, and slow as I began to travel, I still kept asking my way and still kept advancing.

It was drawing on to sundown when I met a stout, dark, sour-looking woman coming trudging down a hill; and she, when I had put my usual question, turned sharp about, accompanied me back to the summit she had just left, and pointed to a great bulk of building standing very bare upon a green in the bottom of the next valley. The country was pleasant round about, running in low hills, pleasantly watered and wooded, and the crops, to my eyes, wonderfully good; but the house itself appeared to be a kind of ruin; no road led up to it; no smoke arose from any of the chimneys; nor was there any semblance of a garden. My heart sank. 'That!' I cried.

The woman's face lit up with a malignant anger. 'That is the house of Shaws!' she cried. 'Blood built it: blood stopped the building of it; blood shall bring it down. See here!' she cried again—'I spit upon the ground, and crack my thumb at it! Black be its fall! If ye see the laird, tell him what ye hear; tell him this makes the twelve hunner and nineteen time that Jennet Clouston has called down the curse on him and his house, byre and stable, man, guest, and master, wife, miss, or bairn—black, black be their fall!'*

And the woman, whose voice had risen to a kind of eldritch sing-song, turned with a skip, and was gone. I stood where she left me, with my hair on end. In these days folk still believed in witches and trembled at a curse; and this one, falling so pat, like a wayside omen, to arrest me ere I carried out my purpose, took the pith out of my legs.

I sat me down and stared at the house of Shaws. The more I looked, the pleasanter that country-side appeared; being all set with hawthorn bushes full of flowers; the fields dotted with sheep; a fine flight of rooks in the sky; and every sign of a kind soil and climate; and yet the barrack in the midst of it went sore against my fancy.

Country folk went by from the fields as I sat there on the side of the ditch, but I lacked the spirit to give them a good-e'en. At last the sun went down, and then, right up against the yellow sky, I saw a scroll of smoke go mounting, not much thicker, as it seemed to me, than the smoke of a candle; but still there it was, and meant a fire, and warmth, and cookery, and some living inhabitant that must have lit it; and this comforted my heart wonderfully—more, I feel sure, than a whole flask of the lily of the valley water that Mrs. Campbell set so great a store by.*

So I set forward by a little faint track in the grass that led in my direction. It was very faint indeed to be the only way to a place of habitation; yet I saw no other. Presently it brought me to stone uprights, with an unroofed lodge beside them, and coats of arms upon the top. A main entrance, it was plainly meant to be, but never finished; instead of gates of wrought iron, a pair of hurdles were tied across with a straw rope; and as there were no park walls, nor any sign of avenue, the track that I was following passed on the right hand of the pillars, and went wandering on toward the house.

The nearer I got to that, the drearier it appeared. It seemed like the one wing of a house that had never been finished. What should have been the inner end stood open on the upper floors, and showed against the sky with steps and stairs of uncompleted masonry. Many of the windows were unglazed, and bats flew in and out like doves out of a dovecote.

The night had begun to fall as I got close; and in three of the lower windows, which were very high up, and narrow, and well barred, the changing light of a little fire began to glimmer.

Was this the palace I had been coming to? Was it within these walls that I was to seek new friends and begin great fortunes? Why, in my father's house on Essen-Waterside, the fire and the bright lights would show a mile away, and the door open to a beggar's knock.

I came forward cautiously, and giving ear as I came, heard someone rattling with dishes, and a little dry, eager cough that came in fits; but there was no sound of speech, and not a dog barked.

The door, as well as I could see it in the dim light, was a great piece of wood all studded with nails; and I lifted my hand with a faint heart under my jacket, and knocked once. Then I stood and waited. The house had fallen into a dead silence; a whole minute passed away, and nothing stirred but the bats overhead. I knocked again, and hearkened again. By this time my ears had grown so accustomed to the quiet, that I could hear the ticking of the clock inside as it slowly counted out the seconds; but whoever was in that house kept deadly still, and must have held his breath.

I was in two minds whether to run away; but anger got the upper hand, and I began instead to rain kicks and buffets on the door, and to shout out aloud for Mr. Balfour. I was in full career, when I heard the cough right overhead, and jumping back and looking up, beheld a man's head in a tall nightcap, and the bell mouth of a blunderbuss, at one of the first-storey windows.

'It's loaded,' said a voice.

'I have come here with a letter,' I said, 'to Mr. Ebenezer Balfour of Shaws. Is he here?'

'From whom is it?' asked the man with the blunderbuss.

'That is neither here nor there,' said I, for I was growing very wroth.

'Well,' was the reply, 'ye can put it down upon the doorstep, and be off with ye.'

'I will do no such thing,' I cried. 'I will deliver it into Mr. Balfour's hands, as it was meant I should. It is a letter of introduction.'

'A what?' cried the voice sharply.

I repeated what I had said.

'Who are ye, yourself?' was the next question, after a considerable pause.

'I am not ashamed of my name,' said I. 'They call me David Balfour.'

At that, I made sure the man started, for I heard the blunderbuss rattle on the windowsill; and it was after quite a long pause, and with a curious change of voice, that the next question followed:

'Is your father dead?'

I was so much surprised at this, that I could find no voice to answer, but stood staring.

'Ay,' the man resumed, 'he'll be dead, no doubt; and that'll be what brings ye chapping to my door.' Another pause, and then, defiantly, 'Well, man,' he said, 'I'll let ye in'; and he disappeared from the window.

CHAPTER III

I MAKE ACQUAINTANCE OF MY UNCLE

PRESENTLY there came a great rattling of chains and bolts, and the door was cautiously opened, and shut to again behind me as soon as I had passed.

'Go into the kitchen and touch naething,' said the voice;

and while the person of the house set himself to replacing the defences of the door, I groped my way forward and entered the kitchen.

The fire had burned up fairly bright, and showed me the barest room I think I ever put my eyes on. Half a dozen dishes stood upon the shelves; the table was laid for supper with a bowl of porridge, a horn spoon, and a cup of small beer. Besides what I have named, there was not another thing in that great, stone-vaulted, empty chamber, but lock-fast chests arranged along the wall and a corner cupboard with a padlock.

As soon as the last chain was up, the man rejoined me. He was a mean, stooping, narrow-shouldered, clay-faced creature; and his age might have been anything between fifty and seventy. His nightcap was of flannel, and so was the nightgown that he wore, instead of coat and waistcoat, over his ragged shirt. He was long unshaved; but what most distressed and even daunted me, he would neither take his eyes away from me nor look me fairly in the face. What he was, whether by trade or birth, was more than I could fathom; but he seemed most like an old, unprofitable serving-man, who should have been left in charge of that big house upon board wages.

'Are ye sharp-set?' he asked, glancing at about the level of my knee. 'You can eat that drop parritch.'

I said I feared it was his own supper.

'O,' said he, 'I can do fine wanting it. I'll take the ale, though, for it slockens[1] my cough.' He drank the cup about half out, still keeping an eye upon me as he drank; and then suddenly held out his hand. 'Let's see the letter,' said he.

I told him the letter was for Mr. Balfour; not for him.

'And who do ye think I am?' says he. 'Give me Alexander's letter!'

'You know my father's name?'

'It would be strange if I didnae,' he returned, 'for he was

[1] Moistens.

my born brother; and little as ye seem to like either me or my house, or my good parritch, I'm your born uncle, Davie, my man, and you my born nephew. So give us the letter, and sit down and fill your kyte.'

If I had been some years younger, what with shame, weariness, and disappointment, I believe I had burst into tears. As it was, I could find no words, neither black nor white, but handed him the letter, and sat down to the porridge with as little appetite for meat as ever a young man had.

Meanwhile, my uncle, stooping over the fire, turned the letter over and over in his hands.

'Do ye ken what's in it?' he asked, suddenly.

'You see for yourself, sir,' said I, 'that the seal has not been broken.'

'Ay,' said he, 'but what brought you here?'

'To give the letter,' said I.

'No,' says he, cunningly, 'but ye'll have had some hopes, nae doubt?'

'I confess, sir,' said I, 'when I was told that I had kinsfolk well-to-do, I did indeed indulge the hope that they might help me in my life. But I am no beggar; I look for no favours at your hands, and I want none that are not freely given. For as poor as I appear, I have friends of my own that will be blithe to help me.'

'Hoot-toot!' said Uncle Ebenezer, 'dinnae fly up in the snuff at me. We'll agree fine yet. And, Davie, my man, if you're done with that bit parritch, I could just take a sup of it myself. Ay,' he continued, as soon as he had ousted me from the stool and spoon, 'they're fine, halesome food—they're grand food, parritch.' He murmured a little grace to himself and fell to. 'Your father was very fond of his meat, I mind; he was a hearty, if not a great eater; but as for me, I could never do mair than pyke at food.' He took a pull at the small beer, which probably reminded him of hospitable duties; for his next speech ran thus: 'If you're dry, ye'll find water behind the door.'

To this I returned no answer, standing stiffly on my two feet, and looking down upon my uncle with a mighty angry heart. He, on his part, continued to eat like a man under some pressure of time, and to throw out little darting glances now at my shoes and now at my homespun stockings. Once only, when he had ventured to look a little higher, our eyes met; and no thief taken with a hand in a man's pockets could have shown more lively signals of distress. This set me in a muse, whether his timidity arose from too long a disuse of any human company; and whether perhaps, upon a little trial, it might pass off, and my uncle change into an altogether different man. From this I was awakened by his sharp voice.

'Your father's been long dead?' he asked.

'Three weeks, sir,' said I.

'He was a secret man, Alexander—a secret, silent man,' he continued. 'He never said muckle when he was young. He'll never have spoken muckle of me?'

'I never knew, sir, till you told it me yourself, that he had any brother.'

'Dear me, dear me!' said Ebenezer. 'Nor yet of Shaws, I daresay?'

'Not so much as the name, sir,' said I.

'To think o' that!' said he. 'A strange nature of a man!' For all that, he seemed singularly satisfied, but whether with himself, or me, or with this conduct of my father's, was more than I could read. Certainly, however, he seemed to be outgrowing that distaste, or ill-will, that he had conceived at first against my person; for presently he jumped up, came across the room behind me, and hit me a smack upon the shoulder. 'We'll agree fine yet!' he cried. 'I'm just as glad I let you in. And now come awa' to your bed.'

To my surprise, he lit no lamp or candle, but set forth into the dark passage, groped his way, breathing deeply, up a flight of steps, and paused before a door, which he unlocked. I was close upon his heels, having stumbled after him as best I might; and he bade me go in, for that was my chamber. I did as he bid, but paused after a few steps, and begged a light to go to bed with.

'Hoot-toot!' said Uncle Ebenezer, 'there's a fine moon.'

'Neither moon nor star, sir, and pit-mirk,'[1] said I. 'I cannae see the bed.'

'Hoot-toot, hoot-toot!' said he. 'Lights in a house is a thing I dinnae agree with. I'm unco feared of fires. Good night to ye, Davie, my man.' And before I had time to add a further protest, he pulled the door to, and I heard him lock me in from the outside.

I did not know whether to laugh or cry. The room was as cold as a well, and the bed, when I found my way to it, as damp as a peat-hag; but by good fortune I had caught up my bundle and my plaid, and rolling myself in the latter, I lay down upon the floor under lee of the big bedstead, and fell speedily asleep.

With the first peep of day I opened my eyes, to find myself in a great chamber, hung with stamped leather, furnished with fine embroidered furniture, and lit by three fair windows. Ten years ago, or perhaps twenty, it must have been as pleasant a room to lie down or to awake in, as a man could wish: but damp, dirt, disuse, and the mice and spiders had done their worst since then. Many of the window-panes, besides, were broken; and indeed this was so common a feature in that house, that I believe my uncle must at some time have stood a siege from his indignant neighbours— perhaps with Jennet Clouston at their head.

Meanwhile the sun was shining outside; and being very cold in that miserable room, I knocked and shouted till my gaoler came and let me out. He carried me to the back of the house, where was a draw-well, and told me to 'wash my face there, if I wanted'; and when that was done, I made the best of my own way back to the kitchen, where he had lit the fire and was making the porridge. The table was laid with two bowls and two horn spoons, but the same single measure of small beer. Perhaps my eye rested on this particular with some surprise, and perhaps my uncle observed it; for he spoke up as if in answer to my thought, asking me if I would like to drink ale—for so he called it.

---

[1] Dark as the pit.

I told him such was my habit, but not to put himself about.

'Na, na,' said he; 'I'll deny you nothing in reason.'

He fetched another cup from the shelf; and then, to my great surprise, instead of drawing more beer, he poured an accurate half from one cup to the other. There was a kind of nobleness in this that took my breath away; if my uncle was certainly a miser, he was one of that thorough breed that goes near to make the vice respectable.

When we had made an end of our meal, my uncle Ebenezer unlocked a drawer, and drew out of it a clay pipe and a lump of tobacco, from which he cut one fill before he locked it up again. Then he sat down in the sun at one of the windows and silently smoked. From time to time his eyes came coasting round to me, and he shot out one of his questions. Once it was, 'And your mother?' and when I had told him that she, too, was dead, 'Ay, she was a bonnie lassie!' Then, after another long pause, 'Whae were these friends o' yours?'

I told him they were different gentlemen of the name of Campbell; though, indeed, there was only one, and that the minister, that had ever taken the least note of me; but I began to think my uncle made too light of my position, and finding myself all alone with him, I did not wish him to suppose me helpless.

He seemed to turn this over in his mind; and then, 'Davie, my man,' said he, 'ye've come to the right bit when ye came to your Uncle Ebenezer. I've a great notion of the family, and I mean to do the right by you; but while I'm taking a bit think to mysel' of what's the best thing to put you to—whether the law, or the meenistry, or maybe the army, whilk is what boys are fondest of—I wouldnae like the Balfours to be humbled before a wheen Hieland Campbells, and I'll ask you to keep your tongue within your teeth. Nae letters; nae messages; no kind of word to onybody; or else—there's my door.'

'Uncle Ebenezer,' said I, 'I've no manner of reason to suppose you mean anything but well by me. For all that, I would have you to know that I have a pride of my own.

It was by no will of mine that I came seeking you; and if you show me your door again, I'll take you at the word.'

He seemed grievously put out. 'Hoots-toots,' said he, 'ca' cannie, man—ca' cannie! Bide a day or two. I'm nae warlock, to find a fortune for you in the bottom of a parritch bowl; but just you give me a day or two, and say naething to naebody, and as sure as sure, I'll do the right by you.'

'Very well,' said I, 'enough said. If you want to help me, there's no doubt but I'll be glad of it, and none but I'll be grateful.'

It seemed to me (too soon, I daresay) that I was getting the upper hand of my uncle; and I began next to say that I must have the bed and bedclothes aired and put to sun-dry; for nothing would make me sleep in such a pickle.

'Is this my house or yours?' said he, in his keen voice, and then all of a sudden broke off. 'Na, na,' said he, 'I didnae mean that. What's mine is yours, Davie, my man, and what's yours is mine. Blood's thicker than water; and there's naebody but you and me that ought the name.' And then on he rambled about the family, and its ancient greatness, and his father that began to enlarge the house, and himself that stopped the building as a sinful waste; and this put it in my head to give him Jennet Clouston's message.

'The limmer!' he cried. 'Twelve hunner and fifteen—that's every day since I had the limmer rowpit![1] Dod, David, I'll have her roasted on red peats before I'm by with it! A witch —a proclaimed witch! I'll aff and see the session clerk.'

And with that he opened a chest, and got out a very old and well-preserved blue coat and waistcoat, and a good enough beaver hat, both without lace. These he threw on anyway, and taking a staff from the cupboard, locked all up again, and was for setting out, when a thought arrested him. 'I cannae leave you by yoursel' in the house,' said he. 'I'll have to lock you out.'

The blood came to my face. 'If you lock me out,' I said, 'it'll be the last you see of me in friendship.'

---

[1] Sold-up.

He turned very pale, and sucked his mouth in. 'This is no the way,' he said, looking wickedly at a corner of the floor—'this is no the way to win my favour, David.'

'Sir,' says I, 'with a proper reverence for your age and our common blood, I do not value your favour at a boddle's purchase. I was brought up to have a good conceit of myself; and if you were all the uncle, and all the family, I had in the world ten times over, I wouldn't buy your liking at such prices.'

Uncle Ebenezer went and looked out of the window for a while. I could see him all trembling and twitching, like a man with palsy. But when he turned round, he had a smile upon his face.

'Well, well,' said he, 'we must bear and forbear. I'll no go; that's all that's to be said of it.'

'Uncle Ebenezer,' I said, 'I can make nothing out of this. You use me like a thief; you hate to have me in this house; you let me see it, every word and every minute; it's not possible that you can like me; and as for me, I've spoken to you as I never thought to speak to any man. Why do you seek to keep me, then? Let me gang back--let me gang back to the friends I have, and that like me!'

'Na, na; na, na,' he said, very earnestly. 'I like you fine; we'll agree fine yet; and for the honour of the house I couldnae let you leave the way ye came. Bide here quiet, there's a good lad; just you bide here quiet a bittie, and ye'll find that we agree.'

'Well, sir,' said I, after I had thought the matter out in silence, 'I'll stay a while. It's more just I should be helped by my own blood than strangers; and if we don't agree, I'll do my best it shall be through no fault of mine.'

CHAPTER IV

I RUN A GREAT DANGER IN THE
HOUSE OF SHAWS

FOR a day that was begun so ill, the day passed fairly well. We had the porridge cold again at noon, and hot porridge at night: porridge and small beer was my uncle's diet. He spoke but little, and that in the same way as before, shooting a question at me after a long silence; and when I sought to lead him in talk about my future, slipped out of it again. In a room next door to the kitchen, where he suffered me to go, I found a great number of books, both Latin and English, in which I took great pleasure all the afternoon. Indeed, the time passed so lightly in this good company, that I began to be almost reconciled to my residence at Shaws; and nothing but the sight of my uncle, and his eyes playing hide and seek with mine, revived the force of my distrust.

One thing I discovered, which put me in some doubt. This was an entry on the flyleaf of a chapbook (one of Patrick Walker's*) plainly written by my father's hand and thus conceived: 'To my brother Ebenezer on his fifth birthday.' Now, what puzzled me was this: That as my father was of course the younger brother, he must either have made some strange error, or he must have written, before he was yet five, an excellent, clear, manly hand of writing.

I tried to get this out of my head; but though I took down many interesting authors, old and new, history, poetry, and story-book, this notion of my father's hand of writing stuck to me; and when at length I went back into the kitchen, and sat down once more to porridge and small beer, the first thing I said to Uncle Ebenezer was to ask him if my father had not been very quick at his book.

'Alexander? No him!' was the reply. 'I was far quicker mysel'; I was a clever chappie when I was young. Why, I could read as soon as he could.'

This puzzled me yet more: and a thought coming into my head, I asked if he and my father had been twins.

He jumped upon his stool, and the horn spoon fell out of his hand upon the floor. 'What gars ye ask that?' he said, and caught me by the breast of the jacket, and looked this time straight into my eyes: his own which were little and light, and bright like a bird's, blinking and winking strangely.

'What do you mean?' I asked, very calmly, for I was far stronger than he, and not easily frightened. 'Take your hand from my jacket. This is no way to behave.'

My uncle seemed to make a great effort upon himself. 'Dod man, David,' he said, 'ye shouldnae speak to me about your father. That's where the mistake is.' He sat a while and shook, blinking in his plate: 'He was all the brother that ever I had,' he added, but with no heart in his voice; and then he caught up his spoon and fell to supper again, but still shaking.

Now this last passage, this laying of hands upon my person and sudden profession of love for my dead father, went so clean beyond my comprehension that it put me into both fear and hope. On the one hand, I began to think my uncle was perhaps insane and might be dangerous; on the other, there came up into my mind (quite unbidden by me and even discouraged) a story like some ballad I had heard folks singing, of a poor lad that was a rightful heir and a wicked kinsman that tried to keep him from his own. For why should my uncle play a part with a relative that came, almost a beggar, to his door, unless in his heart he had some cause to fear him?

With this notion, all unacknowledged, but nevertheless getting firmly settled in my head, I now began to imitate his covert looks; so that we sat at table like a cat and a mouse, each stealthily observing the other. Not another word had he to say to me, black or white, but was busy turning something secretly over in his mind; and the longer we sat and the more I looked at him, the more certain I became that the something was unfriendly to myself.

When he had cleared the platter, he got out a single pipeful of tobacco, just as in the morning, turned round a stool into the chimney corner, and sat a while smoking, with his back to me.

'Davie,' he said, at length, 'I've been thinking;' then he paused and said it again. 'There's a wee bit siller that I half promised ye before ye were born,' he continued; 'promised it to your father. O, naething legal, ye understand; just gentlemen daffing at their wine. Well, I keepit that bit money separate—it was a great expense, but a promise is a promise—and it has grown by now to be a maitter of just precisely—just exactly'— and here he paused and stumbled —'of just exactly forty pounds!' This last he rapped out with a sidelong glance over his shoulder; and the next moment added, almost with a scream, 'Scots!'

The pound Scots being the same thing as an English shilling, the difference made by this second thought was considerable; I could see, besides, that the whole story was a lie, invented with some end which it puzzled me to guess; and I made no attempt to conceal the tone of raillery in which I answered—

'O, think again, sir! Pounds sterling, I believe!'

'That's what I said,' returned my uncle: 'pounds sterling! And if you'll step out-by to the door a minute, just to see what kind of a night it is, I'll get it out to ye and call ye in again.'

I did his will, smiling to myself in my contempt that he should think I was so easily to be deceived. It was a dark night, with a few stars low down; and as I stood just outside the door, I heard a hollow moaning of wind far off among the hills. I said to myself there was something thundery and changeful in the weather, and little knew of what a vast importance that should prove to me before the evening passed.

When I was called in again, my uncle counted out into my hand seven and thirty golden guinea pieces; the rest was in his hand, in small gold and silver; but his heart failed him there, and he crammed the change into his pocket.

'There,' said he, 'that'll show you! I'm a queer man, and

strange wi' strangers; but my word is my bond, and there's the proof of it.'

Now, my uncle seemed so miserly that I was struck dumb by this sudden generosity, and could find no words in which to thank him.

'No a word!' said he. 'Nae thanks; I want nae thanks. I do my duty; I'm no saying that everybody would have done it; but for my part (though I'm a careful body, too) it's a pleasure to me to do the right by my brother's son; and it's a pleasure to me to think that now we'll agree as such near friends should.'

I spoke him in return as handsomely as I was able; but all the while I was wondering what would come next, and why he had parted with his precious guineas; for as to the reason he had given, a baby would have refused it.

Presently, he looked towards me sideways.

'And see here,' says he, 'tit for tat.'

I told him I was ready to prove my gratitude in any reasonable degree, and then waited, looking for some monstrous demand. And yet, when at last he plucked up courage to speak, it was only to tell me (very properly, as I thought) that he was growing old and a little broken, and that he would expect me to help him with the house and the bit garden.

I answered, and expressed my readiness to serve.

'Well,' he said, 'let's begin.' He pulled out of his pocket a rusty key. 'There,' says he, 'there's the key of the stair-tower at the far end of the house. Ye can only win into it from the outside, for that part of the house is no finished. Gang ye in there, and up the stairs, and bring me down the chest that's at the top. 'There's papers in't,' he added.

'Can I have a light, sir?' said I.

'Na,' said he, very cunningly. 'Nae lights in my house.'

'Very well, sir,' said I. 'Are the stairs good?'

'They're grand,' said he; and then as I was going, 'Keep to the wall,' he added; 'there's nae bannisters. But the stairs are grand under foot.'

Out I went into the night. The wind was still moaning

in the distance, though never a breath of it came near the house of Shaws. It had fallen blacker than ever; and I was glad to feel along the wall, till I came the length of the stair-tower door at the far end of the unfinished wing. I had got the key into the keyhole and had just turned it, when all upon a sudden, without sound of wind or thunder, the whole sky lighted up with wild fire and went black again. I had to put my hand over my eyes to get back to the colour of the darkness; and indeed I was already half blinded when I stepped into the tower.

It was so dark inside, it seemed a body could scarce breathe; but I pushed out with foot and hand, and presently struck the wall with the one, and the lowermost round of the stair with the other. The wall, by the touch, was of fine hewn stone; the steps too, though somewhat steep and narrow, were of polished mason-work, and regular and solid under foot. Minding my uncle's word about the bannisters, I kept close to the tower side, and felt my way in the pitch darkness with a beating heart.

The house of Shaws stood some five full storeys high, not counting lofts. Well, as I advanced, it seemed to me the stair grew airier and a thought more lightsome; and I was wondering what might be the cause of this change, when a second blink of the summer lightning came and went. If I did not cry out, it was because fear had me by the throat; and if I did not fall, it was more by Heaven's mercy than my own strength. It was not only that the flash shone in on every side through breaches in the wall, so that I seemed to be clambering aloft upon an open scaffold, but the same passing brightness showed me the steps were of unequal length, and that one of my feet rested that moment within two inches of the well.

This was the grand stair! I thought; and with the thought, a gust of a kind of angry courage came into my heart. My uncle had sent me here, certainly to run great risk, perhaps to die. I swore I would settle that 'perhaps,' if I should break my neck for it; got me down upon my hands and knees; and as slowly as a snail, feeling before me every inch, and testing the solidity of every stone, I continued to ascend the stair. The darkness, by contrast with the flash, appeared to have redoubled; nor was that all, for my ears were now troubled and my mind confounded by a great stir of bats in the top part of the tower, and the foul beasts, flying downward, sometimes beat about my face and body.

The tower, I should have said, was square; and in every corner the step was made of a great stone of a different shape, to join the flights. Well, I had come close to one of these turns, when, feeling forward as usual, my hand slipped upon an edge and found nothing but emptiness beyond it. The stair had been carried no higher: to set a stranger mounting it in the darkness was to send him straight to his death; and (although, thanks to the lightning and my own precautions, I was safe enough) the mere thought of the peril in which I might have stood, and the dreadful height I might have fallen from, brought out the sweat upon my body and relaxed my joints.

But I knew what I wanted now, and turned and groped my way down again with a wonderful anger in my heart. About half way down, the wind sprang up in a clap and shook the tower, and died again; the rain followed; and before I had reached the ground level it fell in buckets. I put out my head into the storm, and looked along towards the kitchen. The door, which I had shut behind me when I left, now stood open, and shed a little glimmer of light; and I thought I could see a figure standing in the rain, quite still, like a man hearkening. And then there came a blinding flash, which showed me my uncle plainly, just where I had fancied him to stand; and hard upon the heels of it, a great tow-row of thunder.

Now, whether my uncle thought the crash to be the sound of my fall, or whether he heard in it God's voice denouncing murder, I will leave you to guess. Certain it is, at least, that he was seized on by a kind of panic fear, and that he ran into the house and left the door open behind him. I followed as softly as I could, and coming unheard into the kitchen, stood and watched him.

He had found time to open the corner cupboard and bring out a great case-bottle of aqua vitæ, and now sat with his back towards me at the table. Ever and again he would be seized with a fit of deadly shuddering and groan aloud, and carrying the bottle to his lips, drink down the raw spirits by the mouthful.

I stepped forward, came close behind him where he sat, and suddenly clapping my two hands down upon his shoulders—'Ah!' cried I.

My uncle gave a kind of broken cry like a sheep's bleat, flung up his arms, and tumbled to the floor like a dead man. I was somewhat shocked at this; but I had myself to look to first of all, and did not hesitate to let him lie as he had fallen. The keys were hanging in the cupboard; and it was my design to furnish myself with arms before my uncle should come again to his senses and the power of devising evil. In the cupboard were a few bottles, some apparently of medicine; a great many bills and other papers, which I should willingly enough have rummaged, had I had the time; and a few necessaries, that were nothing to my purpose. Thence I turned to the chests. The first was full of meal; the second of moneybags and papers tied into sheaves; in the third, with many other things (and these for the most part clothes) I found a rusty, ugly-looking Highland dirk without the scabbard. This, then, I concealed inside my waistcoat, and turned to my uncle.

He lay as he had fallen, all huddled, with one knee up and one arm sprawling abroad; his face had a strange colour of blue, and he seemed to have ceased breathing. Fear came on me that he was dead; then I got water and dashed it in his face; and with that he seemed to come a little to himself, working his mouth and fluttering his eyelids. At last he looked up and saw me, and there came into his eyes a terror that was not of this world.

'Come, come,' said I, 'sit up.'

'Are you alive?' he sobbed. 'O man, are ye alive?'

'That am I,' said I. 'Small thanks to you!'

He had begun to seek for his breath with deep sighs. 'The

blue phial,' said he—'in the aumry—the blue phial.' His breath came slower still.

I ran to the cupboard, and, sure enough, found there a blue phial of medicine, with the dose written on it on a paper, and this I administered to him with what speed I might.

'It's the trouble,' said he, reviving a little; 'I have a trouble, Davie. It's the heart.'

I set him on a chair and looked at him. It is true I felt some pity for a man that looked so sick, but I was full besides of righteous anger; and I numbered over before him the points on which I wanted explanation: why he lied to me at every word; why he feared that I should leave him; why he disliked it to be hinted that he and my father were twins—'Is that because it is true?' I asked; why he had given me money to which I was convinced I had no claim; and, last of all, why he had tried to kill me. He heard me all through in silence; and then, in a broken voice, begged me to let him go to bed.

'I'll tell ye the morn,' he said; 'as sure as death I will.'

And so weak was he that I could do nothing but consent. I locked him into his room, however, and pocketed the key; and then returning to the kitchen, made up such a blaze as had not shone there for many a long year, and wrapping myself in my plaid, lay down upon the chests and fell asleep.

CHAPTER V

I GO TO THE QUEEN'S FERRY

MUCH rain fell in the night; and the next morning there blew a bitter wintry wind out of the north-west, driving scattered clouds. For all that, and before the sun began to peep or the last of the stars had vanished, I made my way to the side of the burn, and had a plunge in a deep whirling pool. All aglow from my bath, I sat down once more beside the fire, which I replenished, and began gravely to consider my position.

There was now no doubt about my uncle's enmity; there

was no doubt I carried my life in my hand, and he would leave no stone unturned that he might compass my destruction. But I was young and spirited, and like most lads that have been country-bred, I had a great opinion of my shrewdness. I had come to his door no better than a beggar and little more than a child; he had met me with treachery and violence; it would be a fine consummation to take the upper hand, and drive him like a herd of sheep.

I sat there nursing my knee and smiling at the fire; and I saw myself in fancy smell out his secrets one after another, and grow to be that man's king and ruler. The warlock of Essendean, they say, had made a mirror in which men could read the future; it must have been of other stuff than burning coal; for in all the shapes and pictures that I sat and gazed at, there was never a ship, never a seaman with a hairy cap, never a big bludgeon for my silly head, or the least sign of all those tribulations that were ripe to fall on me.

Presently, all swollen with conceit, I went upstairs and gave my prisoner his liberty. He gave me good morning civilly; and I gave the same to him, smiling down upon him from the heights of my sufficiency. Soon we were set to breakfast, as it might have been the day before.

'Well, sir,' said I, with a jeering tone, 'have you nothing more to say to me?' And then, as he made no articulate reply, 'it will be time, I think, to understand each other,' I continued. 'You took me for a country Johnnie Raw, with no more mother-wit or courage than a porridge-stick. I took you for a good man, or no worse than others at the least. It seems we were both wrong. What cause you have to fear me, to cheat me, and to attempt my life——'

He murmured something about a jest, and that he liked a bit of fun; and then, seeing me smile, changed his tone, and assured me he would make all clear as soon as we had breakfasted. I saw by his face that he had no lie ready for me, though he was hard at work preparing one; and I think I was about to tell him so, when we were interrupted by a knocking at the door.

Bidding my uncle sit where he was, I went to open it, and

found on the doorstep a half-grown boy in sea-clothes. He had no sooner seen me than he began to dance some steps of the sea-hornpipe (which I had never before heard of, far less seen), snapping his fingers in the air and footing it right cleverly. For all that, he was blue with the cold; and there was something in his face, a look between tears and laughter, that was highly pathetic and consisted ill with this gaiety of manner.

'What cheer, mate?' says he, with a cracked voice.

I asked him soberly to name his pleasure.

'O, pleasure!' says he; and then began to sing:

> 'For it's my delight, of a shiny night,
>   In the season of the year.'*

'Well,' said I, 'if you have no business at all, I will even be so unmannerly as to shut you out.'

'Stay, brother!' he cried. 'Have you no fun about you? or do you want to get me thrashed? I've brought a letter from old Heasy-oasy to Mr. Belflower.' He showed me a letter as he spoke. 'And I say, mate,' he added, 'I'm mortal hungry.'

'Well,' said I, 'come into the house, and you shall have a bite if I go empty for it.'

With that I brought him in and set him down to my own place, where he fell-to greedily on the remains of breakfast, winking to me between-whiles, and making many faces, which I think the poor soul considered manly. Meanwhile, my uncle had read the letter and sat thinking; then, suddenly, he got to his feet with a great air of liveliness, and pulled me apart into the farthest corner of the room.

'Read that,' said he, and put the letter in my hand.

Here it is, lying before me as I write:

'The Hawes Inn,* at the Queen's Ferry.

'Sir,—I lie here with my hawser up and down, and send my cabin-boy to informe. If you have any further commands for over-seas, to-day will be the last occasion, as the wind will serve us well out of the firth. I will not seek to deny that I have had crosses with your doer,[1] Mr. Rankeillor; of which, if not speedily redd up, you may looke to see some losses follow. I have drawn a bill upon you, as per margin, and am, sir, you most obedt., humble servant,

'ELIAS HOSEASON.'

'You see, Davie,' resumed my uncle as soon as he saw that I had done. 'I have a venture with this man Hoseason, the captain of a trading brig, the *Covenant*, of Dysart. Now, if you and me was to walk over with yon lad, I could see the captain at the Hawes, or maybe on board the *Covenant* if there was papers to be signed; and so far from a loss of time, we can jog on to the lawyer, Mr. Rankeillor's. After a' that's come and gone, ye would be swier[2] to believe me upon my naked word: but ye'll believe Rankeillor. He's factor to half the gentry in these parts; an auld man, forby: highly respeckit; and he kenned your father.'

I stood awhile and thought. I was going to some place of shipping, which was doubtless populous, and where my uncle durst attempt no violence, and, indeed, even the society of the cabin-boy so far protected me. Once there, I believed I could force on the visit to the lawyer, even if my uncle were now insincere in proposing it; and, perhaps, in the bottom of my heart, I wished a nearer view of the sea and ships. You are to remember I had lived all my life in the inland hills, and just two days before had my first sight of the firth lying like a blue floor, and the sailed ships moving on the face of it, no bigger than toys. One thing with another, I made up my mind.

'Very well,' says I, 'let us go to the Ferry.'

My uncle got into his hat and coat, and buckled an old rusty cutlass on; and then we trod the fire out, locked the door, and set forth upon our walk.

The wind, being in that cold quarter, the north-west, blew nearly in our faces, as we went. It was the month of June; the grass was all white with daisies and the trees with blossom; but, to judge by our blue nails and aching wrists,

1 Agent.   2 Unwilling.

the time might have been winter and the whiteness a December frost.

Uncle Ebenezer trudged in the ditch, jogging from side to side like an old ploughman coming home from work. He never said a word the whole way; and I was thrown for talk on the cabin-boy. He told me his name was Ransome, and that he had followed the sea since he was nine, but could not say how old he was, as he had lost his reckoning. He showed me tattoo marks, baring his breast in the teeth of the wind and in spite of my remonstrances, for I thought it was enough to kill him; he swore horribly whenever he remembered, but more like a silly schoolboy than a man; and boasted of many wild and bad things that he had done: stealthy thefts, false accusations, ay, and even murder; but all with such a dearth of likelihood in the details, and such a weak and crazy swagger in the delivery, as disposed me rather to pity than to believe him.

I asked him of the brig (which he declared was the finest ship that sailed) and of Captain Hoseason, in whose praise he was equally loud. Heasy-oasy (for so he still named the skipper) was a man, by his account, that minded for nothing either in heaven or earth; one that, as people said, would 'crack on all sail into the day of judgment'; rough, fierce, un-scrupulous, and brutal; and all this my poor cabin-boy had taught himself to admire as something seamanlike and manly. He would only admit one flaw in his idol. 'He ain't no sea-man,' he admitted. 'That's Mr. Shuan that navigates the brig; he's the finest seaman in the trade, only for drink; and I tell you I believe it! Why, look 'ere'; and turning down his stock-ing he showed me a great, raw, red wound that made my blood run cold. 'He done that—Mr. Shuan done it,' he said, with an air of pride.

'What!' I cried, 'do you take such savage usage at his hands? Why, you are no slave, to be so handled!'

'No,' said the poor moon-calf, changing his tune at once, 'and so he'll find! See 'ere'; and he showed me a great case-knife, which he told me was stolen. 'O,' says he, 'let me see him try; I dare him to; I'll do for him! O, he ain't

the first!' And he confirmed it with a poor, silly, ugly
oath.

I have never felt such pity for anyone in this wide world
as I felt for that half-witted creature; and it began to come
over me that the brig *Covenant* (for all her pious name) was
little better than a hell upon the seas.

'Have you no friends?' said I.

He said he had a father in some English seaport, I forget
which. 'He was a fine man, too,' he said; 'but he's dead.'

'In Heaven's name,' cried I, 'can you find no reputable life
on shore?'

'O, no!' says he, winking and looking very sly; 'they
would put me to a trade. I know a trick worth two of that,
I do!'

I asked him what trade could be so dreadful as the one
he followed, where he ran the continual peril of his life,
not alone from wind and sea, but by the horrid cruelty of
those who were his masters. He said it was very true; and
then began to praise the life, and tell what a pleasure it was
to get on shore with money in his pocket, and spend it like
a man, and buy apples, and swagger, and surprise what he
called stick-in-the-mud boys. 'And then it's not all as bad
as that,' says he; 'there's worse off than me: there's the
twenty-pounders. O, laws! you should see them taking on.
Why, I've seen a man as old as you, I dessay'—(to him I
seemed old)—'ah, and he had a beard, too—well, and as soon
as we cleared out of the river, and he had the drug out of his
head—my! how he cried and carried on! I made a fine fool
of him, I tell you! And then there's little uns, too: oh, little
by me! I tell you, I keep them in order. When we carry little
uns, I have a rope's-end of my own to wollop 'em.' And so he
ran on, until it came in on me what he meant by twenty-
pounders were those unhappy criminals who were sent over-
seas to slavery in North America, or the still more unhappy
innocents who were kidnapped or trepanned (as the word
went) for private interest or vengeance.

Just then we came to the top of the hill, and looked down
on the Ferry and the Hope. The Firth of Forth (as is very well

known) narrows at this point to the width of a good-sized river, which makes a convenient ferry going north, and turns the upper reach into a land-locked haven for all manner of ships. Right in the midst of the narrows lies an islet with some ruins; on the south shore they have built a pier for the service of the Ferry: and at the end of the pier, on the other side of the road, and backed against a pretty garden of holly trees and hawthorns, I could see the building which they called the Hawes Inn.

The town of Queensferry lies farther west, and the neighbourhood of the inn looked pretty lonely at that time of day, for the boat had just gone north with passengers. A skiff, however, lay beside the pier, with some seamen sleeping on the thwarts; this, as Ransome told me, was the brig's boat waiting for the captain; and about half a mile off, and all alone in the anchorage, he showed me the *Covenant* herself. There was a seagoing bustle on board; yards were swinging into place; and as the wind blew from that quarter, I could hear the song of the sailors as they pulled upon the ropes. After all I had listened to upon the way, I looked at that ship with an extreme abhorrence; and from the bottom of my heart I pitied all poor souls that were condemned to sail in her.

We had all three pulled up on the brow of the hill; and now I marched across the road and addressed my uncle. 'I think it right to tell you, sir,' says I, 'there's nothing that will bring me on board that *Covenant*.'

He seemed to waken from a dream. 'Eh?' he said. 'What's that?'

I told him over again.

'Well, well,' he said, 'we'll have to please ye, I suppose. But what are we standing here for? It's perishing cold; and if I'm no mistaken, they're busking the *Covenant* for sea.'

CHAPTER VI

WHAT BEFELL AT THE QUEEN'S FERRY

As soon as we came to the inn, Ransome led us up the stair to a small room, with a bed in it, and heated like an oven by a great fire of coal. At a table hard by the chimney, a tall, dark, sober-looking man sat writing. In spite of the heat of the room, he wore a thick sea-jacket, buttoned to the neck, and a tall hairy cap drawn down over his ears; yet I never saw any man, not even a judge upon the bench, look cooler, or more studious and self-possessed, than this ship-captain.

He got to his feet at once, and coming forward, offered his large hand to Ebenezer. 'I am proud to see you, Mr. Balfour,' said he, in a fine deep voice, 'and glad that ye are here in time. The wind's fair, and the tide upon the turn; we'll see the old coal-bucket burning on the Isle of May before to-night.'

'Captain Hoseason,' returned my uncle, 'you keep your room unco hot.'

'It's a habit I have, Mr. Balfour,' said the skipper. 'I'm a cold-rife man by my nature; I have a cold blood, sir. There's neither fur, nor flannel—no, sir, nor hot rum, will warm up what they call the temperature. Sir, it's the same with most men that have been carbonadoed, as they call it, in the tropic seas.'

'Well, well, captain,' replied my uncle, 'we must all be the way we're made.'

But it chanced that this fancy of the captain's had a great share in my misfortunes. For though I had promised myself not to let my kinsman out of sight, I was both so impatient for a nearer look of the sea, and so sickened by the closeness of the room, that when he told me to 'run downstairs and play myself awhile,' I was fool enough to take him at his word.

Away I went, therefore, leaving the two men sitting down to a bottle and a great mass of papers; and crossing the road in front of the inn, walked down upon the beach. With the wind in that quarter, only little wavelets, not much bigger than I had seen upon a lake, beat upon the shore. But the weeds were new to me—some green, some brown and long, and some with little bladders that crackled between my fingers. Even so far up the firth, the smell of the sea water was exceedingly salt and stirring; the *Covenant*, besides, was beginning to shake out her sails, which hung upon the yards in clusters; and the spirit of all that I beheld put me in thoughts of far voyages and foreign places.

I looked, too, at the seamen with the skiff—big brown fellows, some in shirts, some with jackets, some with coloured handkerchiefs about their throats, one with a brace of pistols stuck into his pockets, two or three with knotty bludgeons, and all with their case-knives. I passed the time of day with one that looked less desperate than his fellows, and asked him of the sailing of the brig. He said they would get under way as soon the ebb set, and expressed his gladness to be out of a port where there were no taverns and fiddlers; but all with such horrifying oaths, that I made haste to get away from him.

This threw me back on Ransome, who seemed the least wicked of that gang, and who soon came out of the inn and ran to me, crying for a bowl of punch. I told him I would give him no such thing, for neither he nor I was of an age for such indulgences. 'But a glass of ale you may have, and welcome,' said I. He mopped and mowed at me, and called me names; but he was glad to get the ale, for all that; and presently we were set down at a table in the front room of the inn, and both eating and drinking with a good appetite.

Here it occurred to me that, as the landlord was a man of that county, I might do well to make a friend of him. I offered him a share, as was much the custom in these days; but he was far too great a man to sit with such poor customers as Ransome and myself, and he was leaving the room, when I called him back to ask if he knew Mr. Rankeillor.

'Hoot, ay,' says he, 'and a very honest man. And, O, by-the-bye,' says he, 'was it you that came in with Ebenezer?' And when I had told him yes, 'Ye'll be no friend of his?' he asked, meaning, in the Scottish way, that I would be no relative.

I told him no, none.

'I thought not,' said he; 'and yet ye have a kind of gliff[1] of Mr. Alexander.'

I said it seemed that Ebenezer was ill-seen in the country.

'Nae doubt,' said the landlord. 'He's a wicked auld man, and there's many would like to see him girning in a tow:[2] Jennet Clouston and mony mair that he has harried out of house and hame. And yet he was ance a fine young fellow, too. But that was before the sough[3] gaed abroad about Mr. Alexander; that was like the death of him.'

'And what was it?' I asked.

'Ou, just that he had killed him,' said the landlord. 'Did ye never hear that?'

'And what would he kill him for?' said I.

'And what for, but just to get the place,' said he.

'The place?' said I. 'The Shaws?'

'Nae other place that I ken,' said he.

'Ay, man?' said I. 'Is that so? Was my—was Alexander the eldest son?'

''Deed was he,' said the landlord. 'What else would he have killed him for?'

And with that he went away, as he had been impatient to do from the beginning.

Of course, I had guessed it a long while ago; but it is one thing to guess, another to know; and I sat stunned with my good fortune, and could scarce grow to believe that the same poor lad who had trudged in the dust from Ettrick Forest not two days ago, was now one of the rich of the earth, and had a house and broad lands, and if he but knew how to ride,* might mount his horse to-morrow. All these pleasant things, and a thousand others, crowded into my mind, as I sat staring before me out of the inn window, and paying no heed to what I saw; only I remember that my eye lighted on Captain Hoseason down on the pier among his seamen, and speaking

1 Look.　　2 Rope.　　3 Report.

towards the house, with no mark of a sailor's clumsiness, but with some authority. And presently he came marching back carrying his fine, tall figure with a manly bearing, and still with the same sober, grave expression on his face. I wondered if it was possible that Ransome's stories could be true, and half disbelieved them; they fitted so ill with the man's looks. But indeed, he was neither so good as I supposed him, nor quite so bad as Ransome did; for, in fact, he was two men, and left the better one behind as soon as he set foot on board his vessel.

The next thing, I heard my uncle calling me, and found the pair in the road together. It was the captain who addressed me, and that with an air (very flattering to a young lad) of grave equality.

'Sir,' said he, 'Mr. Balfour tells me great things of you; and for my own part, I like your looks. I wish I was for longer here, that we might make the better friends; but we'll make the most of what we have. Ye shall come on board my brig for half-an-hour, till the ebb sets, and drink a bowl with me.'

Now, I longed to see the inside of a ship more than words can tell; but I was not going to put myself in jeopardy, and I told him my uncle and I had an appointment with a lawyer.

'Ay, ay,' said he, 'he passed me word of that. But, ye see, the boat'll set ye ashore at the town pier, and that's but a penny stone-cast from Rankeillor's house.' And here he suddenly leaned down and whispered in my ear: 'Take care of the old tod;[1] he means mischief. Come aboard till I can get a word with ye.' And then, passing his arm through mine, he continued aloud, as he set off towards his boat: 'But come, what can I bring ye from the Carolinas? Any friend of Mr. Balfour's can command. A roll of tobacco? Indian featherwork? a skin of a wild beast? a stone pipe? the mocking-bird that mews for all the world like a cat? the cardinal bird that is as red as blood?—take your pick and say your pleasure.'

1 Fox.

By this time we were at the boat-side, and he was handing me in. I did not dream of hanging back; I thought (the poor fool!) that I had found a good friend and helper, and I was rejoiced to see the ship. As soon as we were all set in our places, the boat was thrust off from the pier and began to move over the waters; and what with my pleasure in this new movement and my surprise at our low position, and the appearance of the shores, and the growing bigness of the brig as we drew near to it, I could hardly understand what the captain said, and must have answered him at random.

As soon as we were alongside (where I sat fairly gaping at the ship's height, the strong humming of the tide against its sides, and the pleasant cries of the seamen at their work) Hoseason, declaring that he and I must be the first aboard, ordered a tackle to be sent down from the main-yard. In this I was whipped into the air and set down again on the deck, where the captain stood ready waiting for me, and instantly slipped back his arm under mine. There I stood some while, a little dizzy with the unsteadiness of all around me, perhaps a little afraid, and yet vastly pleased with these strange sights; the captain meanwhile pointing out the strangest, and telling me their names and uses.

'But where is my uncle?' said I, suddenly.

'Ay,' said Hoseason, with a sudden grimness, 'that's the point.'

I felt I was lost. With all my strength, I plucked myself clear of him, and ran to the bulwarks. Sure enough, there was the boat pulling for the town, with my uncle sitting in the stern. I gave a piercing cry—'Help, help! Murder!'—so that both sides of the anchorage rang with it, and my uncle turned round where he was sitting, and showed me a face full of cruelty and terror.

It was the last I saw. Already strong hands had been plucking me back from the ship's side; and now a thunder-bolt seemed to strike me; I saw a great flash of fire, and fell senseless.

CHAPTER VII

I GO TO SEA IN THE BRIG 'COVENANT' OF DYSART

I CAME to myself in darkness, in great pain, bound hand and foot, and deafened by many unfamiliar noises. There sounded in my ears a roaring of water as of a huge mill-dam; the thrashing of heavy sprays, the thundering of the sails, and the shrill cries of seamen. The whole world now heaved giddily up, and now rushed giddily downward; and so sick and hurt was I in body, and my mind so much confounded, that it took me a long while, chasing my thoughts up and down, and ever stunned again by a fresh stab of pain, to realise that I must be lying somewhere bound in the belly of that unlucky ship, and that the wind must have strengthened to a gale. With the clear perception of my plight, there fell upon me a blackness of despair, a horror of remorse at my own folly, and a passion of anger at my uncle, that once more bereft me of my senses.

When I returned again to life, the same uproar, the same confused and violent movements, shook and deafened me; and presently, to my other pains and distresses, there was added the sickness of an unused landsman on the sea. In that time of my adventurous youth, I suffered many hardships; but none that was so crushing to my mind and body, or lit by so few hopes, as these first hours on board the brig.

I heard a gun fire, and supposed the storm had proved too strong for us, and we were firing signals of distress. The thought of deliverance, even by death in the deep sea, was welcome to me. Yet it was no such matter; but (as I was afterwards told) a common habit of the captain's, which I here set down to show that even the worst man may have his kindlier side. We were then passing, it appeared, within some miles of Dysart, where the brig was built, and where old Mrs. Hoseason, the captain's mother, had come some years before to live; and whether outward or inward bound, the *Covenant*

was never suffered to go by that place by day, without a gun
fired and colours shown.

I had no measure of time; day and night were alike in that
ill-smelling cavern of the ship's bowels where I lay; and the
misery of my situation drew out the hours to double. How
long, therefore, I lay waiting to hear the ship split upon
some rock, or to feel her reel head-foremost into the depths
of the sea, I have not the means of computation. But sleep
at length stole from me the consciousness of sorrow.

I was wakened by the light of a hand-lantern shining in
my face. A small man of about thirty, with green eyes and
a tangle of fair hair, stood looking down at me.

'Well,' said he, 'how goes it?'

I answered by a sob; and my visitor then felt my pulse and
temples, and set himself to wash and dress the wound upon
my scalp.

'Ay,' said he, 'a sore dunt.[1] What, man? Cheer up! The
world's no done; you've made a bad start of it, but you'll
make a better. Have you had any meat?'

I said I could not look at it; and thereupon he gave me
some brandy and water in a tin pannikin, and left me once
more to myself.

The next time he came to see me, I was lying betwixt
sleep and waking, my eyes wide open in the darkness, the
sickness quite departed, but succeeded by a horrid giddiness
and swimming that was almost worse to bear. I ached,
besides, in every limb, and the cords that bound me seemed
to be of fire. The smell of the hole in which I lay seemed to
have become a part of me; and during the long interval since
his last visit I had suffered tortures of fear, now from the
scurrying of the ship's rats, that sometimes pattered on my
very face, and now from the dismal imaginings that haunt
the bed of fever.

The glimmer of the lantern, as a trap opened, shone in like
the heaven's sunlight; and though it only showed me the
strong, dark beams of the ship that was my prison, I could

1 Stroke.

have cried aloud for gladness. The man with the green eyes
was the first to descend the ladder, and I noticed that he came
somewhat unsteadily. He was followed by the captain.
Neither said a word; but the first set to and examined me,
and dressed my wound as before, while Hoseason looked me
in my face with an odd, black look.

'Now, sir, you see for yourself,' said the first: 'a high fever,
no appetite, no light, no meat: you see for yourself what that
means.'

'I am no conjurer, Mr. Riach,' said the captain.

'Give me leave, sir,' said Riach; 'you've a good head upon
your shoulders, and a good Scotch tongue to ask with; but
I will leave you no manner of excuse: I want that boy taken
out of this hole and put in the forecastle.'

'What ye may want, sir, is a matter of concern to nobody
but yoursel',' returned the captain; 'but I can tell ye that
which is to be. Here he is; here he shall bide.'

'Admitting that you have been paid in a proportion,' said
the other, 'I will crave leave humbly to say that I have not.
Paid I am, and none too much, to be the second officer of this
old tub; and you ken very well if I do my best to earn it. But
I was paid for nothing more.'

'If ye could hold back your hand from the tin-pan, Mr.
Riach, I would have no complaint to make of ye,' returned
the skipper; 'and instead of asking riddles, I make bold to say
that ye would keep your breath to cool your porridge. We'll
be required on deck,' he added, in a sharper note, and set one
foot upon the ladder.

But Mr. Riach caught him by the sleeve.

'Admitting that you have been paid to do a murder——'
he began.

Hoseason turned upon him with a flash.

'What's that?' he cried. 'What kind of talk is that?'

'It seems it is the talk that you can understand,' said
Mr. Riach, looking him steadily in the face.

'Mr. Riach, I have sailed with ye three cruises,' replied
the captain. 'In all that time, sir, ye should have learned to
know me: I'm a stiff man, and a dour man; but for what ye

say the now—fie, fie!—it comes from a bad heart and a black conscience. If ye say the lad will die——'

'Ay, will he!' said Mr. Riach.

'Well, sir, is not that enough?' said Hoseason. 'Flit him where ye please!'

Thereupon the captain ascended the ladder; and I, who had lain silent throughout this strange conversation, beheld Mr. Riach turn after him and bow as low as to his knees in what was plainly a spirit of derision. Even in my then state of sickness, I perceived two things: that the mate was touched with liquor, as the captain hinted, and that (drunk or sober) he was like to prove a valuable friend.

Five minutes afterwards my bonds were cut, I was hoisted on a man's back, carried up to the forecastle, and laid in a bunk on some sea-blankets; where the first thing that I did was to lose my senses.

It was a blessed thing indeed to open my eyes again upon the daylight, and to find myself in the society of men. The forecastle was a roomy place enough, set all about with berths, in which the men of the watch below were seated smoking, or lying down asleep. The day being calm and the wind fair, the scuttle was open, and not only the good daylight, but from time to time (as the ship rolled) a dusty beam of sunlight shone in, and dazzled and delighted me. I had no sooner moved, moreover, than one of the men brought me a drink of something healing which Mr. Riach had prepared, and bade me lie still and I should soon be well again. There were no bones broken, he explained: 'A clour[1] on the head was naething. Man,' said he, 'it was me that gave it ye!'

Here I lay for the space of many days a close prisoner, and not only got my health again, but came to know my companions. They were a rough lot indeed, as sailors mostly are; being men rooted out of all the kindly parts of life, and condemned to toss together on the rough seas, with masters no less cruel. There were some among them that had sailed with the pirates and seen things it would be a shame even

[1] Blow.

to speak of; some were men that had run from the king's ships, and went with a halter round their necks, of which they made no secret; and all, as the saying goes, were 'at a word and a blow' with their best friends. Yet I had not been many days shut up with them before I began to be ashamed of my first judgment, when I had drawn away from them at the Ferry pier, as though they had been unclean beasts. No class of man is altogether bad; but each has its own faults and virtues; and these shipmates of mine were no exception to the rule. Rough they were, sure enough; and bad, I suppose; but they had many virtues. They were kind when it occurred to them, simple even beyond the simplicity of a country lad like me, and had some glimmerings of honesty.

There was one man of maybe forty, that would sit on my berth-side for hours, and tell me of his wife and child. He was a fisher that had lost his boat, and thus been driven to the deep-sea voyaging. Well, it is years ago now; but I have never forgotten him. His wife (who was 'young by him,' as he often told me) waited in vain to see her man return; he would never again make the fire for her in the morning, nor yet keep the bairn when she was sick. Indeed, many of these poor fellows (as the event proved) were upon their last cruise; the deep seas and cannibal fish received them; and it is a thankless business to speak ill of the dead.

Among other good deeds that they did, they returned my money, which had been shared among them; and though it was about a third short, I was very glad to get it, and hoped great good from it in the land I was going to. The ship was bound for the Carolinas; and you must not suppose that I was going to that place merely as an exile. The trade was even then much depressed; since that, and with the rebellion of the colonies and the formation of the United States, it has, of course, come to an end; but in these days of my youth, white men were still sold into slavery on the plantations, and that was the destiny to which my wicked uncle had condemned me.

The cabin-boy Ransome (from whom I had first heard of these atrocities) came in at times from the round-house, where he berthed and served, now nursing a bruised limb in silent agony, now raving against the cruelty of Mr. Shuan. It made my heart bleed; but the men had a great respect for the chief mate, who was, as they said, 'the only seaman of the whole jing-bang, and none such a bad man when he was sober.' Indeed, I found there was a strange peculiarity about our two mates: that Mr. Riach was sullen, unkind, and harsh when he was sober, and Mr. Shuan would not hurt a fly except when he was drinking. I asked about the captain; but I was told drink made no difference upon that man of iron.

I did my best in the small time allowed me to make something like a man, or rather I should say something like a boy, of the poor creature, Ransome. But his mind was scarce truly human. He could remember nothing of the time before he came to sea; only that his father had made clocks, and had a starling in the parlour, which could whistle 'The North Countrie'; all else had been blotted out in these years of hardship and cruelties. He had a strange notion of the dry land, picked up from sailors' stories: that it was a place where lads were put to some kind of slavery called a trade, and where apprentices were continually lashed and clapped into foul prisons. In a town, he thought every second person a decoy, and every third house a place in which seamen would be drugged and murdered. To be sure, I could tell him how kindly I had myself been used upon that dry land he was so much afraid of, and how well fed and carefully taught both by my friends and my parents: and if he had been recently hurt, he would weep bitterly and swear to run away; but if he was in his usual cockbrain humour or (still more) if he had had a glass of spirits in the round-house, he would deride the notion.

It was Mr. Riach (Heaven forgive him!) who gave the boy drink; and it was, doubtless, kindly meant; but besides that it was ruin to his health, it was the pitifullest thing in life to see this unhappy, unfriended creature staggering, and dancing, and talking he knew not what. Some of the men laughed, but not all; others would grow as black as thunder (thinking, perhaps, of their own childhood or their own children) and bid him stop that nonsense, and think what he was doing. As for me, I felt ashamed to look at him, and the poor child still comes about me in my dreams.

All this time, you should know, the *Covenant* was meeting continual head-winds and tumbling up and down against head-seas, so that the scuttle was almost constantly shut, and the forecastle lighted only by a swinging lantern on a beam. There was constant labour for all hands; the sails had to be made and shortened every hour; the strain told on the men's temper; there was a growl of quarrelling all day long from berth to berth; and as I was never allowed to set my foot on deck, you can picture to yourselves how weary of my life I grew to be, and how impatient for a change.

And a change I was to get, as you shall hear; but I must first tell of a conversation I had with Mr. Riach, which put a little heart in me to bear my troubles. Getting him in a favourable stage of drink (for indeed he never looked near me when he was sober) I pledged him to secrecy, and told him my whole story.

He declared it was like a ballad; that he would do his best to help me; that I should have paper, pen, and ink, and write one line to Mr. Campbell and another to Mr. Rankeillor; and that if I had told the truth, ten to one he would be able (with their help) to pull me through and set me in my rights.

'And in the meantime,' says he, 'keep your heart up. You're not the only one, I'll tell you that. There's many a man hoeing tobacco over-seas that should be mounting his horse at his own door at home; many and many! And life is all a variorum, at the best. Look at me: I am a laird's son and more than half a doctor, and here I am, man-Jack to Hoseason!'

I thought it would be civil to ask him for his story.

He whistled loud.

'Never had one,' said he. 'I liked fun, that's all.' And he skipped out of the forecastle.

CHAPTER VIII

THE ROUND-HOUSE

ONE night, about twelve o'clock,* a man of Mr. Riach's
watch (which was on deck) came down for his jacket; and
instantly there began to go a whisper about the forecastle
that 'Shuan had done for him at last.' There was no need
of a name; we all knew who was meant; but we had scarce
time to get the idea rightly in our heads, far less to speak
of it, when the scuttle was again flung open, and Captain
Hoseason came down the ladder. He looked sharply round the
bunks in the tossing light of the lantern; and then, walking
straight up to me, he addressed me, to my surprise, in tones
of kindness.

'My man,' said he, 'we want ye to serve in the round-
house. You and Ransome are to change berths. Run away aft
with ye.'

Even as he spoke, two seamen appeared in the scuttle,
carrying Ransome in their arms; and the ship at that moment
giving a great sheer into the sea, and the lantern swinging,
the light fell direct on the boy's face. It was as white as wax,
and had a look upon it like a dreadful smile. The blood in me
ran cold, and I drew in my breath as if I had been
struck.

'Run away aft; run away aft with ye!' cried Hoseason.

And at that I brushed by the sailors and the boy (who
neither spoke nor moved), and ran up the ladder on deck.

The brig was sheering swiftly and giddily through a long,
cresting swell. She was on the starboard tack, and on the
left hand, under the arched foot of the foresail, I could see
the sunset still quite bright. This, at such an hour of the
night, surprised me greatly; but I was too ignorant to draw
the true conclusion—that we were going north-about round
Scotland, and were now on the high sea between the Orkney
and the Shetland Islands, having avoided the dangerous cur-
rents of the Pentland Firth. For my part, who had been so

long shut in the dark and knew nothing of headwinds, I thought we might be half-way or more across the Atlantic. And indeed (beyond that I wondered a little at the lateness of the sunset light) I gave no heed to it, and pushed on across the decks, running between the seas, catching at ropes, and only saved from going overboard by one of the hands on deck, who had been always kind to me.

The round-house, for which I was bound, and where I was now to sleep and serve, stood some six feet above the decks, and considering the size of the brig, was of good dimensions. Inside were a fixed table and bench, and two berths, one for the captain and the other for the two mates, turn and turn about. It was all fitted with lockers from top to bottom, so as to stow away the officers' belongings and a part of the ship's stores; there was a second store-room underneath, which you entered by a hatchway in the middle of the deck; indeed, all the best of the meat and drink and the whole of the powder were collected in this place; and all the firearms, except the two pieces of brass ordnance, were set in a rack in the aftermost wall of the round-house. The most of the cutlasses were in another place.

A small window with a shutter on each side, and a sky-light in the roof, gave it light by day; and after dark there was a lamp always burning. It was burning when I entered, not brightly, but enough to show Mr. Shuan sitting at the table, with the brandy bottle and a tin pannikin in front of him. He was a tall man, strongly made and very black; and he stared before him on the table like one stupid.

He took no notice of my coming in; nor did he move when the captain followed and leant on the berth beside me, looking darkly at the mate. I stood in great fear of Hoseason, and had my reasons for it; but something told me I need not be afraid of him just then; and I whispered in his ear, 'How is he?' He shook his head like one that does not know and does not wish to think, and his face was very stern.

Presently Mr. Riach came in. He gave the captain a glance that meant the boy was dead as plain as speaking, and took his place like the rest of us; so that we all three stood without a word, staring down at Mr. Shuan, and Mr. Shuan (on his side) sat without a word, looking hard upon the table.

All of a sudden he put out his hand to take the bottle; and at that Mr. Riach started forward and caught it away from him, rather by surprise than violence, crying out, with an oath, that there had been too much of this work altogether, and that a judgment would fall upon the ship. And as he spoke (the weather sliding-doors standing open) he tossed the bottle into the sea.

Mr. Shuan was on his feet in a trice; he still looked dazed, but he meant murder, aye, and would have done it, for the second time that night, had not the captain stepped in between him and his victim.

'Sit down!' roars the captain. 'Ye sot and swine, do ye know what ye've done? Ye've murdered the boy!'

Mr. Shuan seemed to understand; for he sat down again and put up his hand to his brow.

'Well,' he said, 'he brought me a dirty pannikin!'

At that word, the captain and I and Mr. Riach all looked at each other for a second with a kind of frightened look; and then Hoseason walked up to his chief officer, took him by the shoulder, led him across to his bunk, and bade him lie down and go to sleep, as you might speak to a bad child. The murderer cried a little, but he took off his sea-boots and obeyed.

'Ah!' cried Mr. Riach, with a dreadful voice, 'ye should have interfered long syne. It's too late now.'

'Mr. Riach,' said the captain, 'this night's work must never be kennt in Dysart. The boy went overboard, sir; that's what the story is; and I would give five pounds out of my pocket it was true!' He turned to the table. 'What made ye throw the good bottle away?' he added. 'There was nae sense in that, sir. Here, David, draw me another. They're in the bottom locker;' and he tossed me a key. 'Ye'll need a glass yourself, sir,' he added, to Riach. 'Yon was an ugly thing to see.'

So the pair sat down and hob-a-nobbed; and while they did so, the murderer, who had been lying and whimpering in his birth, raised himself upon his elbow and looked at them and at me.

That was the first night of my new duties; and in the course of the next day I had got well into the run of them. I had to serve at the meals, which the captain took at regular hours, sitting down with the officer who was off duty; all the day through I would be running with a dram to one or the other of my three masters; and at night I slept on a blanket thrown on the deck boards at the aftermost end of the round-house, and right in the draught of the two doors. It was a hard and a cold bed; nor was I suffered to sleep without interruption; for someone would be always coming in from deck to get a dram, and when a fresh watch was to be set, two and sometimes all three would sit down and brew a bowl together. How they kept their health, I know not, any more than how I kept my own.

And yet in other ways it was an easy service. There was no cloth to lay; the meals were either of oatmeal porridge or salt junk, except twice a week, when there was duff: and though I was clumsy enough and (not being firm on my sea-legs) sometimes fell with what I was bringing them, both Mr. Riach and the captain were singularly patient. I could not but fancy they were making up lee-way with their consciences, and that they would scarce have been so good with me if they had not been worse with Ransome.

As for Mr. Shuan, the drink, or his crime, or the two together, had certainly troubled his mind. I cannot say I ever saw him in his proper wits. He never grew used to my being there, stared at me continually (sometimes, I could have thought, with terror) and more than once drew back from my hand when I was serving him. I was pretty sure from the first that he had no clear mind of what he had done, and on my second day in the round-house I had the proof of it. We were alone, and he had been staring at me a long time, when, all at once, up he got, as pale as death, and came close up to me, to my great terror. But I had no cause to be afraid of him.

'You were not here before?' he asked.

'No, sir,' said I.

'There was another boy?' he asked again; and when I had answered him, 'Ah!' says he, 'I thought that,' and went and sat down, without another word, except to call for brandy.

You may think it strange, but for all the horror I had, I was still sorry for him. He was a married man, with a wife in Leith; but whether or no he had a family, I have now forgotten; I hope not.

Altogether it was no very hard life for the time it lasted, which (as you are to hear) was not long. I was as well fed as the best of them; even their pickles, which were the great dainty, I was allowed my share of; and had I liked, I might have been drunk from morning to night, like Mr. Shuan. I had company, too, and good company of its sort. Mr. Riach, who had been to the college, spoke to me like a friend when he was not sulking, and he told me many curious things, and some that were informing; and even the captain, though he kept me at the stick's end the most part of the time, would sometimes unbuckle a bit, and tell me of the fine countries he had visited.

The shadow of poor Ransome, to be sure, lay on all four of us, and on me and Mr. Shuan, in particular, most heavily. And then I had another trouble of my own. Here I was, doing dirty work for three men that I looked down upon, and one of whom, at least, should have hung upon a gallows; that was for the present; and as for the future, I could only see myself slaving alongside of negroes in the tobacco fields. Mr. Riach, perhaps from caution, would never suffer me to say another word about my story; the captain, whom I tried to approach, rebuffed me like a dog and would not hear a word; and as the days came and went, my heart sank lower and lower, till I was even glad of the work which kept me from thinking.

CHAPTER IX

THE MAN WITH THE BELT OF GOLD

MORE than a week went by, in which the ill-luck that had hitherto pursued the *Covenant* upon this voyage grew yet more strongly marked. Some days she made a little way; others, she was driven actually back. At last we were beaten so far to the south that we tossed and tacked to and fro the whole of the ninth day, within sight of Cape Wrath and the wild, rocky coast on either hand of it. There followed on that a council of the officers, and some decision which I did not rightly understand, seeing only the result: that we had made a fair wind of a foul one and were running south.

The tenth afternoon, there was a falling swell and a thick, wet, white fog that hid one end of the brig from the other. All afternoon, when I went on deck, I saw men and officers listening hard over the bulwarks—'for breakers,' they said; and though I did not so much as understand the word, I felt danger in the air, and was excited.

Maybe about ten at night, I was serving Mr. Riach and the captain at their supper, when the ship struck something with a great sound, and we heard voices singing out. My two masters leaped to their feet.

'She's struck,' said Mr. Riach.

'No, sir,' said the captain. 'We've only run a boat down.' And they hurried out.

The captain was in the right of it. We had run down a boat in the fog, and she had parted in the midst and gone to the bottom with all her crew, but one. This man (as I heard afterwards) had been sitting in the stern as a passenger, while the rest were on the benches rowing. At the moment of the blow, the stern had been thrown into the air, and the man (having his hands free, and for all he was encumbered with a frieze overcoat that came below his knees) had leaped up and caught hold of the brig's bowsprit. It showed he had luck and much agility and unusual strength, that he should have thus saved himself from such a pass. And yet, when the captain brought him into the round-house, and I set eyes on him for the first time, he looked as cool as I did.

He was smallish in stature, but well set and as nimble as a goat; his face was of a good open expression, but sunburnt very dark, and heavily freckled and pitted with the smallpox; his eyes were unusually light and had a kind of dancing madness in them, that was both engaging and alarming; and when he took off his great-coat, he laid a pair of fine, silver-mounted pistols on the table, and I saw that he was belted with a great sword.* His manners, besides, were elegant, and he pledged the captain handsomely. Altogether I thought of him, at the first sight, that here was a man I would rather call my friend than my enemy.

The captain, too, was taking his observations, but rather of the man's clothes than his person. And to be sure, as soon as he had taken off the great-coat, he showed forth mighty fine for the round-house of a merchant brig: having a hat with feathers, a red waistcoat, breeches of black plush, and a blue coat with silver buttons and handsome silver lace: costly clothes, though somewhat spoiled with the fog and being slept in.

'I'm vexed, sir, about the boat,' says the captain.

'There are some pretty men gone to the bottom,' said the stranger, 'that I would rather see on the dry land again than half a score of boats.'

'Friends of yours?' said Hoseason.

'You have none such friends in your country,' was the reply. 'They would have died for me like dogs.'

'Well, sir,' said the captain, still watching him, 'there are more men in the world than boats to put them in.'

'And that's true too,' cried the other, 'and ye seem to be a gentleman of great penetration.'

'I have been in France, sir,' says the captain, so that it was plain he meant more by the words than showed upon the face of them.

'Well, sir,' says the other, 'and so has many a pretty man, for the matter of that.'

'No doubt, sir,' says the captain; 'and fine coats.'

'Oho!' says the stranger, 'is that how the wind sets?' And he laid his hand quickly on his pistols.

'Don't be hasty,' said the captain. 'Don't do a mischief, before ye see the need of it. Ye've a French soldier's coat upon your back and a Scotch tongue in your head, to be sure; but so has many an honest fellow in these days, and I dare say none the worse of it.'

'So?' said the gentleman in the fine coat: 'are ye of the honest party?' (meaning, Was he a Jacobite? for each side, in these sort of civil broils, takes the name of honesty for its own).

'Why, sir,' replied the captain, 'I am a true-blue Protestant, and I thank God for it.' (It was the first word of any religion I had ever heard from him, but I learnt afterwards he was a great church-goer while on shore.) 'But, for all that,' says he, 'I can be sorry to see another man with his back to the wall.'

'Can ye so, indeed?' asks the Jacobite. 'Well, sir, to be quite plain with ye, I am one of those honest gentlemen that were in trouble about the years forty-five and six; and (to be still quite plain with ye) if I got into the hands of any of the red-coated gentry, it's like it would go hard with me. Now, sir, I was for France; and there was a French ship cruising here to pick me up; but she gave us the go-by in the fog—as I wish from the heart that ye had done yoursel'! And the best that I can say is this: If ye can set me ashore where I was going, I have that upon me will reward you highly for your trouble.'

'In France?' says the captain. 'No, sir; that I cannot do. But where ye come from—we might talk of that.'

And then, unhappily, he observed me standing in my corner, and packed me off to the galley to get supper for the gentleman. I lost no time, I promise you; and when I came back into the round-house, I found the gentleman had taken a money-belt from about his waist, and poured out a guinea or two upon the table. The captain was looking at the guineas, and then at the belt, and then at the gentleman's face; and I thought he seemed excited.

'Half of it,' he cried, 'and I'm your man!'

The other swept back the guineas into the belt, and put

it on again under his waistcoat. 'I have told ye, sir,' said he, 'that not one doit of it belongs to me. It belongs to my chieftain'—and here he touched his hat—'and while I would be but a silly messenger to grudge some of it that the rest might come safe, I should show myself a hound indeed if I bought my own carcase any too dear. Thirty guineas on the seaside, or sixty if ye set me on the Linnhe loch. Take it, if ye will; if not, ye can do your worst.'

'Ay,' said Hoseason. 'And if I give ye over to the soldiers?'

'Ye would make a fool's bargain,' said the other. 'My chief, let me tell you, sir, is forfeited, like every honest man in Scotland. His estate is in the hands of the man they call King George; and it is his officers that collect the rents, or try to collect them. But for the honour of Scotland, the poor tenant bodies take a thought upon their chief lying in exile; and this money is a part of that very rent for which King George is looking. Now, sir, ye seem to me to be a man that understands things: bring this money within the reach of Government, and how much of it'll come to you?'

'Little enough, to be sure,' said Hoseason; and then: 'If they knew,' he added, drily. 'But I think, if I was to try, that I could hold my tongue about it.'

'Ah, but I'll begowk[1] ye there!' cried the gentleman. 'Play me false, and I'll play you cunning. If a hand's laid upon me, they shall ken what money it is.'

'Well,' returned the captain, 'what must be must. Sixty guineas, and done. Here's my hand upon it.'

'And here's mine,' said the other.

And thereupon the captain went out (rather hurriedly, I thought), and left me alone in the round-house with the stranger.

At that period (so soon after the forty-five) there were many exiled gentlemen coming back at the peril of their lives, either to see their friends or to collect a little money; and as for the Highland chiefs that had been forfeited, it was a common matter of talk how their tenants would stint

1 Befool.

themselves to send them money, and their clansmen outface the soldiery to get it in, and run the gauntlet of our great navy to carry it across. All this I had, of course, heard tell of; and now I had a man under my eyes whose life was forfeit on all these counts and upon one more; for he was not only a rebel and a smuggler of rents, but had taken service with King Louis of France. And as if all this were not enough, he had a belt full of golden guineas round his loins. Whatever my opinions, I could not look on such a man without a lively interest.

'And so you're a Jacobite?' said I, as I set meat before him.

'Ay,' said he, beginning to eat. 'And you by your long face, should be a Whig?'[1]

'Betwixt and between,' said I, not to annoy him; for indeed I was as good a Whig as Mr. Campbell could make me.

'And that's naething,' said he. 'But I'm saying, Mr. Betwixt-and-Between,' he added, 'this bottle of yours is dry; and it's hard if I'm to pay sixty guineas and be grudged a dram upon the back of it.'

'I'll go and ask for the key,' said I, and stepped on deck.

The fog was as close as ever, but the swell almost down. They had laid the brig to, not knowing precisely where they were, and the wind (what little there was of it) not serving well for their true course. Some of the hands were still hearkening for breakers; but the captain and the two officers were in the waist with their heads together. It struck me, I don't know why, that they were after no good; and the first word I heard, as I drew softly near, more than confirmed me.

It was Mr. Riach, crying out as if upon a sudden thought:

'Couldn't we wile him out of the round-house?'

'He's better where he is,' returned Hoseason; 'he hasn't room to use his sword.'

'Well, that's true,' said Riach; 'but he's hard to come at.'

'Hut!' said Hoseason. 'We can get the man in talk, one

1 Whig or Whigamore was the cant name for those who were loyal to King George.

upon each side, and pin him by the two arms; or if that'll not hold, sir, we can make a run by both the doors and get him under hand before he has the time to draw.'

At this hearing, I was seized with both fear and anger at these treacherous, greedy, bloody men that I sailed with. My first mind was to run away; my second was bolder.

'Captain,' said I, 'the gentleman is seeking a dram, and the bottle's out. Will you give me the key?'

They all started and turned about.

'Why, here's our chance to get the firearms!' Riach cried; and then to me: 'Hark ye, David,' he said, 'do ye ken where the pistols are?'

'Ay, ay,' put in Hoseason. 'David kens; David's a good lad. Ye see, David my man, yon wild Hielandman is a danger to the ship besides being a rank foe to King George, God bless him!'

I had never been so be-Davided since I came on board; but I said Yes, as if all I heard were quite natural.

'The trouble is,' resumed the captain, 'that all our firelocks, great and little, are in the round-house under this man's nose; likewise the powder. Now, if I, or one of the officers, was to go in and take them, he would fall to thinking. But a lad like you, David, might snap up a horn and a pistol or two without remark. And if ye can do it cleverly, I'll bear it in mind when it'll be good for you to have friends; and that's when we come to Carolina.'

Here Mr. Riach whispered him a little.

'Very right, sir,' said the captain; and then to myself: 'And see here, David, yon man has a beltful of gold, and I give you my word that you shall have your fingers in it.'

I told him I would do as he wished, though indeed I had scarce breath to speak with; and upon that he gave me the key of the spirit-locker, and I began to go slowly back to the round-house. What was I to do? They were dogs and thieves; they had stolen me from my own country; they had killed poor Ransome; and was I to hold the candle to another murder? But then, upon the other hand, there was the fear of death very plain before me; for what could a boy and a man, if they were as brave as lions, against a whole ship's company?

I was still arguing it back and forth, and getting no great clearness, when I came into the round-house and saw the Jacobite eating his supper under the lamp; and at that my mind was made up all in a moment. I have no credit by it; it was by no choice of mine, but as if by compulsion, that I walked right up to the table and put my hand on his shoulder.

'Do ye want to be killed?' said I.

He sprang to his feet, and looked a question at me as clear as if he had spoken.

'O!' cried I, 'they're all murderers here; it's a ship full of them! They've murdered a boy already. Now it's you.'

'Ay, ay,' said he; 'but they haven't got me yet.' And then looking at me curiously, 'Will ye stand with me?'

'That will I!' said I. 'I am no thief, nor yet murderer. I'll stand by you.'

'Why, then,' said he, 'what's your name?'

'David Balfour,' said I; and then thinking that a man with so fine a coat must like fine people, I added for the first time 'of Shaws.'

It never occurred to him to doubt me, for a Highlander is used to see great gentlefolk in great poverty; but as he had no estate of his own, my words nettled a very childish vanity he had.

'My name is Stewart,' he said, drawing himself up. 'Alan Breck* they call me. A king's name is good enough for me, though I bear it plain and have the name of no farm-midden to clap to the hind end of it.'

And having administered this rebuke, as though it were something of a chief importance, he turned to examine our defences.

The round-house was built very strong, to support the breaching of the seas. Of its five apertures, only the skylight and the two doors were large enough for the passage of a man. The doors, besides, could be drawn close: they were of stout oak, and ran in grooves, and were fitted with hooks to keep them either shut or open, as the need arose. The one that was already shut, I secured in this fashion; but when I was proceeding to slide to the other, Alan stopped me.

'David,' said he—'for I cannae bring to mind the name of your landed estate, and so will make so bold as call you David—that door, being open, is the best part of my defences.'

'It would be yet better shut,' says I.

'Not so, David,' says he. 'Ye see, I have but one face; but so long as that door is open and my face to it, the best part of my enemies will be in front of me, where I would aye wish to find them.'

Then he gave me from the rack a cutlass (of which there were a few besides the firearms), choosing it with great care, shaking his head and saying he had never in all his life seen poorer weapons; and next he set me down to the table with a powder-horn, a bag of bullets, and all the pistols, which he bade me charge.

'And that will be better work, let me tell you,' said he, 'for a gentleman of decent birth, than scraping plates and raxing[1] drams to a wheen tarry sailors.'

Thereupon he stood up in the midst with his face to the door, and drawing his great sword, made trial of the room he had to wield it in.

'I must stick to the point,' he said, shaking his head; 'and that's a pity, too. It doesn't set my genius, which is all for the upper guard. And now,' said he, 'do you keep on charging the pistols, and give heed to me.'

I told him I would listen closely. My chest was tight, my mouth dry, the light dark to my eyes; the thought of the numbers that were soon to leap in upon us kept my heart in a flutter; and the sea, which I heard washing round the brig, and where I thought my dead body would be cast ere morning, ran in my mind strangely.

'First of all,' said he, 'how many are against us?'

---

[1] Reaching.

I reckoned them up; and such was the hurry of my mind, I had to cast the numbers twice. 'Fifteen,' said I.

Alan whistled. 'Well,' said he, 'that can't be cured. And now follow me. It is my part to keep this door, where I look for the main battle. In that, ye have no hand. And mind and dinnae fire to this side unless they get me down; for I would rather have ten foes in front of me than one friend like you cracking pistols at my back.'

I told him, indeed I was no great shot.

'And that's very bravely said,' he cried, in a great admiration of my candour. 'There's many a pretty gentleman that wouldnae dare to say it.'

'But then, sir,' said I, 'there is the door behind you, which they may perhaps break in.'

'Ay,' said he, 'and that is a part of your work. No sooner the pistols charged, than ye must climb up into yon bed where ye're handy at the window; and if they lift hand against the door, ye're to shoot. But that's not all. Let's make a bit of a soldier of ye, David. What else have ye to guard?'

'There's the skylight,' said I. 'But indeed, Mr. Stewart, I would need to have eyes upon both sides to keep the two of them; for when my face is at the one, my back is to the other.'

'And that's very true,' said Alan. 'But have ye no ears to your head?'

'To be sure,' cried I. 'I must hear the bursting of the glass!'

'Ye have some rudiments of sense,' said Alan, grimly.

CHAPTER X

THE SIEGE OF THE ROUND-HOUSE*

BUT now our time of truce was come to an end. Those on deck had waited for my coming till they grew impatient; and scarce had Alan spoken, when the captain showed face in the open door.

'Stand!' cried Alan, and pointed his sword at him.

The captain stood, indeed; but he neither winced nor drew back a foot.

'A naked sword?' says he. 'This is a strange return for hospitality.'

'Do ye see me?' said Alan. 'I am come of kings; I bear a king's name. My badge is the oak. Do ye see my sword? It has slashed the heads off mair Whigamores than you have toes upon your feet. Call up your vermin to your back, sir, and fall on! The sooner the clash begins, the sooner ye'll taste this steel throughout your vitals.'

The captain said nothing to Alan, but he looked over at me with an ugly look. 'David,' said he, 'I'll mind this'; and the sound of his voice went through me with a jar.

Next moment he was gone.

'And now,' said Alan, 'let your hand keep your head, for the grip is coming.'

Alan drew a dirk, which he held in his left hand in case they should run in under his sword. I, on my part, clambered up into the berth with an armful of pistols and something of a heavy heart, and set open the window where I was to watch. It was a small part of the deck that I could overlook, but enough for our purpose. The sea had gone down, and the wind was steady and kept the sails quiet; so that there was a great stillness in the ship, in which I made sure I heard the sound of muttering voices. A little after, and there came a clash of steel upon the deck, by which I knew they were dealing out the cutlasses and one had been let fall; and after that, silence again.

I do not know if I was what you call afraid; but my heart beat like a bird's, both quick and little; and there was a dimness came before my eyes which I continually rubbed away, and which continually returned. As for hope, I had none; but only a darkness of despair and a sort of anger against all the world that made me long to sell my life as dear as I was able. I tried to pray, I remember, but that same hurry of my mind, like a man running, would not suffer me to think upon the words; and my chief wish was to have the thing begin and be done with it.

It came all of a sudden when it did, with a rush of feet and a roar, and then a shout from Alan, and a sound of blows and someone crying out as if hurt. I looked back over my shoulder, and saw Mr. Shuan in the doorway, crossing blades with Alan.

'That's him that killed the boy!' I cried.

'Look to your window!' said Alan; and as I turned back to my place, I saw him pass his sword through the mate's body.

It was none too soon for me to look to my own part; for my head was scarce back at the window, before five men carrying a spare yard for a battering-ram, ran past me and took post to drive the door in. I had never fired with a pistol in my life, and not often with a gun; far less against a fellow-creature. But it was now or never; and just as they swang the yard, I cried out, 'Take that!' and shot into their midst.

I must have hit one of them, for he sang out and gave back a step, and the rest stopped as if a little disconcerted. Before they had time to recover, I sent another ball over their heads; and at my third shot (which went as wide as the second) the whole party threw down the yard and ran for it.

Then I looked round again into the deck-house. The whole place was full of the smoke of my own firing, just as my ears seemed to be burst with the noise of the shots. But there was Alan, standing as before; only now his sword was running blood to the hilt, and himself so swelled with triumph and fallen into so fine an attitude, that he looked to be invincible. Right before him on the floor was Mr. Shuan, on his hands and knees; the blood was pouring from his mouth, and he was sinking slowly lower, with a terrible, white face; and just as I looked, some of those from behind caught hold of him by the heels and dragged him bodily out of the round-house. I believe he died as they were doing it.

'There's one of your Whigs for ye!' cried Alan; and then turning to me, he asked if I had done much execution.

I told him I had winged one, and thought it was the captain.

'And I've settled two,' says he. 'No, there's not enough

blood let; they'll be back again. To your watch, David. This was but a dram before meat.'

I settled back to my place, re-charging the three pistols I had fired, and keeping watch with both eye and ear.

Our enemies were disputing not far off upon the deck, and that so loudly that I could hear a word or two above the washing of the seas.

'It was Shuan bauchled[1] it,' I heard one say.

And another answered him with a 'Wheesht, man! He's paid the piper.'

After that the voices fell again into the same muttering as before. Only now, one person spoke most of the time, as though laying down a plan, and first one and then another answered him briefly, like men taking orders. By this, I made sure they were coming on again, and told Alan.

'It's what we have to pray for,' said he. 'Unless we can give them a good distaste of us, and done with it, there'll be nae sleep for either you or me. But this time, mind, they'll be in earnest.'

By this, my pistols were ready, and there was nothing to do but listen and wait. While the brush lasted, I had not the time to think if I was frighted; but now, when all was still again, my mind ran upon nothing else. The thought of the sharp swords and the cold steel was strong in me; and presently, when I began to hear stealthy steps and a brushing of men's clothes against the round-house wall, and knew they were taking their places in the dark, I could have found it in my mind to cry out aloud.

All this was upon Alan's side; and I had begun to think my share of the fight was at an end, when I heard someone drop softly on the roof above me.

Then there came a single call on the sea-pipe, and that was the signal. A knot of them made one rush of it, cutlass in hand, against the door; and at the same moment, the glass of the skylight was dashed in a thousand pieces, and a man leaped through and landed on the floor. Before he got his

---

[1] Bungled.

feet, I had clapped a pistol to his back, and might have shot him, too; only at the touch of him (and him alive) my whole flesh misgave me, and I could no more pull the trigger than I could have flown.

He had dropped his cutlass as he jumped, and when he felt the pistol, whipped straight round and laid hold of me, roaring out an oath; and at that either my courage came again, or I grew so much afraid as came to the same thing; for I gave a shriek and shot him in the midst of the body. He gave the most horrible, ugly groan and fell to the floor. The foot of a second fellow, whose legs were dangling through the skylight, struck me at the same time upon the head; and at that I snatched another pistol and shot this one through the thigh, so that he slipped through and tumbled in a lump on his companion's body. There was no talk of missing, any more than there was time to aim; I clapped the muzzle to the very place and fired.

I might have stood and stared at them for long, but I heard Alan shout as if for help, and that brought me to my senses.

He had kept the door so long; but one of the seamen, while he was engaged with others, had run in under his guard and caught him about the body. Alan was dirking him with his left hand, but the fellow clung like a leech. Another had broken in and had his cutlass raised. The door was thronged with their faces. I thought we were lost, and catching up my cutlass, fell on them in flank.

But I had not time to be of help. The wrestler dropped at last; and Alan, leaping back to get his distance, ran upon the others like a bull, roaring as he went. They broke before him like water, turning, and running, and falling one against another in their haste. The sword in his hands flashed like quicksilver into the huddle of our fleeing enemies; and at every flash there came the scream of a man hurt. I was still thinking we were lost, when lo! they were all gone, and Alan was driving them along the deck as a sheep-dog chases sheep.

Yet he was no sooner out than he was back again, being as cautious as he was brave; and meanwhile the seamen continued running and crying out as if he was still behind them;

and we heard them tumble one upon another into the forecastle, and clap-to the hatch upon the top.

The round-house was like a shambles; three were dead inside, another lay in his death agony across the threshold; and there were Alan and I victorious and unhurt.

He came up to me with open arms. 'Come to my arms!' he cried, and embraced and kissed me hard upon both cheeks. 'David,' said he, 'I love you like a brother. And O, man,' he cried in a kind of ecstasy, 'am I no a bonny fighter?'

Thereupon he turned to the four enemies, passed his sword clean through each of them, and tumbled them out of doors one after the other. As he did so, he kept humming and singing and whistling to himself, like a man trying to recall an air; only what *he* was trying, was to make one. All the while, the flush was in his face, and his eyes were as bright as a five-year-old child's with a new toy. And presently he sat down upon the table, sword in hand; the air that he was making all the time began to run a little clearer, and then clearer still; and then out he burst with a great voice into a Gaelic song.

I have translated it here, not in verse (of which I have no skill) but at least in the king's English. He sang it often afterwards, and the thing became popular; so that I have heard it, and had it explained to me, many's the time.

> 'This is the song of the sword of Alan:
> The smith made it,
> The fire set it;
> Now it shines in the hand of Alan Breck.
>
> 'Their eyes were many and bright,
> Swift were they to behold,
> Many the hands they guided:
> The sword was alone.
>
> 'The dun deer troop over the hill,
> They are many, the hill is one;
> The dun deer vanish,
> The hill remains.

'Come to me from the hills of heather,
Come from the isles of the sea.
O far-beholding eagles,
Here is your meat.'

Now this song which he made (both words and music) in
the hour of our victory, is something less than just to me,
who stood beside him in the tussle. Mr. Shuan and five more
were either killed outright or thoroughly disabled; but of
these, two fell by my hand, the two that came by the skylight. Four more were hurt, and of that number, one (and he
not the least important) got his hurt from me. So that, altogether, I did my fair share both of the killing and the
wounding, and might have claimed a place in Alan's verses.
But poets (as a very wise man once told me)* have to think
upon their rhymes; and in good prose talk, Alan always did
me more than justice.

In the meanwhile, I was innocent of any wrong being done
me. For not only I knew no word of the Gaelic; but what
with the long suspense of the waiting, and the scurry and
strain of our two spirts of fighting, and, more than all, the
horror I had of some of my own share in it, the thing was
no sooner over than I was glad to stagger to a seat. There was
that tightness on my chest that I could hardly breathe; the
thought of the two men I had shot sat upon me like a nightmare; and all upon a sudden, and before I had a guess of what
was coming, I began to sob and cry like any child.

Alan clapped my shoulder, and said I was a brave lad and
wanted nothing but a sleep.

'I'll take the first watch,' said he. 'Ye've done well by me,
David, first and last; and I wouldn't lose you for all Appin—
no, nor for Breadalbane.'

So he made up my bed on the floor, and took the first spell,
pistol in hand and sword on knee; three hours by the
captain's watch upon the wall. Then he roused me up, and
I took my turn of three hours; before the end of which it was
broad day, and a very quiet morning, with a smooth, rolling
sea that tossed the ship and made the blood run to and fro

on the round-house floor, and a heavy rain that drummed
upon the roof. All my watch there was nothing stirring; and
by the banging of the helm, I knew they had even no one
at the tiller. Indeed (as I learned afterwards) there were so
many of them hurt or dead, and the rest in so ill a temper,
that Mr. Riach and the captain had to take turn and turn like
Alan and me, or the brig might have gone ashore and nobody
the wiser. It was a mercy the night had fallen so still, for the
wind had gone down as soon as the rain began. Even as it
was, I judged by the wailing of a great number of gulls that
went crying and fishing round the ship, that she must have
drifted pretty near the coast or one of the islands of the
Hebrides; and at last, looking out of the door of the round-
house, I saw the great stone hills of Skye on the right hand,
and, a little more astern, the strange isle of Rum.

CHAPTER XI

THE CAPTAIN KNUCKLES UNDER

ALAN and I sat down to breakfast about six of the clock. The
floor was covered with broken glass and in a horrid mess of
blood, which took away my hunger. In all other ways we
were in a situation not only agreeable but merry; having
ousted the officers from their own cabin, and having at command all the drink in the ship—both wine and spirits—and
all the dainty part of what was eatable, such as the pickles
and the fine sort of biscuit.* This, of itself, was enough to set
us in good humour; but the richest part of it was this, that
the two thirstiest men that ever came out of Scotland (Mr.
Shuan being dead) were now shut in the fore-part of the ship
and condemned to what they hated most—cold water.

'And depend upon it,' Alan said, 'we shall hear more of
them ere long. Ye may keep a man from the fighting but
never from his bottle.'

We made good company for each other. Alan, indeed,
expressed himself most lovingly; and taking a knife from

the table, cut me off one of the silver buttons from his coat.

'I had them,' says he, 'from my father, Duncan Stewart; and now give ye one of them to be keepsake for last night's work. And wherever ye go and show the button, the friends of Alan Breck will come around you.'

He said this as if he had been Charlemagne, and commanded armies; and indeed, much as I admired his courage, I was always in danger of smiling at his vanity: in danger, I say, for had I not kept my countenance, I would be afraid to think what a quarrel might have followed.

As soon as we were through with our meal, he rummaged in the captain's locker till he found a clothes-brush; and then taking off his coat, began to visit his suit and brush away the stains, with such care and labour as I supposed to have been only usual with women. To be sure, he had no other; and besides (as he said), it belonged to a King and so behoved to be royally looked after.

For all that, when I saw what care he took to pluck out the threads where the button had been cut away, I put a higher value on his gift.

He was still so engaged, when we were hailed by Mr. Riach from the deck, asking for a parley; and I, climbing through the skylight and sitting on the edge of it, pistol in hand and with a bold front, though inwardly in fear of broken glass, hailed him back again and bade him speak out. He came to the edge of the round-house, and stood on a coil of rope, so that his chin was on a level with the roof; and we looked at each other a while in silence. Mr. Riach, as I do not think he had been very forward in the battle, so he had got off with nothing worse than a blow upon the cheek: but he looked out of heart and very weary, having been all night afoot, either standing watch or doctoring the wounded.

'This is a bad job,' said he at last, shaking his head.

'It was none of our choosing,' said I.

'The captain,' says he, 'would like to speak with your friend. They might speak at the window.'

'And how do we know what treachery he means?' cried I.

'He means none, David,' returned Mr. Riach; 'and if he

did, I'll tell ye the honest truth, we couldnae get the men to follow.'

'Is that so?' said I.

'I'll tell ye more than that,' said he. 'It's not only the men; it's me, I'm frich'ened, Davie.' And he smiled across at me. 'No,' he continued, 'what we want is to be shut of him.'

Thereupon I consulted with Alan, and the parley was agreed to and parole given upon either side; but this was not the whole of Mr. Riach's business, and he now begged me for a dram with such instancy and such reminders of his former kindness, that at last I handed him a pannikin with about a gill of brandy. He drank a part, and then carried the rest down upon the deck to share it (I suppose) with his superior.

A little after, the captain came (as was agreed) to one of the windows, and stood there in the rain, with his arm in a sling, and looking stern and pale, and so old that my heart smote me for having fired upon him.

Alan at once held a pistol in his face.

'Put that thing up!' said the captain. 'Have I not passed my word, sir? or do ye seek to affront me?'

'Captain,' says Alan, 'I doubt your word is a breakable. Last night ye haggled and arglebargled like an apple-wife; and then passed me your word, and gave me your hand to back it; and ye ken very well what was the upshot. Be damned to your word!' says he.

'Well, well, sir,' said the captain, 'ye'll get little good by swearing.' (And truly that was a fault of which the captain was quite free.) 'But we have other things to speak,' he continued, bitterly. 'Ye've made a sore hash of my brig; I haven't hands enough left to work her; and my first officer (whom I could ill spare) has got your sword throughout his vitals, and passed without speech. There is nothing left me, sir, but to put back into the port of Glasgow after hands; and there (by your leave) ye will find them that are better able to talk to you.'

'Ay?' said Alan; 'and faith, I'll have a talk with them mysel'! Unless there's naebody speaks English in that town, I have a bonny tale for them. Fifteen tarry sailors upon the one side, and a man and a halfling boy upon the other! O, man, it's peetiful!'

Hoseason flushed red.

'No,' continued Alan, 'that'll no do. Ye'll just have to set me ashore as we agreed.'

'Ay,' said Hoseason, 'but my first officer is dead—ye ken best how. There's none of the rest of us acquaint with this coast, sir; and it's one very dangerous to ships.'

'I give ye your choice,' says Alan. 'Set me on dry ground in Appin, or Ardgour, or in Morven, or Arisaig, or Morar; or, in brief where ye please, within thirty miles of my own country; except in a country of the Campbells. That's a broad target. If ye miss that, ye must be as feckless at the sailoring as I have found ye at the fighting. Why, my poor country people in their bit cobles¹ pass from island to island in all weathers—ay, and by night too, for the matter of that.'

'A coble's not a ship, sir,' said the captain. 'It has nae draught of water.'

'Well, then, to Glasgow if ye list!' says Alan. 'We'll have the laugh of ye at the least.'

'My mind runs little upon laughing,' said the captain. 'But all this will cost money, sir.'

'Well, sir,' says Alan, 'I am nae weathercock. Thirty guineas, if ye land me on the sea-side; and sixty, if ye put me in the Linnhe Loch.'

'But see, sir, where we lie, we are but a few hours' sail from Ardnamurchan,' said Hoseason. 'Give me sixty, and I'll set ye there.'

'And I'm to wear my brogues and run jeopardy of the red coats to please you?' cries Alan. 'No, sir, if ye want sixty guineas, earn them, and set me in my own country.'

'It's to risk the brig, sir,' said the captain, 'and your own lives along with her.'

'Take it or want it,' says Alan.

'Could ye pilot us at all?' asked the captain, who was frowning to himself.

¹ Coble: a small boat used in fishing.

'Well, it's doubtful,' said Alan. 'I'm more of a fighting man (as ye have seen for yoursel') than a sailor-man. But I have been often enough picked up and set down upon this coast, and should ken something of the lie of it.'

The captain shook his head, still frowning.

'If I had lost less money on this unchancy cruise,' says he, 'I would see you in a rope's end before I risked my brig, sir. But be it as ye will. As soon as I get a slant of wind (and there's some coming, or I'm the more mistaken) I'll put it in hand. But there's one thing more. We may meet in with a king's ship and she may lay us aboard, sir, with no blame of mine: they keep the cruisers thick upon this coast, ye ken who for. Now, sir, if that was to befall, ye might leave the money.'

'Captain,' says Alan, 'if ye see a pennant, it shall be your part to run away. And now, as I hear you're a little short of brandy in the fore-part, I'll offer ye a change: a bottle of brandy against two buckets of water.'

That was the last clause of the treaty, and was duly executed on both sides; so that Alan and I could at last wash out the round-house and be quit of the memorials of those whom we had slain, and the captain and Mr. Riach could be happy again in their own way, the name of which was drink.

CHAPTER XII

I HEAR OF THE 'RED FOX'*

BEFORE we had done cleaning out the round-house, a breeze sprang up from a little to the east of north. This blew off the rain and brought out the sun.

And here I must explain; and the reader would do well to look at a map. On the day when the fog fell and we ran down Alan's boat, we had been running through the Little Minch. At dawn after the battle, we lay becalmed to the east of the Isle of Canna or between that and Isle Eriska in the chain of the Long Island. Now to get from there to the

Linnhe Loch, the straight course was through the narrows of the Sound of Mull. But the captain had no chart; he was afraid to trust his brig so deep among the islands; and the wind serving well, he preferred to go by west of Tiree and come up under the southern coast of the great Isle of Mull.

All day the breeze held in the same point, and rather freshened than died down; and towards afternoon, a swell began to set in from round the outer Hebrides. Our course, to go round about the inner isles, was to the west of south, so that at first we had this swell upon our beam, and were much rolled about. But after nightfall, when we had turned the end of Tiree and began to head more to the east, the sea came right astern.

Meanwhile, the early part of the day, before the swell came up, was very pleasant; sailing, as we were, in a bright sunshine and with many mountainous islands upon different sides. Alan and I sat in the round-house with the doors open on each side (the wind being straight astern) and smoked a pipe or two of the captain's fine tobacco. It was at this time we heard each other's stories, which was the more important to me, as I gained some knowledge of that wild Highland country, on which I was so soon to land. In those days, so close on the back of the great rebellion, it was needful a man should know what he was doing when he went upon the heather.

It was I that showed the example, telling him all my misfortune; which he heard with great good-nature. Only, when I came to mention that good friend of mine, Mr. Campbell the minister, Alan fired up and cried out that he hated all that were of that name.

'Why,' said I, 'he is a man you should be proud to give your hand to.'

'I know nothing I would help a Campbell to,' says he, 'unless it was a leaden bullet. I would hunt all of that name like blackcocks. If I lay dying, I would crawl upon my knees to my chamber window for a shot at one.'

'Why, Alan,' I cried, 'what ails ye at the Campbells?'

'Well,' says he, 'ye ken very well that I am an Appin

Stewart, and the Campbells have long harried and wasted
those of my name; ay, and got lands of us by treachery—but
never with the sword,' he cried loudly, and with the word
brought down his fist upon the table. But I paid the less
attention to this, for I knew it was usually said by those who
have the underhand. 'There's more than that,' he continued,
'and all in the same story: lying words, lying papers, tricks fit
for a pedlar, and the show of what's legal over all, to make a
man the more angry.'

'You that are so wasteful of your buttons;' said I,' I can
hardly think you would be a good judge of business.'

'Ah!' says he, falling again to smiling, 'I got my wasteful-
ness from the same man I got the buttons from: and that was
my poor father, Duncan Stewart, grace be to him! He was
the prettiest man of his kindred; and the best swordsman in
the Hielands, David, and that is the same as to say, in all the
world, I should ken, for it was him that taught me. He was
in the Black Watch, when first it was mustered; and like other
gentleman privates, had a gillie at his back to carry his firelock for him on the march. Well, the king, it appears, was
wishful to see Hieland swordsmanship; and my father and
three more were chosen out and sent to London town, to let
him see it at the best. So they were had into the palace and
showed the whole art of the sword for two hours at a stretch,
before King George and Queen Carline, and the Butcher
Cumberland, and many more of whom I havenae mind. And
when they were through, the King (for all he was a rank
usurper) spoke them fair and gave each man three guineas in
his hand. Now, as they were going out of the palace, they
had a porter's lodge to go by; and it came in on my father,
as he was perhaps the first private Hieland gentleman that
had ever gone by that door, it was right he should give the
poor porter a proper notion of their quality. So he gives the
King's three guineas into the man's hand, as if it was his
common custom; the three others that came behind him did
the same; and there they were on the street, never a penny the
better for their pains. Some say it was one, that was the first
to fee the King's porter; and some say it was another; but

the truth of it is, that it was Duncan Stewart, as I am willing to prove with either sword or pistol. And that was the father that I had, God rest him!'

'I think he was not the man to leave you rich,' said I.

'And that's true,' said Alan. 'He left me my breeks to cover me, and little besides. And that was how I came to enlist, which was a black spot upon my character at the best of times, and would still be a sore job for me if I fell among the red-coats.'

'What,' cried I, 'were you in the English army?'

'That was I,' said Alan. 'But I deserted to the right side at Prestonpans*—and that's some comfort.'

I could scarcely share this view: holding desertion under arms for an unpardonable fault in honour. But for all I was so young, I was wiser than say my thought. 'Dear, dear,' says I, 'the punishment is death.'

'Ay,' said he, 'if they got hands on me, it would be a short shrift and a lang tow for Alan! But I have the King of France's commission in my pocket, which would aye be some protection.'

'I misdoubt it much,' said I.

'I have doubts mysel',' said Alan, drily.

'And, good heaven, man,' cried I, 'that you are a condemned rebel, and a deserter, and a man of the French King's —what tempts ye back into this country? It's a braving of Providence.'

'Tut,' says Alan, 'I have been back every year since forty-six!'

'And what brings ye, man?' cried I.

'Well, ye see, I weary for my friends and country,' said he. 'France is a braw place, nae doubt; but I weary for the heather and the deer. And then I have bit things that I attend to. Whiles I pick up a few lads to serve the King of France: recruits, ye see; and that's aye a little money. But the heart of the matter is the business of my chief, Ardshiel.'

'I thought they called your chief Appin,' said I.

'Ay, but Ardshiel is the captain of the clan,' said he, which scarcely cleared my mind. 'Ye see, David, he that was all his life so great a man, and come of the blood and bearing the name of kings, is now brought down to live in a French town like a poor and private person. He that had four hundred swords at his whistle, I have seen, with these eyes of mine, buying butter in the market-place, and taking it home in a kale-leaf. This is not only a pain but a disgrace to us of his family and clan. There are the bairns forby, the children and the hope of Appin, that must be learned their letters and how to hold a sword, in that far country. Now, the tenants of Appin have to pay a rent to King George; but their hearts are staunch, they are true to their chief; and what with love and a bit of pressure, and maybe a threat or two, the poor folk scrape up a second rent for Ardshiel. Well, David, I'm the hand that carries it.' And he struck the belt about his body, so that the guineas rang.

'Do they pay both?' cried I.

'Ay, David, both,' says he.

'What? two rents?' I repeated.

'Ay, David,' said he. 'I told a different tale to yon captain man; but this is the truth of it. And it's wonderful to me how little pressure is needed. But that's the handiwork of my good kinsman and my father's friend, James of the Glens; James Stewart, that is: Ardshiel's half-brother. He it is that gets the money in, and does the management.'

This was the first time I heard the name of that James Stewart, who was afterwards so famous at the time of his hanging. But I took little heed at the moment, for all my mind was occupied with the generosity of these poor Highlanders.

'I call it noble,' I cried. 'I'm a Whig, or little better; but I call it noble.'

'Ay,' said he, 'ye're a Whig, but ye're a gentleman; and that's what does it. Now, if ye were one of the cursed race of Campbell, ye would gnash your teeth to hear tell of it. If ye were the Red Fox.' . . . And at that name, his teeth shut together, and he ceased speaking. I have seen many a grim face, but never a grimmer than Alan's when he had named the Red Fox.

'And who is the Red Fox?' I asked, daunted, but still curious.

'Who is he?' cried Alan. 'Well, and I'll tell you that. When the men of the clans were broken at Culloden,* and the good cause went down, and the horses rode over the fetlocks in the best blood of the north, Ardshiel had to flee like a poor deer upon the mountains—he and his lady and his bairns. A sair job we had of it before we got him shipped; and while he still lay in the heather, the English rogues, that couldnae come at his life, were striking at his rights. They stripped him of his powers; they stripped him of his lands; they plucked the weapons from the hands of his clansmen, that had borne arms for thirty centuries; ay, and the very clothes off their backs—so that it's now a sin to wear a tartan plaid, and a man may be cast into a gaol if he has but a kilt about his legs. One thing they couldnae kill. That was the love the clansmen bore their chief. These guineas are the proof of it. And now, in there steps a man, a Campbell, red-headed Colin of Glenure——'

'Is that him you call the Red Fox?' said I.

'Will ye bring me his brush?' cries Alan, fiercely. 'Ay, that's the man. In he steps, and gets papers from King George, to be so-called King's factor on the lands of Appin. And at first he sings small, and is hail-fellow-well-met with Sheamus—that's James of the Glens, my chieftain's agent. But by-and-bye, that came to his ears that I have just told you; how the poor commons of Appin, the farmers and the crofters and the boumen, were wringing their very plaids to get a second rent, and send it over-seas for Ardshiel and his poor bairns. What was it ye called it, when I told ye?'

'I called it noble, Alan,' said I.

'And you little better than a common Whig!' cried Alan. 'But when it came to Colin Roy, the black Campbell blood in him ran wild. He sat gnashing his teeth at the wine table. What! should a Stewart get a bite of bread, and him not be able to prevent it? Ah! Red Fox, if ever I hold you at a gun's end, the Lord have pity upon ye!' (Alan stopped to swallow down his anger.) 'Well, David, what does he do? He declares all the farms to let. And thinks he, in his black heart, "I'll soon get other tenants that'll overbid these Stewarts, and Maccolls, and Macrobs" (for these are all names in my clan, David) "and then," thinks he, "Ardshiel will have to hold his bonnet on a French roadside." '

'Well,' said I, 'what followed?'

Alan laid down his pipe, which he had long since suffered to go out, and set his two hands upon his knees.

'Ay,' said he, 'ye'll never guess that! For these same Stewarts, and Maccolls, and Macrobs (that had two rents to pay, one to King George by stark voice, and one to Ardshiel by natural kindness), offered him a better price than any Campbell in all broad Scotland; and far he sent seeking them —as far as to the sides of Clyde and the cross of Edinburgh— seeking, and fleeching, and begging them to come, where there was a Stewart to be starved and a red-headed hound of a Campbell to be pleasured!'

'Well, Alan,' said I, 'that is a strange story, and a fine one too. And Whig as I may be, I am glad the man was beaten.'

'Him beaten?' echoed Alan. 'It's little ye ken of Campbells and less of the Red Fox. Him beaten? No: nor will be, till his blood's on the hillside! But if the day comes, David man, that I can find time and leisure for a bit of hunting, there grows not enough heather in all Scotland to hide him from my vengeance!'

'Man Alan,' said I, 'ye are neither very wise nor very Christian to blow off so many words of anger. They will do the man ye call the Fox no harm, and yourself no good. Tell me your tale plainly out. What did he next?'

'And that's a good observe, David,' said Alan. 'Troth and indeed, they will do him no harm; the more's the pity! And barring that about Christianity (of which my opinion is quite otherwise, or I would be nae Christian) I am much of your mind.'

'Opinion here or opinion there,' said I, 'it's a kent thing that Christianity forbids revenge.'

'Ay,' said he, 'it's well seen it was a Campbell taught ye! It would be a convenient world for them and their sort, if there was no such a thing as a lad and a gun behind a heather bush! But that's nothing to the point. This is what he did.'

'Ay,' said I, 'come to that.'

'Well, David,' said he, 'since he couldnae be rid of the loyal commons by fair means, he swore he would be rid of them by foul. Ardshiel was to starve: that was the thing he aimed at. And since them that fed him in his exile wouldnae be bought out—right or wrong, he would drive them out. Therefore he sent for lawyers, and papers, and red-coats to stand at his back. And the kindly folk of that country must all pack and tramp, every father's son out of his father's house, and out of the place where he was bred and fed, and played when he was a callant. And who are to succeed them? Bare-leggit beggars! King George is to whistle for his rents; he maun dow with less; he can spread his butter thinner: what cares Red Colin? If he can hurt Ardshiel, he has his wish; if he can pluck the meat from my chieftain's table, and the bit toys out if his children's hands, he will gang hame singing to Glenure!'

'Let me have a word,' said I. 'Be sure, if they take less rents, be sure Government has a finger in the pie. It's not this Campbell's fault, man—it's his orders. And if ye killed this Colin to-morrow, what better would ye be? There would be another factor in his shoes, as fast as spur can drive.'

'Ye're a good lad in a fight,' said Alan; 'but man! ye have Whig blood in ye!'

He spoke kindly enough, but there was so much anger under his contempt that I thought it was wise to change the conversation. I expressed my wonder how, with the Highlands covered with troops and guarded like a city in a siege, a man in his situation could come and go without arrest.

'It's easier than ye would think,' said Alan. 'A bare hillside (ye see) is like all one road; if there's a sentry at one place, ye just go by another. And then heather's a great help. And everywhere there are friends' houses and friends' byres and haystacks. And besides, when folk talk of a country covered with troops, it's but a kind of a byword at the best. A soldier covers nae mair of it than his boot-soles. I have fished a water with a sentry on the other side of the brae, and killed a fine trout; and I have sat in a heather bush within six feet of another, and learned a real bonny tune from his whistling. This was it,' said he, and whistled me the air.

'And then, besides,' he continued, 'it's no sae bad now as it was in forty-six. The Hielands are what they call pacified. Small wonder, with never a gun or a sword left from Cantyre to Cape Wrath, but what tenty[1] folk have hidden in their thatch! But what I would like to ken, David, is just how long? Not long, ye would think, with men like Ardshiel in exile and men like the Red Fox sitting birling the wine and oppressing the poor at home. But it's a kittle thing to decide what folk'll bear, and what they will not. Or why would Red Colin be riding his horse all over my poor country of Appin, and never a pretty lad to put a bullet in him?'

And with this Alan fell into a muse, and for a long time sate very sad and silent.

I will add the rest of what I have to say about my friend, that he was skilled in all kinds of music, but principally pipe-music; was a well-considered poet in his own tongue; had read several books both in French and English; was a dead shot, a good angler, and an excellent fencer with the small sword as well as with his own particular weapon. For his faults, they were on his face, and I now knew them all. But the worst of them, his childish propensity to take offence and to pick quarrels, he greatly laid aside in my case, out of regard for the battle of the round-house. But whether it was because I had done well myself, or because I had been a witness of his own much greater prowess, is more than I can tell. For though he had a great taste for courage in other men, yet he admired it most in Alan Breck.

1 Careful.

CHAPTER XIII

THE LOSS OF THE BRIG

IT was already late at night, and as dark as it ever would be at that season of the year (and that is to say, it was still pretty bright), when Hoseason clapped his head into the round-house door.

'Here,' said he, 'come out and see if ye can pilot.'

'Is this one of your tricks?' asked Alan.

'Do I look like tricks?' cries the captain. 'I have other things to think of—my brig's in danger!'

By the concerned look of his face, and above all, by the sharp tones in which he spoke of his brig, it was plain to both of us he was in deadly earnest; and so Alan and I, with no great fear of treachery, stepped on deck.

The sky was clear; it blew hard, and was bitter cold; a great deal of daylight lingered; and the moon, which was nearly full, shone brightly. The brig was close hauled, so as to round the south-west corner of the Island of Mull; the hills of which (and Ben More above them all, with a wisp of mist upon the top of it) lay full upon the larboard bow. Though it was no good point of sailing for the *Covenant*, she tore through the seas at a great rate, pitching and straining, and pursued by the westerly swell.

Altogether it was no such ill night to keep the seas in; and I had begun to wonder what it was that sat so heavily upon the captain, when the brig rising suddenly on the top of a high swell, he pointed and cried to us to look. Away on the lee bow, a thing like a fountain rose out of the moonlit sea, and immediately after we heard a low sound of roaring.

'What do ye call that?' asked the captain, gloomily.

'The sea breaking on a reef,' said Alan. 'And now ye ken where it is; and what better would ye have?'

'Ay,' said Hoseason, 'if it was the only one.'

And sure enough, just as he spoke there came a second fountain further to the south.

'There!' said Hoseason. 'Ye see for yourself. If I had kent of these reefs, if I had had a chart, or if Shuan had been spared, it's not sixty guineas, no, nor six hundred, would have made me risk my brig in sic a stoneyard! But you, sir, that was to pilot us, have ye never a word?'

'I'm thinking,' said Alan, 'these'll be what they call the Torran Rocks.'*

'Are there many of them?' says the captain.

'Truly, sir, I am nae pilot,' said Alan; 'but it sticks in my mind there are ten miles of them.'

Mr. Riach and the captain looked at each other.

'There's a way through them, I suppose?' said the captain.

'Doubtless,' said Alan; 'but where? But it somehow runs in my mind once more, that it is clearer under the land.'

'So?' said Hoseason. 'We'll have to haul our wind then, Mr. Riach; we'll have to come as near in about the end of Mull as we can take her, sir; and even then we'll have the land to kep the wind off us, and that stoneyard on our lee. Well, we're in for it now, and may as well crack on.'

With that he gave an order to the steersman, and sent Riach to the foretop. There were only five men on deck, counting the officers; these were all that were fit (or, at least, both fit and willing) for their work; and two of these were hurt.* So, as I say, it fell to Mr. Riach to go aloft, and he sat there looking out and hailing the deck with news of all he saw.

'The sea to the south is thick,' he cried; and then, after a while; 'It does seem clearer in by the land.'

'Well, sir,' said Hoseason to Alan, 'we'll try your way of it. But I think I might as well trust to a blind fiddler. Pray God you're right.'

'Pray God I am!' says Alan to me. 'But where did I hear it? Well, well, it will be as it must.'

As we got nearer to the turn of the land the reefs began to be sown here and there on our very path; and Mr. Riach sometimes cried down to us to change the course. Sometimes, indeed, none too soon; for one reef was so close on the brig's weather board that when a sea burst upon it the lighter sprays fell upon her deck and wetted us like rain.

The brightness of the night showed us these perils as clearly as by day, which was, perhaps, the more alarming. It showed me, too, the face of the captain as he stood by the steersman, now on one foot, now on the other, and sometimes blowing in his hands, but still listening and looking and as steady as steel. Neither he or Mr. Riach had shown well in the fighting; but I saw they were brave in their own trade, and admired them all the more because I found Alan very white.

'Ochone, David,' says he, 'this is no the kind of death I fancy.'

'What, Alan!' I cried, 'you're not afraid?'

'No,' said he, wetting his lips, 'but you'll allow yourself, it's a cold ending.'

By this time, now and then sheering to one side or the other to avoid a reef, but still hugging the wind and the land, we had got round Iona and begun to come alongside Mull. The tide at the tail of the land ran very strong, and threw the brig about. Two hands were put to the helm, and Hoseason himself would sometimes lend a help; and it was strange to see three strong men throw their weight upon the tiller, and it (like a living thing) struggle against and drive them back. This would have been the greater danger, had not the sea been for some while free of obstacles. Mr. Riach, besides, announced from the top that he saw clear water ahead.

'Ye were right,' said Hoseason to Alan. 'Ye have saved the brig, sir; I'll mind that when we come to clear accounts.' And I believe he not only meant what he said, but would have done it; so high a place did the *Covenant* hold in his affections.

But this is matter only for conjecture, things have gone otherwise than he forecast.

'Keep her away a point,' sings out Mr. Riach. 'Reef to windward!'

And just at the same time the tide caught the brig, and

threw the wind out of her sails. She came round into the wind like a top, and the next moment struck the reef with such a dunch as threw us all flat upon the deck, and came near to shake Mr. Riach from his place upon the mast.

I was on my feet in a minute. The reef on which we had struck was close in under the south-west end of Mull, off a little isle they call Earraid, which lay low and black upon the larboard. Sometimes the swell broke clean over us; sometimes it only ground the poor brig upon the reef, so that we could hear her beat herself to pieces; and what with the great noise of the sails, and the singing of the wind, and the flying of the spray in the moonlight, and the sense of danger, I think my head must have been partly turned, for I could scarcely understand the things I saw.

Presently I observed Mr. Riach and the seamen busy round the skiff; and still in the same blank, ran over to assist them; and as soon as I set my hand to work, my mind came clear again. It was no very easy task, for the skiff lay amidships and was full of hamper, and the breaking of the heavier seas continually forced us to give over and hold on; but we all wrought like horses while we could.

Meanwhile such of the wounded as could move came clambering out of the fore-scuttle and began to help; while the rest that lay helpless in their bunks harrowed me with screaming and begging to be saved.

The captain took no part. It seemed he was struck stupid. He stood holding by the shrouds, talking to himself and groaning out aloud whenever the ship hammered on the rock. His brig was like wife and child to him; he had looked on, day by day, at the mishandling of poor Ransome; but when it came to the brig, he seemed to suffer along with her.

All the time of our working at the boat, I remember only one other thing; that I asked Alan, looking across at the shore, what country it was; and he answered, it was the worst possible for him, for it was a land of the Campbells.

We had one of the wounded men told off to keep a watch upon the seas and cry us warning. Well, we had the boat

about ready to be launched, when this man sang out pretty
shrill: 'For God's sake, hold on!' We knew by his tone that
it was something more than ordinary; and sure enough, there
followed a sea so huge that it lifted the brig right up and
canted her over on her beam. Whether the cry came too late
or my hold was too weak, I know not; but at the sudden
tilting of the ship I was cast clean over the bulwarks into
the sea.

I went down, and drank my fill; and then came up, and
got a blink of the moon; and then down again. They say
a man sinks a third time for good. I cannot be made like other
folk, then; for I would not like to write how often I went
down or how often I came up again. All the while, I was
being hurled along, and beaten upon and choked, and then
swallowed whole; and the thing was so distracting to my
wits, that I was neither sorry nor afraid.

Presently, I found I was holding to a spar, which helped
me somewhat. And then all of a sudden I was in quiet water,
and began to come to myself.

It was the spare yard I had got hold of, and I was amazed
to see how far I had travelled from the brig. I hailed her,
indeed; but it was plain she was already out of cry. She was
still holding together; but whether or not they had yet
launched the boat, I was too far off and too low down to
see.

While I was hailing the brig, I spied a tract of water lying
between us, where no great waves came, but which yet boiled
white all over and bristled in the moon with rings and
bubbles. Sometimes the whole tract swung to one side, like
the tail of a live serpent; sometimes, for a glimpse, it would
all disappear and then boil up again. What it was I had no
guess, which for the time increased my fear of it; but I now
know it must have been the roost or tide race, which had
carried me away so fast and tumbled me about so cruelly,
and at last, as if tired of that play, had flung out me and
the spare yard upon its landward margin.

I now lay quite becalmed, and began to feel that a man
can die of cold as well as of drowning. The shores of Earraid

were close in; I could see in the moonlight the dots of heather and the sparkling of the mica in the rocks.

'Well,' thought I to myself, 'if I cannot get as far as that, it's strange!'

I had no skill of swimming, Essen Water being small in our neighbourhood; but when I laid hold upon the yard with both arms, and kicked out with both feet, I soon begun to find that I was moving. Hard work it was, and mortally slow; but in about an hour of kicking and splashing, I had got well in between the points of a sandy bay surrounded by low hills.

The sea was here quite quiet; there was no sound of any surf; the moon shone clear; and I thought in my heart I had never seen a place so desert and desolate. But it was dry land; and when at last it grew so shallow that I could leave the yard and wade ashore upon my feet, I cannot tell if I was more tired or more grateful. Both at least, I was: tired as I never was before that night; and grateful to God as I trust I have been often, though never with more cause.

CHAPTER XIV

THE ISLET*

WITH my stepping ashore I began the most unhappy part of my adventures. It was half-past twelve in the morning, and though the wind was broken by the land, it was a cold night. I dared not sit down (for I thought I should have frozen), but took off my shoes and walked to and fro upon the sand, barefoot, and beating my breast, with infinite weariness. There was no sound of man or cattle; not a cock crew, though it was about the hour of their first waking; only the surf broke outside in the distance, which put me in mind of my perils and those of my friend. To walk by the sea at that hour of the morning, and in a place so desert-like and lonesome, struck me with a kind of fear.

As soon as the day began to break I put on my shoes and climbed a hill—the ruggedest scramble I ever undertook—

falling, the whole way, between big blocks of granite or leaping from one to another. When I got to the top the dawn was come. There was no sign of the brig, which must have lifted from the reef and sunk. The boat, too, was nowhere to be seen. There was never a sail upon the ocean; and in what I could see of the land, was neither house nor man.

I was afraid to think what had befallen my shipmates, and afraid to look longer at so empty a scene. What with my wet clothes and weariness, and my belly that now began to ache with hunger, I had enough to trouble me without that. So I set off eastward along the south coast, hoping to find a house where I might warm myself, and perhaps get news of those I had lost And at the worst, I considered the sun would soon rise and dry my clothes.

After a little, my way was stopped by a creek or inlet of the sea, which seemed to run pretty deep into the land: and as I had no means to get across, I must needs change my direction to go about the end of it. It was still the roughest kind of walking; indeed the whole, not only of Earraid, but of the neighbouring part of Mull (which they call the Ross) is nothing but a jumble of granite rocks with heather in among. At first the creek kept narrowing as I had looked to see; but presently to my surprise it began to widen out again. At this I scratched my head, but had still no notion of the truth; until at last I came to a rising ground, and it burst upon me all in a moment that I was cast upon a little, barren isle, and cut off on every side by the salt seas.

Instead of the sun rising to dry me, it came on to rain, with a thick mist; so that my case was lamentable.

I stood in the rain, and shivered, and wondered what to do, till it occurred to me that perhaps the creek was fordable. Back I went to the narrowest point and waded in. But not three yards from shore, I plumped in head over ears; and if ever I was heard of more it was rather by God's grace than my own prudence. I was no wetter (for that could hardly be) but I was all the colder for this mishap; and having lost another hope, was the more unhappy.

And now, all at once, the yard came in my head. What
had carried me through the roost, would surely serve me to
cross this little quiet creek in safety. With that I set off,
undaunted, across the top of the isle, to fetch and carry it
back. It was a weary tramp in all ways, and if hope had not
buoyed me up, I must have cast myself down and given up.
Whether with the sea salt, or because I was growing fevered,
I was distressed with thirst, and had to stop, as I went, and
drink the peaty water out of the hags.

I came to the bay at last, more dead than alive; and at the
first glance, I thought the yard was something further out
than when I left it. In I went, for the third time, into the sea.
The sand was smooth and firm and shelved gradually down;
so that I could wade out till the water was almost to my neck
and the little waves splashed into my face. But at that
depth my feet began to leave me and I durst venture in no
further. As for the yard, I saw it bobbing very quietly some
twenty feet in front of me.

I had borne up well until this last disappointment; but at
that I came ashore, and flung myself down upon the sands
and wept.

The time I spent upon the island is still so horrible a
thought to me, that I must pass it lightly over. In all the
books I have read of people cast away, they had either their
pockets full of tools, or a chest of things would be thrown
upon the beach along with them, as if on purpose. My case
was very different. I had nothing in my pockets but money
and Alan's silver button; and being inland bred, I was as
much short of knowledge as of means.

I knew indeed that shell-fish were counted good to eat;
and among the rocks of the isle I found a great plenty of
limpets, which at first I could scarcely strike from their places,
not knowing quickness to be needful. There were, besides,
some of the little shells that we call buckies; I think peri-
winkle is the English name. Of these two I made my whole
diet, devouring them cold and raw as I found them; and so
hungry was I, that at first they seemed to me delicious.

Perhaps they were out of season, or perhaps there was

something wrong in the sea about my island. But at least I had no sooner eaten my first meal than I was seized with giddiness and retching, and lay for a long time no better than dead. A second trial of the same food (indeed I had no other) did better with me and revived my strength. But as long as I was on the island, I never knew what to expect when I had eaten; sometimes all was well, and sometimes I was thrown into a miserable sickness;; nor could I ever distinguish what particular fish it was that hurt me.

All day it streamed rain; the island ran like a sop; there was no dry spot to be found; and when I lay down that night, between two boulders that made a kind of roof, my feet were in a bog.

The second day I crossed the island to all sides. There was no one part of it better than another; it was all desolate and rocky; nothing living on it but game birds which I lacked the means to kill, and the gulls which haunted the outlying rocks in a prodigious number. But the creek, or straits, that cut off the isle from the main land of the Ross, opened out on the north into a bay, and the bay again opened into the Sound of Iona; and it was the neighbourhood of this place that I chose to be my home; though if I had thought upon the very name of home in such a spot, I must have burst out weeping.

I had good reasons for my choice. There was in this part of the isle a little hut of a house like a pig's hut, where fishers used to sleep when they came there upon their business; but the turf roof of it had fallen entirely in; so that the hut was of no use to me, and gave me less shelter than my rocks. What was more important, the shell-fish on which I lived grew there in great plenty; when the tide was out I could gather a peck at a time: and this was doubtless a convenience. But the other reason went deeper. I had become in no way used to the horrid solitude of the isle, but still looked round me on all sides (like a man that was hunted) between fear and hope that I might see some human creature coming. Now, from a little up the hillside over the bay, I could catch a sight of the great, ancient church and the roofs of the people's houses

in Iona. And on the other hand, over the low country of the
Ross, I saw smoke go up, morning and evening, as if from
a homestead in a hollow of the land.

I used to watch this smoke, when I was wet and cold, and
had my head half turned with loneliness; and think of the
fireside and the company, till my heart burned. It was the
same with the roofs of Iona. Altogether, this sight I had of
men's homes and comfortable lives, although it put a point
on my own sufferings, yet it kept hope alive, and helped me
to eat my raw shell-fish (which had soon grown to be a
disgust) and saved me from the sense of horror I had whenever I was quite alone with dead rocks, and fowls, and the
rain, and the cold sea.

I say it kept hope alive; and indeed it seemed impossible
that I should be left to die on the shores of my own country,
and within view of a church tower and the smoke of men's
houses. But the second day passed; and though as long as the
light lasted I kept a bright look-out for boats on the Sound
or men passing on the Ross, no help came near me. It still
rained; and I turned in to sleep, as wet as ever and with a
cruel sore throat, but a little comforted, perhaps, by having
said good-night to my next neighbours, the people of Iona.

Charles the Second declared a man could stay outdoors
more days in the year in the climate of England than in any
other. This was very like a king with a palace at his back
and changes of dry clothes. But he must have had better luck
on his flight from Worcester* than I had on that miserable
isle. It was the height of the summer; yet it rained for more
than twenty-four hours, and did not clear until the afternoon
of the third day.

This was the day of incidents. In the morning I saw a red
deer, a buck with a fine spread of antlers, standing in the rain
on the top of the island; but he had scarce seen me rise from
under my rock, before he trotted off upon the other side.
I supposed he must have swum the straits; though what
should bring any creature to Earraid, was more than I could
fancy.

A little after, as I was jumping about after my limpets, I

was startled by a guinea-piece, which fell upon a rock in front of me and glanced off into the sea. When the sailors gave me my money again, they kept back not only about a third of the whole sum, but my father's leather purse; so that from that day out, I carried my gold loose in a pocket with a button. I now saw there must be a hole, and clapped my hand to the place in a great hurry. But this was to lock the stable door after the steed was stolen. I had left the shore at Queensferry with near on fifty pounds; now I found no more than two guinea-pieces and a silver shilling.

It is true I picked up a third guinea a little after, where it lay shining on a piece of turf. That made a fortune of three pounds and four shillings, English money, for a lad, the rightful heir of an estate, and now starving on an isle at the extreme end of the wild Highlands.

This state of my affairs dashed me still further; and indeed my plight on that third morning was truly pitiful. My clothes were beginning to rot; my stockings in particular were quite worn through, so that my shanks went naked; my hands had grown quite soft with the continual soaking; my throat was very sore, my strength had much abated, and my heart so turned against the horrid stuff I was condemned to eat, that the very sight of it came near to sicken me.

And yet the worst was not yet come.

There is a pretty high rock on the north-west of Earraid, which (because it had a flat top and overlooked the Sound) I was much in the habit of frequenting; not that ever I stayed in one place, save when asleep, my misery giving me no rest. Indeed I wore myself down with continual and aimless goings and comings in the rain.

As soon, however, as the sun came out, I lay down on the top of that rock to dry myself. The comfort of the sunshine is a thing I cannot tell. It set me thinking hopefully of my deliverance, of which I had begun to despair; and I scanned the sea and the Ross with a fresh interest. On the south of my rock, a part of the island jutted out and hid the open ocean, so that a boat could thus come quite near me upon that side, and I be none the wiser.

Well, all of a sudden, a coble with a brown sail and a pair
of fishers aboard of it, came flying round that corner of the
isle, bound for Iona. I shouted out, and then fell on my knees
on the rock and reached up my hands and prayed to them.
They were near enough to hear—I could even see the colour
of their hair; and there was no doubt but they observed me,
for they cried out in the Gaelic tongue, and laughed. But
the boat never turned aside, and flew on, right before my
eyes, for Iona.

I could not believe such wickedness, and ran along the
shore from rock to rock, crying on them piteously; even after
they were out of reach of my voice, I still cried and waved
to them; and when they were quite gone, I thought my heart
would have burst. All the time of my troubles I wept only
twice. Once, when I could not reach the yard, and now the
second time, when these fishers turned a deaf ear to my cries.
But this time I wept and roared like a wicked child, tearing
up the turf with my nails and grinding my face in the earth.
If a wish would kill men, those two fishers would never have
seen morning, and I should likely have died upon my
island.

When I was a little over my anger, I must eat again, but
with such loathing of the mess as I could now scarce control.
Sure enough, I should have done as well to fast, for my fishes
poisoned me again. I had all my first pains; my throat was
so sore I could scarce swallow; I had a fit of strong shuddering, which clucked my teeth together; and there came on me
that dreadful sense of illness, which we have no name for
either in Scotch or English. I thought I should have died, and
made my peace with God, forgiving all men, even my uncle
and the fishers; and as soon as I had thus made up my mind
to the worst, clearness came upon me: I observed the night
was falling dry; my clothes were dried a good deal; truly, I
was in a better case than ever before, since I had landed on
the isle; and so I got to sleep at last, with a thought of
gratitude.

The next day (which was the fourth of this horrible life
of mine) I found my bodily strength run very low. But the

sun shone, the air was sweet, and what I managed to eat of
the shell-fish agreed well with me and revived my courage.

I was scarce back on my rock (where I went always the
first thing after I had eaten) before I observed a boat coming
down the Sound, and with her head, as I thought, in my
direction.

I began at once to hope and fear exceedingly; for I thought
these men might have thought better of their cruelty and
be coming back to my assistance. But another disappointment, such as yesterday's, was more than I could bear. I
turned my back, accordingly, upon the sea, and did not look
again till I had counted many hundreds. The boat was still
heading for the island. The next time I counted the full
thousand, as slowly as I could, my heart beating so as to
hurt me. And then it was out of all question. She was coming
straight to Earraid!

I could no longer hold myself back, but ran to the seaside
and out, from one rock to another, as far as I could go. It is a
marvel I was not drowned; for when I was brought to a stand
at last, my legs shook under me, and my mouth was so dry,
I must wet it with the sea-water before I was able to shout.

All this time the boat was coming on; and now I was able
to perceive it was the same boat and the same two men as
yesterday. This I knew by their hair, which the one had of
a bright yellow and the other black. But now there was a
third man along with them, who looked to be of a better class.

As soon as they were come within easy speech, they let
down their sail and lay quiet. In spite of my supplications,
they drew no nearer in, and what frightened me most of all,
the new man tee-heed'd with laughter as he talked and looked
at me.

Then he stood up in the boat and addressed me a long
while, speaking fast and with many wavings of his hand.
I told him I had no Gaelic; and at this he became very angry,
and I began to suspect he thought he was talking English.
Listening very close, I caught the word 'whateffer' several
times; but all the rest was Gaelic and might have been Greek
and Hebrew for me.

'Whatever,' said I, to show him I had caught a word.

'Yes, yes—yes, yes,' says he, and then he looked at the other men, as much as to say, 'I told you I spoke English,' and began again as hard as ever in the Gaelic.

This time I picked out another word, 'tide.' Then I had a flash of hope. I remembered he was always waving his hand towards the mainland of the Ross.

'Do you mean when the tide is out——?' I cried, and could not finish.

'Yes, yes,' said he. 'Tide.'

At that I turned tail upon their boat (where my adviser had once more begun to tee-hee with laughter) leaped back the way I had come, from one stone to another, and set off running across the isle as I had never run before. In about half an hour I came out upon the shores of the creek; and, sure enough, it was shrunk into a little trickle of water, through which I dashed, not above my knees, and landed with a shout on the main island.

A sea-bred boy would not have stayed a day on Earraid; which is only what they call a tidal islet, and except in the bottom of the neaps, can be entered and left twice in every twenty-four hours, either dry-shod, or at the most by wading. Even I, who had the tide going out and in before me in the bay, and even watched for the ebbs, the better to get my shell-fish—even I (I say) if I had sat down to think, instead of raging at my fate, must have soon guessed the secret, and got free. It was no wonder the fishers had not understood me. The wonder was rather that they had ever guessed my pitiful illusion, and taken the trouble to come back. I had starved with cold and hunger on that island for close upon one hundred hours. But for the fishers, I might have left my bones there, in pure folly. And even as it was, I had paid for it pretty dear, no only in past sufferings, but in my present case; being clothed like a beggar-man, scarce able to walk, and in great pain of my sore throat.

I have seen wicked men and fools, a great many of both; and I believe they both get paid in the end; but the fools first.

CHAPTER XV

THE LAD WITH THE SILVER BUTTON: THROUGH THE ISLE OF MULL

THE Ross of Mull, which I had now got upon, was rugged and trackless, like the isle I had just left; being all bog, and brier, and big stone. There may be roads for them that know the country well; but for my part I had no better guide than my own nose, and no other landmark than Ben More.

I aimed as well as I could for the smoke I had seen so often from the island; and with all my great weariness and the difficulty of the way, came upon the house in the bottom of a little hollow, about five or six at night. It was low and longish, roofed with turf and built of unmortared stones; and on a mound in front of it, an old gentleman sat smoking his pipe in the sun.

With what little English he had, he gave me to understand that my shipmates had got safe ashore, and had broken bread in that very house on the day after.

'Was there one,' I asked, 'dressed like a gentleman?'

He said they all wore rough great-coats; but to be sure, the first of them, the one that came alone, wore breeches and stockings, while the rest had sailors' trousers.

'Ah,' said I, 'and he would have a feathered hat?'

He told me, no, that he was bareheaded like myself.

At first I thought Alan might have lost his hat; and then the rain came in my mind, and I judged it more likely he had it out of harm's way under his great-coat. This set me smiling, partly because my friend was safe, partly to think of his vanity in dress.

And then the old gentleman clapped his hand to his brow, and cried out that I must be the lad with the silver button.

'Why, yes!' said I, in some wonder.

'Well, then,' said the old gentleman, 'I have a word for you that you are to follow your friend to his country, by Torosay.'

He then asked me how I had fared, and I told him my tale. A south-country man would certainly have laughed; but this old gentleman (I call him so because of his manners, for his clothes were dropping off his back) heard me all through with nothing but gravity and pity. When I had done, he took me by the hand, led me into his hut (it was no better) and presented me before his wife, as if she had been the Queen and I a duke.

The good woman set oat-bread before me and a cold grouse, patting my shoulder and smiling to me all the time, for she had no English; and the old gentleman (not to be behind) brewed me a strong punch out of their country spirit. All the while I was eating, and after that when I was drinking the punch, I could scarce come to believe in my good fortune; and the house, though it was thick with the peat smoke and as full of holes as a colander, seemed like a palace.

The punch threw me in a strong sweat and a deep slumber; the good people let me lie; and it was near noon of the next day before I took the road, my throat already easier and my spirits quite restored by good fare and good news. The old gentleman, although I pressed him hard, would take no money, and gave me an old bonnet for my head; though I'm free to own I was no sooner out of view of the house, than I very jealously washed this gift of his in a wayside fountain.

Thought I to myself: 'If these are the wild Highlanders, I could wish my own folk wilder.'

I not only started late, but I must have wandered nearly half the time. True, I met plenty of people, grubbing in little miserable fields that would not keep a cat, or herding little kine about the bigness of asses. The Highland dress being forbidden by law since the rebellion, and the people condemned to the Lowland habit, which they much disliked, it was strange to see the variety of their array. Some went bare, only for a hanging cloak or great-coat, and carried their trousers on their backs like a useless burthen; some had made an imitation of the tartan with little parti-coloured stripes patched together like an old wife's quilt; others, again, still wore the Highland philabeg, but by putting a few stitches between the legs, transformed it into a pair of trousers like a Dutchman's. All those makeshifts were condemned and punished, for the law was harshly applied, in hopes to break up the clan spirit; but in that out-of-the-way, sea-bound isle, there were few to make remarks and fewer to tell tales.

They seemed in great poverty; which was no doubt natural, now that rapine was put down, and the chiefs kept no longer an open house; and the roads (even such a wandering, country by-track as the one I followed) were infested with beggars. And here again I marked a difference from my own part of the country. For our Lowland beggars—even the gownsmen themselves, who beg by patent—had a louting, flattering way with them, and if you gave them a plack and asked change, would very civilly return you a boddle. But these Highland beggars stood on their dignity, asked alms only to buy snuff (by their account) and would give no change.

To be sure, this was no concern of mine, except in so far as it entertained me by the way. What was much more to the purpose, few had any English, and these few (unless they were of the brotherhood of beggars) not very anxious to place it at my service. I knew Torosay to be my destination, and repeated the name to them and pointed; but instead of simply pointing in reply, they would give me a screed of the Gaelic that set me foolish; so it was small wonder if I went out of my road as often as I stayed in it.

At last, about eight at night, and already very weary, I came to a lone house, where I asked admittance, and was refused, until I bethought me of the power of money in so poor a country, and held up one of my guineas in my finger and thumb. Thereupon, the man of the house, who had hitherto pretended to have no English, and driven me from his door by signals, suddenly began to speak as clearly as was needful, and agreed for five shillings to give me a night's lodging and guide me the next day to Torosay.

I slept uneasily that night, fearing I should be robbed; but I might have spared myself the pain; for my host was no robber, only miserably poor and a great cheat. He was not alone in his poverty; for the next morning, we must go five miles about to the house of what he called a rich man to have one of my guineas changed. This was perhaps a rich man for Mull; he would have scarce been thought so in the south; for it took all he had, the whole house was turned upside down, and a neighbour brought under contribution, before he could scrape together twenty shillings in silver. The odd shilling he kept for himself, protesting that he could ill afford to have so great a sum of money lying 'locked up.' For all that he was very courteous and well spoken, made us both sit down with his family to dinner, and brewed punch in a fine china bowl, over which my rascal guide grew so merry that he refused to start.

I was for getting angry, and appealed to the rich man (Hector Maclean was his name) who had been a witness to our bargain and to my payment of the five shillings. But Maclean had taken his share of the punch, and vowed that no gentleman should leave his table after the bowl was brewed; so there was nothing for it but to sit and hear Jacobite toasts and Gaelic songs, till all were tipsy and staggered off to the bed or the barn for their night's rest.

Next day (the fourth of my travels) we were up before five upon the clock; but my rascal guide got to the bottle at once, and it was three hours before I had him clear of the house, and then (as you shall hear) only for a worse disappointment.

As long as we went down a heathery valley that lay before Mr. Maclean's house, all went well; only my guide looked constantly over his shoulder, and when I asked him the cause, only grinned at me. No sooner, however, had we crossed the back of the hill, and got out of sight of the house windows, than he told me Torosay lay right in front, and that hilltop (which he pointed out) was my best landmark.

'I care very little for that,' said I, 'since you are going with me.'

The impudent cheat answered me in the Gaelic that he had no English.

'My fine fellow,' I said, 'I know very well your English

comes and goes. Tell me what will bring it back? Is it more money you wish?'

'Five shillings mair,' said he, 'and hersel' will bring ye there.'

I reflected a while and then offered him two, which he accepted greedily, and insisted on having in his hands at once—'for luck,' he said, but I think it was rather for my misfortune.

The two shillings carried him not quite as many miles; at the end of which distance, he sat down upon the wayside and took off his brogues from his feet, like a man about to rest.

I was now red-hot. 'Ha!' said I, 'have you no more English?'

He said impudently, 'no.'

At that I boiled over and lifted my hand to strike him; and he, drawing a knife from his rags, squatted back and grinned at me like a wild cat. At that, forgetting everything but my anger, I ran in upon him, put aside his knife with my left, and struck him in the mouth with the right. I was a strong lad and very angry, and he but a little man; and he went down before me heavily. By good luck, his knife flew out of his hand as he fell.

I picked up both that and his brogues, wished him a good morning and set off upon my way, leaving him barefoot and disarmed. I chuckled to myself as I went, being sure I was done with that rogue, for a variety of reasons. First, he knew he could have no more of my money; next, the brogues were worth in that country only a few pence; and lastly the knife, which was really a dagger, it was against the law for him to carry.

In about half-an-hour of walk, I overtook a great, ragged man, moving pretty fast but feeling before him with a staff. He was quite blind and told me he was a catechist, which should have put me at my ease. But his face went against me; it seemed dark and dangerous and secret; and presently, as we began to go on alongside, I saw the steel butt of a pistol sticking from under the flap of his coat-pocket. To carry such a thing meant a fine of fifteen pounds sterling upon a first offence, and transportation to the colonies upon a second. Nor could I quite see why a religious teacher should go armed, or what a blind man could be doing with a pistol.

I told him about my guide, for I was proud of what I had done, and my vanity for once got the heels of my prudence. At the mention of the five shillings he cried out so loud that I made up my mind I should say nothing of the other two, and was glad he could not see my blushes.

'Was it too much?' I asked a little faltering.

'Too much!' cried he. 'Why, I will guide you to Torosay myself for a dram of brandy. And give you the great pleasure of my company (me that is a man of some learning) in the bargain.'

I said I did not see how a blind man could be a guide; but at that he laughed aloud, and said his stick was eyes enough for an eagle.

'In the Isle of Mull, at least,' says he, 'where I knew every stone and heather-bush by mark of head. See, now,' he said, striking right and left, as if to make sure, 'down there a burn is running; and at the head of it there stands a bit of a small hill with a stone cocked upon the top of that; and it's hard at the foot of the hill, that the way runs by to Torosay; and the way here, being for droves, is plainly trodden, and will show grassy through the heather.'

I had to own he was right in every feature, and told my wonder.

'Ha!' says he, 'that's nothing. Would ye believe me now, that before the Act came out, and when there were weapons in this country, I could shoot? Ay, could I!' cries he, and then with a leer: 'If ye have such a thing as a pistol here to try with, I would show ye how it's done.'

I told him I had nothing of the sort, and gave him a wider berth. If he had known, his pistol stuck at the time quite plainly out of his pocket, and I could see the sun twinkle on the steel of the butt. But by the better luck for me, he knew nothing, thought all was covered, and lied on in the dark.

He then began to question me cunningly, where I came

from, whether I was rich, whether I could change a five-shilling piece for him (which he declared he had that moment in his sporran) and all the time he kept edging up to me, and I avoiding him. We were now upon a sort of green cattle-track which crossed the hills towards Torosay, and we kept changing sides upon that like dancers in a reel. I had so plainly the upper-hand that my spirits rose, and indeed I took a pleasure in this game of blind-man's buff; but the catechist grew angrier and angrier, and at last began to swear in Gaelic and to strike for my legs with his staff.

Then I told him that, sure enough, I had a pistol in my pocket as well as he, and if he did not strike across the hill due south I would even blow his brains out.

He became at once very polite; and after trying to soften me for some time, but quite in vain, he cursed me once more in the Gaelic and took himself off. I watched him striding along, through bog and brier, tapping with his stick, until he turned the end of a hill and disappeared in the next hollow. Then I struck on again for Torosay, much better pleased to be alone than to travel with that man of learning. This was an unlucky day; and these two, of whom I had just rid myself one after the other, were the two worst men I met with in the Highlands.

At Torosay, on the Sound of Mull and looking over to the mainland of Morven, there was an inn with an innkeeper, who was a Maclean, it appeared, of a very high family; for to keep an inn is thought even more genteel in the Highlands than it is with us, perhaps as partaking of hospitality, or perhaps because the trade is idle and drunken. He spoke good English and finding me to be something of a scholar, tried me first in French, where he easily beat me, and then in the Latin, in which I don't know which of us did best. This pleasant rivalry put us at once upon friendly terms; and I sat up and drank punch with him (or to be more correct, sat up and watched him drink it) until he was so tipsy that he wept upon my shoulder.

I tried him, as if by accident, with a sight of Alan's button; but it was plain he had never seen or heard of it. Indeed, he bore some grudge against the family and friends of Ardshiel, and before he was drunk he read me a lampoon, in very good Latin, but with a very ill meaning, which he had made in elegiac verses upon a person of that house.

When I told him of my catechist, he shook his head, and said I was lucky to have got clear off. 'That is a very dangerous man,' he said; 'Duncan Mackiegh is his name; he can shoot by the ear at several yards, and has been often accused of highway robberies, and once of murder.'

'The cream of it is,' says I, 'that he called himself a catechist.'

'And why should he not?' says he, 'when that is what he is. It was Maclean of Duart gave it to him because he was blind. But, perhaps, it was a peety,' says my host, 'for he is always on the road, going from one place to another to hear the young folk say their religion; and doubtless, that is a great temptation to the poor man.'

At last, when my landlord could drink no more, he showed me to a bed, and I lay down in very good spirits; having travelled the greater part of that big and crooked Island of Mull, from Earraid to Torosay, fifty miles as the crow flies and (with my wanderings) much nearer a hundred, in four days and with little fatigue. Indeed I was by far in better heart and health of body at the end of that long tramp than I had been at the beginning.

CHAPTER XVI

THE LAD WITH THE SILVER BUTTON:
ACROSS MORVEN

THERE is a regular ferry from Torosay to Kinlochaline on the mainland. Both shores of the Sound are in the country of the strong clan of the Macleans, and the people that passed the ferry with me were almost all of that clan. The skipper of the boat, on the other hand, was called Neil Roy Macrob; and since Macrob was one of the names of Alan's clansmen, and Alan himself had sent me to that ferry, I was eager to come to private speech of Neil Roy.

In the crowded boat this was of course impossible, and the passage was a very slow affair. There was no wind, and as the boat was wretchedly equipped, we could pull but two oars on one side, and one on the other. The men gave way, however, with a good will, the passengers taking spells to help them, and the whole company giving the time in Gaelic boat-songs. And what with the songs, and the sea air, and the good-nature and spirit of all concerned, and the bright weather, the passage was a pretty thing to have seen.

But there was one melancholy part. In the mouth of Loch Aline we found a great sea-going ship at anchor; and this I supposed at first to be one of the King's cruisers which were kept along that coast, both summer and winter, to prevent communication with the French. As we got a little nearer, it became plain she was a ship of merchandise; and what still more puzzled me, not only her decks, but the sea-beach also, were quite black with people, and skiffs were continually plying to and fro between them. Yet nearer, and there began to come to our ears a great sound of mourning, the people on board and those on the shore crying and lamenting one to another so as to pierce the heart.

Then I understood this was an emigrant ship bound for the American colonies.

We put the ferry-boat alongside, and the exiles leaned over the bulwarks, weeping and reaching out their hands to my fellow-passengers, among whom they counted some near friends. How long this might have gone on I do not know, for they seemed to have no sense of time: but at last the captain of the ship, who seemed near beside himself (and no great wonder) in the midst of this crying and confusion, came to the side and begged us to depart.

Thereupon Neil sheered off; and the chief singer in our boat struck into a melancholy air, which was presently taken up both by the emigrants and their friends upon the beach, so that it sounded from all sides like a lament for the dying. I saw the tears run down the cheeks of the men and women

in the boat, even as they bent at the oars; and the circumstances, and the music of the song (which is one called
'Lochaber no more'*) were highly affecting even to myself.

At Kinlochaline I got Neil Roy upon one side on the beach,
and said I made sure he was one of Appin's men.

'And what for no?' said he.

'I am seeking somebody,' said I; 'and it comes in my mind
that you will have news of him. Alan Breck Stewart is his
name.' And very foolishly, instead of showing him the
button, I sought to pass a shilling in his hand.

At this he drew back. 'I am very much affronted,' he said;
'and this is not the way that one shentleman should behave
to another at all. The man you ask for is in France; but if he
was in my sporran,' says he, 'and your belly full of shillings,
I would not hurt a hair upon his body.'

I saw I had gone the wrong way to work, and without
wasting time upon apologies, showed him the button lying
in the hollow of my palm.

'Aweel, aweel,' said Neil; 'and I think ye might have begun
with that end of the stick, whatever! But if ye are the lad
with the silver button, all is well, and I have the word to see
that ye come safe. But if ye will pardon me to speak plainly,'
says he, 'there is a name that you should never take into your
mouth, and that is the name of Alan Breck; and there is a
thing that ye would never do, and that is to offer your dirty
money to a Hieland shentleman.'

It was not very easy to apologise; for I could scarce tell
him (what was the truth) that I had never dreamed he would
set up to be a gentleman until he told me so. Neil on his part
had no wish to prolong his dealings with me, only to fulfil
his orders and be done with it; and he made haste to give my
route. This was to lie the night in Kinlochaline in the public
inn; to cross Morven the next day to Ardgour, and lie the
night in the house of one John of the Claymore, who was
warned that I might come; the third day, to be set across
one loch at Corran and another at Balachulish, and then ask
my way to the house of James of the Glens, at Aucharn in
Duror of Appin. There was a good deal of ferrying, as you

hear; the sea in all this part running deep into the mountains and winding about their roots. It makes the country strong to hold and difficult to travel, but full of prodigious wild and dreadful prospects.

I had some other advice from Neil; to speak with no one by the way, to avoid Whigs, Campbells, and the 'red-soldiers'; to leave the road and lie in a bush if I saw any of the latter coming 'for it was never chancy to meet in with them'; and in brief, to conduct myself like a robber or a Jacobite agent, as perhaps Neil thought me.

The inn at Kinlochaline was the most beggarly vile place that ever pigs were styed in, full of smoke, vermin, and silent Highlanders. I was not only discontented with my lodging, but with myself for my mismanagement of Neil, and thought I could hardly be worse off. But very wrongly, as I was soon to see; for I had not been half an hour at the inn (standing in the door most of the time, to ease my eyes from the peat smoke) when a thunderstorm came close by, the springs broke in a little hill on which the inn stood, and one end of the house became a running water. Places of public entertainment were bad enough all over Scotland in those days; yet it was a wonder to myself, when I had to go from the fireside to the bed in which I slept, wading over the shoes.

Early in my next day's journey I overtook a little, stout, solemn man, walking very slowly with his toes turned out, sometimes reading in a book and sometimes marking the place with his finger, and dressed decently and plainly in something of a clerical style.

This I found to be another catechist, but of a different order from the blind man of Mull: being indeed one of those sent out by the Edinburgh Society for Propagating Christian Knowledge, to evangelise the more savage places of the Highlands. His name was Henderland;* he spoke with the broad south-country tongue, which I was beginning to weary for the sound of; and besides common countryship, we soon found we had a more particular bond of interest. For my good friend, the minister of Essendean, had translated into the Gaelic in his by-time a number of hymns and pious books, which Henderland used in his work, and held in great esteem. Indeed it was one of these he was carrying and reading when we met.

We fell in company at once, our ways lying together as far as to Kingairloch. As we went, he stopped and spoke with all the wayfarers and workers that we met or passed; and though of course I could not tell what they discoursed about, yet I judged Mr. Henderland must be well liked in the countryside, for I observed many of them to bring out their mulls and share a pinch of snuff with him.

I told him as far in my affairs as I judged wise: as far, that is, as they were none of Alan's; and gave Balachulish as the place I was travelling to, to meet a friend; for I thought Aucharn, or even Duror, would be too particular, and might put him on the scent.

On his part, he told me much of his work and the people he worked among, the hiding priests and Jacobites, the Disarming Act,* the dress, and many other curiosities of the time and place. He seemed moderate; blaming Parliament in several points, and especially because they had framed the Act more severely against those who wore the dress than against those who carried weapons.

This moderation put it in my mind to question him of the Red Fox and the Appin tenants; questions which, I thought, would seem natural enough in the mouth of one travelling to that country.

He said it was a bad business. 'It's wonderful,' said he, 'where the tenants find the money, for their life is mere starvation. (Ye don't carry such a thing as snuff, do ye, Mr. Balfour? No. Well, I'm better wanting it.) But these tenants (as I was saying) are doubtless partly driven to it. James Stewart in Duror (that's him they call James of the Glens) is half-brother to Ardshiel, the captain of the clan; and he is a man much looked up to, and drives very hard. And then there's one they call Alan Breck——'

'Ah!' cried I, 'what of him?'

'What of the wind that bloweth where it listeth?' said Henderland. 'He's here and awa; here to-day and gone to-morrow: a fair heather-cat. He might be glowering at the two of us out of yon whin-bush, and I wouldnae wonder! Ye'll no carry such a thing as snuff, will ye?'

I told him no, and that he had asked the same thing more than once.

'It's highly possible,' said he, sighing. 'But it seems strange ye shouldnae carry it. However, as I was saying, this Alan Breck is a bold, desperate customer, and well kent to be James's right hand. His life is forfeit already; he would boggle at naething; and maybe, if a tenant-body was to hang back he would get a dirk in his wame.'

'You make a poor story of it all, Mr. Henderland,' said I. 'If it is all fear upon both sides, I care to hear no more of it.'

'Na,' said Mr. Henderland, 'but there's love too, and self-denial that should put the like of you and me to shame. There's something fine about it; no perhaps Christian, but humanly fine. Even Alan Breck, by all that I hear, is a chield to be respected. There's many a lying sneck-draw sits close in kirk in our own part of the country, and stands well in the world's eye, and maybe is a far worse man, Mr. Balfour, than yon misguided shedder of man's blood. Ay, ay, we might take a lesson by them.—Ye'll perhaps think I've been too long in the Hielands?' he added, smiling to me.

I told him not at all; that I had seen much to admire among the Highlanders; and if he came to that, Mr. Campbell himself was a Highlander.

'Ay,' said he, 'that's true. It's a fine blood.'

'And what is the King's agent about?' I asked.

'Colin Campbell?' says Henderland. 'Putting his head in a bees' byke!'

'He is to turn the tenants out by force, I hear?' said I.

'Yes,' says he, 'but the business has gone back and forth as folks say. First, James of the Glens rode to Edinburgh, and got some lawyer (a Stewart, nae doubt--they all hing together like bats in a steeple) and had the proceedings stayed. And then Colin Campbell cam' in again, and had the upper hand before the Barons of Exchequer. And now they tell me the first of the tenants are to flit to-morrow. It's to begin at

Duror under James's very windows, which doesnae seem wise by my humble way of it.'

'Do you think they'll fight?' I asked.

'Well,' says Henderland, 'they're disarmed—or supposed to be—for there's still a good deal of cold iron lying by in quiet places. And then Colin Campbell has the sogers coming. But for all that, if I was his lady wife, I wouldnae be well pleased till I got him home again. They're queer customers, the Appin Stewarts.'

I asked if they were worse than their neighbours.

'No they,' said he. 'And that's the worst part of it. For if Colin Roy can get his business done in Appin, he has it all to begin again in the next country, which they call Mamore, and which is one of the countries of the Camerons. He's King's factor upon both, and from both he has to drive out the tenants; and indeed, Mr. Balfour (to be open with ye) it's my belief that if he escapes the one lot, he'll get his death by the other.'

So we continued talking and walking the great part of the day; until at last, Mr. Henderland, after expressing his delight in my company, and satisfaction in meeting with a friend of Mr. Campbell's ('whom,' says he, 'I will make bold to call that sweet singer of our covenanted Zion') proposed that I should make a short stage, and lie the night in his house a little beyond Kingairloch. To say truth, I was overjoyed; for I had no great desire for John of the Claymore, and since my double misadventure, first with the guide and next with the gentleman skipper, I stood in some fear of any Highland stranger. Accordingly we shook hands upon the bargain, and came in the afternoon to a small house, standing alone by the shore of the Linnhe Loch. The sun was already gone from the desert mountains of Ardgour upon the hither side, but shone on those of Appin on the farther; the loch lay as still as a lake, only the gulls were crying round the sides of it; and the whole place seemed solemn and uncouth.

We had no sooner come to the door of Mr. Henderland's dwelling, than to my great surprise (for I was now used to the politeness of Highlanders) he burst rudely past me, dashed into the room, caught up a jar and a small horn spoon, and began ladling snuff into his nose in most excessive quantities. Then he had a hearty fit of sneezing, and looked round upon me with a rather silly smile.

'It's a vow I took,' says he. 'I took a vow upon me that I wouldnae carry it. Doubtless it's a great privation; but when I think upon the martyrs, not only to the Scottish Covenant but to other points of Christianity, I think shame to mind it.'

As soon as we had eaten (and porridge and whey was the best of the good man's diet) he took a grave face and said he had a duty to perform by Mr. Campbell, and that was to inquire into my state of mind towards God. I was inclined to smile at him, since the business of the snuff; but he had not spoken long before he brought the tears into my eyes. There are two things that men should never weary of, goodness and humility; we get none too much of them in this rough world among cold, proud people; but Mr. Henderland had their very speech upon his tongue. And though I was a good deal puffed up with my adventures and with having come off, as the saying is, with flying colours; yet he soon had me on my knees beside a simple, poor old man, and both proud and glad to be there.

Before we went to bed he offered me sixpence to help me on my way, out of a scanty store he kept in the turf wall of his house; at which excess of goodness I knew not what to do. But at last he was so earnest with me, that I thought it the more mannerly part to let him have his way, and so left him poorer than myself.

CHAPTER XVII

THE DEATH OF THE 'RED FOX'

THE next day Mr. Henderland found for me a man who had a boat of his own and was to cross the Linnhe Loch that afternoon into Appin, fishing. Him he prevailed on to take me, for he was one of his flock; and in this way I saved a long day's travel and the price of the two public ferries I must otherwise have passed.

It was near noon before we set out; a dark day, with clouds, and the sun shining upon little patches. The sea was here very deep and still, and had scarce a wave upon it; so that I must put the water to my lips before I could believe it to be truly salt. The mountains on either side were high, rough and barren, very black and gloomy in the shadow of the clouds, but all silver-laced with little water-courses where the sun shone upon them. It seemed a hard country, this of Appin, for people to care as much about as Alan did.

There was but one thing to mention. A little after we had started, the sun shone upon a little moving clump of scarlet close in along the waterside to the north. It was much of the same red as soldiers' coats; every now and then, too, there came little sparks and lightnings, as though the sun had struck upon bright steel.

I asked my boatman what it should be; and he answered he supposed it was some of the red soldiers coming from Fort William into Appin, against the poor tenantry of the country. Well, it was a sad sight to me; and whether it was because of my thoughts of Alan, or from something prophetic in my bosom, although this was but the second time I had seen King George's troops, I had no good will to them.

At last we came so near the point of land at the entering in of Loch Leven that I begged to be set on shore. My boatman (who was an honest fellow and mindful of his promise to the catechist) would fain have carried me on to Balachulish; but as this was to take me farther from my secret destination, I insisted, and was set on shore at last under the wood of Lettermore (or Lettervore, for I have heard it both ways) in Alan's country of Appin.

This was a wood of birches, growing on a steep, craggy side of a mountain that overhung the loch. It had many openings and ferny howes;* and a road or bridle track ran north and south through the midst of it, by the edge of which where was a spring, I sat down to eat some oatbread of Mr. Henderland's, and think upon my situation.

Here I was not only troubled by a cloud of stinging midges, but far more by the doubts of my mind. What I ought to do, why I was going to join myself with an outlaw and a would-be murderer like Alan, whether I should not be acting more like a man of sense to tramp back to the south country direct, by my own guidance and at my own charges, and what Mr. Campbell or even Mr. Henderland would think of me if they should ever learn my folly and presumption: these were the doubts that now began to come in on me stronger than ever.

As I was so sitting and thinking, a sound of men and horses came to me through the wood; and presently after, at a turning of the road, I saw four travellers come into view. The way was in this part so rough and narrow that they came single and led their horses by the reins. The first was a great, red-headed gentleman, of an imperious and flushed face, who carried his hat in his hand and fanned himself, for he was in a breathing heat. The second, by his decent black garb and white wig, I correctly took to be a lawyer. The third was a servant, and wore some part of his clothes in tartan, which showed that his master was of a Highland family, and either an outlaw or else in singular good odour with the Government, since the wearing of tartan was against the Act. If I had been better versed in these things, I would have known the tartan to be of the Argyle (or Campbell) colours. This servant had a good-sized portmanteau strapped on his horse, and a net of lemons (to brew punch with) hanging at the saddle-bow; as was often enough the custom with luxurious travellers in that part of the country.

As for the fourth, who brought up the tail, I had seen his like before, and knew him at once to be a sheriff's officer.

I had no sooner seen these people coming than I made up my mind (for no reason that I can tell) to go through with my adventure; and when the first came alongside of me, I rose up from the bracken and asked him the way to Aucharn.

He stopped and looked at me, as I thought, a little oddly; and then, turning to the lawyer. 'Mungo,' said he, 'there's many a man would think this more of a warning than two pyats. Here am I on my road to Duror on the job ye ken; and here is a young lad starts up out of the bracken, and speers if I am on the way to Aucharn.'

'Glenure,' said the other, 'this is an ill subject for jesting.'

These two had now drawn close up and were gazing at me, while the two followers had halted about a stonecast in the rear.

'And what seek ye in Aucharn?' said Colin Roy Campbell of Glenure; him they called the 'Red Fox'; for he it was that I had stopped.

'The man that lives there,' said I.

'James of the Glens,' says Glenure, musingly;; and then to the lawyer: 'Is he gathering his people, think ye?'

'Anyway,' says the lawyer, 'we shall do better to bide where we are, and let the soldiers rally us.'

'If you are concerned for me,' said I, 'I am neither of his people nor yours, but an honest subect of King George, owing no man and fearing no man.'

'Why, very well said,' replies the Factor. 'But if I may make so bold as ask, what does this honest man so far from his country? and why does he come seeking the brother of Ardshiel? I have power here, I must tell you. I am King's Factor upon several of these estates, and have twelve files of soldiers at my back.'

'I have heard a waif word in the country,' said I, a little nettled, 'that you were a hard man to drive.'

He still kept looking at me, as if in doubt.

'Well,' said he, at last, 'your tongue is bold; but I am no unfriend to plainness. If ye had asked me the way to the door of James Stewart on any other day but this, I would have set ye right and bidden ye God speed. But to-day—eh, Mungo?' And turned again to look at the lawyer.

But just as he turned there came the shot of a firelock from higher up the hill; and with the very sound of it Glenure fell upon the road.

'O, I am dead!' he cried, several times over.

The lawyer had caught him up and held him in his arms, the servant standing over and clasping his hands. And now the wounded man looked from one to another with scared eyes, and there was a change in his voice that went to the heart.

'Take care of yourselves,' says he. 'I am dead.'

He tried to open his clothes as if to look for the wound, but his fingers slipped on the buttons. With that he gave a great sigh, his head rolled on his shoulder, and he passed away.

The lawyer said never a word, but his face was as sharp as a pen and as white as the dead man's; the servant broke out into a great noise of crying and weeping, like a child; and I, on my side, stood staring at them in a kind of horror. The sheriff's officer had run back at the first sound of the shot, to hasten the coming of the soldiers.

At last the lawyer laid down the dead man in his blood upon the road, and got to his own feet with a kind of stagger.

I believe it was his movement that brought me to my senses; for he had no sooner done so than I began to scramble up the hill, crying out, 'The murderer! the murderer!'

So little a time had elapsed, that when I got to the top of the first steepness, and could see some part of the open mountain, the murderer was still moving away at no great distance. He was a big man, in a black coat, with metal buttons, and carried a long fowling-piece.

'Here!' I cried. 'I see him!'

At that the murderer gave a little, quick look over his shoulder, and began to run. The next moment he was lost in a fringe of birches; then he came out again on the upper side, where I could see him climbing like a jackanapes, for that part was again very steep; and then he dipped behind a shoulder, and I saw him no more.

All this time I had been running on my side, and had got a good way up, when a voice cried upon me to stand.

I was at the edge of the upper wood, and so now, when I halted and looked back, I saw all the open part of the hill below me.

The lawyer and the sheriff's officer were standing just above the road, crying and waving on me to come back; and on their left, the red-coats, musket in hand, were beginning to struggle singly out of the lower wood.

'Why should I come back?' I cried. 'Come you on!'

'Ten pounds if ye take that lad!' cried the lawyer. 'He's an accomplice. He was posted here to hold us in talk.'

At that word (which I could hear quite plainly, though it was to the soldiers and not to me that he was crying it) my heart came in my mouth with quite a new kind of terror. Indeed, it is one thing to stand the danger of your life, and quite another to run the peril of both life and character. The thing, besides, had come so suddenly, like thunder out of a clear sky, that I was all amazed and helpless.

The soldiers began to spread, some of them to run, and others to put up their pieces and cover me; and still I stood.

'Jouk[1] in here among the trees,' said a voice, close by.

Indeed, I scarce knew what I was doing, but I obeyed; and as I did so, I heard the firelocks bang and the balls whistle in the birches.

Just inside the shelter of the trees I found Alan Breck standing, with a fishing-rod. He gave me no salutation; indeed it was no time for civilities; only 'Come!' says he, and set off running along the side of the mountain towards Balachulish; and I, like a sheep, to follow him.

Now we ran among the birches; now stopping behind low humps upon the mountain side; now crawling on all fours among the heather. The pace was deadly; my heart seemed bursting against my ribs; and I had neither time to think nor breath to speak with. Only I remember seeing with wonder, that Alan every now and then would straighten himself to his full height and look back; and every time he did so, there came a great far-away cheering and crying of the soldiers.

Quarter of an hour later, Alan stopped, clapped down flat in the heather, and turned to me.

'Now,' said he, 'it's earnest. Do as I do, for your life.'

And at the same speed, but now with infinitely more

---

[1] Duck.

precaution, we traced back again across the mountain side by the same way that we had come, only perhaps higher; till at last Alan threw himself down in the upper wood of Lettermore, where I had found him at the first, and lay, with his face in the bracken, panting like a dog.

My own sides so ached, my head so swam, my tongue so hung out of my mouth with heat and dryness, that I lay beside him like one dead.

CHAPTER XVIII

I TALK WITH ALAN IN THE WOOD OF LETTERMORE

ALAN was the first to come round. He rose, went to the border of the wood, peered out a little, and then returned and sat down.

'Well,' said he, 'yon was a hot burst, David.'

I said nothing, nor so much as lifted my face. I had seen murder done, and a great, ruddy, jovial gentleman struck out of life in a moment; the pity of that sight was still sore within me, and yet that was but a part of my concern. Here was murder done upon the man Alan hated; here was Alan skulking in the trees and running from the troops; and whether his was the hand that fired or only the head that ordered, signified but little. By my way of it, my only friend in that wild country was blood-guilty in the first degree; I held him in horror; I could not look upon his face; I would have rather lain alone in the rain on my cold isle, than in that warm wood beside a murderer.

'Are ye still wearied?' he asked again.

'No,' said I, still with my face in the bracken; 'no, I am not wearied now, and I can speak. You and me must twine,'[1] I said. 'I liked you very well, Alan; but your ways are not mine, and they're not God's: and the short and long of it is just that we must twine.'

1 Part.

'I will hardly twine from ye, David, without some kind of reason for the same,' said Alan, mighty gravely. 'If ye ken anything against my reputation, it's the least thing that ye should do, for old acquaintance sake, to let me hear the name of it; and if ye have only taken a distaste to my society, it will be proper for me to judge if I'm insulted.'

'Alan,' said I, 'what is the sense of this? Ye ken very well yon Campbellman lies in his blood upon the road.'

He was silent for a little; then says he, 'Did ever ye hear tell of the story of the Man and the Good People?'—by which he meant the fairies.

'No,' said I, 'nor do I want to hear it.'

'With your permission, Mr. Balfour, I will tell it you, whatever,' says Alan. 'The man, ye should ken, was cast upon a rock in the sea, where it appears the Good People were in use to come and rest as they went through to Ireland. The name of this rock is called the Skerryvore, and it's not far from where we suffered shipwreck. Well, it seems the man cried so sore, if he could just see his little bairn before he died! that at last the king of the Good People took peety upon him, and sent one flying that brought back the bairn in a poke[1] and laid it down beside the man where he lay sleeping. So when the man woke, there was a poke beside him and something into the inside of it that moved. Well, it seems he was one of these gentry that think aye the worst of things; and for greater security, he stuck his dirk throughout that poke before he opened it, and there was his bairn dead. I am thinking to myself, Mr. Balfour, that you and the man are very much alike.'

'Do you mean you had no hand in it?' cried I, sitting up.

'I will tell you first of all, Mr. Balfour of Shaws, as one friend to another,' said Alan, 'that if I were going to kill a gentleman, it would not be in my own country, to bring trouble on my clan; and I would not go wanting sword and gun, and with a long fishing-rod upon my back.'

'Well,' said I, 'that's true!'

[1] Bag.

'And now,' continued Alan, taking out his dirk and laying his hand upon it in a certain manner, 'I swear upon the Holy Iron I had neither art nor part, act nor thought in it.'

'I thank God for that!' cried I, and offered him my hand.

He did not appear to see it.

'And here is a great deal of work about a Campbell!' said he. 'They are not so scarce, that I ken!'

'At least,' said I, 'you cannot justly blame me, for you know very well what you told me in the brig. But the temptation and the act are different, I thank God again for that. We may all be tempted; but to take a life in cold blood, Alan!' And I could say no more for the moment. 'And do you know who did it?' I added. 'Do you know that man in the black coat?'

'I have nae clear mind about his coat,' said Alan, cunningly; 'but it sticks in my head that it was blue.'

'Blue or black, did ye know him?' said I.

'I couldnae just conscientiously swear to him,' says Alan. 'He gaed very close by me, to be sure, but it's a strange thing that I should just have been tying my brogues.'

'Can you swear that you don't know him, Alan?' I cried, half angered, half in a mind to laugh at his evasions.

'Not yet,' says he; 'but I've a grand memory for forgetting, David.'

'And yet there was one thing I saw clearly,' said I; 'and that was, that you exposed yourself and me to draw the soldiers.'

'It's very likely,' said Alan; 'and so would any gentleman. You and me were innocent of that transaction.'

'The better reason, since we were falsely suspected, that we should get clear,' I cried. 'The innocent should surely come before the guilty.'

'Why, David,' said he, 'the innocent have aye a chance to get assoiled in court; but for the lad that shot the bullet, I think the best place for him will be the heather. Them that havenae dipped their hands in any little difficulty, should be very mindful of the case of them that have. And that is the good Christianity. For if it was the other way about, and the lad whom I could just clearly see had been in our shoes, and we in his (as might very well have been), I think we would be a good deal obliged to him oursel's if he would draw the soldiers.'

When it came to this, I gave Alan up. But he looked so innocent all the time, and was in such clear good faith in what he said, and so ready to sacrifice himself for what he deemed his duty, that my mouth was closed. Mr. Henderland's words came back to me: that we ourselves might take a lesson by these wild Highlanders. Well, here I had taken mine. Alan's morals were all tail-first; but he was ready to give his life for them, such as they were.

'Alan,' said I, 'I'll not say it's the good Christianity as I understand it, but it's good enough. And here I offer ye my hand for the second time.'

Whereupon he gave me both of his, saying surely I had cast a spell upon him, for he could forgive me anything. Then he grew very grave, and said we had not much time to throw away, but must both flee that country: he, because he was a deserter, and the whole of Appin would now be searched like a chamber, and every one obliged to give a good account of himself; and I, because I was certainly involved in the murder.

'O!' says I, willing to give him a little lesson, 'I have no fear of the justice of my country.'

'As if this was your country!' said he. 'Or as if ye would be tried here, in a country of Stewarts!'

'It's all Scotland,' said I.

'Man, I whiles wonder at ye,' said Alan. 'This is a Campbell that's been killed. Well, it'll be tried in Inverara, the Campbells' head place; with fifteen Campbells in the jury-box, and the biggest Campbell of all (and that's the Duke) sitting cocking on the bench. Justice, David? The same justice, by all the world, as Glenure found a while ago at the roadside.'

This frighted me a little, I confess, and would have frighted me more if I had known how nearly exact were Alan's predictions; indeed it was but in one point that he exaggerated, there being but eleven Campbells on the jury; though as the other four were equally in the Duke's dependence, it mattered less than might appear. Still, I cried out that he was unjust to the Duke of Argyle, who (for all he was a Whig), was yet a wise and honest nobleman.

'Hoot!' said Alan, 'the man's a Whig, nae doubt; but I would never deny he was a good chieftain to his clan. And what would the clan think if there was a Campbell shot, and naebody hanged, and their own chief the Justice General? But I have often observed,' says Alan, 'that you Low-country bodies have no clear idea of what's right and wrong.'

At this I did at last laugh out aloud; when to my surprise, Alan joined in and laughed as merrily as myself.

'Na, na,' said he, 'we're in the Hielands, David; and when I tell ye to run, take my word and run. Nae doubt it's a hard thing to skulk and starve in the heather, but it's harder yet to lie shackled in a red-coat prison.'

I asked him whither we should flee; and as he told me 'to the Lowlands,' I was a little better inclined to go with him; for indeed I was growing impatient to get back and have the upper hand of my uncle. Besides, Alan made so sure there would be no question of justice in the matter, that I began to be afraid he might be right. Of all deaths, I would truly like least to die by the gallows; and the picture of that uncanny instrument came into my head with extraordinary clearness (as I had once seen it engraved at the top of a pedlar's ballad) and took away my appetite for courts of justice.

'I'll chance it, Alan,' said I. 'I'll go with you.'

'But mind you,' said Alan, 'it's no small thing. Ye maun lie bare and hard, and brook many an empty belly. Your bed shall be the moorcock's, and your life shall be like the hunted deer's, and ye shall sleep with your hand upon your weapons. Ay, man, ye shall taigle many a weary foot, or we get clear! I tell ye this at the start, for it's a life that I ken well. But if ye ask what other chance ye have, I answer: Nane. Either take to the heather with me, or else hang.'

'And that's a choice very easily made,' said I; and we shook hands upon it.

'And now let's take another keek at the red-coats,' says Alan, and he led me to the north-eastern fringe of the wood.

Looking out between the trees, we could see a great side of mountain, running down exceeding steep into the waters of the loch. It was a rough part, all hanging stone, and heather, and bit scrags of birchwood; and away at the far end towards Balachulish, little wee red soldiers were dipping up and down over hill and howe, and growing smaller every minute. There was no cheering now, for I think they had other uses for what breath was left them; but they still stuck to the trail, and doubtless thought that we were close in front of them.

Alan watched them, smiling to himself.

'Ay,' said he, 'they'll be gey weary before they've got to the end of that employ! And so you and me, David, can sit down and eat a bite, and breathe a bit longer, and take a dram from my bottle. Then we'll strike for Aucharn, the house of my kinsman, James of the Glens, where I must get my clothes, and my arms, and money to carry us along; and then David, we'll cry "Forth, Fortune!" and take a cast among the heather.'

So we sat again and ate and drank, in a place where we could see the sun going down into a field of great, wild and houseless mountains, such as I was now condemned to wander in with my companion. Partly as we so sat, and partly afterwards, on the way to Aucharn, each of us narrated his adventures; and I shall here set down so much of Alan's as seems either curious or needful.

It appears he ran to the bulwarks as soon as the wave was passed; saw me, and lost me, and saw me again, as I tumbled in the roost; and at last had one glimpse of me clinging on the yard. It was this that put him in some hope I would maybe get to land after all, and made him leave those clues and messages which had brought me (for my sins) to that unlucky country of Appin.

In the meanwhile, those still on the brig had got the skiff

launched, and one or two were on board of her already, when there came a second wave greater than the first, and heaved the brig out of her place, and would certainly have sent her to the bottom, had she not struck and caught on some projection of the reef. When she had struck first, it had been bows-on, so that the stern had hitherto been lowest. But now her stern was thrown in the air, and the bows plunged under the sea; and with that, the water began to pour into the forescuttle like the pouring of a mill-dam.

It took the colour out of Alan's face even to tell what followed. For there were still two men lying impotent in their bunks; and there, seeing the water pour in and thinking the ship had foundered, begun to cry out aloud, and that with such harrowing cries that all who were on deck tumbled one after another into the skiff and fell to their oars. They were not two hundred yards away, when there came a third great sea; and at that the brig lifted clean over the reef; her canvas filled for a moment, and she seemed to sail in chase of them, but settling all the while; and presently she drew down and down, as if a hand was drawing her; and the sea closed over the *Covenant* of Dysart.

Never a word they spoke as they pulled ashore, being stunned with the horror of that screaming; but they had scarce set foot upon the beach when Hoseason woke up, as if out of a muse, and bade them lay hands upon Alan. They hung back indeed, having little taste for the employment; but Hoseason was like a fiend; crying that Alan was alone, that he had a great sum about him, that he had been the means of losing the brig and drowning all their comrades, and that here was both revenge and wealth upon a single cast. It was seven against one; in that part of the shore there was no rock that Alan could set his back to; and the sailors began to spread out and come behind him.

'And then,' said Alan, 'the little man with the red head—I havenae mind of the name that he is called.'

'Riach,' said I.

'Ay,' said Alan, 'Riach!' Well, it was him that took up the clubs for me, asked the men if they werenae feared of a judgment, and says he, "Dod, I'll put my back to the Hieland-man's mysel'." That's none such an entirely bad little man with the red head,' said Alan. 'He has some spunks of decency.'

'Well,' said I, 'he was kind to me in his way.'

'And so he was to Alan,' said he; 'and by my troth, I found his way a very good one! But ye see, David, the loss of the ship and the cries of these poor lads sat very ill upon the man; and I'm thinking that would be the cause of it.'

'Well, I would think so,' says I; 'for he was as keen as any of the rest at the beginning. But how did Hoseason take it?'

'It sticks in my mind that he would take it very ill,' says Alan. 'But the little man cried to me to run, and indeed I thought it was a good observe, and ran. The last that I saw they were all in a knot upon the beach, like folk that were not agreeing very well together.'

'What do you mean by that?' said I.

'Well, the fists were going,' said Alan; 'and I saw one man go down like a pair of breeks. But I thought it would be better no to wait. Ye see there's a strip of Campbells in that end of Mull, which is no good company for a gentleman like me. If it hadnae been for that I would have waited and looked for ye mysel', let alone giving a hand to the little man.' (It was droll how Alan dwelt on Mr. Riach's stature, for, to say the truth, the one was not much smaller than the other.) 'So,' says he, continuing, 'I set my best foot forward, and when-ever I met in with anyone I cried out there was a wreck ashore. Man, they didnae stop to fash with me! Ye should have seen them linking for the beach! And when they got there they found they had had the pleasure of a run, which is aye good for a Campbell. I'm thinking it was a judgment on the clan that the brig went down in the lump and didnae break. But it was a very unlucky thing for you, that same; for if any wreck had come ashore they would have hunted high and low, and would soon have found ye.'

CHAPTER XIX

THE HOUSE OF FEAR

NIGHT fell as we were walking, and the clouds, which had broken up in the afternoon, settled in and thickened, so that it fell, for the season of the year, extremely dark. The way we went was over rough mountain sides; and though Alan pushed on with an assured manner, I could by no means see how he directed himself.

At last, about half-past ten of the clock, we came to the top of a brae, and saw lights below us. It seemed a house door stood open and let out a beam of fire and candle-light; and all round the house and steading five or six persons were moving hurriedly about, each carrying a lighted brand.

'James must have tint his wits,' said Alan. 'If this was the soldiers instead of you and me, he would be in a bonny mess. But I dare say he'll have a sentry on the road, and he would ken well enough no soldiers would find the way that we came.'

Hereupon he whistled three times, in a particular manner. It was strange to see how, at the first sound of it, all the moving torches came to a stand, as if the bearers were affrighted; and how, at the third, the bustle began again as before.

Having thus set folks' minds at rest, we came down the brae, and were met at the yard gate (for this place was like a well-doing farm) by a tall, handsome man of more than fifty, who cried out to Alan in the Gaelic.

'James Stewart,' said Alan, 'I will ask ye to speak in Scotch, for here is a young gentleman with me that has nane of the other. This is him,' he added, putting his arm through mine, 'a young gentleman of the Lowlands, and a laird in his country too, but I am thinking it will be the better for his health if we give his name the go-by.'

James of the Glens turned to me for a moment, and greeted me courteously enough; the next he had turned to Alan.

'This has been a dreadful accident,' he cried. 'It will bring trouble on the country.' And he wrung his hands.

'Hoots!' said Alan, 'ye must take the sour with the sweet, man. Colin Roy is dead, and be thankful for that!'

'Ay,' said James, 'and by my troth, I wish he was alive again! It's all very fine to blow and boast beforehand; but now it's done, Alan; and who's to bear the wyte[1] of it? The accident fell out in Appin—mind ye that, Alan; it's Appin that must pay; and I am a man that has a family.'

While this was going on I looked about me at the servants. Some were on ladders, digging in the thatch of the house or the farm buildings, from which they brought out guns, swords, and different weapons of war; others carried them away; and by the sound of mattock blows from somewhere further down the brae, I suppose they buried them. Though they were all so busy, there prevailed no kind of order in their efforts; men struggled together for the same gun and ran into each other with their burning torches; and James was continually turning about from his talk with Alan, to cry out orders which were apparently never understood. The faces in the torchlight were like those of people overborne with hurry and panic; and though none spoke above his breath, their speech sounded both anxious and angry.

It was about this time that a lassie came out of the house carrying a pack or bundle; and it has often made me smile to think how Alan's instinct awoke at the mere sight of it.

'What's that the lassie has?' he asked.

'We're just setting the house in order, Alan,' said James, in his frightened and somewhat fawning way. 'They'll search Appin with candles, and we must have all things straight. We're digging the bit guns and swords into the moss, ye see; and these, I am thinking will be your ain French clothes.'*

'Bury my French clothes!' cried Alan. 'Troth, no!' And he laid a hold upon the packet and retired into the barn to

---

1 Blame.

shift himself, recommending me in the meanwhile to his kinsman.

James carried me accordingly into the kitchen, and sat down with me at table, smiling and talking at first in a very hospitable manner. But presently the gloom returned upon him; he sat frowning, and biting his fingers; only remembered me from time to time; and then gave me but a word or two and a poor smile, and back into his private terrors. His wife sat by the fire and wept, with her face in her hands; his eldest son was crouched upon the floor, running over a great mass of papers and now and again setting one alight and burning it to the bitter end; all the while a servant lass with a red face was rummaging about the room, in a blind hurry of fear, and whimpering as she went; and every now and again one of the men would thrust in his face from the yard, and cry for orders.

At last James could keep his seat no longer, and begged my permission to be so unmannerly as walk about. 'I am but poor company altogether, sir,' says he, 'but I can think of nothing but this dreadful accident, and the trouble it is like to bring upon quite innocent persons.'

A little after he observed his son burning a paper, which he thought should have been kept; and at that his excitement burst out so that it was painful to witness. He struck the lad repeatedly.

'Are you gone gyte[1]?' he cried. 'Do you wish to hang your father?' and forgetful of my presence, carried on at him a long time together in the Gaelic, the young man answering nothing; only the wife, at the name of hanging, throwing her apron over her face and sobbing out louder than before.

This was all wretched for a stranger like myself to hear and see; and I was right glad when Alan returned, looking like himself in his fine French clothes, though (to be sure) they were now grown almost too battered and withered to deserve the name of fine. I was then taken out in my turn by another of the sons, and given that change of clothing

1 Mad.

of which I had stood so long in need, and a pair of Highland brogues made of deer-leather, rather strange at first, but after a little practice very easy to the feet.

By the time I came back Alan must have told his story; for it seemed understood that I was to fly with him, and they were all busy upon our equipment. They gave us each a sword and pistols, though I professed my inability to use the former; and with these, and some ammunition, a bag of oatmeal, an iron pan, and a bottle of right French brandy, we were ready for the heather. Money, indeed, was lacking. I had about two guineas left; Alan's belt having been despatched by another hand, that trusty messenger had no more than seventeen-pence to his whole fortune; and as for James, it appears he had brought himself so low with journeys to Edinburgh and legal expenses on behalf of the tenants, that he could only scrape together three-and-fivepence-halfpenny, the most of it in coppers.

'This'll no do,' said Alan.

'Ye must find a safe bit somewhere near by,' said James, 'and get word sent to me. Ye see, ye'll have to get this business prettily off, Alan. This is no time to be stayed for a guinea or two. They're sure to get wind of ye, sure to seek ye, and by my way of it, sure to lay on ye the wyte of this day's accident. If it falls on you, it falls on me that am your near kinsman and harboured ye while ye were in the country. And if it comes on me——' he paused, and bit his fingers, with a white face. 'It would be a painful thing for our friends if I was to hang,' said he.

'It would be an ill day for Appin,' says Alan.

'It's a day that sticks in my throat,' said James. 'O man, man, man—man Alan! you and me have spoken like two fools!' he cried, striking his hand upon the wall so that the house rang again.

'Well, and that's true, too,' said Alan; 'and my friend from the Lowlands here' (nodding at me) 'gave me a good word upon that head, if I would only have listened to him.'

'But see here,' said James, returning to his former manner, 'if they lay me by the heels, Alan, it's then that you'll be needing the money. For with all that I have said and that you have said, it will look very black against the two of us; do ye mark that? Well, follow me out, and ye'll see that I'll have to get a paper out against ye mysel'; I'll have to offer a reward for ye; ay, will I! It's a sore thing to do between such near friends; but if I get the dirdum[1] of this dreadful accident, I'll have to fend for myself, man. Do ye see that?'

He spoke with a pleading earnestness, taking Alan by the breast of the coat.

'Ay,' said Alan, 'I see that.'

'And ye'll have to be clear of the country, Alan—ay, and clear of Scotland—you and your friend from the Lowlands, too. For I'll have to paper your friend from the Lowlands. Ye see that, Alan—say that ye see that!'

I thought Alan flushed a bit. 'This is unco hard on me that brought him here, James,' said he, throwing his head back. 'It's like making me a traitor!'

'Now, Alan, man!' cried James. 'Look things in the face! He'll be papered anyway; Mungo Campbell'll be sure to paper him; what matters if I paper him too? And then, Alan, I am a man that has a family.' And then, after a little pause on both sides: 'And, Alan, it'll be a jury of Campbells,' said he.

'There's one thing,' said Alan, musingly, 'that naebody kens his name.'

'Nor yet they shallnae, Alan! There's my hand on that,' cried James, for all the world as if he had really known my name and was foregoing some advantage. 'But just the habit he was in, and what he looked like, and his age, and the like? I couldnae well do less.'

'I wonder at your father's son,' cried Alan, sternly. 'Would ye sell the lad with a gift? Would ye change his clothes and then betray him?'

'No, no, Alan,' said James. 'No, no: the habit he took off—the habit Mungo saw him in.' But I thought he seemed crest-fallen; indeed, he was clutching at every straw, and all the

1 Blame.

time, I daresay, saw the faces of his hereditary foes on the bench and in the jury-box, and the gallows in the background.

'Well, sir,' says Alan, turning to me, 'what say ye to that? Ye are here under the safeguard of my honour; and it's my part to see nothing done but what shall please you.'

'I have but one word to say,' said I; 'for to all this dispute I am a perfect stranger. But the plain commonsense is to set the blame where it belongs, and that is on the man that fired the shot. Paper him, as ye call it, set the hunt on him; and let honest, innocent folk show their faces in safety.'

But at this both Alan and James cried out in horror; bidding me hold my tongue, for that was not to be thought of; and asking me what the Camerons would think? (which confirmed me, it must have been a Cameron from Mamore that did the act) and if I did not see that the lad might be caught? 'Ye havenae surely thought of that?' said they, with such innocent earnestness, that my hands dropped at my side and I despaired of argument.

'Very well, then,' said I, 'paper me, if you please, paper Alan, paper King George! We're all three innocent, and that seems to be what's wanted! But at least, sir,' said I to James, recovering from my little fit of annoyance, 'I am Alan's friend, and if I can be helpful to friends of his, I will not stumble at the risk.'

I thought it best to put a fair face on my consent, for I saw Alan troubled; and besides (thinks I to myself) as soon as my back is turned, they will paper me, as they call it, whether I consent or not. But in this I saw I was wrong; for I had no sooner said the words, than Mrs. Stewart leaped out of her chair, came running over to us, and wept first upon my neck and then on Alan's, blessing God for our goodness to her family.

'As for you, Alan, it was no more than your bounden duty,' she said. 'But for this lad that has come here and seen us at our worst, and seen the goodman fleeching like a suitor, him that by rights should give his commands like any king—as for you, my lad,' she says, 'my heart is wae not to have your name, but I have your face; and as long as my heart beats under my bosom, I will keep it, and think of it, and bless it.' And with that she kissed me, and burst once more into such sobbing, that I stood abashed.

'Hoot, hoot,' said Alan, looking mighty silly. 'The day comes unco soon in this month of July; and to-morrow there'll be a fine to-do in Appin, a fine riding of dragoons, and crying of "Cruachan!"[1] and running of red-coats; and it behoves you and me to be the sooner gone.'

Thereupon we said farewell, and set out again, bending somewhat eastwards, in a fine mild dark night, and over much the same broken country as before.

CHAPTER XX

THE FLIGHT IN THE HEATHER:
THE ROCKS

SOMETIMES we walked, sometimes ran; and as it drew on to morning, walked ever the less and ran the more. Though, upon its face, that country appeared to be a desert, yet there were huts and houses of the people, of which we must have passed more than twenty, hidden in quiet places of the hills. When we came to one of these, Alan would leave me in the way, and go himself and rap upon the side of the house and speak a while at the window with some sleeper awakened. This was to pass the news; which, in that country, was so much of a duty that Alan must pause to attend to it even while fleeing for his life; and so well attended to by others, that in more than half of the houses where we called they had heard already of the murder. In the others, as well as I could make out (standing back at a distance and hearing a strange tongue) the news was received with more of consternation than surprise.

For all our hurry, day began to come in while we were

1 The rallying-word of the Campbells.

still far from any shelter. It found us in a prodigious valley, strewn with rocks and where ran a foaming river. Wild mountains stood around it; there grew there neither grass nor trees; and I have sometimes thought since then, that it may have been the valley called Glencoe,* where the massacre was in the time of King William. But for the details of our itinerary, I am all to seek; our way lying now by short cuts, now by great detours; our pace being so hurried; our time of journeying usually by night; and the names of such places as I asked and heard, being in the Gaelic tongue and the more easily forgotten.

The first peep of morning, then, showed us this horrible place, and I could see Alan knit his brow.

'This is no fit place for you and me,' he said. 'This is a place they're bound to watch.'

And with that he ran harder than ever down to the waterside, in a part where the river was split in two among three rocks. It went through with a horrid thundering that made my belly quake; and there hung over the lynn a little mist of spray. Alan looked neither to the right nor to the left, but jumped clean upon the middle rock and fell there on his hands and knees to check himself, for that rock was small and he might have pitched over on the far side. I had scarce time to measure the distance or to understand the peril, before I had followed him, and he had caught and stopped me.

So there we stood, side by side upon a small rock slippery with spray, a far broader leap in front of us, and the river dinning upon all sides. When I saw where I was, there came on me a deadly sickness of fear, and I put my hand over my eyes. Alan took me and shook me; I saw he was speaking, but the roaring of the falls and the trouble of my mind prevented me from hearing; only I saw his face was red with anger, and that he stamped upon the rock. The same look showed me the water raging by, and the mist hanging in the air; and with that, I covered my eyes again and shuddered.

The next minute Alan had set the brandy bottle to my lips, and forced me to drink about a gill, which sent the blood into my head again. Then, putting his hands to his mouth and his mouth to my ear, he shouted 'Hang or drown!' and turning his back upon me, leaped over the farther branch of the stream, and landed safe.

I was now alone upon the rock, which gave me the more room; the brandy was singing in my ears; I had this good example fresh before me, and just wit enough to see that if I did not leap at once, I should never leap at all. I bent low on my knees and flung myself forth, with that kind of anger of despair that has sometimes stood me in stead of courage. Sure enough, it was but my hands that reached the full length; these slipped, caught again, slipped again; and I was sliddering back into the lynn, when Alan seized me, first by the hair, then by the collar, and with a great strain dragged me into safety.

Never a word he said, but set off running again for his life, and I must stagger to my feet and run after him. I had been weary before, but now I was sick and bruised, and partly drunken with the brandy; I kept stumbling as I ran, I had a stitch that came near to overmaster me; and when at last Alan paused under a great rock that stood there among a number of others, it was none too soon for David Balfour.

A great rock, I have said; but by rights it was two rocks leaning together at the top, both some twenty feet high, and at the first sight inaccessible. Even Alan (though you may say he had as good as four hands) failed twice in an attempt to climb them; and it was only at the third trial, and then by standing on my shoulders and leaping up with such force as I thought must have broken my collar-bone, that he secured a lodgment. Once there, he let down his leathern girdle; and with the aid of that and a pair of shallow foot-holds in the rock, I scrambled up beside him.

Then I saw why we had come there; for the two rocks, being both somewhat hollow on the top and sloping one to the other, made a kind of dish or saucer, where as many as three or four men might have lain hidden.

All this while Alan had not said a word, and had run and climbed with such a savage, silent frenzy of hurry, that I

knew that he was in mortal fear of some miscarriage. Even
now we were on the rock he said nothing, nor so much as
relaxed the frowning look upon his face; but clapped flat
down, and keeping only one eye above the edge of our place
of shelter, scouted all round the compass. The dawn had come
quite clear; we could see the stony sides of the valley, and its
bottom, which was bestrewed with rocks, and the river, which
went from one side to another, and made white falls; but
nowhere the smoke of a house, nor any living creature but
some eagles screaming round a cliff.

Then at last Alan smiled.

'Ay,' said he, 'now we have a chance'; and then looking
at me with some amusement, 'Ye're no very gleg[1] at the
jumping,' said he.

At this I suppose I coloured with mortification, for he
added at once, 'Hoots! small blame to ye! To be feared of a
thing and yet to do it, is what makes the prettiest kind of a
man. And then there was water there, and water's a thing
that dauntons even me. No, no,' said Alan, 'it's no you that's
to blame, it's me.'

I asked him why.

'Why,' said he, 'I have proved myself a gomeral this night.
For first of all I take a wrong road, and that in my own
country of Appin; so that the day has caught us where we
should never have been; and thanks to that, we lie here in
some danger and mair discomfort. And next (which is the
worst of the two, for a man that has been so much among
the heather as myself) I have come wanting a water-bottle,
and here we lie for a long summer's day with naething but
neat spirit. Ye may think that a small matter; but before it
comes night, David, ye'll give me news of it.'

I was anxious to redeem my character, and offered, if he
would pour out the brandy, to run down and fill the bottle
at the river.

'I wouldnae waste the good spirit either,' says he. 'It's been
a good friend to you this night; or in my poor opinion, ye

1 Brisk.

would still be cocking on yon stone. And what's mair,' says he, 'ye may have observed (you that's a man of so much penetration) that Alan Breck Stewart was perhaps walking quicker than his ordinar'.'

'You!' I cried, 'you were running fit to burst.'

'Was I so?' said he. 'Well, then, ye may depend upon it, there was nae time to be lost. And now here is enough said; gang you to your sleep, lad, and I'll watch.'

Accordingly, I lay down to sleep; a little peaty earth had drifted in between the top of the two rocks, and some bracken grew there, to be a bed to me; the last thing I heard was still the crying of the eagles.

I dare say it would be nine in the morning when I was roughly awakened, and found Alan's hand pressed upon my mouth.

'Wheesht!' he whispered. 'Ye were snoring.'

'Well,' said I, surprised at his anxious and dark face, 'and why not?'

He peered over the edge of the rock, and signed to me to do the like.

It was now high day, cloudless, and very hot. The valley was as clear as in a picture. About half a mile up the water was a camp of red-coats; a big fire blazed in their midst, at which some were cooking; and near by, on the top of a rock about as high as ours, there stood a sentry, with the sun sparkling on his arms. All the way down along the riverside were posted other sentries; here near together, there widelier scattered; some planted like the first, on places of command, some on the ground level and marching and countermarching, so as to meet half-way. Higher up the glen, where the ground was more open, the chain of posts was continued by horse-soldiers, whom we could see in the distance riding to and fro. Lower down, the infantry continued; but as the stream was suddenly swelled by the confluence of a considerable burn, they were more widely set, and only watched the fords and stepping-stones.

I took but one look at them, and ducked again into my

place. It was strange indeed to see this valley, which had laid so solitary in the hour of dawn, bristling with arms and dotted with the red coats and breeches.

'Ye see,' said Alan, 'this was what I was afraid of, Davie: that they would watch the burn-side. They began to come in about two hours ago, and, man! but ye're a grand hand at the sleeping! We're in a narrow place. If they get up the sides of the hill, they could easy spy us with a glass; but if they'll only keep in the foot of the valley, we'll do yet. The posts are thinner down the water; and, come night, we'll try our hand at getting by them.'

'And what are we to do till night?' I asked.

'Lie here,' says he, 'and birstle.'

That one good Scotch word, 'birstle,' was indeed the most of the story of the day that we had now to pass. You are to remember that we lay on the bare top of a rock, like scones upon a girdle; the sun beat upon us cruelly; the rock grew so heated, a man could scarce endure the touch of it; and the little patch of earth and fern, which kept cooler, was only large enough for one at a time. We took turn about to lie on the naked rock, which was indeed like the position of that saint that was martyred on a gridiron; and it ran in my mind how strange it was, that in the same climate and at only a few days' distance, I should have suffered so cruelly, first from cold upon my island, and now from heat upon this rock.

All the while we had no water, only raw brandy for a drink, which was worse than nothing; but we kept the bottle as cool as we could, burying it in the earth, and got some relief by bathing our breasts and temples.

The soldiers kept stirring all day in the bottom of the valley, now changing guard, now in patrolling parties hunting among the rocks. These lay round in so great a number, that to look for men among them was like looking for a needle in a bottle of hay; and being so hopeless a task, it was gone about with the less care. Yet we could see the soldiers pike their bayonets among the heather, which sent a cold thrill into my vitals; and thy would sometimes hang about our rock, so that we scarce dared to breathe.

It was in this way that I first heard the right English speech; one fellow as he went by actually clapping his hand upon the sunny face of the rock on which we lay, and plucking it off again with an oath.

'I tell you it's 'ot,' says he; and I was amazed at the clipping tones and the odd sing-song in which he spoke, and no less at that strange trick of dropping out the letter h. To be sure, I had heard Ransome; but he had taken his ways from all sorts of people, and spoke so imperfectly at the best, that I set down the most of it to childishness. My surprise was all the greater to hear that manner of speaking in the mouth of a grown man; and indeed I have never grown used to it; nor yet altogether with the English grammar,* as perhaps a very critical eye might here and there spy out even in these memoirs.

The tediousness and pain of these hours upon the rock grew only the greater as the day went on; the rock getting still hotter and the sun fiercer. There were giddiness, and sickness, and sharp pangs like rheumatism, to be supported. I minded then, and have often minded since, on the lines in our Scotch psalm:—

'The moon by night thee shall not smite,
     Nor yet the sun by day';

and indeed it was only by God's blessing that we were neither of us sun-smitten.

At last, about two, it was beyond men's bearing, and there was now temptation to resist, as well as pain to thole. For the sun being now got a little into the west, there came a patch of shade on the east side of our rock, which was the side sheltered from the soldiers.

'As well one death as another,' said Alan, and slipped over the edge and dropped on the ground on the shadowy side.

I followed him at once, and instantly fell all my length, so weak was I and so giddy with that long exposure. Here, then, we lay for an hour or two, aching from head to foot, as weak as water, and lying quite naked to the eye of any soldier who should have strolled that way. None came, how-

ever, all passing by on the other side; so that our rock
continued to be our shield even in this new position.

Presently we began again to get a little strength; and as
the soldiers were now lying closer along the riverside, Alan
proposed that we should try a start. I was by this time afraid
of but one thing in the world; and that was to be set back
upon the rock; anything else was welcome to me; so we got
ourselves at once in marching order, and began to slip from
rock to rock one after the other, now crawling flat on our
bellies in the shade, now making a run for it, heart in mouth.

The soldiers, having searched this side of the valley after
a fashion, and being perhaps somewhat sleepy with the sultri-
ness of the afternoon, had now laid by much of their vigilance, and stood dozing at their posts or only kept a look-out
along the banks of the river; so that in this way, keeping
down the valley and at the same time towards the mountains,
we drew steadily away from their neighbourhood. But the
business was the most wearing I had ever taken part in. A
man had need of a hundred eyes in every part of him, to
keep concealed in that uneven country and within cry of so
many and scattered sentries. When we must pass an open
place, quickness was not all, but a swift judgment not only
of the lie of the whole country, but of the solidity of every
stone on which we must set foot; for the afternoon was now
fallen so breathless that the rolling of a pebble sounded
abroad like a pistol shot, and would start the echo calling
among the hills and cliffs.

By sundown we had made some distance, even by our slow
rate of progress, though to be sure the sentry on the rock was
still plainly in our view. But now we came on something that
put all fears out of season; and that was a deep rushing burn,
that tore down, in that part, to join the glen river. At the
sight of this we cast ourselves on the ground and plunged
head and shoulders in the water; and I cannot tell which was
the more pleasant, the great shock as the cool stream went
over us, or the greed with which we drank of it.

We lay there (for the banks hid us), drank again and again,
bathed our chests, let our wrists trail in the running water

till they ached with the chill; and at last, being wonderfully renewed, we got out the meal-bag and made drammach in the iron pan. This, though it is but cold water mingled with oatmeal, yet makes a good enough dish for a hungry man; and where there are no means of making fire, or (as in our case) good reason for not making one, it is the chief stand-by of those who have taken to the heather.

As soon as the shadow of the night had fallen, we set forth again, at first with the same caution, but presently with more boldness, standing our full height and stepping out at a good pace of walking. The way was very intricate, lying up the steep sides of mountains and along the brows of cliffs; clouds had come in with the sunset, and the night was dark and cool; so that I walked without much fatigue, but in continual fear of falling and rolling down the mountains, and with no guess at our direction.

The moon rose at last and found us still on the road; it was in its last quarter and was long beset with clouds; but after a while shone out, and showed me many dark heads of mountains, and was reflected far underneath us on the narrow arm of a sea-loch.

At this sight we both paused: I struck with wonder to find myself so high and walking (as it seemed to me) upon clouds: Alan to make sure of his direction.

Seemingly he was well pleased, and he must certainly have judged us out of ear-shot of all our enemies; for throughout the rest of our night-march, he beguiled the way with whistling of many tunes, warlike, merry, plaintive; reel tunes that made the foot go faster; tunes of my own south country that made me fain to be home from my adventures; and all these, on the great, dark, desert mountains, making company upon the way.

CHAPTER XXI

THE FLIGHT IN THE HEATHER: THE HEUGH
OF CORRYNAKIEGH

EARLY as day comes in the beginning of July, it was still dark when we reached our destination, a cleft in the head of a great mountain, with water running through the midst, and upon the one hand a shallow cave in a rock. Birches grew there in a thin, pretty wood, which a little farther on was changed into a wood of pines. The burn was full of trout; the wood of cushat-doves; on the open side of the mountain beyond, whaups would be always whistling, and cuckoos were plentiful. From the mouth of the cleft we looked down upon a part of Mamore, and on the sea-loch that divides that country from Appin; and this from so great a height, as made it my continual wonder and pleasure to sit and behold them.

The name of the cleft was the Heugh of Corrynakiegh; and although from its height being so near upon the sea, it was often beset with clouds, yet it was on the whole a pleasant place, and the five days we lived in it went happily.

We slept in the cave, making our bed of heather bushes which we cut for that purpose, and covering ourselves with Alan's great-coat. There was a low concealed place, in a turning of the glen, where we were so bold as to make fire: so that we could warm ourselves when the clouds set in, and cook hot porridge, and grill the little trouts that we caught with our hands under the stones and overhanging banks of the burn. This was indeed our chief pleasure and business; and not only to save our meal against worse times, but with a rivalry that much amused us, we spent a great part of our days at the water side, stripped to the waist and groping about or (as they say) guddling for these fish. The largest we got might have been a quarter of a pound; but they were of good flesh and flavour, and when broiled upon the coals, lacked only a little salt to be delicious.

In any by-time Alan must teach me to use my sword, for my ignorance had much distressed him; and I think besides, as I had sometimes the upper-hand of him in the fishing, he was not sorry to turn to an exercise where he had so much the upper-hand of me. He made it somewhat more of a pain than need have been, for he stormed at me all through the lessons in a very violent manner of scolding, and would push me so close that I made sure he must run me through the body. I was often tempted to turn tail, but held my ground for all that, and got some profit of my lessons; if it was but to stand on guard with an assured countenance, which is often all that is required. So, though I could never in the least please my master, I was not altogether displeased with myself.

In the meanwhile, you are not to suppose that we neglected our chief business, which was to get away.

'It will be many a long day,' Alan said to me on our first morning, 'before the red-coats think upon seeking Corrynakiegh; so now we must get word sent to James, and he must find the siller for us.'

'And how shall we send that word?' says I. 'We are here in a desert place, which yet we dare not leave; and unless ye get the fowls of the air to be your messengers, I see not what we shall be able to do.'

'Ay?' said Alan. 'Ye're a man of small contrivance, David.'

Thereupon he fell in a muse, looking in the embers of the fire; and presently, getting a piece of wood, he fashioned it in a cross, the four ends of which he blackened on the coals. Then he looked at me a little shyly.

'Could ye lend me my button?' says he. 'It seems a strange thing to ask a gift again, but I own I am laith to cut another.'

I gave him the button; whereupon he strung it on a strip of his great-coat which he had used to bind the cross; and tying in a little sprig of birch and another of fir, he looked upon his work with satisfaction.

'Now,' said he, 'there is a little clachan' (what is called a hamlet in the English) 'not very far from Corrynakiegh, and it has the name of Koalisnacoan. There, there are living many

friends of mine whom I could trust with my life, and some
that I am no just so sure of. Ye see, David, there will be
money set upon our heads; James himsel' is to set money on
them; and as for the Campbells, they would never spare siller
where there was a Stewart to be hurt. If it was otherwise,
I would go down to Koalisnacoan whatever, and trust my life
into these people's hands as lightly as I would trust another
with my glove.'

'But being so?' said I.

'Being so,' said he, 'I would as lief they didnae see me.
There's bad folk everywhere, and what's far worse, weak
ones. So when it comes dark again, I will steal down into
that clachan, and set this that I have been making in the
window of a good friend of mine, John Breck Maccoll, a
bouman[1] of Appin's.'

'With all my heart,' says I; 'and if he finds it, what is he
to think?'

'Well,' says Alan, 'I wish he was a man of more penetration, for by my troth I am afraid he will make little enough
of it! But this is what I have in mind. This cross is something
in the nature of the crosstarrie,* or fiery cross, which is the
signal of gathering in our clans; yet he will know well enough
the clan is not to rise, for there it is standing in his window,
and no word with it. So he will say to himsel', *The clan is not
to rise, but there is something*. Then he will see my button,
and that was Duncan Stewart's. And then he will say to
himsel', *The son of Duncan is in the heather, and has need
of me.*'

'Well,' said I, 'it may be. But even supposing so, there is a
good deal of heather between here and the Forth.'

'And that is a very true word,' says Alan. 'But then John
Breck will see the sprig of birch and the sprig of pine; and
he will say to himsel' (if he is a man of any penetration
at all, which I misdoubt) *Alan will be lying in a wood which
is both of pines and birches*. Then he will think to himsel',
That is not so very rife hereabout; and then he will come

---

1 A bouman is a tenant who takes stock from the landlord and
shares with him the increase.

and give us a look up in Corrynakiegh. And if he does not, David, the devil may fly away with him, for what I care; for he will no be worth the salt to his porridge.'

'Eh, man,' said I, drolling with him a little, 'you're very ingenious! But would it not be simpler for you to write him a few words in black and white?'

'And that is an excellent observe, Mr. Balfour of Shaws,' says Alan, drolling with me; 'and it would certainly be much simpler for me to write to him, but it would be a sore job for John Breck to read it. He would have to go to the school for two-three years; and it's possible we might be wearied waiting on him.'

So that night Alan carried down his fiery cross and set it in the bouman's window. He was troubled when he came back; for the dogs had barked and the folk run out from their houses; and he thought he had heard a clatter of arms and seen a red-coat come to one of the doors. On all accounts, we lay the next day in the borders of the wood and kept a close look-out; so that if it was John Breck that came, we might be ready to guide him, and if it was the red-coats, we should have time to get away.

About noon a man was to be spied, straggling up the open side of the mountain in the sun, and looking round him as he came, from under his hand. No sooner had Alan seen him than he whistled; the man turned and came a little towards us: then Alan would give another 'peep!' and the man would come still nearer; and so by the sound of whistling, he was guided to the spot where we lay.

He was a ragged, wild, bearded man, about forty, grossly disfigured with the smallpox, and looked both dull and savage. Although his English was very bad and broken, yet Alan (according to his very handsome use, whenever I was by) would suffer him to speak no Gaelic. Perhaps the strange language made him appear more backward than he really was; but I thought he had little good-will to serve us, and what he had was the child of terror.

Alan would have had him carry a message to James; but the bouman would hear of no message. 'She was forget it,'

he said in his screaming voice; and would either have a letter
or wash his hands of us.

I thought Alan would be gravelled at that, for we lacked
the means of writing in that desert. But he was a man of more
resources than I knew; searched the wood until he found a
quill of a cushat-dove, which he shaped into a pen; made
himself a kind of ink with gunpowder from his horn and
water from the running stream; and tearing a corner from
his French military commission (which he carried in his
pocket, like a talisman to keep him from the gallows) he sat
down and wrote as follows:

'DEAR KINSMAN,—Please send the money by the bearer to the
place he kens of.

'Your affectionate cousin,
'A. S.'

This he entrusted to the bouman, who promised to make
what manner of speed he best could, and carried it off with
him down the hill.

He was three full days gone, but about five in the evening
of the third, we heard a whistling in the wood, which Alan
answered: and presently the bouman came up the waterside, looking for us, right and left. He seemed less sulky
than before, and indeed he was no doubt well pleased to have
got to the end of such a dangerous commission.

He gave us the news of the country; that it was alive
with red-coats; that arms were being found, and poor folk
brought in trouble daily; and that James and some of his
servants were already clapped in prison at Fort William,
under strong suspicion of complicity. It seemed, it was
noised on all sides that Alan Breck had fired the shot; and
there was a bill issued for both him and me, with one
hundred pounds reward.

This was all as bad as could be; and the little note the
bouman had carried us from Mrs. Stewart was of a miserable
sadness. In it she besought Alan not to let himself be cap-
tured, assuring him, if he fell in the hands of the troops,
both he and James were no better than dead men. The money

she had sent was all that she could beg or borrow, and she prayed heaven we could be doing with it. Lastly, she said she enclosed us one of the bills in which we were described.

This we looked upon with great curiosity and not a little fear, partly as a man may look in a mirror, partly as he might look into the barrel of an enemy's gun to judge if it be truly aimed. Alan was advertised as 'a small, pock-marked, active man of thirty-five or thereby, dressed in a feathered hat, a French side-coat of blue with silver buttons and lace a great deal tarnished, a red waistcoat and breeches of black shag'; and I as 'a tall strong lad of about eighteen, wearing an old blue coat, very ragged, an old Highland bonnet, a long home-spun waistcoat, blue breeches; his legs bare, low-country shoes, wanting the toes; speaks like a Lowlander, and has no beard.'

Alan was well enough pleased to see his finery so fully remembered and set down; only when he came to the word tarnish, he looked upon his lace like one a little mortified. As for myself, I thought I cut a miserable figure in the bill; and yet was well enough pleased too, for since I had changed these rags, the description had ceased to be a danger and become a source of safety.

'Alan,' said I, 'you should change your clothes.'

'Na, troth' said Alan, 'I have nae others. A fine sight I would be, if I went back to France in a bonnet!'

This put a second reflection in my mind: that if I were to separate from Alan and his tell-tale clothes I should be safe against arrest, and might go openly about my business. Nor was this all; for suppose I was arrested when I was alone, there was little against me; but suppose I was taken in company with the reputed murderer, my case would begin to be grave. For generosity's sake, I dare not speak my mind upon this head; but I thought of it none the less.

I thought of it all the more, too, when the bouman brought out a green purse with four guineas in gold, and the best part of another in small change. True, it was more than I had. But then Alan, with less than five guineas, had to get as far as France; I, with my less than two, not beyond Queensferry;

so that, taking things in their proportion, Alan's society was
not only a peril to my life but a burden on my purse.

But there was no thought of the sort in the honest head
of my companion. He believed he was serving, helping, and
protecting me. And what could I do but hold my peace, and
chafe, and take my chance of it?

'It's little enough,' said Alan, putting the purse in his
pocket, 'but it'll do my business. And now John Breck, if ye
will hand me over my button, this gentleman and me will be
for taking the road.'

But the bouman, after feeling about in a hairy purse that
hung in front of him in the Highland manner (though he
wore otherwise the Lowland habit, with sea-trousers) began
to roll his eyes strangely, and at last said, 'Her nainsel' will
loss it,' meaning he thought he had lost it.

'What!' cried Alan, 'you will lose my button, that was my
father's before me? Now, I will tell you what is in my mind,
John Breck: it is in my mind this is the worse day's work that
ever ye did since ye were born.'

And as Alan spoke, he set his hands on his knees and
looked at the bouman with a smiling mouth, and that dancing
light in his eyes that meant mischief to his enemies.

Perhaps the bouman was honest enough; perhaps he had
meant to cheat and then, finding himself alone with two
of us in a desert-place, cast back to honesty as being safer;
at least, and all at once, he seemed to find that button and
handed it to Alan.

'Well, and it is a good thing for the honour of the Maccolls,' said Alan, and then to me, 'Here is my button back
again, and I thank you for parting with it, which is of a piece
with all your friendships to me.' Then he took the warmest
parting of the bouman. 'For,' says he, 'ye have done very well
by me, and set your neck at a venture, and I will always give
you the name of a good man.'

Lastly, the bouman took himself off by one way; and Alan
and I (getting our chattels together) struck into another to
resume our flight.

CHAPTER XXII

THE FLIGHT IN THE HEATHER:
THE MOOR

MORE than eleven hours of incessant, hard travelling brought us early in the morning to the end of a range of mountains. In front of us there lay a piece of low, broken, desert land, which we must now cross. The sun was not long up, and shone straight in our eyes; a little, thin mist went up from the face of the moorland like a smoke; so that (as Alan said) there might have been twenty squadron of dragoons there and we none the wiser.

We sat down, therefore, in a howe of the hillside till the mist should have risen, and made ourselves a dish of drammach, and held a council of war.

'David,' said Alan, 'this is the kittle bit. Shall we lie here till it comes night, or shall we risk it and stave on ahead?'

'Well,' said I, 'I am tired indeed, but I could walk as far again, if that was all.'

'Ay, but it isnae,' said Alan, 'nor yet the half. This is how we stand: Appin's fair death to us. To the south it's all Campbells, and no to be thought of. To the north; well, there's no muckle to be gained by going north; neither for you, that wants to get to Queensferry, not yet for me, that wants to get to France. Well then, we'll can strike east.'

'East be it!' says I, quite cheerily; but I was thinking, in to myself: 'O, man, if you would only take one point of the compass and let me take any other, it would be the best for both of us.'

'Well, then, east, ye see, we have the muirs,' said Alan. 'Once there, David, it's mere pitch-and-toss. Out on yon bald, naked, flat place, where can a body turn to? Let the red-coats come over a hill, they can spy you miles away; and the sorrow's in their horses' heels, they would soon ride you down. It's no good place, David; and I'm free to say, it's worse by daylight than by dark.'

'Alan,' said I, 'hear my way of it. Appin's death for us; we have none too much money, nor yet meal; the longer they seek, the nearer they may guess where we are; it's all a risk; and I give my word to go ahead until we drop.'

Alan was delighted. 'There are whiles,' said he, 'when ye are altogether too canny and Whiggish to be company for a gentleman like me; but there come other whiles when ye show yoursel' a mettle spark; and it's then, David, that I love ye like a brother.'

The mist rose and died away, and showed us that country lying as waste as the sea; only the moorfowl and the peewees crying upon it, and far over to the east a herd of deer, moving like dots. Much of it was red with heather; much of the rest broken up with bogs and hags and peaty pools; some had been burnt black in a heath fire; and in another place there was quite a forest of dead firs, standing like skeletons. A wearier-looking desert man never saw; but at least it was clear of troops, which was our point.

We went down accordingly into the waste, and began to make our toilsome and devious travel towards the eastern verge. There were the tops of mountains all round (you are to remember) from whence we might be spied at any moment; so it behoved us to keep in the hollow parts of the moor, and when these turned aside from our direction, to move upon its naked face with infinite care. Sometimes, for half an hour together, we must crawl from one heather bush to another, as hunters do when they are hard upon the deer. It was a clear day again, with a blazing sun; the water in the brandy bottle was soon gone; and altogether, if I had guessed what it would be to crawl half the time upon my belly and to walk much of the rest stooping nearly to the knees, I should certainly have held back from such a killing enterprise.

Toiling and resting and toiling again, we wore away the morning; and about noon lay down in a thick bush of heather to sleep. Alan took the first watch; and it seemed to me I had scarce closed my eyes before I was shaken up to take the second. We had no clock to go by; and Alan stuck a sprig of heath in the ground to serve instead; so that as soon as the shadow of the bush should fall so far to the east, I might know to rouse him. But I was by this time so weary that I could have slept twelve hours at a stretch; I had the taste of sleep in my throat; my joints slept even when my mind was waking; the hot smell of the heather, and the drone of the wild bees, were like possets to me; and every now and again I would give a jump and find I had been dozing.

The last time I woke I seemed to come back from further away, and thought the sun had taken a great start in the heavens. I looked at the sprig of heath, and at that I could have cried aloud; for I saw I had betrayed my trust. My head was nearly turned with fear and shame; and at what I saw, when I looked out around me on the moor, my heart was like dying in my body. For sure enough, a body of horse-soldiers had come during my sleep, and were drawing near to us from the south-east, spread out in the shape of a fan and riding their horses to and fro in the deep parts of the heather.

When I waked Alan, he glanced first at the soldiers, then at the mark and the position of the sun, and knitted his brows with a sudden, quick look, both ugly and anxious, which was all the reproach I had of him.

'What are we to do now?' I asked.

'We'll have to play at being hares,' said he. 'Do ye see yon mountain?' pointing to one on the north-eastern sky.

'Ay,' said I.

'Well, then,' says he, 'let us strike for that. Its name is Ben Alder; it is a wild, desert mountain full of hills and hollows, and if we can win to it before the morn, we may do yet.'

'But, Alan,' cried I, 'that will take us across the very coming of the soldiers!'

'I ken that fine,' said he; 'but if we are driven back on Appin, we are two dead men. So now, David man, be brisk!'

With that he began to run forward on his hands and knees with an incredible quickness, as though it were his natural way of going. All the time, too, he kept winding in and out in the lower parts of the moorland where we were the best concealed. Some of these had been burned or at least scathed with fire; and there rose in our faces (which were close to the ground) a blinding, choking dust as fine as smoke. The water was long out; and this posture of running on the hands and knees brings an overmastering weakness and weariness, so that the joints ache and the wrists faint under your weight.

Now and then, indeed, where was a big bush of heather, we lay awhile, and panted, and putting aside the leaves, looked back at the dragoons. They had not spied us, for they held straight on; a half-troop, I think, covering about two miles of ground, and beating it mighty thoroughly as they went. I had awakened just in time; a little later, and we must have fled in front of them, instead of escaping on one side. Even as it was, the least misfortune might betray us; and now and again, when a grouse rose out of the heather with a clap of wings, we lay as still as the dead and were afraid to breathe.

The aching and faintness of my body, the labouring of my heart, the soreness of my hands, and the smarting of my throat and eyes in the continual smoke of dust and ashes, had soon grown to be so unbearable that I would gladly have given up. Nothing but the fear of Alan lent me enough of a false kind of courage to continue. As for himself (and you are to bear in mind that he was cumbered with a great-coat) he had first turned crimson, but as time went on, the redness began to be mingled with patches of white; his breath cried and whistled as it came; and his voice, when he whispered his observations in my ear during our halts, sounded like nothing human. Yet he seemed in no way dashed in spirits, nor did he at all abate in his activity; so that I was driven to marvel at the man's endurance.

At length, in the first gloaming of the night, we heard a trumpet sound, and looking back from among the heather, saw the troop beginning to collect. A little after, they had built a fire and camped for the night, about the middle of the waste.

At this I begged and besought that we might lie down and sleep.

'There shall be no sleep the night!' said Alan. 'From now on, these weary dragoons of yours will keep the crown of the muirland, and none will get out of Appin but winged fowls. We got through in the nick of time, and shall we jeopard what we've gained? Na, na, when the day comes, it shall find you and me in a fast place on Ben Alder.'

'Alan,' I said, 'it's not the want of will: it's the strength that I want. If I could, I would; but as sure as I'm alive I cannot.'

'Very well, then,' said Alan. 'I'll carry ye.'

I looked to see if he were jesting; but no, the little man was in dead earnest; and the sight of so much resolution shamed me.

'Lead away!' said I. 'I'll follow.'

He gave me one look, as much as to say 'Well done, David!' and off he set again at his top speed.

It grew cooler and even a little darker (but not much) with the coming of the night. The sky was cloudless; it was still early in July, and pretty far north; in the darkest part of that night you would have needed pretty good eyes to read, but for all that, I have often seen it darker in a winter midday. Heavy dew fell and drenched the moor like rain; and this refreshed me for a while. When we stopped to breathe, and I had time to see all about me, the clearness and sweetness of the night, the shapes of the hills like things asleep, and the fire dwindling away behind us, like a bright spot in the midst of the moor, anger would come upon me in a clap that I must still drag myself in agony and eat the dust like a worm.

By what I have read in books, I think few that have held a pen were ever really wearied, or they would write of it more strongly. I had no care of my life, neither past nor future, and I scarce remembered there was such a lad as David Balfour. I did not think of myself, but just of each fresh step which I was sure would be my last, with despair—and of Alan, who was the cause of it, with hatred. Alan was in the right trade as a soldier; this is the officer's part to make men continue to do things, they know not wherefore, and when, if the choice was offered, they would lie down where they were and be killed. And I dare say I would have made a good enough private; for in these last hours, it never occurred to me that I had any choice, but just to obey as long as I was able, and die obeying.

Day began to come in, after years, I thought; and by that time we were past the greatest danger, and could walk upon our feet like men, instead of crawling like brutes. But, dear heart have mercy! what a pair we must have made, going double like old grandfathers, stumbling like babes, and as white as dead folk. Never a word passed between us; each set his mouth and kept his eyes in front of him, and lifted up his foot and set it down again, like people lifting weights at a country play;[1] all the while, with the moorfowl crying 'peep!' in the heather, and the light coming slowly clearer in the east.

I say Alan did as I did. Not that ever I looked at him, for I had enough ado to keep my feet; but because it is plain he must have been as stupid with weariness as myself, and looked as little where we were going, or we should not have walked into an ambush like blind men.

It fell in this way. We were going down a heathery brae, Alan leading and I following a pace or two behind, like a fiddler and his wife; when upon a sudden the heather gave a rustle, three or four ragged men leaped out, and the next moment we were lying on our backs, each with a dirk at his throat.

I don't think I cared: the pain of this rough handling was quite swallowed up by the pains of which I was already full; and I was too glad to have stopped walking to mind about a dirk. I lay looking up in the face of the man that held me; and I mind his face was black with the sun and his eyes very light, but I was not afraid of him. I heard Alan and another whispering in the Gaelic; and what they said was all one to me.

---

1 Village fair.

Then the dirks were put up, our weapons were taken away, and we were set face to face, sitting in the heather.

'They are Cluny's men,' said Alan. 'We couldnae have fallen better. We're just to bide here with these, which are his out-sentries, till they can get word to the chief of my arrival.'

Now Cluny Macpherson,* the chief of the clan Vourich, had been one of the leaders of the great rebellion six years before; there was a price on his life; and I had supposed him long ago in France, with the rest of the heads of that desperate party. Even tired as I was, the surprise of what I heard half-wakened me.

'What?' I cried, 'is Cluny still here?'

'Ay is he so!' said Alan. 'Still in his own country, and kept by his own clan. King George can do no more.'

I think I would have asked farther, but Alan gave me the put-off. 'I am rather wearied,' he said, 'and I would like fine to get a sleep.' And without more words, he rolled on his face in a deep heather bush, and seemed to sleep at once.

There was no such thing possible for me. You have heard grasshoppers whirring in the grass in the summer time? Well, I had no sooner closed my eyes, than my body, and above all my head, belly, and wrists, seemed to be filled with whirring grasshoppers; and I must open my eyes again at once, and tumble and toss, and sit up and lie down; and look at the sky which dazzled me, or at Cluny's wild and dirty sentries, peering out over the top of the brae and chattering to each other in the Gaelic.

That was all the rest I had, until the messenger returned; when, as it appeared that Cluny would be glad to receive us, we must get once more upon our feet and set forward. Alan was in excellent good spirits, much refreshed by his sleep, very hungry, and looking pleasantly forward to a dram and a dish of hot collops, of which, it seems, the messenger had brought him word. For my part, it made me sick to hear of eating. I had been dead-heavy before, and now I felt a kind of dreadful lightness, which would not suffer me to walk. I drifted like a gossamer; the ground seemed to me a cloud, the hills a feather-weight, the air to have a current, like a running burn, which carried me to and fro. With all that, a sort of horror of despair sat on my mind, so that I could have wept at my own helplessness.

I saw Alan knitting his brows at me, and supposed it was in anger; and that gave me a pang of light-headed fear, like what a child may have. I remember, too, that I was smiling, and could not stop smiling, hard as I tried; for I thought it was out of place at such a time. But my good companion had nothing in his mind but kindness; and the next moment, two of the gillies had me by the arms, and I began to be carried forward with great swiftness (or so it appeared to me, although I dare say it was slowly enough in truth) through a labyrinth of dreary glens and hollows and into the heart of that dismal mountain of Ben Alder.

CHAPTER XXIII
CLUNY'S CAGE

WE came at last to the foot of an exceeding steep wood, which scrambled up a craggy hill-side, and was crowned by a naked precipice.

'It's here,' said one of the guides, and we struck up hill.

The trees clung upon the slope, like sailors on the shrouds of a ship; and their trunks were like the rounds of a ladder, by which we mounted.

Quite at the top, and just before the rocky face of the cliff sprang above the foliage, we found that strange house which was known in the country as 'Cluny's Cage.' The trunks of several trees had been wattled across, the intervals streng-thened with stakes, and the ground behind this barricade levelled up with earth to make the floor. A tree, which grew out from the hillside, was the living centre-beam of the roof. The walls were of wattle and covered with moss. The whole house had something of an egg shape; and it half hung, half stood in that steep, hillside thicket, like a wasp's nest in a green hawthorn.

Within, it was large enough to shelter five or six persons with some comfort. A projection of the cliff had been cunningly employed to be the fireplace; and the smoke rising against the face of the rock, and being not dissimilar in colour, readily escaped notice from below.

This was but one of Cluny's hiding places; he had caves, besides, and underground chambers in several parts of his country; and following the reports of his scouts, he moved from one to another as the soldiers drew near or moved away. By this manner of living, and thanks to the affection of his clan, he had not only stayed all this time in safety, while so many others had fled or been taken and slain; but stayed four or five years longer, and only went to France at last by the express command of his master. There he soon died; and it is strange to reflect that he may have regretted his Cage upon Ben Alder.

When we came to the door he was seated by his rock chimney, watching a gillie about some cookery. He was mighty plainly habited, with a knitted nightcap drawn over his ears, and smoked a foul cutty pipe. For all that he had the manners of a king, and it was quite a sight to see him rise out of his place to welcome us.

'Well, Mr. Stewart, come awa' sir!' said he, 'and bring in your friend that as yet I dinna ken the name of.'

'And how is yourself, Cluny?' said Alan. 'I hope ye do brawly, sir. And I am proud to see ye, and to present to ye my friend the Laird of Shaws, Mr. David Balfour.'

Alan never referred to my estate without a touch of a sneer, when we were alone; but with strangers, he rang the words out like a herald.

'Step in by, the both of ye, gentlemen,' says Cluny. 'I make ye welcome to my house, which is a queer, rude place for certain, but one where I have entertained a royal personage, Mr. Stewart—ye doubtless ken the personage I have in my eye. We'll take a dram for luck, and as soon as this handless man of mine has the collops ready, we'll dine and take a hand

at the cartes as gentlemen should. My life is a bit driegh,'
says he, pouring out the brandy; 'I see little company, and
sit and twirl my thumbs, and mind upon a great day that is
gone by, and weary for another great day that we all hope
will be upon the road. And so here's a toast to ye: The
Restoration!'

Thereupon we all touched glasses and drank. I am sure
I wish no ill to King George; and if he had been there himself in proper person, it's like he would have done as I did.
No sooner had I taken out the dram than I felt hugely better,
and could look on and listen, still a little mistily perhaps, but
no longer with the same groundless horror and distress of
mind.

It was certainly a strange place, and we had a strange host.
In his long hiding, Cluny had grown to have all manner of
precise habits, like those of an old maid. He had a particular
place, where no one else must sit; the Cage was arranged in a
particular way, which none must disturb; cookery was one
of his chief fancies, and even while he was greeting us in,
he kept an eye to the collops.

It appears, he sometimes visited or received visits from his
wife and one or two of his nearest friends, under the cover
of night; but for the more part lived quite alone, and communicated only with his sentinels and the gillies that waited
on him in the Cage. The first thing in the morning, one of
them, who was a barber, came and shaved him, and gave him
the news of the country, of which he was immoderately
greedy. There was no end to his questions; he put them as
earnestly as a child; and at some of the answers, laughed out
of all bounds of reason, and would break out again laughing
at the mere memory, hours after the barber was gone.

To be sure, there might have been a purpose in his questions; for though he was thus sequestered, and like the other
landed gentlemen of Scotland, stripped by the late Act of
Parliament of legal powers, he still exercised a patriarchal
justice in his clan. Disputes were brought to him in his
hiding-hole to be decided; and the men of his country, who
would have snapped their fingers at the Court of Session, laid

aside revenge and paid down money at the bare word of this forfeited and hunted outlaw. When he was angered, which was often enough, he gave his commands and breathed threats of punishment like any king; and his gillies trembled and crouched away from him like children before a hasty father. With each of them, as he entered, he ceremoniously shook hands, both parties touching their bonnets at the same time in a military manner. Altogether, I had a fair chance to see some of the inner workings of a Highland clan; and this with a proscribed, fugitive chief; his country conquered; the troops riding upon all sides in quest of him, sometimes within a mile of where he lay; and when the least of the ragged fellows whom he rated and threatened, could have made a fortune by betraying him.

On that first day, as soon as the collops were ready, Cluny gave them with his own hand a squeeze of a lemon (for he was well supplied with luxuries) and bade us draw in to our meal.

'They,' said he, meaning the collops, 'are such as I gave his Royal Highness in this very house; bating the lemon juice, for at that time we were glad to get the meat and never fashed for kitchen.[1] Indeed, there were mair dragoons than lemons in my country in the year forty-six.'

I do not know if the collops were truly very good, but my heart rose against the sight of them, and I could eat but little. All the while Cluny entertained us with stories of Prince Charlie's stay in the Cage, giving us the very words of the speakers, and rising from his place to show us where they stood. By these, I gathered the Prince was a gracious, spirited boy, like the son of a race of polite kings, but not so wise as Solomon. I gathered, too, that while he was in the Cage, he was often drunk; so the fault that has since, by all accounts, made such a wreck of him, had even then begun to show itself.

We were no sooner done eating than Cluny brought out an old, thumbed, greasy pack of cards, such as you may find

---

1 Condiment.

in a mean inn; and his eyes brightened in his face as he proposed that we should fall to playing.

Now this was one of the things I had been brought up to eschew like disgrace; it being held by my father neither the part of a Christian nor yet of a gentleman, to set his own livelihood and fish for that of others, on the cast of painted pasteboard. To be sure, I might have pleaded my fatigue, which was excuse enough; but I thought it behoved that I should bear a testimony. I must have got very red in the face, but I spoke steadily, and told them I had no call to be a judge of others, but for my own part, it was a matter in which I had no clearness.

Cluny stopped mingling the cards. 'What in deil's name is this?' says he. 'What kind of Whiggish, canting talk is this, for the house of Cluny Macpherson?'

'I will put my hand in the fire for Mr. Balfour,' says Alan. 'He is an honest and a mettle gentleman, and I would have ye bear in mind who says it. I bear a king's name,' says he, cocking his hat; 'and I and any that I call friend are company for the best. But the gentleman is tired, and should sleep; if he has no mind to the cartes, it will never hinder you and me. And I'm fit and willing, sir, to play ye any game that ye can name.'

'Sir,' says Cluny, 'in this poor house of mine I would have you to ken that any gentleman may follow his pleasure. If your friend would like to stand on his head, he is welcome. And if either he, or you, or any other man, is not preceesely satisfied, I will be proud to step outside with him.'

I had no will that these two friends should cut their throats for my sake.

'Sir,' said I, 'I am very wearied, as Alan says; and what's more, as you are a man that likely has sons of your own, I may tell you it was a promise to my father.'

'Say nae mair, say nae mair,' said Cluny, and pointed me to a bed of heather in a corner of the Cage. For all that he was displeased enough, looked at me askance, and grumbled when he looked. And indeed it must be owned that both my scruples and the words in which I declared them, smacked somewhat of the Covenanter, and were little in their place among wild Highland Jacobites.

What with the brandy and the venison, a strange heaviness had come over me; and I had scarce lain down upon the bed before I fell into a kind of trance, in which I continued almost the whole time of our stay in the Cage. Sometimes I was broad awake and understood what passed; sometimes I only heard voices, or men snoring, like the voice of a silly river; and the plaids upon the wall dwindled down and swelled out again, like firelight shadows on the roof. I must sometimes have spoken or cried out, for I remember I was now and then amazed at being answered; yet I was conscious of no particular nightmare, only of a general, black, abiding horror—a horror of the place I was in, and the bed I lay in, and the plaids on the wall, and the voices, and the fire, and myself.

The barber-gillie, who was a doctor too, was called in to prescribe for me; but as he spoke in the Gaelic, I understood not a word of his opinion, and was too sick even to ask for a translation. I knew well enough I was ill, and that was all I cared about.

I paid little heed while I lay in this poor pass. But Alan and Cluny were most of the time at the cards, and I am clear that Alan must have begun by winning; for I remember sitting up, and seeing them hard at it, and a great glittering pile of as much as sixty or a hundred guineas on the table. It looked strange enough, to see all this wealth in a nest upon a cliff-side, wattled about growing trees. And even then, I thought it seemed deep water for Alan to be riding, who had no better battle-horse than a green purse and a matter of five pounds.

The luck, it seems, changed on the second day. About noon I was awakened as usual for dinner, and as usual refused to eat, and was given a dram with some bitter infusion which the barber had prescribed. The sun was shining in at the open door of the Cage, and this dazzled and offended me. Cluny sat at the table, biting the pack of cards. Alan had stooped over the bed, and had his face close to my eyes; to which, troubled as they were with the fever, it seemed of the most shocking bigness.

He asked me for a loan of my money.

'What for?' said I.

'O, just for a loan,' said he.

'But why?' I repeated. 'I don't see.'

'Hut, David!' said Alan, 'ye wouldnae grudge me a loan?'

I would though, if I had had my senses! But all I thought of then was to get his face away, and I handed him my money.

On the morning of the third day, when we had been forty-eight hours in the Cage, I awoke with a great relief of spirits, very weak and weary indeed, but seeing things of the right size with their honest, everyday appearance. I had a mind to eat, moreover; rose from bed of my own movement; and as soon as we had breakfasted, stepped to the entry of the Cage and sat down outside in the top of the wood. It was a grey day with a cool, mild air: and I sat in a dream all morning, only disturbed by the passing by of Cluny's scouts and servants coming with provisions and reports; for as the coast was at that time clear, you might almost say he held court openly.

When I returned, he and Alan had laid the cards aside, and were questioning a gillie; and the chief turned about and spoke to me in the Gaelic.

'I have no Gaelic, sir,' said I.

Now since the card question, everything I said or did had the power of annoying Cluny. 'Your name has more sense than yourself, then,' said he, angrily; 'for it's good Gaelic. But the point is this. My scout reports all clear in the south, and the question is have ye the strength to go?'

I saw cards on the table, but no gold; only a heap of little written papers and these all on Cluny's side. Alan, besides, had an odd look, like a man not very well content; and I began to have a strong misgiving.

'I do not know if I am as well as I should be,' said I, looking at Alan; 'but the little money we have has a long way to carry us.'

Alan took his underlip into his mouth, and looked upon the ground.

'David,' says he at last, 'I've lost it; there's the naked truth.'

'My money too?' said I.

'Your money too,' says Alan, with a groan. 'Ye shouldnae have given it me. I'm daft when I get to the cartes.'

'Hoot-toot, hoot-toot,' said Cluny. 'It was all daffing; it's all nonsense. Of course, you'll have your money back again, and the double of it, if ye'll make so free with me. It would be a singular thing for me to keep it. It's not to be supposed that I would be any hindrance to gentlemen in your situation; that would be a singular thing!' cries he, and began to pull gold out of his pocket, with a mighty red face.

Alan said nothing, only looked on the ground.

'Will you step to the door with me, sir?' said I.

Cluny said he would be very glad, and followed me readily enough, but he looked flustered and put out.

'And now, sir,' says I, 'I must first acknowledge your generosity.'

'Nonsensical nonsense!' cries Cluny. 'Where's the generosity? This is just a most unfortunate affair; but what would ye have me do—boxed up in this beeskep of a cage of mine—but just set my friends to the cartes, when I can get them? And if they lose, of course, it's not to be supposed——' And here he came to a pause.

'Yes,' said I, 'if they lose, you give them back their money; and if they win, they carry away yours in their pouches! I have said before that I grant your generosity; but to me, sir, it's a very painful thing to be placed in this position.'

There was a little silence, in which Cluny seemed always as if he was about to speak, but said nothing. All the time he grew redder and redder in the face.

'I am a young man,' said I, 'and I ask your advice. Advise me as you would your son. My friend fairly lost this money, after having fairly gained a far greater sum of yours; can I accept it back again? Would that be the right part for me to play? Whatever I do, you can see for yourself it must be hard upon a man of any pride.'

'It's rather hard on me, too, Mr. Balfour,' said Cluny, 'and ye give me very much the look of a man that has entrapped poor people to their hurt. I wouldnae have my friends come to any house of mine to accept affronts; no,' he cried, with a sudden heat of anger, 'nor yet to give them!'

'And so you see, sir,' said I, 'there is something to be said upon my side; and this gambling is a very poor employ for gentlefolks. But I am still waiting your opinion.'

I am sure if ever Cluny hated any man it was David Balfour. He looked me all over with a warlike eye, and I saw the challenge at his lips. But either my youth disarmed him, or perhaps his own sense of justice. Certainly it was a mortifying matter for all concerned, and not least for Cluny; the more credit that he took it as he did.

'Mr. Balfour,' said he, 'I think you are too nice and covenanting, but for all that you have the spirit of a very pretty gentleman. Upon my honest word, ye may take this money—it's what I would tell my son—and here's my hand along with it!'

CHAPTER XXIV

THE FLIGHT IN THE HEATHER:
THE QUARREL

ALAN and I were put across Loch Errocht under cloud of night, and went down its eastern shore to another hiding-place near the head of Loch Rannoch, whither we were led by one of the gillies from the Cage. This fellow carried all our luggage and Alan's great-coat in the bargain, trotting along under the burthen, far less than the half of which used to weigh me to the ground, like a stout hill pony with a feather; yet he was a man that, in plain contest, I could have broken on my knee.

Doubtless it was a great relief to walk disencumbered; and perhaps without that relief, and the consequent sense of liberty and lightness, I could not have walked at all. I was but new arisen from a bed of sickness; and there was nothing in the state of our affairs to hearten me for much exertion; travelling, as we did, over the most dismal deserts in Scotland, under a cloudy heaven, and with divided hearts among the travellers.

For long, we said nothing; marching alongside or one behind the other, each with a set countenance; I, angry and proud, and drawing what strength I had from these two violent and sinful feelings: Alan angry and ashamed, ashamed that he had lost my money, angry that I should take it so ill.

The thought of a separation ran always the stronger in my mind; and the more I approved of it, the more ashamed I grew of my approval. It would be a fine, handsome, generous thing, indeed, for Alan to turn round and say to me: 'Go, I am in the most danger, and my company only increases yours.' But for me to turn to the friend who certainly loved me, and say to him: 'You are in great danger, I am in but little; your friendship is a burden; go take your risks and bear your hardships alone——' no, that was impossible; and even to think of it privily to myself, made my cheeks to burn.

And yet Alan had behaved like a child and (what is worse) a treacherous child. Wheedling my money from me while I lay half-conscious, was scarce better than theft; and yet here he was trudging by my side, without a penny to his name, and by what I could see, quite blithe to sponge upon the money he had driven me to beg. True, I was ready to share it with him; but it made me rage to see him count upon my readiness.

These were the two things uppermost in my mind; and I could open my mouth upon neither without black ungenerosity. So I did the next worse, and said nothing, nor so much as looked once at my companion, save with the tail of my eye.

At last, upon the other side of Loch Errocht, going over a smooth, rushy place, where the walking was easy, he could bear it no longer, and came close to me.

'David,' says he, 'this is no way for two friends to take

a small accident. I have to say that I'm sorry; and so that's said. And now if you have anything, ye'd better say it.'

'O,' says I, 'I have nothing.'

He seemed disconcerted; at which I was meanly pleased.

'No,' said he, with rather a trembling voice, 'but when I say I was to blame?'

'Why, of course, ye were to blame,' said I, coolly; 'and you will bear me out that I have never reproached you.'

'Never,' says he; 'but ye ken very well that ye've done worse. Are we to part? Ye said so once before. Are ye to say it again? There's hills and heather enough between here and the two seas, David; and I will own I'm no very keen to stay where I'm no wanted.'

This pierced me like a sword, and seemed to lay bare my private disloyalty.

'Alan Breck!' I cried; and then: 'Do you think I am one to turn my back on you in your chief need? You dursn't say it to my face. My whole conduct's there to give the lie to it. It's true, I fell asleep upon the muir; but that was from weariness, and you do wrong to cast it up to me——'

'Which is what I never did,' said Alan.

'But aside from that,' I continued, 'what have I done that you should even me to dogs by such a supposition? I never yet failed a friend, and it's not likely I'll begin with you. There are things between us that I can never forget, even if you can.'

'I will only say this to ye, David,' said Alan, very quietly, 'that I have long been owing ye my life, and now I owe ye money. Ye should try to make that burden light for me.'

This ought to have touched me, and in a manner it did, but the wrong manner. I felt I was behaving badly; and was now not only angry with Alan, but angry with myself in the bargain; and it made me the more cruel.

'You asked me to speak,' said I. 'Well, then, I will. You own yourself that you have done me a disservice; I have had to swallow an affront; I have never reproached you, I never named the thing till you did. And now you blame me,' cried I, 'because I cannae laugh and sing as if I was glad to be affronted. The next thing will be that I'm to go down upon my knees and thank you for it! Ye should think more of others, Alan Breck. If ye thought more of others, ye would perhaps speak less about yourself; and when a friend that likes you very well, has passed over an offence without a word, you would be blithe to let it lie, instead of making it a stick to break his back with. By your own way of it, it was you that was to blame; then it shouldnae be you to seek the quarrel.'

'Aweel,' said Alan, 'say nae mair.'

And we fell back into our former silence; and came to our journey's end, and supped, and lay down to sleep, without another word.

The gillie put us across Loch Rannoch in the dusk of the next day, and gave us his opinion as to our best route. This was to get us up at once into the tops of the mountains: to go round by a circuit, turning the heads of Glen Lyon, Glen Lochay, and Glen Dochart, and come down upon the Lowlands by Kippen and the upper waters of the Forth. Alan was little pleased with a route which led us through the country of his blood-foes, the Glenorchy Campbells. He objected that by turning to the east, we should come almost at once among the Athole Stewarts, a race of his own name and lineage although following a different chief, and come besides by a far easier and swifter way to the place whither we were bound. But the gillie, who was indeed the chief man of Cluny's scouts, had good reasons to give him on all hands, naming the force of troops in every district, and alleging finally (as well as I could understand) that we should no-where be so little troubled as in a country of the Campbells.

Alan gave way at last, but with only half a heart. 'It's one of the dowiest countries in Scotland,' said he. 'There's naething there that I ken, but heath, and crows, and Campbells. But I see that ye're a man of some penetration; and be it as ye please!'

We set forth accordingly by this itinerary; and for the best part of three nights travelled on eerie mountains and among the well-heads of wild rivers; often buried in mist, almost continually blown and rained upon, and not once cheered by any glimpse of sunshine. By day, we lay and slept in the drenching heather; by night, incessantly clambered upon breakneck hills and among rude crags. We often wandered; we were often so involved in fog, that we must lie quiet till it lightened. A fire was never to be thought of. Our only food was drammach and a portion of cold meat that we had carried from the Cage; and as for drink, Heaven knows we had no want of water.

This was a dreadful time, rendered the more dreadful by the gloom of the weather and the country. I was never warm; my teeth chattered in my head; I was troubled with a very sore throat, such as I had on the isle; I had a painful stitch in my side, which never left me; and when I slept in my wet bed, with the rain beating above and the mud oozing below me, it was to live over again in fancy the worst part of my adventures—to see the tower of Shaws lit by lightning, Ransome carried below on the men's backs, Shuan dying on the round-house floor, or Colin Campbell grasping at the bosom of his coat. From such broken slumbers, I would be aroused in the gloaming, to sit up in the same puddle where I had slept, and sup cold drammach; the rain driving sharp in my face or running down my back in icy trickles; the mist enfolding us like as in a gloomy chamber—or perhaps, if the wind blew, falling suddenly apart and showing us the gulf of some dark valley where the streams were crying aloud.

The sound of an infinite number of rivers came up from all round. In this steady rain the springs of the mountain were broken up; every glen gushed water like a cistern; every stream was in high spate, and had filled and overflowed its channel. During our night tramps, it was solemn to hear the voice of them below in the valleys, now booming like thunder, now with an angry cry. I could well understand the story of the Water Kelpie, that demon of the streams, who is fabled to keep wailing and roaring at the ford until the coming of the doomed traveller. Alan I saw believed it, or half believed it; and when the cry of the river rose more than usually sharp, I was little surprised (though, of course, I would still be shocked) to see him cross himself in the manner of the Catholics.

During all these horrid wanderings we had no familiarity, scarcely even that of speech. The truth is that I was sickening for my grave, which is my best excuse. But besides that I was of an unforgiving disposition from my birth, slow to take offence, slower to forget it, and now incensed both against my companion and myself. For the best part of two days he was unweariedly kind; silent, indeed, but always ready to help, and always hoping (as I could very well see) that my displeasure would blow by. For the same length of time I stayed in myself, nursing my anger, roughly refusing his services, and passing him over with my eyes as if he had been a bush or a stone.

The second night, or rather the peep of the third day, found us upon a very open hill, so that we could not follow our usual plan and lie down immediately to eat and sleep. Before we had reached a place of shelter, the grey had come pretty clear, for though it still rained, the clouds ran higher; and Alan, looking in my face, showed some marks of concern.

'Ye had better let me take your pack,' said he, for perhaps the ninth time since we had parted from the scout beside Loch Rannoch.

'I do very well, I thank you,' said I, as cold as ice.

Alan flushed darkly. 'I'll not offer it again,' he said. 'I'm not a patient man, David.'

'I never said you were,' said I, which was exactly the rude, silly speech of a boy of ten.

Alan made no answer at the time, but his conduct answered for him. Henceforth, it is to be thought, he quite forgave himself for the affair at Cluny's; cocked his hat again, walked jauntily, whistled airs, and looked at me upon one side with a provoking smile.

The third night we were to pass through the western end of the country of Balquidder. It came clear and cold, with a touch in the air like frost, and a northerly wind that blew the clouds away and made the stars bright. The streams were full, of course, and still made a great noise among the hills;

but I observed that Alan thought no more upon the Kelpie, and was in high good spirits. As for me, the change of weather came too late; I had lain in the mire so long that (as the Bible has it) my very clothes 'abhorred me'; I was dead weary, deadly sick and full of pains and shiverings; the chill of the wind went through me, and the sound of it confused my ears. In this poor state I had to bear from my companion something in the nature of a persecution. He spoke a good deal, and never without a taunt. 'Whig' was the best name he had to give me. 'Here,' he would say, 'here's a dub for ye to jump, my Whiggie! I kent you're a fine jumper!' And so on; all the time with a gibing voice and face.

I knew it was my own doing, and no one else's; but I was too miserable to repent. I felt I could drag myself but little farther; pretty soon, I must lie down and die on these wet mountains like a sheep or a fox, and my bones must whiten there like the bones of a beast. My head was light, perhaps; but I began to love the prospect, I began to glory in the thought of such a death, alone in the desert, with the wild eagles besieging my last moments. Alan would repent then, I thought; he would remember, when I was dead, how much he owed me, and the remembrance would be torture. So I went like a sick, silly, and bad-hearted schoolboy, feeding my anger against a fellow-man, when I would have been better on my knees, crying on God for mercy. And at each of Alan's taunts, I hugged myself. 'Ah!' thinks I to myself, 'I have a better taunt in readiness; when I lie down and die, you will feel it like a buffet in your face; ah, what a revenge! ah, how you will regret your ingratitude and cruelty!'

All the while, I was growing worse and worse. Once I had fallen, my legs simply doubling under me, and this had struck Alan for the moment; but I was afoot so briskly, and set off again with such a natural manner, that he soon forgot the incident. Flushes of heat went over me, and then spasms of shuddering. The stitch in my side was hardly bearable. At last I began to feel that I could trail myself no farther: and with that, there came on me all at once the wish to have it out with Alan, let my anger blaze, and be done with my life in a more sudden manner. He had just called me 'Whig.' I stopped.

'Mr. Stewart,' said I, in a voice that quivered like a fiddle-string, 'you are older than I am, and should know your manners. Do you think it either very wise or very witty to cast my politics in my teeth? I thought, where folk differed, it was the part of gentlemen to differ civilly; and if I did not, I may tell you I could find a better taunt than some of yours.'

Alan had stopped opposite to me, his hat cocked, his hands in his breeches pockets, his head a little on one side. He listened, smiling evilly, as I could see by the starlight; and when I had done he began to whistle a Jacobite air. It was the air made in mockery of General Cope's defeat at Prestonpans:—

> 'Hey, Johnnie Cope, are ye waukin' yet?
> And are your drums a-beatin' yet?'*

And it came in my mind that Alan, on the day of that battle, had been engaged upon the royal side.

'Why do ye take that air, Mr. Stewart?' said I. 'Is that to remind me you have been beaten on both sides?'

The air stopped on Alan's lips. 'David!' said he.

'But it's time these manners ceased,' I continued; 'and I mean you shall henceforth speak civilly of my King and my good friends the Campbells.'

'I am a Stewart——' began Alan.

'O!' says I, 'I ken ye bear a king's name. But you are to remember, since I have been in the Highlands, I have seen a good many of those that bear it; and the best I can say of them is this, that they would be none the worse of washing.'

'Do you know that you insult me?'* said Alan, very low.

'I am sorry for that,' said I, 'for I am not done; and if you distaste the sermon, I doubt the pirliecue[1] will please you as little. You have been chased in the field by the grown men of my party; it seems a poor kind of pleasure to outface a boy.

---

1 A second sermon.

Both the Campbells and the Whigs have beaten you; you have run before them like a hare. It behoves you to speak of them as of your betters.'

Alan stood quite still, the tails of his great-coat clapping behind him in the wind.

'This is a pity,' he said at last. 'There are things said that cannot be passed over.'

'I never asked you to,' said I. 'I am as ready as yourself.'

'Ready?' said he.

'Ready,' I repeated. 'I am no blower and boaster like some that I could name. Come on!' And drawing my sword, I fell on guard as Alan himself had taught me.

'David!' he cried. 'Are ye daft? I cannae draw upon ye, David. It's fair murder.'

'That was your look-out when you insulted me,' said I.

'It's the truth!' cried Alan, and he stood for a moment, wringing his mouth in his hand like a man in sore perplexity. 'It's the bare truth,' he said, and drew his sword. But before I could touch his blade with mine, he had thrown it from him and fallen to the ground. 'Na, na,' he kept saying, 'na, na—I cannae, I cannae.'

At this the last of my anger oozed all out of me; and I found myself only sick, and sorry, and blank, and wondering at myself. I would have given the world to take back what I had said; but a word once spoken, who can recapture it? I minded me of all Alan's kindness and courage in the past, how he had helped and cheered and borne with me in our evil days; and then recalled my own insults, and saw that I had lost for ever that doughty friend. At the same time, the sickness that hung upon me seemed to redouble, and the pang in my side was like a sword for sharpness. I thought I must have swooned where I stood.

This it was that gave me a thought. No apology could blot out what I had said; it was needless to think of one, none could cover the offence; but where an apology was vain, a mere cry for help might bring Alan back to my side. I put my pride away from me. 'Alan!' I said; 'if you cannae help me, I must just die here.'

He started up sitting, and looked at me.

'It's true,' said I. 'I'm by with it. O, let me get into the bield of a house—I'll can die there easier.' I had no need to pretend; whether I chose or not, I spoke in a weeping voice that would have melted a heart of stone.

'Can ye walk?' asked Alan.

'No,' said I, 'not without help. This last hour, my legs have been fainting under me; I've stitch in my side like a red-hot iron; I cannae breathe right. If I die, ye'll can forgive me, Alan? In my heart, I liked ye fine—even when I was the angriest.'

'Wheesht, wheesht!' cried Alan. 'Dinnae say that! David man, ye ken——' He shut his mouth upon a sob. 'Let me get my arm about ye,' he continued; 'that's the way! Now lean upon me hard. Gude kens where there's a house! We're in Balwhidder, too; there should be no want of houses, no, nor friends' houses here. Do ye gang easier so, Davie?'

'Ay,' said I, 'I can be doing this way'; and I pressed his arm with my hand.

Again he came near sobbing. 'Davie,' said he, 'I'm no a right man at all; I have neither sense nor kindness; I couldnae remember ye were just a bairn, I couldnae see ye were dying on your feet; Davie, ye'll have to try and forgive me.'

'Oh man, It's say no more about it!' said I. 'We're neither one of us to mend the other—that's the truth! We must just bear and forbear, man Alan! O, but my stitch is sore! Is there nae house?'

'I'll find a house to ye, David,' he said stoutly. 'We'll follow down the burn, where there's bound to be houses. My poor man, will ye no be better on my back?'

'Oh, Alan,' says I, 'and me a good twelve inches taller?'

'Ye're no such a thing,' cried Alan, with a start. 'There may a trifling matter of an inch or two; I'm no saying I'm just exactly what ye would call a tall man, whatever; and I dare say,' he added, his voice tailing off in a laughable manner, 'now when I come to think of it, I dare say ye'll be just about right. Ay, it'll be a foot, or near hand; or may be even mair!'

It was sweet and laughable to hear Alan eat his words up in the fear of some fresh quarrel. I could have laughed, had not my stitch caught me so hard; but if I had laughed, I think I must have wept too.

'Alan,' cried I, 'what makes ye so good to me? What makes ye care for such a thankless fellow?'

''Deed, and I don't know,' said Alan. 'For just precisely what I thought I liked about ye, was that ye never quarrelled;—and now I like ye better!'

CHAPTER XXV

IN BALQUIDDER

AT the door of the first house we came to, Alan knocked, which was no very safe enterprise in such a part of the Highlands as the Braes of Balquidder. No great clan held rule there; it was filled and disputed by small septs, and broken remnants, and what they call 'chiefless folk,' driven into the wild country about the springs of Forth and Teith by the advance of the Campbells. Here were Stewarts and Maclarens, which came to the same thing, for the Maclarens followed Alan's chief in war, and made but one clad with Appin. Here, too, were many of that old proscribed, nameless, red-handed clan of the Macgregors.* They had always been ill-considered, and now worse than ever, having credit with no side or party in the whole country of Scotland. Their chief, Macgregor of Macgregor, was in exile; the more immediate leader of that part of them about Balquidder, James More, Rob Roy's eldest son, lay waiting his trial in Edinburgh Castle; they were in ill-blood with Highlander and Lowlander, with the Grahames, the Maclarens and the Stewarts; and Alan, who took up the quarrel of any friend however distant, was extremely wishful to avoid them.

Chance served us very well; for it was a household of Maclarens that we found, where Alan was not only welcome for his name's sake but known by reputation. Here then

I was got to bed without delay, and a doctor fetched, who found me in a sorry plight. But whether because he was a very good doctor, or I a very young, strong man, I lay bedridden for no more than a week, and before a month I was able to take the road again with a good heart.

All this time Alan would not leave me; though I often pressed him, and indeed his foolhardiness in staying was a common subject of outcry with the two or three friends that were let into the secret. He hid by day in a hole of the braes under a little wood; and at night when the coast was clear, would come into the house to visit me. I need not say if I was pleased to see him; Mrs. Maclaren, our hostess, thought nothing good enough for such a guest; and as Duncan Dhu (which was the name of our host) had a pair of pipes in his house and was much a lover of music, the time of my recovery was quite a festival, and we commonly turned night into day.

The soldiers let us be; although once a party of two companies and some dragoons went by in the bottom of the valley, where I could see them through the window as I lay in bed. What was much more astonishing, no magistrate came near me, and there was no question put of whence I came or whither I was going; and in that time of excitement, I was as free of all inquiry as though I had lain in a desert. Yet my presence was known before I left to all the people in Balquidder and the adjacent parts; many coming about the house on visits and these (after the custom of the country) spreading the news among their neighbours. The bills, too, had now been printed. There was one pinned near the foot of my bed, where I could read my own not very flattering portrait and, in larger characters, the amount of the blood money that had been set upon my life. Duncan Dhu and the rest that knew that I had come there in Alan's company, could have entertained no doubt of who I was; and many others must have had their guess. For though I had changed my clothes, I could not change my age or person; and Lowland boys of eighteen were not so rife in these parts of the world, and above all about that time, that they could fail to put one thing with another and connect me with the bill. So it was, at least. Other folk keep a secret among two or three near friends, and somehow it leaks out; but among these clansmen, it is told to a whole countryside, and they will keep it for a century.

There was but one thing happened worth narrating; and that is the visit I had of Robin Oig,* one of the sons of the notorious Rob Roy. He was sought upon all sides on a charge of carrying a young woman from Balfron and marrying her (as was alleged) by force; yet he stepped about Balquidder like a gentleman in his own walled policy. It was he who had shot James Maclaren at the plough stilts, a quarrel never satisfied; yet he walked into the house of his blood enemies as a rider[1] might into a public inn.

Duncan had time to pass me word of who it was; and we looked at one another in concern. You should understand, it was then close upon the time of Alan's coming; the two were little likely to agree; and yet if we sent word or sought to make a signal, it was sure to arouse suspicion in a man under so dark a cloud as the Macgregor.

He came in with a great show of civility, but like a man among inferiors; took off his bonnet to Mrs. Maclaren, but clapped it on his head again to speak to Duncan; and having thus set himself (as he would have thought) in a proper light, came to my bedside and bowed.

'I am given to know, sir,' says he, 'that your name is Balfour.'

'They call me David Balfour,' said I, 'at your service.'

'I would give ye my name in return, sir,' he replied, 'but it's one somewhat blown upon of late days; and it'll perhaps suffice if I tell ye that I am own brother to James More Drummond or Macgregor, of whom ye will scarce have failed to hear.'

'No, sir,' said I, a little alarmed; 'nor yet of your father, Macgregor-Campbell.' And I sat up and bowed in bed; for I thought best to compliment him, in case he was proud of having had an outlaw to his father.

1 Commercial traveller.

He bowed in return. 'But what I am come to say, sir,' he went on, 'is this. In the year '45, my brother raised a part of the "Gregara," and marched six companies to strike a stroke for the good side; and the surgeon that marched with our clan and cured my brother's leg when it was broken in the brush at Preston Pans, was a gentleman of the same name precisely as yourself. He was brother to Balfour of Baith; and if you are in any reasonable degree of nearness one of that gentleman's kin, I have come to put myself and my people at your command.'

You are to remember that I knew no more of my descent than any cadger's dog; my uncle, to be sure, had prated of some of our high connections, but nothing to the present purpose; and there was nothing left me but that bitter disgrace of owning that I could not tell.

Robin told me shortly he was sorry he had put himself about, turned his back upon me without a sign of salutation, and as he went towards the door, I could hear him telling Duncan that I was 'only some kinless loon that didn't know his own father.' Angry as I was at these words, and ashamed of my own ignorance, I could scarce keep from smiling that a man who was under the lash of the law (and was indeed hanged some three years later) should be so nice as to the descent of his acquaintances.

Just in the door he met Alan coming in; and the two drew back and looked at each other like strange dogs. They were neither of them big men, but they seemed fairly to swell out with pride. Each wore a sword, and by a movement of his haunch, thrust clear the hilt of it, so that it might be the more readily grasped and the blade drawn.

'Mr. Stewart, I am thinking,' says Robin.

'Troth, Mr. Macgregor, it's not a name to be ashamed of,' answered Alan.

'I did not know ye were in my country, sir,' says Robin.

'It sticks in mind that I am in the country of my friends the Maclarens,' says Alan.

'That's a kittle point,' returned the other. 'There may be

two words to say to that. But I think I will have heard that
you are a man of your sword?'

'Unless ye were born deaf, Mr. Macgregor, ye will have
heard a good deal more than that,' says Alan. 'I am not the
only man that can draw steel in Appin; and when my kinsman and captain, Ardshiel, had a talk with a gentleman of
your name, not so many years back, I could never hear that
the Macgregor had the best of it.'

'Do ye mean my father, sir?' says Robin.

'Well, I wouldnae wonder,' said Alan. 'The gentleman I
have in my mind had the ill-taste to clap Campbell to his
name.'

'My father was an old man,' returned Robin. 'The match
was unequal. You and me would make a better pair, sir.'

'I was thinking that,' said Alan.

I was half out of bed, and Duncan had been hanging at
the elbow of these fighting cocks, ready to intervene upon the
least occasion. But when that word was uttered, it was a case
of now or never; and Duncan, with something of a white face
to be sure, thrust himself between.

'Gentleman,' said he, 'I will have been thinking of a very
different matter, whateffer. Here are my pipes, and here are
you two gentlemen who are baith acclaimed pipers. It's an
auld dispute which one of ye's the best. Here will be a braw
chance to settle it.'

'Why, sir,' said Alan, still addressing Robin, from whom
indeed he had not so much as shifted his eyes, nor yet Robin
from him, 'why, sir,' says Alan, 'I think I will have heard
some sough[1] of the sort. Have ye music, as folk say? Are ye a
bit of a piper?'

'I can pipe like a Macrimmon!'* cries Robin.

'And that is a very bold word,' quoth Alan.

'I have made bolder words good before now,' returned
Robin, 'and that against better adversaries.'

'It is easy to try that,' says Alan.

Duncan Dhu made haste to bring out the pair of pipes that

---

[1] Rumour.

was his principal possession, and to set before his guests a mutton-ham and a bottle of that drink which they call Athole brose, and which is made of old whiskey, strained honey and sweet cream, slowly beaten together in the right order and proportion. The two enemies were still on the very breach of a quarrel; but down they sat, one upon each side of the peat fire, with a mighty show of politeness. Maclaren pressed them to taste his mutton-ham and 'the wife's brose,' reminding them the wife was out of Athole, and had a name far and wide for her skill in that confection. But Robin put aside these hospitalities as bad for the breath.

'I would have ye to remark, sir,' said Alan, 'that I havenae broken bread for near upon ten hours, which will be worse for the breath than any brose in Scotland.'

'I will take no advantages, Mr. Stewart,' replied Robin. 'Eat and drink; I'll follow you.'

Each ate a small portion of the ham and drank a glass of the brose to Mrs. Maclaren; and then after a great number of civilities, Robin took the pipes and played a little spring in a very ranting manner.

'Ay, ye can blow,' said Alan; and taking the instrument from his rival, he first played the same spring in a manner identical with Robin's; and then wandered into variations, which, as he went on, he decorated with a perfect flight of grace notes, such as pipers love, and call the 'warblers.'

I had been pleased with Robin's playing, Alan's ravished me.

'That's no very bad, Mr. Stewart,' said the rival, 'but ye show a poor device in your warblers.'

'Me!' cried Alan, the blood starting to his face. 'I give ye the lie.'

'Do ye own yourself beaten at the pipes, then,' said Robin, 'that ye seek to change them for the sword?'

'And that's very well said, Mr. Macgregor,' returned Alan; 'and in the meantime' (laying a strong accent on the word) 'I take back the lie. I appeal to Duncan.'

'Indeed, ye need appeal to naebody,' said Robin. 'Ye're a far better judge than any Maclaren in Balquidder: for it's a God's truth that you're a very creditable piper for a Stewart. Hand me the pipes.'

Alan did as he asked; and Robin proceeded to imitate and correct some part of Alan's variations, which it seemed that he remembered perfectly.

'Ay, ye have music,' said Alan, gloomily.

'And now be the judge yourself, Mr. Stewart,' said Robin; and taking up the variations from the beginning, he worked them throughout to so new a purpose, with such ingenuity and sentiment, and with so odd a fancy and so quick a knack in the grace-notes, that I was amazed to hear him.

As for Alan, his face grew dark and hot, and he sat and gnawed his fingers, like a man under some deep affront. 'Enough!' he cried. 'Ye can blow the pipes—make the most of that.' And he made as if to rise.

But Robin only held out his hand as if to ask for silence, and struck into the slow measure of a pibroch. It was a fine piece of music in itself and nobly played; but it seems, besides, it was a piece peculiar to the Appin Stewarts and a chief favourite with Alan. The first notes were scarce out, before there came a change in his face; when the time quickened, he seemed to grow restless in his seat; and long before that piece was at an end, the last signs of his anger died from him, and he had no thought but for the music.

'Robin Oig,' he said, when it was done, 'ye are a great piper. I am not fit to blow in the same kingdom with ye. Body of me! ye have mair music in your sporran than I have in my head; And though it still sticks in my mind that I could maybe show ye another of it with the cold steel, I warn ye beforehand—it'll no be fair! It would go against my heart to haggle a man that can blow the pipes as you can!'

Thereupon that quarrel was made up; all night long the brose was going and the pipes changing hands; and the day had come pretty bright, and the three men were none the better for what they had been taking, before Robin as much as thought upon the road.

It was the last I saw of him, for I was in the Low Countries at the University of Leyden, when he stood his trial, and was hanged in the Grassmarket. And I have told this at so great length, partly because it was the last incident of any note that befell me on the wrong side of the Highland Line,* and, partly because (as the man came to be hanged) it's in a manner history.*

CHAPTER XXVI

END OF THE FLIGHT: WE PASS
THE FORTH

THE month, as I have said, was not yet out, but it was already far through August, and beautiful warm weather, with every sign of an early and great harvest, when I was pronounced able for my journey. Our money was now run to so low an ebb that we must think first of all on speed; for if we came not soon to Mr. Rankeillor's, or if when we came there he should fail to help me, we must surely starve. In Alan's view, besides, the hunt must have now greatly slackened; and the line of the Forth and even Stirling Bridge, which is the main pass over that river, would be watched with little interest.

'It's a chief principle in military affairs,' said he, 'to go where ye are least expected. Forth is our trouble; ye ken the saying, "Forth bridles the wild Hielandman." Well, if we seek to creep round about the head of that river and come down by Kippen or Balfron it's just precisely there that they'll be looking to lay hands on us. But if we stave on straight to the auld Brig of Stirling, I'll lay my sword they let us pass unchallenged.'

The first night, accordingly, we pushed to the house of a Maclaren in Strathire, a friend of Duncan's, where we slept the twenty-first of the month, and whence we set forth again about the fall of night to make another easy stage. The twenty-second we lay in a heather bush on the hillside in Uam Var, within view of a herd of deer, the happiest ten hours of sleep in a fine, breathing sunshine and on bone-dry ground, that I have ever tasted. That night we struck Allan Water, and followed it down; and coming to the edge of the hills saw the whole Carse of Stirling underfoot, as flat as a pancake, with the town and castle on a hill in the midst of it, and the moon shining on the Links of Forth.

'Now,' said Alan, 'I kenna if ye care, but ye're in your own land again. We passed the Hieland Line in the first hour; and now if we could but pass yon crooked water, we might cast our bonnets in the air.'

In Allan Water, near by where it falls into the Forth, we found a little sandy islet, overgrown with burdock, butterbur and the like low plants, that would just cover us if we lay flat. Here it was we made our camp, within plain view of Stirling Castle, whence we could hear the drums beat as some part of the garrison paraded. Shearers worked all day in a field on one side of the river, and we could hear the stones going on the hooks and the voices and even the words of the men talking. It behoved to lie close and keep silent. But the sand of the little isle was sun-warm, and green plants gave us shelter for our heads, we had food and drink in plenty; and to crown all, we were within sight of safety.

As soon as the shearers quit their work and the dusk began to fall, we waded ashore and struck for the Bridge of Stirling, keeping to the fields and under the field fences.

The bridge is close under the castle hill, an old, high, narrow bridge with pinnacles along the parapet; and you may conceive with how much interest I looked upon it, not only as a place famous in history, but as the very doors of salvation to Alan and myself. The moon was not yet up when we came there; a few lights shone along the front of the fortress, and lower down a few lighted windows in the town; but it was all mighty still, and there seemed to be no guard upon the passage.

I was for pushing straight across; but Alan was more wary.

'It looks unco' quiet,' said he; 'but for all that we'll lie down here cannily behind a dyke, and make sure.'

So we lay for about a quarter of an hour, whiles whispering, whiles lying still and hearing nothing earthly but the washing of the water on the piers. At last there came by an old, hobbling woman with a crutch stick; who first stopped a little, close to where we lay, and bemoaned herself and the long way she had travelled; and then set forth again up the steep spring of the bridge. The woman was so little, and the night still so dark, that we soon lost sight of her; only heard the sound of her steps, and her stick, and a cough that she had by fits, draw slowly farther away.

'She's bound to be across now,' I whispered.

'Na,' said Alan, 'her foot still sounds boss[1] upon the bridge.'

And just then—'Who goes?' cried a voice, and we heard the butt of a musket rattle on the stones. I must suppose the sentry had been sleeping, so that had we tried, we might have passed unseen; but he was awake now, and the chance forfeited.

'This'll never do,' said Alan. 'This'll never, never do for us, David.'

And without another word, he began to crawl away through the fields; and a little after, being well out of eye-shot, got to his feet again, and struck along a road that led to the eastward. I could not conceive what he was doing; and indeed I was so sharply cut by the disappointment, that I was little likely to be pleased with anything. A moment back, and I had seen myself knocking at Mr. Rankeillor's door to claim my inheritance, like a hero in a ballad; and here was I back again, a wandering, hunted blackguard, on the wrong side of Forth.

'Well?' said I.

'Well,' said Alan, 'what would ye have? They're none such fools as I took them for. We have still the Forth to pass, Davie—weary fall the rains that fed and the hillsides that guided it!'

'And why go east?' said I.

'Ou, just upon the chance!' said he. 'If we cannae pass the river, we'll have to see what we can do for the firth.'

1 Hollow.

'There are fords upon the river, and none upon the firth,' said I.

'To be sure there are fords, and a bridge forbye,' quoth Alan; 'and of what service, when they are watched?'

'Well,' said I, 'but a river can be swum.'

'By them that have the skill of it,' returned he; 'but I have yet to hear that either you or me is much of a hand at that exercise; and for my own part, I swim like a stone.'

'I'm not up to you in talking back, Alan,' I said; 'but I can see we're making bad worse. If it's hard to pass a river, it stands to reason it must be worse to pass a sea.'

'But there's such a thing as a boat,' says Alan, 'or I'm the more deceived.'

'Ay, and such a thing as money,' says I. 'But for us that have neither one nor other, they might just as well not have been invented.'

'Ye think so?' said Alan.

'I do that,' said I.

'David,' says he, 'ye're a man of small invention and less faith. But let me set my wits upon the hone, and if I cannae beg, borrow, nor yet steal a boat, I'll make one!'

'I think I see ye!' said I. 'And what's more than all that: if ye pass a bridge, it can tell no tales; but if we pass the firth, there's the boat on the wrong side—somebody must have brought it—the countryside will all be in a bizz——'

'Man!' cried Alan, 'if I make a boat, I'll make a body to take it back again! So deave me with no more of your nonsense, but walk (for that's what you've got to do)—and let Alan think for ye.'

All night, then, we walked through the north side of the Carse under the high line of the Ochil mountains; and by Alloa and Clackmannan and Culross, all of which we avoided; and about ten in the morning, mighty hungry and tired, came to the little clachan of Limekilns. This is a place that sits near in by the waterside, and looks across the Hope to the town of the Queensferry. Smoke went up from both of these, and from other villages and farms upon all hands. The fields were being reaped; two ships lay anchored, and boats were coming and going on the Hope. It was altogether a right pleasant sight to me; and I could not take my fill of gazing at these comfortable, green, cultivated hills and the busy people both of the field and sea.

For all that, there was Mr. Rankeillor's house on the south shore, where I had no doubt wealth awaited me; and here was I upon the north, clad in poor enough attire of an outlandish fashion, with three silver shillings left to me of all my fortune, a price set upon my head, and an outlawed man for my sole company.

'O, Alan!' said I, 'to think of it! Over there, there's all that heart could want waiting me; and the birds go over, and the boats go over—all that please can go, but just me only! O, man, but it's a heart-break!'

In Limekilns we entered a small change-house, which we only knew to be a public by the wand over the door, and bought some bread and cheese from a good-looking lass that was the servant. This we carried with us in a bundle, meaning to sit and eat it in a bush of wood on the sea-shore, that we saw some third part of a mile in front. As we went, I kept looking across the water and sighing to myself; and though I took no heed of it, Alan had fallen into a muse. At last he stopped in the way.

'Did ye take heed of the lass we bought this of?' says he, tapping on the bread and cheese.

'To be sure,' said I, 'and a bonny lass she was.'

'Ye thought that?' cried he. 'Man David, that's good news.'

'In the name of all that's wonderful, why so?' says I. 'What good can that do?'

'Well,' said Alan, with one of his droll looks, 'I was rather in hopes it would maybe get us that boat.'

'If it were the other way about, it would be liker it,' said I.

'That's all that you ken, ye see,' said Alan. 'I don't want the lass to fall in love with ye, I want her to be sorry for ye, David; to which end, there is no manner of need that she should take you for a beauty. Let me see' (looking me curiously over). 'I wish ye were a wee thing paler; but apart from that ye'll do fine for my purpose—ye have a fine, hang-dog, rag-and-tatter, clappermaclaw kind of a look to ye, as if ye had stolen the coat from a potato-bogle. Come; right about, and back to the change-house for that boat of ours.'

I followed him laughing.

'David Balfour,' said he, 'ye're a very funny gentleman by your way of it, and this is a very funny employ for ye, no doubt. For all that, if ye have any affection for my neck (to say nothing of your own) ye will perhaps be kind enough to take this matter responsibly. I am going to do a bit of play-acting, the bottom ground of which is just exactly as serious as the gallows for the pair of us. So bear it, if ye please, in mind, and conduct yourself according.'

'Well, well,' said I, 'have it as you will.'

As we got near the clachan, he made me take his arm and hang upon it like one almost helpless with weariness; and by the time he pushed open the change-house door, he seemed to be half carrying me. The maid appeared surprised (as well she might be) at our speedy return; but Alan had no words to spare for her in explanation, helped me to a chair, called for a tass of brandy with which he fed me little sips, and then breaking up the bread and cheese helped me to eat it like a nursery-lass; the whole with that grave, concerned, affectionate countenance, that might have imposed upon a judge. It was small wonder if the maid were taken with the picture we presented, of a poor, sick, overwrought lad and his most tender comrade. She drew quite near, and stood leaning with her back on the next table.

'What's like wrong with him?' said she at last.

Alan turned upon her, to my great wonder, with a kind of fury. 'Wrong?' cries he. 'He's walked more hundreds of miles than he has hairs upon his chin, and slept oftener in wet heather than dry sheets. Wrong, quo' she! Wrong enough, I would think! Wrong, indeed!' and he kept grumbling to himself as he fed me, like a man ill-pleased.

'He's young for the like of that,' said the maid.

'Ower young,' said Alan, with his back to her.

'He would be better riding,' says she.

'And where could I get a horse to him?' cried Alan, turning on her with the same appearance of fury. 'Would ye have me steal?'

I thought this roughness would have sent her off in dudgeon, as indeed it closed her mouth for the time. But my companion knew very well what he was doing; and for as simple as he was in some things of life, had a great fund of roguishness in such affairs as these.

'Ye neednae tell me,' she said at last—'ye're gentry.'

'Well,' said Alan, softened a little (I believe against his will) by this artless comment, 'and suppose we were? Did ever you hear that gentrice put money in folks' pockets?'

She sighed at this, as if she were herself some disinherited great lady. 'No,' says she, 'that's true indeed.'

I was all this while chafing at the part I played, and sitting tongue-tied between shame and merriment; but somehow at this I could hold in no longer, and bade Alan let me be, for I was better already. My voice stuck in my throat, for I ever hated to take part in lies; but my very embarrassment helped on the plot, for the lass no doubt set down my husky voice to sickness and fatigue.

'Has he nae friends?' said she, in a tearful voice.

'That has he so!' cried Alan, 'if we could but win to them!—friends and rich friends, beds to lie in, food to eat, doctors to see him—and here he must tramp in the dubs and sleep in the heather like a beggarman.'

'And why that?' says the lass.

'My dear,' says Alan, 'I cannae very safely say; but I'll tell ye what I'll do instead,' says he, 'I'll whistle ye a bit tune.' And with that he leaned pretty far over the table, and in a mere breath of a whistle, but with a wonderful pretty sentiment, gave her a few bars of 'Charlie is my darling.'*

'Wheesht,' says she, and looked over her shoulder to the door.

'That's it,' said Alan.

'And him so young!' cries the lass.

'He's old enough to——' and Alan struck his forefinger

on the back of his neck, meaning that I was old enough to lose my head.

'It would be a black shame,' she cried, flushing high.

'It's what will be, though,' said Alan, 'unless we manage the better.'

At this the lass turned and ran out of that part of the house, leaving us alone together, Alan in high good humour at the furthering of his schemes, and I in bitter dudgeon at being called a Jacobite and treated like a child.

'Alan,' I cried, 'I can stand no more of this.'

'Ye'll have to sit it then, Davie,' said he. 'For if ye upset the pot now, ye may scrape your own life out of the fire, but Alan Breck is a dead man.'

This was so true that I could only groan; and even my groan served Alan's purpose, for it was overheard by the lass as she came flying in again with a dish of white puddings and a bottle of strong ale.

'Poor lamb!' says she, and had no sooner set the meat before us, than she touched me on the shoulder with a little friendly touch, as much as to bid me cheer up. Then she told us to fall to, and there would be no more to pay; for the inn was her own, or at least her father's, and he was gone for the day to Pittencrieff. We waited for no second bidding, for bread and cheese is but cold comfort and the puddings smelt excellently well; and while we sat and ate, she took up that same place by the next table, looking on, and thinking, and frowning to herself, and drawing the string of her apron through her hand.

'I'm thinking ye have rather a long tongue,' she said at last to Alan.

'Ay,' said Alan; 'but ye see I ken the folk I speak to.'

'I would never betray ye,' said she, 'if ye mean that.'

'No,' said he, 'ye're not that kind. But I'll tell ye what ye would do, ye would help.'

'I couldnae,' said she, shaking her head. 'Na, I couldnae.'

'No,' said he, 'but if ye could?'

She answered him nothing.

'Look here, my lass,' said Alan, 'there are boats in the

kingdom of Fife, for I saw two (no less) upon the beach,
as I came in by your town's end. Now if we could have the
use of a boat to pass under cloud of night into Lothian, and
some secret, decent kind of a man to bring that boat back
again and keep his counsel, there would be two souls saved—
mine to all likelihood—his to a dead surety. If we lack that
boat, we have but three shillings left in this wide world; and
where to go, and how to do, and what other place there is for
us except the chains of a gibbet—I give you my naked word,
I kenna! Shall we go wanting, lassie? Are ye to lie in your
warm bed and think upon us, when the wind gowls in the
chimney and the rain tirls on the roof? Are ye to eat your
meat by the cheeks of a red fire, and think upon this poor
sick lad of mine, biting his finger ends on a blae muir for cauld
and hunger? Sick or sound, he must aye be moving; with the
death grapple at his throat he must aye be trailing in the rain
on the lang roads; and when he gants his last on a rickle
of cauld stanes, there will be nae friends near him but only
me and God.'*

At this appeal, I could see the lass was in great trouble
of mind, being tempted to help us, and yet in some fear she
might be helping malefactors; and so now I determined to
step in myself and to allay her scruples with a portion of the
truth.

'Did ever you hear,' said I, 'of Mr. Rankeillor of the Ferry?'

'Rankeillor the writer?' said she. 'I daursay that!'

'Well,' said I, 'it's to his door that I am bound, so you
may judge by that if I am an ill-doer; and I will tell you more,
that though I am indeed, by a dreadful error, in some peril
of my life, King George has no truer friend in all Scotland
than myself.'

Her face cleared up mightily at this, although Alan's
darkened.

'That's more than I would ask,' said she. 'Mr. Rankeillor
is a kennt man.' And she bade us finish our meat, get clear
of the clachan as soon as might be, and lie close in the bit
wood on the sea beach. 'And ye can trust me,' says she, 'I'll
find some means to put you over.'

At this we waited for no more, but shook hands with her upon the bargain, made short work of the puddings, and set forth again from Limekilns as far as to the wood. It was a small piece of perhaps a score of elders and hawthorns and a few young ashes, not thick enough to veil us from passers-by upon the road or beach. Here we must lie, however, making the best of the brave warm weather and the good hopes we now had of a deliverance, and planning more particularly what remained for us to do.

We had but one trouble all day: when a strolling piper came and sat in the same wood with us; a red-nosed, blear-eyed, drunken dog, with a great bottle of whiskey in his pocket, and a long story of wrongs that had been done him by all sorts of persons, from the Lord President of the Court of Session who had denied him justice, down to the Bailies of Inverkeithing who had given him more of it than he desired. It was impossible but he should conceive some suspicion of two men lying all day concealed in a thicket and having no business to allege. As long as he stayed there, he kept us in hot water with prying questions; and after he was gone, as he was a man not very likely to hold his tongue, we were in the greater impatience to be gone ourselves.

The day came to an end with the same brightness; the night fell quiet and clear; lights came out in houses and hamlets and then, one after another, began to be put out; but it was past eleven, and we were long since strangely tortured with anxieties, before we heard the grinding of oars upon the rowing pins. At that, we looked out and saw the lass herself coming rowing to us in a boat. She had trusted no one with our affairs, not even her sweetheart, if she had one; but as soon as her father was asleep, had left the house by a window, stolen a neighbour's boat, and come to our assistance single-handed.

I was abashed how to find expression for my thanks; but she was no less abashed at the thought of hearing them; begged us to lose no time and to hold our peace, saying (very properly) that the heart of our matter was in haste and silence; and so, what with one thing and another, she had set us on the Lothian shore not far from Carriden, had shaken hands with us, and was out again at sea and rowing for Limekilns, before there was one word said either of her service or our gratitude.

Even after she was gone, we had nothing to say, as indeed nothing was enough for such a kindness. Only Alan stood a great while upon the shore shaking his head.

'It is a very fine lass,' he said at last. 'David, it is a very fine lass.' And a matter of an hour later, as we were lying in a den on the seashore and I had been already dozing, he broke out again in commendations of her character. For my part, I could say nothing, she was so simple a creature that my heart smote me both with remorse and fear; remorse because we had traded upon her ignorance; and fear lest we should have anyway involved her in the dangers of our situation.

CHAPTER XXVII

I COME TO MR. RANKEILLOR

THE next day it was agreed that Alan should fend for himself till sunset; but as soon as it began to grow dark, he should lie in the fields by the roadside near to Newhalls, and stir for naught until he heard me whistling. At first I proposed I should give him for a signal the 'Bonnie House of Airlie,' which was a favourite of mine; but he objected that as the piece was very commonly known, any ploughman might whistle it by accident; and taught me instead a little fragment of a Highland air, which has run in my head from that day to this, and will likely run in my head when I lie dying. Every time it comes to me, it takes me off to that last day of my uncertainty, with Alan sitting up in the bottom of the den, whistling and beating the measure with a finger, and the grey of the dawn coming on his face.

I was in the long street of Queensferry before the sun was up. It was a fairly built burgh, the houses of good stone, many slated; the town hall not so fine, I thought, as that of Peebles, nor yet the street so noble; but take it altogether, it put me to shame for my foul tatters.

As the morning went on, and the fires began to be kindled, and the windows to open, and the people to appear out of the houses, my concern and despondency grew ever the blacker. I saw now that I had no grounds to stand upon; and no clear proof of my rights, nor so much as of my own identity. If it was all a bubble, I was indeed sorely cheated and left in a sore pass. Even if things were as I conceived, it would in all likelihood take time to establish my contentions; and what time had I to spare with less than three shillings in my pocket, and a condemned, hunted man upon my hands to ship out of the country? Truly, if my hope broke with me, it might come to the gallows yet for both of us. And as I continued to walk up and down, and saw people looking askance at me upon the street or out of windows, and nudging or speaking one to another with smiles, I began to take a fresh apprehension: that it might be no easy matter even to come to speech of the lawyer, far less to convince him of my story.

For the life of me I could not muster up the courage to address any of these reputable burghers; I thought shame even to speak with them in such a pickle of rags and dirt; and if I had asked for the house of such a man as Mr. Rankeillor, I supposed they would have burst out laughing in my face. So I went up and down, and through the street, and down to the harbour-side, like a dog that has lost its master, with a strange gnawing in my inwards, and every now and then a movement of despair. It grew to be high day at last, perhaps nine in the forenoon; and I was worn with these wanderings, and chanced to have stopped in front of a very good house on the landward side, a house with beautiful, clear glass windows, flowering knots upon the sills, the walls new-harled,[1] and a chase-dog sitting yawning on the step like one that was at home. Well, I was even envying this dumb brute, when the door fell open and there issued forth a

---

1 Newly rough-cast.

shrewd, ruddy, kindly consequential man in a well-powdered wig and spectacles. I was in such a plight that no one set eyes on me once, but he looked at me again; and this gentleman, as it proved, was so much struck with my poor appearance that he came straight up to me and asked me what I did.

I told him I was come to the Queensferry on business, and taking heart of grace, asked him to direct me to the house of Mr. Rankeillor.

'Why,' said he, 'that is his house that I have just come out of; and for a rather singular chance, I am that very man.'

'Then, sir,' said I, 'I have to beg the favour of an interview.'

'I do not know your name,' said he, 'nor yet your face.'

'My name is David Balfour,' said I.

'David Balfour?' he repeated, in rather a high tone, like one surprised. 'And where have you come from, Mr. David Balfour?' he asked, looking me pretty drily in the face.

'I have come from a great many strange places, sir,' said I; 'but I think it would be as well to tell you where and how in a more private manner.'

He seemed to muse awhile, holding his lip in his hand, and looking now at me and now upon the causeway of the street.

'Yes,' says he, 'that will be the best, no doubt.' And he led me back with him into his house, cried out to someone whom I could not see that he would be engaged all morning, and brought me into a little dusty chamber full of books and documents. Here he sate down, and bade me be seated; though I thought he looked a little ruefully from his clean chair to my muddy rags. 'And now,' says he, 'if you have any business, pray be brief and come swiftly to the point. *Nec gemino bellum Trojanum orditur ab ovo**—do you understand that?' says he, with a keen look.

'I will even do as Horace says, sir,' I answered, smiling, 'and carry you *in medias res*.' He nodded as if he was well pleased, and indeed his scrap of Latin had been set to test me. For all that, and though I was somewhat encouraged, the blood came in my face when I added: 'I have reason to believe myself some rights on the estate of Shaws.'

He got a paper book out of a drawer and set it before him open. 'Well?' said he.

But I had shot my bolt and sat speechless.

'Come, come, Mr. Balfour,' said he, 'you must continue. Where were you born?'

'In Essendean, sir,' said I, 'the year 1734,* the 12th of March.'

He seemed to follow this statement in his paper book; but what that meant I knew not. 'Your father and mother?' said he.

'My father was Alexander Balfour, schoolmaster of that place,' said I, 'and my mother Grace Pitarrow; I think her people were from Angus.'

'Have you any papers proving your identity?' asked Mr. Rankeillor.

'No, sir,' said I, 'but they are in the hands of Mr. Campbell, the minister, and could be readily produced. Mr. Campbell, too, would give me his word; and for that matter, I do not think my uncle would deny me.'

'Meaning Mr. Ebenezer Balfour?' says he.

'The same,' said I.

'Whom you have seen?' he asked.

'By whom I was received into his own house,' I answered.

'Did you ever meet a man of the name of Hoseason?' asked Mr. Rankeillor.

'I did so, sir, for my sins,' said I; 'for it was by his means and the procurement of my uncle, that I was kidnapped within sight of this town, carried to sea, suffered shipwreck and a hundred other hardships, and stand before you to-day in this poor accoutrement.'

'You say you were shipwrecked,' said Rankeillor; 'where was that?'

'Off the south end of the Isle of Mull,' said I. 'The name of the isle on which I was cast up is the Island Earraid.'

'Ah!' says he smiling, 'you are deeper than me in geography. But so far, I may tell you, this agrees pretty exactly with other informations that I hold. But you say you were kidnapped; in what sense?'

'In the plain meaning of the word, sir,' said I. 'I was on my way to your house, when I was trepanned on board the brig, cruelly struck down, thrown below, and knew no more of anything till we were far at sea. I was destined for the plantations; a fate that, in God's providence, I have escaped.'

'The brig was lost on June the 27th,' says he, looking in his book, 'and we are now at August the 24th. Here is a considerable hiatus, Mr. Balfour, of near upon two months. It has already caused a vast amount of trouble to your friends; and I own I shall not be very well contented until it is set right.'

'Indeed, sir,' said I, 'these months are very easily filled up; but yet before I told my story, I would be glad to know that I was talking to a friend.'

'This is to argue in a circle,' said the lawyer. 'I cannot be convinced till I have heard you. I cannot be your friend till I am properly informed. If you were more trustful, it would better befit your time of life. And you know, Mr. Balfour, we have a proverb in the country that evil-doers are aye evil-dreaders.'

'You are not to forget, sir,' said I, 'that I have already suffered by my trustfulness; and was shipped off to be a slave by the very man that (if I rightly understand) is your employer.'

All this while I had been gaining ground with Mr. Rankeillor, and in proportion as I gained ground, gaining confidence. But at this sally, which I made with something of a smile myself, he fairly laughed aloud.

'No, no,' said he, 'it is not so bad as that. *Fui, non sum.** I *was* indeed your uncle's man of business; but while you (*imberbis juvenis custode remoto*)* were gallivanting in the west, a good deal of water has run under the bridges; and if your ears did not sing, it was not for lack of being talked about. On the very day of your sea disaster, Mr. Campbell stalked into my office, demanding you from all the winds. I had never heard of your existence; but I had known your father; and from matters in my competence (to be touched upon hereafter) I was disposed to fear the worst. Mr. Ebenezer admitted having seen you; declared (what seemed improbable) that he had given you considerable sums; and that you had started for the continent of Europe, intending to fulfil your education, which was probable and praiseworthy. Interrogated how you had come to send no word to Mr. Campbell, he deponed that you had expressed a great desire to break with your past life. Further interrogated where you now were, protested ignorance, but believed you were in Leyden. That is a close sum of his replies. I am not exactly sure that anyone believed him,' continued Mr. Rankeillor with a smile; 'and in particular he so much disrelished some expressions of mine that (in a word) he showed me to the door. We were then at a full stand; for whatever shrewd suspicions we might entertain, we had no shadow of probation. In the very article, comes Captain Hoseason with the story of your drowning; whereupon all fell through; with no consequences but concern to Mr. Campbell, injury to my pocket, and another blot upon your uncle's character, which could very ill afford it. And now, Mr. Balfour,' said he, 'you understand the whole process of these matters, and can judge for yourself to what extent I may be trusted.'

Indeed he was more pedantic that I can represent him, and placed more scraps of Latin in his speech; but it was all uttered with a fine geniality of eye and manner which went far to conquer my distrust. Moreover, I could see he now treated me as if I was myself beyond a doubt; so that first point of my identity seemed fully granted.

'Sir,' said I, 'if I tell you my story, I must commit a friend's life to your discretion. Pass me your word it shall be sacred; and for what touches myself, I would ask no better guarantee than just your face.'

He passed me his word very seriously. 'But,' said he, 'these are rather alarming prolocutions; and if there are in your story any little jostles to the law, I would beg you to bear in mind that I am a lawyer, and pass lightly.'

Thereupon I told him my story from the first, he listening with his spectacles thrust up and his eyes closed, so that I sometimes feared he was asleep. But no such matter! he heard

every word (as I found afterward) with such quickness of
hearing and precision of memory as often surprised me. Even
strange, outlandish Gaelic names, heard for that time only,
he remembered and would remind me of, years after. Yet
when I called Alan Breck in full, we had an odd scene. The
name of Alan had of course rung through Scotland, with
the news of the Appin murder and the offer of the reward;
and it had no sooner escaped me than the lawyer moved in
his seat and opened his eyes.

'I would name no unnecessary names, Mr. Balfour,' said
he; 'above all of Highlanders, many of whom are obnoxious
to the law.'

'Well, it might have been better not,' said I; 'but since
I have let it slip, I may as well continue.'

'Not at all,' said Mr. Rankeillor. 'I am somewhat dull of
hearing, as you may have remarked; and I am far from sure
I caught the name exactly. We will call your friend, if you
please, Mr. Thomson—that there may be no reflections. And
in future, I would take some such way with any Highlander
that you may have to mention—dead or alive.'

By this, I saw he must have heard the name all too clearly
and had already guessed I might be coming to the murder.
If he chose to play this part of ignorance, it was no matter
of mine; so I smiled, said it was no very Highland-sounding
name, and consented. Through all the rest of my story Alan
was Mr. Thomson; which amused me the more, as it was a
piece of policy after his own heart. James Stewart, in like
manner, was mentioned under the style of Mr. Thomson's
kinsman; Colin Campbell passed as a Mr. Glen; and to Cluny,
when I came to that part of my tale, I gave the name of 'Mr.
Jameson, a Highland Chief.' It was truly the most open farce,
and I wondered that the lawyer should care to keep it up; but
after all it was quite in the taste of that age, when there were
two parties in the State, and quiet persons, with no very high
opinions of their own, sought out every cranny to avoid
offence to either.

'Well, well,' said the lawyer, when I had quite done, 'This
is a great epic, a great Odyssey of yours. You must tell it, sir,

in a sound Latinity when your scholarship is riper; or in English if you please, though for my part I prefer the stronger tongue. You have rolled much; *quæ regio in terris**—what parish in Scotland (to make a homely translation) has not been filled with your wanderings? You have shown, besides, a singular aptitude for getting into false positions; and, yes, upon the whole, for behaving well in them. This Mr. Thomson seems to me a gentleman of some choice qualities, though perhaps a trifle bloody-minded. It would please me none the worse, if (with all his merits) he were soused in the North Sea; for the man, Mr. David, is a sore embarrassment. But you are doubtless quite right to adhere to him; indubitably, he adhered to you. *It comes*—we may say—he was your true companion; nor less, *paribus curis vestigia figit,** for I daresay you would both take an orra thought upon the gallows. Well, well, these days are fortunately by; and I think (speaking humanly) that you are near the end of your troubles.'

As he thus moralised on my adventures, he looked upon me with so much humour and benignity that I could scarce contain my satisfaction. I had been so long wandering with lawless people, and making by bed upon the hills and under the bare sky, that to sit once more in a clean, covered house, and to talk amicably with a gentleman in broadcloth, seemed mighty elevations. Even as I thought so, my eye fell on my unseemly tatters, and I was once more plunged in confusion. But the lawyer saw and understood me. He rose, called over the stair to lay another plate, for Mr. Balfour would stay to dinner, and led me into a bedroom in the upper part of the house. Here he set before me water and soap and a comb; and laid out some clothes that belonged to his son; and here, with another apposite tag, he left me to my toilet.

CHAPTER XXVIII

I GO IN QUEST OF MY INHERITANCE

I MADE what change I could in my appearance; and blithe was I to look in the glass and find the beggar-man a thing of the past, and David Balfour came to life again. And yet I was ashamed of the change too, and, above all, of the borrowed clothes. When I had done, Mr. Rankeillor caught me on the stair, made me his compliments, and had me again into the cabinet.

'Sit ye down, Mr. David,' said he, 'and now that you are looking a little more like yourself, let me see if I can find you any news. You will be wondering, no doubt, about your father and your uncle? To be sure it is a singular tale; and the explanation is one that I blush to have to offer you. For,' says he, really with embarrassment, 'the matter hinges on a love affair.'

'Truly,' said I, 'I cannot very well join that notion with my uncle.'

'But your uncle, Mr. David, was not always old,' replied the lawyer, 'and what may perhaps surprise you more, not always ugly. He had a fine, gallant air; people stood in their doors to look after him, as he went by upon a mettle horse. I have seen it with these eyes, and I ingenuously confess, not altogether without envy; for I was a plain lad myself and a plain man's son; and in those days it was a case of *Odi te, qui bellus es, Sabelle.*'*

'It sounds like a dream,' said I.

'Ay, ay,' said the lawyer, 'that is how it is with youth and age. Nor was that all, but he had a spirit of his own that seemed to promise great things in the future. In 1715, what must he do but run away to join the rebels? It was your father that pursued him, found him in a ditch, and brought him back *multum gementem;** to the mirth of the whole county. However, *majora canamus**—the two lads fell in love, and that with the same lady. Mr. Ebenezer, who was the admired and the beloved, and the spoiled one, made, no doubt, mighty certain of the victory, and when he found he had deceived himself, screamed like a peacock. The whole country heard of it; now he lay sick at home, with his silly family standing round the bed in tears; now he rode from public-house to public-house, and shouted his sorrows into the lug of Tom, Dick, and Harry. Your father, Mr. David, was a kind gentleman; but he was weak, dolefully weak; took all this folly with a long countenance; and one day—by your leave—resigned the lady. She was no such fool, however; it's from her you must inherit your excellent good sense; and she refused to be bandied from one to another. Both got upon their knees to her; and the upshot of the matter for that while was that she showed both of them the door. That was in August; dear me! the same year I came from college. The scene must have been highly farcical.'

I thought myself it was a silly business, but I could not forget my father had a hand in it. 'Surely, sir, it had some note of tragedy,' said I.

'Why, no, sir, not at all,' returned the lawyer. 'For tragedy implies some ponderable matter in dispute, some *dignus vindice nodus;** and this piece of work was all about the petulance of a young ass that had been spoiled, and wanted nothing so much as to be tied up and soundly belted. However, that was not your father's view; and the end of it was, that from concession to concession on your father's part, and from one height to another of squalling, sentimental selfishness upon your uncle's, they came at last to drive a sort of bargain, from whose ill results you have recently been smarting. The one man took the lady, the other the estate. Now, Mr. David, they talk a great deal of charity and generosity; but in this disputable state of life, I often think the happiest consequences seem to flow when a gentleman consults his lawyer and takes all the law allows him. Anyhow, this piece of Quixotry upon your father's part, as it was unjust in itself, has brought forth a monstrous family of injustices. Your father and mother lived and died poor folk; you were poorly reared; and in the meanwhile, what a time it has been for the tenants on the estate of Shaws! And I might add (if it was a matter I cared much about)) what a time for Mr. Ebenezer!'

'And yet that is certainly the strangest part of all,' said I, 'that a man's nature should thus change.'

'True,' said Mr. Rankeillor. 'And yet I imagine it was natural enough. He could not think that he had played a handsome part. Those who knew the story gave him the cold shoulder; those who knew it not, seeing one brother disappear, and the other succeed in the estate, raised a cry of murder; so that upon all sides, he found himself evited. Money was all he got by his bargain; well, he came to think the more of money. He was selfish when he was young, he is selfish now that he is old; and the latter end of all these pretty manners and fine feelings you have seen for yourself.'

'Well sir,' said I, 'and in all this, what is my position?'

'The estate is yours beyond a doubt,' replied the lawyer. 'It matters nothing what your father signed, you are the heir of entail. But your uncle is a man to fight the indefensible; and it would be likely your identity that he would call in question. A lawsuit is always expensive, and a family lawsuit always scandalous; besides which, if any of your doings with your friend Mr. Thomson* were to come out, we might find that we had burned our fingers. The kidnapping, to be sure, would be a court card upon our side, if we could only prove it. But it may be difficult to prove; and my advice (upon the whole) is to make a very easy bargain with your uncle, perhaps even leaving him at Shaws where he has taken root for a quarter of a century, and contenting yourself in the meanwhile with a fair provision.'

I told him I was very willing to be easy, and that to carry family concerns before the public was a step from which I was naturally much averse. In the meantime (thinking to myself) I began to see the outlines of that scheme on which we afterwards acted.

'The great affair,' I asked, 'is to bring home to him the kidnapping?'

'Surely,' said Mr. Rankeillor, 'and if possible, out of court.

For mark you here, Mr. David: we could no doubt find some men of the *Covenant* who would swear to your reclusion; but once they were in the box, we could no longer check their testimony, and some word of your friend Mr. Thomson must certainly crop out. Which (from what you have let fall) I cannot think to be desirable.'

'Well, sir,' said I, 'here is my way of it.' And I opened my plot to him.

'But this would seem to involve my meeting the man Thomson?' says he, when I had done.

'I think so, indeed, sir,' said I.

'Dear doctor!' cries he, rubbing his brow. 'Dear doctor! No, Mr. David, I am afraid your scheme is inadmissible. I say nothing against your friend Mr. Thomson; I know nothing against him; and if I did—mark this, Mr. David!—it would be my duty to lay hands on him. Now I put it to you: is it wise to meet? He may have matters to his charge. He may not have told you all. His name may not be even Thomson!' cries the lawyer, twinkling; 'for some of these fellows will pick up names by the roadside as another would gather haws.'

'You must be the judge, sir,' said I.

But it was clear my plan had taken hold upon his fancy, for he kept musing to himself till we were called to dinner and the company of Mrs. Rankeillor; and that lady had scarce left us again to ourselves and a bottle of wine, ere he was back harping on my proposal. When and where was I to meet my friend Mr. Thomson; was I sure of Mr. T.'s discretion; supposing we could catch the old fox tripping, would I consent to such and such a term of an agreement—these and the like questions he kept asking at long intervals, while he thoughtfully rolled his wine upon his tongue. When I had answered all of them, seemingly to his content-ment, he fell into a still deeper muse, even the claret being now forgotten. Then he got a sheet of paper and a pencil, and set to work writing and weighing every word; and at last touched a bell and had his clerk into the chamber.

'Torrance,' said he, 'I must have this written out fair against to-night; and when it is done, you will be so kind as put on your hat and be ready to come along with this gentleman and me, for you will probably be wanted as a witness.'

'What, sir,' cried I, as soon as the clerk was gone, 'are you to venture it?'

'Why, so it would appear,' says he, filling his glass. 'But let us speak no more of business. They very sight of Torrance brings in my head a little, droll matter of some years ago, when I had made a tryst with the poor oaf at the cross of Edinburgh. Each had gone his proper errand; and when it came four o'clock, Torrance had been taking a glass and did not know his master, and I, who had forgot my spectacles, was so blind without them, that I give you my word I did not know my own clerk.' And thereupon he laughed heartily.

I said it was an odd chance, and smiled out of politeness; but what held me all the afternoon in wonder, he kept returning and dwelling on this story, and telling it again with fresh details and laughter, so that I began at last to be quite put out of countenance* and feel ashamed for my friend's folly.

Towards the time I had appointed with Alan, we set out from the house, Mr. Rankeillor and I arm in arm, and Torrance following behind with the deed in his pocket and a covered basket in his hand. All through the town, the lawyer was bowing right and left, and continually being button-holed by gentlemen on matters of burgh or private business; and I could see he was one greatly looked up to in the county. At last we were clear of the houses, and began to go along the side of the haven and towards the Hawes Inn and the ferry pier, the scene of my misfortune. I could not look upon the place without emotion, recalling how many that had been there with me that day were now no more: Ransome taken, I could hope, from the evil to come; Shuan passed where I dared not follow him; and the poor souls that had gone down with the brig in her last plunge. All these, and the brig herself, I had outlived; and come through these hardships and fearful perils without scathe.

My only thought should have been of gratitude; and yet I could not behold the place without sorrow for others and a chill of recollected fear.

I was so thinking when, upon a sudden, Mr. Rankeillor cried out, clapped his hand to his pockets, and began to laugh.

'Why,' he cries, 'if this be not a farcical adventure! After all that I said, I have forgot my glasses!'

At that, of course, I understood the purpose of his anecdote, and knew that if he had left his spectacles at home, it had been done on purpose, so that he might have the benefit of Alan's help without the awkwardness of recognising him. And indeed it was well thought upon; for now (suppose things to go the very worst) how could Rankeillor swear to my friend's identity, or how be made to bear damaging evidence against myself? For all that, he had been a long while finding out his want, and had spoken to and recognised a good few persons as we came through the town; and I had little doubt myself that he saw reasonably well.

As soon as we were past the Hawes (where I recognised the landlord smoking his pipe in the door, and was amazed to see him look no older) Mr. Rankeillor changed the order of march, walking behind with Torrance and sending me forward in the manner of a scout. I went up the hill, whistling from time to time my Gaelic air; and at length I had the pleasure to hear it answered and to see Alan rise from behind a bush. He was somewhat dashed in spirits, having passed a long day alone skulking in the county, and made but a poor meal in an alehouse near Dundas. But at the mere sight of my clothes, he began to brighten up; and as soon as I had told him in what a forward state our matters were, and the part I looked to him to play in what remained, he sprang into a new man.

'And that is a very good notion of yours,' says he; 'and I dare to say that you could lay your hands upon no better man to put it through, than Alan Breck. It is not a thing (mar' ye) that anyone could do, but takes a gentleman of penetration. But it sticks in my head your lawyer-man will be somewhat wearying to see me,' says Alan.

Accordingly I cried and waved on Mr. Rankeillor, who came up alone and was presented to my friend, Mr. Thomson.

'Mr. Thomson, I am pleased to meet you,' said he. 'But I have forgotten my glasses; and our friend, Mr. David here' (clapping me on the shoulder), 'will tell you that I am little better than blind, and that you must not be surprised if I pass you by to-morrow.'

This he said thinking that Alan would be pleased; but the Highlandman's vanity was ready to startle at a less matter than that.

'Why, sir,' says he, stiffly, 'I would say it mattered the less as we are met here for a particular end, to see justice done to Mr. Balfour; and by what I can see, not very likely to have much else in common. But I accept your apology, which was a very proper one to make.'

'And that is more than I could look for, Mr. Thomson,' said Rankeillor, heartily. 'And now as you and I are the chief actors in this enterprise, I think we should come into a nice agreement; to which end, I propose that you should lend me your arm, for (what with the dusk and the want of my glasses) I am not very clear as to the path; and as for you, Mr. David, you will find Torrance a pleasant kind of body to speak with. Only let me remind you it's quite needless he should hear more of your adventures or those of—ahem—Mr. Thomson.'

Accordingly these two went on ahead in very close talk, and Torrance and I brought up the rear.

Night was quite come when we came in view of the house of Shaws. Ten had been gone some time; it was dark and mild, with a pleasant, rustling wind in the south-west that covered the sound of our approach; and as we drew near we saw no glimmer of light in any portion of the building. It seemed my uncle was already in bed, which was indeed the best thing for our arrangements. We made our last whispered consultations some fifty yards away; and then the lawyer and Torrance and I crept quietly up and crouched down beside the corner of the house; and as soon as we were in our places, Alan strode to the door without concealment and began to knock.

CHAPTER XXIX

I COME INTO MY KINGDOM

FOR some time Alan volleyed upon the door, and his knocking only roused the echoes of the house and neighbourhood. At last, however, I could hear the noise of a window gently thrust up, and knew that my uncle had come to his observatory. By what light there was, he would see Alan standing, like a dark shadow, on the steps; the three witnesses were hidden quite out of his view; so that there was nothing to alarm an honest man in his own house. For all that, he studied his visitor awhile in silence, and when he spoke his voice had a quaver of misgiving.

'What's this?' says he. 'This is nae kind of time of night for decent folk; and I hae nae trokings[1] wi' nighthawks. What brings ye here? I have a blunderbush.'

'Is that yoursel', Mr. Balfour?' returned Alan, stepping back and looking up into the darkness. 'Have a care with that blunderbuss; they're nasty things to burst.'

'What brings ye here? and whae are ye?' says my uncle, angrily.

'I have no manner of inclination to rowt out my name to the countryside,' said Alan; 'but what brings me here is another story, being more of your affairs than mine; and if ye're sure it's what ye would like, I'll set it to a tune and sing it to you.'

'And what is't?' asked my uncle.

'David,' says Alan.

'What was that?' cried my uncle, in a mighty changed voice.

[1] Dealings.

'Shall I give ye the rest of the name, then?' said Alan.

There was a pause; and then, 'I'm thinking I'll better let ye in,' says my uncle, doubtfully.

'I daresay that,' said Alan; 'but the point is, Would I go? Now I will tell you what I am thinking. I am thinking that it is here upon this doorstep that we must confer upon this business; and it shall be here or nowhere at all whatever; for I would have you to understand that I am as stiff-necked as yoursel', and a gentleman of better family.'

This change of note disconcerted Ebenezer; he was a little while digesting it; and then says he, 'Weel, weel, what must be must,' and shut the window. But it took him a long time to get down-stairs, and a still longer to undo the fastenings, repenting (I dare say) and taken with fresh claps of fear at every second step and every bolt and bar. At last, however, we heard the creak of the hinges, and it seems my uncle slipped gingerly out and (seeing that Alan had stepped back a pace or two) sate him down on the top doorstep with the blunderbuss ready in his hands.

'And now,' says he, 'mind I have my blunderbush, and if ye take a step nearer ye're as good as deid.'

'And a very civil speech,' says Alan, 'to be sure.'

'Na,' says my uncle, 'but this is no a very chancy kind of a proceeding, and I'm bound to be prepared. And now that we understand each other, ye'll can name your business.'

'Why,' says Alan, 'you that are a man of so much understanding, will doubtless have perceived that I am an Hieland gentleman. My name has nae business in my story; but the country of my friends is no very far from the Isle of Mull, of which ye will have heard. It seems there was a ship lost in those parts; and the next day a gentleman of my family was seeking wreck-wood for his fire along the sands, when he came upon a lad that was half drowned. Well, he brought him to; and he and some other gentlemen took and clapped him in an auld, ruined castle, where from that day to this he has been a great expense to my friends. My friends are a wee wild-like, and not so particular about the law as some

that I could name; and finding that the lad owned some
decent folk, and was your born nephew, Mr. Balfour, they
asked me to give ye a bit call and to confer upon the matter.
And I may tell ye at the off-go, unless we can agree upon
some terms, ye are little likely to set eyes upon him. For my
friends,' added Alan, simply, 'are no very well off.'

My uncle cleared his throat. 'I'm no very caring,' says
he. 'He wasnae a good lad at the best of it, and I've nae call
to interfere.'

'Ay, ay,' said Alan, 'I see what ye would be at: pretending ye don't care, to make the ransom smaller.'

'Na,' said my uncle, 'it's the mere truth. I take nae
manner of interest in the lad, and I'll pay nae ransom, and
ye can make a kirk and a mill of him for what I care.'

'Hoot, sir,' says Alan. 'Blood's thicker than water, in the
deil's name! Ye cannae desert your brother's son for the fair
shame of it; and if ye did, and it came to be kennt, ye
wouldnae be very popular in your countryside, or I'm the
more deceived.'

'I'm no just very popular the way it is,' returned
Ebenezer; 'and I dinnae see how it would come to be kennt.
No by me, onyway; nor yet by you or your friends. So that's
idle talk, my buckie,' says he.

'Then it'll have to be David that tells it,' said Alan.

'How that?' says my uncle, sharply.

'Ou, just this way,' says Alan. 'My friends would doubtless keep your nephew as long as there was any likelihood
of siller to be made of it, but there was nane, I am clearly
of opinion they would let him gang where he pleased, and
be damned to him!'

'Ay, but I'm no very caring about that either,' said my
uncle. 'I wouldnae be muckle made up with that.'

'I was thinking that,' said Alan.

'And what for why?' asked Ebenezer.

'Why, Mr. Balfour,' replied Alan, 'by all that I could
hear, there were two ways of it: either ye liked David and
would pay to get him back; or else ye had very good reasons
for not wanting him, and would pay for us to keep him. It

seems it's not the first; well then, it's the second; and blythe am I to ken it, for it should be a pretty penny in my pocket and the pockets of my friends.'

'I dinnae follow ye there,' said my uncle.

'No?' said Alan. 'Well, see here: you dinnae want the lad back; well, what do ye want done with him, and how much will ye pay?'

My uncle made no answer, but shifted uneasily on his seat.

'Come, sir,' cried Alan. 'I would have ye to ken that I am a gentleman; I bear a king's name; I am nae rider to kick my shanks at your hall-door. Either give me an answer in civility, and that out of hand; or by the top of Glencoe, I will ram three feet of iron through your vitals.'

'Eh, man,' cried my uncle, scrambling to his feet, 'give me a meenit! What's like wrong with ye? I'm just a plain man, and nae dancing-master; and I'm trying to be as ceevil as it's morally possible. As for that wild talk, it's fair disrepitable. Vitals, says you! And where would I be with my blunder-bush?' he snarled.

'Powder and your auld hands are but as the snail to the swallow against the bright steel in the hands of Alan,' said the other. 'Before your jottering finger could find the trigger, the hilt would dirl on your breast bane.'

'Eh, man, whae's denying it?' said my uncle. 'Pit it as ye please, hae't your ain way; I'll do naething to cross ye. Just tell me what like ye'll be wanting, and ye'll see that we'll can agree fine.'

'Troth, sir,' said Alan, 'I ask for nothing but plain deal-ing. In two words: do ye want the lad killed or kept?'

'Or, sirs!' cried Ebenezer. 'O, sirs, me! that's no kind of language!'

'Killed or kept?' repeated Alan.

'O keepit, keepit!' wailed my uncle. 'We'll have nae blood shed, if you please.'

'Well,' says Alan, 'as ye please; that'll be the dearer.'

'The dearer?' cries Ebenezer. 'Would ye fyle your hands wi' crime?'

'Hoot!' said Alan, 'they're baith crime, whatever! And the killing's easier, and quicker, and surer. Keeping the lad'll be a fashious[1] job, a fashious, kittle business.'

'I'll have him keepit, though,' returned my uncle. 'I never had naething to do with onything morally wrong; and I'm no gaun to begin to pleasure a wild Hielandman.'

'Ye're unco scrupulous,' sneered Alan.

'I'm a man o' principle,' said Ebenezer, simply; 'and if I have to pay for it, I'll have to pay for it. And besides,' says he, 'ye forget the lad's my brother's son.'

'Well, well,' said Alan, 'and now about the price. It's no very easy for me to set a name upon it; I would first have to ken some small matters. I would have to ken, for instance, what ye gave Hoseason at the first off-go?'

'Hoseason!' cries my uncle, struck aback. 'What for?'

'For kidnapping David,' says Alan.

'It's a lee, it's a black lee!' cried my uncle. 'He was never kidnapped. He leed in his throat that tauld ye that. Kidnapped? He never was!'

'That's no fault of mine nor yet of yours,' said Alan; 'nor yet of Hoseason's, if he's a man that can be trusted.'

'What do ye mean?' cried Ebenezer. 'Did Hoseason tell ye?'

'Why, ye donnered auld runt, how else would I ken?' cried Alan. 'Hoseason and I are partners; we gang shares; so ye can see for yoursel', what good ye can do leeing. And I must plainly say ye drove a fool's bargain when ye let a man like the sailor-man so far forward in your private matters. But that's past praying for; and ye must lie on your bed the way ye made it. And the point in hand is just this: what did ye pay him?'

'Has he tauld ye himsel',' asked my uncle.

'That's my concern,' said Alan.

'Weel,' said my uncle, 'I dinnae care what he said, he leed, and the solemn God's truth is this, that I gave him twenty pound. But I'll be perfec'ly honest with ye: forby that, he

1 Troublesome.

was to have the selling of the lad in Caroliny, whilk would be as muckle mair, but no from my pocket, ye see.'

'Thank you, Mr. Thomson. That will do excellently well,' said the lawyer, stepping forward; and then mighty civilly, 'Good evening, Mr. Balfour,' said he.

And, 'Good evening, uncle Ebenezer,' said I.

And 'It's a braw nicht, Mr. Balfour,' added Torrance.

Never a word said my uncle, neither black nor white; but just sat where he was on the top doorstep and stared upon us like a man turned to stone. Alan filched away his blunderbuss; and the lawyer, taking him by the arm, plucked him up from the doorstep, led him into the kitchen, whither we all followed, and set him down in a chair beside the hearth, where the fire was out and only a rushlight burning.

There we all looked upon him for awhile, exulting greatly in our success, but yet with a sort of pity for the man's shame.

'Come, come, Mr. Ebenezer,' said the lawyer, 'you must not be down-hearted, for I promise you we shall make easy terms. In the meanwhile give us the cellar key, and Torrance shall draw us a bottle of your father's wine in honour of the event.' Then, turning to me and taking me by the hand, 'Mr. David,' says he, 'I wish you all joy in your good fortune, which I believe to be deserved.' And then to Alan, with a spice of drollery, 'Mr. Thomson, I pay you my compliment; it was most artfully conducted; but in one point you somewhat outran my comprehension. Do I understand your name to be James? or Charles? or is it George perhaps?'

'And why should it be any of the three, sir?' quoth Alan, drawing himself up, like one who smelt an offence.

'Only, sir, that you mentioned a king's name,' replied Rankeillor; 'and as there has never yet been a King Thomson, or his fame at least has never come my way, I judged you must refer to that you had in baptism.'

This was just the stab that Alan would feel keenest, and I am free to confess he took it very ill. Not a word would he answer, but stepped off to the far end of the kitchen, and sat down and sulked; and it was not till I stepped after him, and gave him my hand, and thanked him by title as the chief spring of my success, that he began to smile a bit, and was at last prevailed upon to join our party.

By that time we had the fire lighted, and a bottle of wine uncorked; a good supper came out of the basket, to which Torrance and I and Alan set ourselves down; while the lawyer and my uncle passed into the next chamber to consult. They stayed there closeted about an hour; at the end of which period they had come to a good understanding, and my uncle and I set our hands to the agreement in a formal manner. By the terms of this, my uncle bound himself to satisfy Rankeillor as to his intromissions, and to pay me two clear thirds of the yearly income of Shaws.

So the beggar in the ballad had come home; and when I lay down that night on the kitchen chests, I was a man of means and had a name in the country. Alan and Torrance and Rankeillor slept and snored on their hard beds; but for me, who had lain out under heaven and upon dirt and stones, so many days and nights, and often with an empty belly, and in fear of death, this good change in my case unmanned me more than any of the former evil ones; and I lay till dawn, looking at the fire on the roof and planning the future.

CHAPTER XXX

GOOD-BYE

So far as I was concerned myself, I had come to port; but I had still Alan, to whom I was much beholden, on my hands; and I felt besides a heavy charge in the matter of the murder and James of the Glens. On both these heads I unbosomed to Rankeillor the next morning, walking to and fro about six of the clock before the house of Shaws, and with nothing in view but the fields and woods that had been

my ancestors' and were now mine. Even as I spoke on these
grave subjects, my eye would take a glad bit of a run over
the prospect, and my heart jump with pride.

About my clear duty to my friend, the lawyer had no
doubt; I must help him out of the county at whatever risk;
but in the case of James, he was of a different mind.

'Mr. Thomson,' says he, 'is one thing, Mr. Thomson's
kinsman quite another. I know little of the facts; but I
gather that a great noble (whom we will call, if you like, the
D. of A.)[1] has some concern and is even supposed to feel
some animosity in the matter. The D. of A. is doubtless an
excellent nobleman; but, Mr. David, *timeo qui nocuere
deos*.* If you interfere to baulk his vengeance, you should
remember there is one way to shut your testimony out; and
that is to put you in the dock. There, you would be in the
same pickle as Mr. Thomson's kinsman. You will object that
you are innocent; well, but so is he. And to be tried for your
life before a Highland jury, on a Highland quarrel and with
a Highland judge upon the bench, would be a brief transition to the gallows.'

Now I had made all these reasonings before and found no
very good reply to them; so I put on all the simplicity I
could. 'In that case, sir,' said I, 'I would just have to be
hanged—would I not?'

'My dear boy,' cries he, 'go in God's name, and do what
you think is right. It is a poor thought that at my time of
life I should be advising you to choose the safe and shameful; and I take it back with an apology. Go and do your
duty; and be hanged, if you must, like a gentleman. There
are worse things in the world than to be hanged.'

'Not many, sir,' said I, smiling.

'Why, yes, sir,' he cried, 'very many. And it would be ten
times better for your uncle (to go no farther afield) if he
were dangling decently upon a gibbet.'

Thereupon he turned into the house (still in a great
fervour of mind, so that I saw I had pleased him heartily)

1 The Duke of Argyle.

and there he wrote me two leetters, making his comments on them as he wrote.

'This,' says he, 'is to my bankers, the British Linen Company, placing a credit to your name. Consult Mr. Thomson, he will know of ways; and you, with this credit, can supply the means. I trust you will be a good husband of your money; but in the affair of a friend like Mr. Thomson, I would be even prodigal. Then, for his kinsman, there is no better way than that you should seek the Advocate, tell him your tale, and offer testimony; whether he may take it or not, is quite another matter, and will turn on the D. of A. Now that you may reach the Lord Advocate well recommended, I give you here a letter to a namesake of your own, the learned Mr. Balfour of Pilrig,* a man whom I esteem. It will look better that you should be presented by one of your own name; and the laird of Pilrig is much looked up to in the Faculty and stands well with Lord Advocate Grant;* I would not trouble him, if I were you, with any particulars; and (do you know?) I think it would be needless to refer to Mr. Thomson. Form yourself upon the laird, he is a good model; when you deal with the Advocate, be discreet; and in all these matters, may the Lord guide you, Mr. David!'

Thereupon he took his farewell, and set out with Torrance for the Ferry, while Alan and I turned our faces for the city of Edinburgh. As we went by the footpath and beside the gateposts and the unfinished lodge, we kept looking back at the house of my fathers. It stood there, bare and great and smokeless, like a place not lived in; only in one of the top windows, there was the peak of a nightcap bobbing up and down and back and forward, like the head of a rabbit from a burrow. I had little welcome when I came, and less kindness while I stayed; but at least I was watched as I went away.

Alan and I went slowly forward upon our way, having little heart either to walk or speak. The same thought was uppermost in both, that we were near the time of our parting; the remembrance of all the bygone days sate upon us sorely. We talked indeed of what should be done; and it was resolved that Alan should keep to the county, biding now here, now there, but coming once in a day to a particular place where I might be able to communicate with him, either in my own person or by messenger. In the meanwhile, I was to seek out a lawyer, who was an Appin Stewart, and a man therefore to be wholly trusted; and it should be his part to find a ship and to arrange for Alan's safe embarkation. No sooner was this business done, than the words seemed to leave us; and though I would seek to jest with Alan under the name of Mr. Thomson, and he with me on my new clothes and my estate, you could feel very well that we were nearer tears than laughter.

We came the by-way over the hill of Corstorphine; and when we got near to the place called Rest-and-be-Thankful, and looked down on Corstorphine bogs and over to the city and the castle on the hill, we both stopped, for we both knew without a word said, that we had come to where our ways parted. Here he repeated to me once again what had been agreed upon between us: the address of the lawyer, the daily hour at which Alan might be found, and the signals that were to be made by any that came seeking him. Then I gave what money I had (a guinea or two of Rankeillor's) so that he should not starve in the meanwhile; and then we stood a space, and looked over at Edinburgh in silence.

'Well, good-bye,' said Alan, and held out his left hand.

'Good-bye,' said I, and gave the hand a little grasp, and went off down hill.

Neither one of us looked the other in the face, nor so long as he was in my view did I take one back glance at the friend I was leaving. But as I went on my way to the city, I felt so lost and lonesome, that I could have found it in my heart to sit down by the dyke, and cry and weep like any baby.

It was coming near noon when I passed in by the West Kirk and the Grassmarket into the streets of the capital. The huge height of the buildings, running up to ten and fifteen storeys, the narrow arched entries that continually vomited

CATRIONA

Being Memoirs of the Further Adventures of David
Balfour at Home and Abroad; In which are set forth
his Misfortunes anent the Appin Murder; his
Troubles with Lord Advocate Grant; Captivity on
the Bass Rock; Journey into Holland and France;
and singular Relations with James More Drummond or Macgregor, a Son of the notorious Rob
Roy, and his Daughter Catriona. Written by
Himself, and now set forth by

ROBERT LOUIS STEVENSON

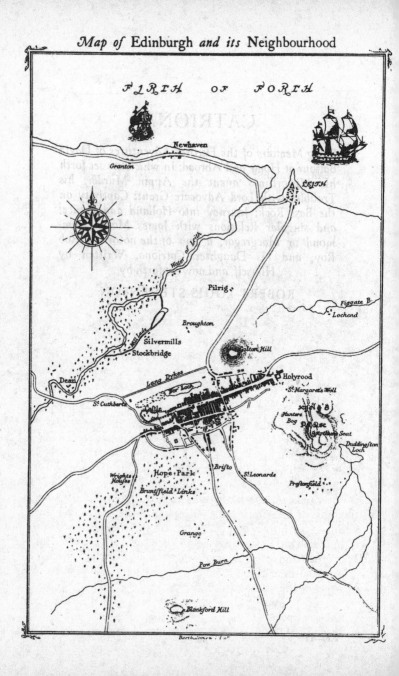

FIRTH OF FORTH

Newhaven

Granton

LEITH

Water of Leith

Pilrig

Figgate B.
Lochend

Broughton

Mill Lade

Silvermills

Stockbridge

Calton Hill

Holyrood

St. Margaret's Well

Dean

Lang Dykes

Nor' Loch

St. Cuthbert's

Castle

Hunter's Bog

Arthur's Seat

Duddingston Loch

Wrights Houses

Hope Park

Bristo

St. Leonards

Prestonfield

Bruntsfield Links

Grange

Pow Burn

Blackford Hill

Bartholomew Edr.

DEDICATION

To

CHARLES BAXTER, Writer to the Signet.

MY DEAR CHARLES,

It is the fate of sequels to disappoint those who have waited for them; and my David, having been left to kick his heels for more than a lustre in the British Linen Company's office, must expect his late re-appearance to be greeted with hoots, if not with missiles. Yet, when I remember the days of our explorations, I am not without hope. There should be left in our native city some seed of the elect; some long-legged, hot-headed youth must repeat to-day our dreams and wanderings of so many years ago; he will relish the pleasure, which should have been ours, to follow among named streets and numbered houses the country walks of David Balfour, to identify Dean, and Silvermills, and Broughton, and Hope Park, and Pilrig, and poor old Lochend—if it still be standing, and the Figgate Whins—if there be any of them left; or to push (on a long holiday) so far afield as Gillane or the Bass. So, perhaps, his eye shall be opened to behold the series of the generations, and he shall weigh with surprise his momentous and nugatory gift of life.

You are still—as when first I saw, as when I last addressed you—in the venerable city which I must always think of as my home. And I have come so far; and the sights and thoughts of my youth pursue me; and I see like a vision the youth of my father, and of his father, and the whole stream of lives flowing down there far in the north, with the sound of laughter and tears, to cast me out in the end, as by a sudden freshet, on these ultimate islands. And I admire and bow my head before the romance of destiny.

R. L. S.

Vailima, Upolu,
Samoa, 1892.

CONTENTS

PART I

THE LORD ADVOCATE

PART II

FATHER AND DAUGHTER

CATRIONA

PART I

THE LORD ADVOCATE

CHAPTER I

A BEGGAR ON HORSEBACK

THE 25th day of August, 1751, about two in the afternoon, I, David Balfour, came forth of the British Linen Company, a porter attending me with a bag of money, and some of the chief of these merchants bowing me from their doors. Two days before, and even so late as yester-morning, I was like a beggar-man by the wayside, clad in rags, brought down to my last shillings, my companion a condemned traitor, a price set on my own head for a crime with the news of which the country rang. To-day I was served heir to my position in life, a landed laird, a bank porter by me carrying my gold, recommendations in my pocket, and (in the words of the saying) the ball directly at my foot.

There were two circumstances that served me as ballast to so much sail. The first was the very difficult and deadly business I had still to handle; the second, the place that I was in. The tall, black city,* and the numbers and movement and noise of so many folk, made a new world for me, after the moorland braes, the sea-sands and the still countrysides that I had frequented up to then. The throng of the citizens in particular abashed me. Rankeillor's son was short and small in the girth; his clothes scarce held on me; and it was plain I was ill qualified to strut in the front of a bank-porter. It was plain, if I did so, I should but set folk laughing, and (what was worse in my case) set them asking questions. So that I behoved to come by some clothes of my own, and in the meanwhile to walk by the porter's side, and put my hand on his arm as though we were a pair of friends.

At a merchant's in the Luckenbooths I had myself fitted out: none too fine, for I had no idea to appear like a beggar on horseback; but comely and responsible, so that servants should respect me. Thence to an armourer's, where I got a plain sword, to suit with my degree in life. I felt safer with the weapon, though (for one so ignorant of defence) it might be called an added danger. The porter, who was naturally a man of some experience, judged my accoutrement to be well chosen.

'Naething kenspeckle,'[1] said he; 'plain, dacent claes. As for the rapier, nae doubt it sits wi' your degree; but an I had been you, I would hae waired my siller better-gates than that.' And he proposed I should buy winter-hosen from a wife in the Cowgate-back, that was a cousin of his own, and made them 'extraordinar endurable.'

But I had other matters on my hand more pressing. Here I was in this old, black city, which was for all the world like a rabbit-warren, not only by the number of its indwellers, but the complication of its passages and holes. It was indeed a place where no stranger had a chance to find a friend, let be another stranger. Suppose him even to hit on the right close, people dwelt so thronged in these tall houses, he might very well seek a day before he chanced on the right door. The ordinary course was to hire a lad they called a *caddie*, who was like a guide or pilot, led you where you had occasion, and (your errands being done) brought you again where you were lodging. But these caddies, being always employed in the same sort of services, and having it for obligation to be well informed of every house and person in the city, had grown to form a brotherhood of spies; and I knew from tales of Mr. Campbell's how they communicated one with another, what a rage of curiosity they conceived as to their employer's business, and how they were like eyes and fingers to the police. It would be a piece of little wisdom, the way I was now

---

1 Conspicuous.

placed, to tack such a ferret to my tails. I had three visits to
make, all immediately needful: to my kinsman Mr. Balfour of
Pilrig, to Stewart the Writer that was Appin's agent, and to
William Grant Esquire of Prestongrange,* Lord Advocate of
Scotland. Mr. Balfour's was a non-committal visit; and besides
(Pilrig being in the country) I made bold to find the way to it
myself, with the help of my two legs and a Scots tongue. But
the rest were in a different case. Not only was the visit to
Appin's agent, in the midst of the cry about the Appin
murder, dangerous in itself, but it was highly inconsistent
with the other. I was like to have a bad enough time of it with
my Lord Advocate Grant, the best of ways; but to go to him
hot-foot from Appin's agent, was little likely to mend my
own affairs, and might prove the mere ruin of friend Alan's.
The whole thing, besides, gave me a look of running with the
hare and hunting with the hounds that was little to my
fancy. I determined, therefore, to be done at once with Mr.
Stewart and the whole Jacobitical side of my business, and to
profit for that purpose by the guidance of the porter at my
side. But it chanced I had scarce given him the address, when
there came a sprinkle of rain—nothing to hurt, only for my
new clothes—and we took shelter under a pend at the head
of a close or alley.

Being strange to what I saw, I stepped a little farther in.
The narrow paved way descended swiftly. Prodigious tall
houses sprang upon each side and bulged out, one storey
beyond another, as they rose. At the top only a ribbon of
sky showed in. By what I could spy in the windows, and by
the respectable persons that passed out and in, I saw the
houses to be very well occupied; and the whole appearance of
the place interested me like a tale.

I was still gazing, when there came a sudden brisk tramp
of feet in time and clash of steel behind me. Turning quickly,
I was aware of a party of armed soldiers, and, in their midst,
a tall man in a great-coat. He walked with a stoop that was
like a piece of courtesy, genteel and insinuating: he waved
his hands plausibly as he went, and his face was sly and
handsome. I thought his eye took me in, but could not meet

it. This procession went by to a door in the close, which a serving-man in a fine livery set open; and two of the soldier-lads carried the prisoner within, the rest lingering with their firelocks by the door.

There can nothing pass in the streets of a city without some following of idle folk and children. It was so now; but the more part melted away incontinent until but three were left. One was a girl; she was dressed like a lady, and had a screen of the Drummond colours on her head; but her comrades or (I should say) followers were ragged gillies, such as I have seen the matches of by the dozen in my Highland journey. They all spoke together earnestly in Gaelic, the sound of which was pleasant in my ears for the sake of Alan; and, though the rain was by again, and my porter plucked at me to be going, I even drew nearer where they were, to listen. The lady scolded sharply, the others making apologies and cringing before her, so that I made sure she was come of a chief's house. All the while the three of them sought in their pockets, and by what I could make out, they had the matter of half a farthing among the party; which made me smile a little to see all Highland folk alike for fine obeisances and empty sporrans.

It chanced the girl turned suddenly about, so that I saw her face for the first time. There is no greater wonder than the way the face of a young woman fits in a man's mind, and stays there, and he could never tell you why; it just seems it was the thing he wanted. She had wonderful bright eyes like stars, and I dare say the eyes had a part in it; but what I remember the most clearly was the way her lips were a trifle open as she turned. And, whatever was the cause, I stood there staring like a fool. On her side, as she had not known there was anyone so near, she looked at me a little longer, and perhaps with more surprise, than was entirely civil.

It went through my country head she might be wondering at my new clothes; with that, I blushed to my hair, and at the sight of my colouring it is to be supposed she drew her own conclusions, for she moved her gillies farther down the close, and they fell again to this dispute where I could hear no more of it.

I had often admired a lassie before then, if scarce so sudden and strong; and it was rather my disposition to withdraw than to come forward, for I was much in fear of mockery from the womenkind. You would have thought I had now all the more reason to pursue my common practice, since I had met this lady in the city street, seemingly following a prisoner, and accompanied with two very ragged indecent-like Highlandmen. But there was here a different ingredient; it was plain the girl thought I had been prying in her secrets; and with my new clothes and sword, and at the top of my new fortunes, this was more than I could swallow. The beggar on horseback could not bear to be thrust down so low, or, at the least of it, not by this young lady.

I followed, accordingly, and took off my new hat to her the best that I was able.

'Madam,' said I, 'I think it is only fair to myself to let you understand I have no Gaelic. It is true I was listening, for I have friends of my own across the Highland line, and the sound of that tongue comes friendly; but for your private affairs, if you had spoken Greek, I might have had more guess at them.'

She made me a little, distant curtsy. 'There is no harm done,' said she, with a pretty accent, most like the English (but more agreeable). 'A cat may look at a king.'

'I do not mean to offend,' said I. 'I have no skill of city manners; I never before this day set foot inside the doors of Edinburgh. Take me for a country lad—it's what I am; and I would rather I told you than you found it out.'

'Indeed, it will be a very unusual thing for strangers to be speaking to each other on the causeway,' she replied. 'But if you are landward[1] bred it will be different. I am as landward as yourself; I am Highland, as you see, and think myself the farther from my home.'

---

1 Country.

'It is not yet a week since I passed the line,' said I. 'Less than a week ago I was on the braes of Balwhidder.'

'Balwhither?' she cries. 'Come ye from Balwhither? The name of it makes all there is of me rejoice. You will not have been long there, and not known some of our friends or family?'

'I lived with a very honest, kind man called Duncan Dhu Maclaren,' I replied.

'Well I know Duncan, and you give him the true name!' she said; 'and if he is an honest man, his wife is honest indeed.'

'Ay,' said I, 'they are fine people, and the place is a bonny place.'

'Where in the great world is such another?' she cries; 'I am loving the smell of that place and the roots that grow there.'

I was infinitely taken with the spirit of the maid. 'I could be wishing I had brought you a spray of that heather,' says I. 'And though I did ill to speak with you at the first, now it seems we have common acquaintance, I make it my petition you will not forget me. David Balfour is the name I am known by. This is my lucky day, when I have just come into a landed estate, and am not very long out of a deadly peril. I wish you would keep my name in mind for the sake of Balwhidder,' said I, 'and I will yours for the sake of my lucky day.'

'My name is not spoken,' she replied, with a great deal of haughtiness. 'More than a hundred years it has not gone upon men's tongues, save for a blink. I am nameless like the Folk of Peace.[1] Catriona Drummond is the one I use.'

Now indeed I knew where I was standing. In all broad Scotland there was but the one name proscribed. In all broad Scotland there was but the one name proscribed, and that was the name of the Macgregors.* Yet so far from fleeing this undesirable acquaintancy, I plunged the deeper in.

'I have been sitting with one who was in the same case with yourself,' said I, 'and I think he will be one of your friends. They called him Robin Oig.'

1 The Fairies.

'Did ye so?' cries she. 'Ye met Rob?'

'I passed the night with him,' said I.

'He is a fowl of the night,' said she.

'There was a set of pipes there,' I went on, 'so you may judge if the time passed.'

'You should be no enemy, at all events,' said she. 'That was his brother there, a moment since, with the red soldiers round him. It is him that I call father.'

'Is it so?' cried I. 'Are you a daughter of James More's?'

'All the daughter that he has,' says she: 'the daughter of a prisoner; that I should forget it so, even for one hour, to talk with strangers!'

Here one of the gillies addressed her in what he had of English, to know what 'she' (meaning by that himself) was to do about 'ta sneeshin.'* I took some note of him for a short, bandy-legged, red-haired, big-headed man, that I was to know more of to my cost.

'There can be none the day, Neil,' she replied. 'How will you get "sneeshin," wanting siller? It will teach you another time to be more careful; and I think James More will not be very well pleased with Neil of the Tom.'

'Miss Drummond,' I said, 'I told you I was in my lucky day. Here I am, and a bank-porter at my tail. And remember I have had the hospitality of your own country of Balwhidder.'

'It was not one of my people gave it,' said she.

'Ah, well,' said I, ' but I am owing your uncle at least for some springs upon the pipes. Besides which, I have offered myself to be your friend, and you have been so forgetful that you did not refuse me in the proper time.'

'If it had been a great sum, it might have done you honour,' said she; 'but I will tell you what this is. James More lies shackled in prison; but this time past, they will be bringing him down here daily to the Advocate's. . . .'

"The Advocate's?' I cried. 'Is that . . .?'

'It is the house of the Lord Advocate Grant of Prestongrange,' said she. 'There they bring my father one time and another, for what purpose I have no thought in my mind;

but it seems there is some hope dawned for him. All this same time they will not let me be seeing him, nor yet him write; and we wait upon the King's street to catch him; and now we give him his snuff as he goes by, and now something else. And here is this son of trouble, Neil, son of Duncan, has lost my four-penny piece that was to buy that snuff, and James More must go wanting, and will think his daughter has forgotten him.'

I took sixpence from my pocket, gave it to Neil, and bade him go about his errand. Then to her, 'That sixpence came with me by Balwhidder,' said I.

'Ah!' she said, 'you are a friend to the Gregara!'

'I would not like to deceive you either,' said I. 'I know very little of the Gregara and less of James More and his doings, but since the while I have been standing in this close, I seem to know something of yourself; and if you will just say "a friend to Miss Catriona" I will see you are the less cheated.'

'The one cannot be without the other,' said she.

'I will even try,' said I.

'And what will you be thinking of myself?' she cried, 'to be holding my hand to the first stranger!'

'I am thinking nothing but that you are a good daughter,' said I.

'I must not be without repaying it,' she said; 'where is it you stop?'

'To tell the truth, I am stopping nowhere yet,' said I, 'being not full three hours in the city; but if you will give me your direction, I will be so bold as come seeking my sixpence for myself.'

'Will I can trust you for that?' she asked.

'You need have little fear,' said I.

'James More could not bear it else,' said she. 'I stop beyond the village of Dean, on the north side of the water, with Mrs. Drummond-Ogilvy of Allardyce, who is my near friend and will be glad to thank you.'

'You are to see me, then, so soon as what I have to do permits,' said I; and the remembrance of Alan rolling in again upon my mind, I made haste to say farewell.

I could not but think, even as I did so, that we had made extraordinary free upon short acquaintance, and that a really wise young lady would have shown herself more backward. I think it was the bank-porter that put me from this ungallant train of thought.

'I thoucht ye had been a lad of some kind o' sense,' he began, shooting out his lips. 'Ye're no likely to gang far this gate. A fule and his siller's shune parted. Eh, but ye're a green callant!' he cried, 'an' a veecious, tae! Cleikin' up wi' baubeejoes!'

'If you dare to speak of the young lady. . . .' I began.

'Leddy!' he cried. 'Haud us and safe us, whatten leddy? Ca' *thon* a leddy? The toun's fu' o' them. Leddies! Man, it's well seen ye're no very acquaint in Embro!'

A clap of anger took me.

'Here,' said I, 'lead me where I told you, and keep your foul mouth shut!'

He did not wholly obey me for, though he no more addressed me directly, he sang at me as he went in a very impudent manner of innuendo, and with an exceedingly ill voice and ear—

'As Mally Lee cam doun the street, her capuchin did flee,
She cuist a look ahint her to see her negligee.
And we're a' gaun east and wast, we're a' gaun ajee,
We're a' gaun east and wast courtin' Mally Lee.'

CHAPTER II

THE HIGHLAND WRITER

MR. CHARLES STEWART the Writer dwelt at the top of the longest stair that ever mason set a hand to; fifteen flights of it, no less; and when I had come to his door, and a clerk had opened it, and told me his master was within, I had scarce breath enough to send my porter packing.

'Awa' east and wast wi' ye!' said I, took the money bag out of his hands, and followed the clerk in.

The outer room was an office with the clerk's chair at a table spread with law papers. In the inner chamber, which opened from it, a little brisk man sat poring on a deed, from which he scarce raised his eyes upon my entrance; indeed, he still kept his finger in the place, as though prepared to show me out and fall again to his studies. This pleased me little enough; and what pleased me less, I thought the clerk was in a good posture to overhear what should pass between us.

I asked if he was Mr. Charles Stewart the Writer.

'The same,' says he; 'and if the question is equally fair, who may you be yourself?'

'You never heard tell of my name nor of me either,' said I, 'but I bring you a token from a friend that you know well. That you know well,' I repeated, lowering my voice, 'but maybe are not just so keen to hear from at this present being. And the bits of business that I have to propone to you are rather in the nature of being confidential. In short, I would like to think we were quite private.'

He rose without more words, casting down his paper like a man ill-pleased, sent forth his clerk on an errand, and shut-to the house-door behind him.

'Now, sir,' said he, returning, 'speak out your mind and fear nothing; though before you begin,' he cries out, 'I tell you mine misgives me! I tell you beforehand, ye're either a Stewart or a Stewart sent ye. A good name it is, and one it would ill-become my father's son to lightly. But I begin to grue at the sound of it.'

'My name is called Balfour,' said I, 'David Balfour of Shaws. As for him that sent me, I will let his token speak.' And I showed the silver button.

'Put it in your pocket, sir!' cries he. 'Ye need name no names. The deevil's buckie, I ken the button of him! And deil hae't! Where is he now?'

I told him I knew not where Alan was, but he had some sure place (or thought he had) about the north side, where he was to lie until a ship was found for him; and how and where he had appointed to be spoken with.

'It's been always my opinion that I would hang in a tow for this family of mine,' he cried, 'and, dod! I believe the day's come now! Get a ship for him, quot' he! And who's to pay for it? The man's daft!'

'That is my part of the affair, Mr. Stewart,' said I. 'Here is a bag of good money, and if more be wanted, more is to be had where it came from.'

'I needn't ask your politics,' said he.

'Ye need not,' said I, smiling, 'for I'm as big a Whig as grows.'

'Stop a bit, stop a bit,' says Mr. Stewart. 'What's all this? A Whig? Then why are you here with Alan's button? and what kind of a black-foot traffic is this that I find ye out in, Mr. Whig? Here is a forfeited rebel and an accused murderer, with two hundred pounds on his life, and ye ask me to meddle in his business, and then tell me ye're a Whig! I have no mind of any such Whigs before, though I've kent plenty of them.'

'He's a forfeited rebel, the more's the pity,' said I, 'for the man's my friend. I can only wish he had been better guided. And an accused murderer, that he is too, for his misfortune; but wrongfully accused.'

'I hear you say so,' said Stewart.

'More than you are to hear me say so, before long,' said I. 'Alan Breck is innocent, and so is James.'

'Oh!' says he, 'the two cases hang together. If Alan is out, James can never be in.'

Hereupon I told him briefly of my acquaintance with Alan, of the accident that brought me present at the Appin murder, and the various passages of our escape among the heather, and my recovery of my estate. 'So, sir, you have now the whole train of these events,' I went on, 'and can see for yourself how I come to be so much mingled up with the affairs of your family and friends, which (for all of our sakes) I wish had been plainer and less bloody. You can see for yourself, too, that I have certain pieces of business depending, which were scarcely fit to lay before a lawyer chosen at random. No more remains, but to ask you if you will undertake my service.'

'I have no great mind to it; but coming as you do with Alan's button, the choice is scarcely left me,' said he. 'What are your instructions?' he added, and took up his pen

'The first point is to smuggle Alan forth of this country,' said I, 'but I need not be repeating that.'

'I am little likely to forget it,' said Stewart.

'The next thing is the bit money I am owing to Cluny,' I went on. 'It would be ill for me to find a conveyance, but that should be no stick to you. It was two pounds five shilling and three-halfpence farthing sterling.'

He noted it.

'Then,' said I, 'there's a Mr. Henderland, a licensed preacher and missionary in Ardgour, that I would like well to get some snuff into the hands of; and as I daresay you keep touch with your friends in Appin (so near by), it's a job you could doubtless overtake with the other.'

'How much snuff are we to say?' he asked.

'I was thinking of two pounds,' said I.

'Two,' said he.

'Then there's the lass Alison Hastie, in Limekilns,' said I. 'Her that helped Alan and me across the Forth. I was thinking if I could get her a good Sunday gown, such as she could wear with decency in her degree, it would be an ease to my conscience; for the mere truth is, we owe her our two lives.'

'I am glad to see you are thrifty, Mr. Balfour,' says he, making his notes.

'I would think shame to be otherwise the first day of my fortune,' said I. 'And now, if you will compute the outlay and your own proper charges, I would be glad to know if I could get some spending money back. It's not that I grudge the whole of it to get Alan safe; it's not that I lack more; but having drawn so much the one day, I think it would have a very ill appearance if I was back again seeking, the next. Only be sure you have enough,' I added, 'for I am very undesirous to meet with you again.'

'Well, and I'm pleased to see you're cautious too,' said the Writer. 'But I think ye take a risk to lay so considerable a sum at my discretion.'

He said this with a plain sneer.

'I'll have to run the hazard,' I replied. 'O, and there's another service I would ask, and that's to direct me to a lodging, for I have no roof to my head. But it must be a lodging I may seem to have hit upon by accident, for it would never do if the Lord Advocate were to get any jealousy of our acquaintance.'

'Ye may set your weary spirit at rest,' said he. 'I will never name your name, sir; and it's my belief the Advocate is still so much to be sympathised with that he doesnae ken of your existence.'

I saw I had got to the wrong side of the man.

'There's a braw day coming for him, then,' said I, 'for he'll have to learn of it on the deaf side of his head no later than to-morrow, when I call on him.'

'When ye *call* on him!' repeated Mr. Stewart. 'Am I daft, or are you? What takes ye near the Advocate?'

'O, just to give myself up,' said I.

'Mr. Balfour,' he cried, 'are ye making a mock of me?'

'No, sir,' said I, 'though I think you have allowed yourself some such freedom with myself. But I give you to understand once and for all that I am in no jesting spirit.'

'Nor yet me,' says Stewart. 'And I give you to understand (if that's to be the word) that I like the looks of your behaviour less and less. You come here to me with all sorts of propositions, which will put me in a train of very doubtful acts and bring me among very undesirable persons this many a day to come. And then you tell me you're going straight out of my office to make your peace with the Advocate! Alan's button here or Alan's button there, the four quarters of Alan wouldnae bribe me further in.'

'I would take it with a little more temper,' said I, 'and perhaps we can avoid what you object to, I can see no way for it but to give myself up, but perhaps you can see another; and if you could, I could never deny but what I would be rather relieved. For I think my traffic with his lordship is little likely to agree with my health. There's just the one thing clear, that I have to give my evidence; for I hope it'll save Alan's character (what's left of it), and James's neck, which is the more immediate.'

He was silent for a breathing-space, and then, 'My man,' said he, 'you'll never be allowed to give such evidence.'

'We'll have to see about that,' said I; 'I'm stiff-necked when I like.'

'Ye muckle ass!' cried Stewart, 'it's James they want; James has got to hang—Alan too, if they could catch him—but James whatever! Go near the Advocate with any such business, and you'll see! he'll find a way to muzzle ye.'

'I think better of the Advocate than that,' said I.

'The Advocate be damned!' cries he. 'It's the Campbells, man! You'll have the whole clanjamfry of them on your back; and so will the Advocate too, poor body! It's extraordinar ye cannot see where ye stand! If there's no fair way to stop your gab, there's a foul one gaping. They can put ye in the dock, do ye no see that?' he cried, and stabbed me with one finger in the leg.

'Ay,' said I, 'I was told that same no further back than this morning by another lawyer.'

'And who was he?' asked Stewart. 'He spoke sense at least.'

I told him I must be excused from naming him, for he was a decent stout old Whig, and had little mind to be mixed up in such affairs.

'I think all the world seems to be mixed up in it!' cried Stewart. 'But what said you?'

I told him what had passed between Rankeillor and myself before the house of Shaws.

'Well, and so ye will hang!' said he. 'Ye'll hang beside James Stewart. There's your fortune told.'

'I hope better of it yet than that,' said I; 'but I could never deny there was a risk.'

'Risk!' says he, and then sat silent again. 'I ought to thank you for your staunchness to my friends, to whom you show a very good spirit,' he says, 'if you have the strength to stand by it. But I warn you that you're wading deep. I wouldn't put myself in your place (me that's a Stewart born!) for all the Stewarts that ever there were since Noah. Risk! ay, I take over-many: but to be tried in court before a Campbell jury and a Campbell judge, and that in a Campbell country and upon a Campbell quarrel—think what you like of me, Balfour, it's beyond me.'

'It's a different way of thinking, I suppose,' said I; 'I was brought up to this one by my father before me.'

'Glory to his bones! he has left a decent son to his name,' says he. 'Yet I would not have you judge me over-sorely. My case is dooms hard. See, sir, ye tell me ye're a Whig: I wonder what I am. No Whig to be sure; I couldnae be just that. But laigh in your ear, man—I'm maybe no very keen on the other side.'

'Is that a fact?' cried I. 'It's what I would think of a man of your intelligence.'

'Hut! none of your whillywhas!'[1] cries he. 'There's intelligence upon both sides. But for my private part I have no particular desire to harm King George; and as for King James, God bless him! he does very well for me across the water. I'm a lawyer, ye see: fond of my books and my bottle, a good plea, a well-drawn deed, a crack in the Parliament House with other lawyer bodies, and perhaps a turn at the golf on a Saturday at e'en. Where do ye come in with your Hieland plaids and claymores?'

'Well,' said I, 'it's a fact ye have little of the wild Highlandman.'

'Little?' quoth he. 'Nothing, man! And yet I'm Hieland born, and when the clan pipes, who but me has to dance? The clan and the name, that goes by all. It's just what you said yourself; my father learned it to me, and a bonny trade I have of it. Treason and traitors, and the smuggling of them out and in; and the French recruiting, weary fall it! and the smuggling through of the recruits; and their please—a sorrow of their pleas! Here have I been moving one for young Ardshiel, my cousin; claimed the estate under the marriage contract—a forfeited estate! I told them it was nonsense; muckle they cared! And there was I cocking behind a yadvocate that

---

[1] Flatteries.

liked the business as little as myself, for it was fair run to the
pair of us—a black mark, *disaffected*, branded on our hurdies
like folks' names upon their kye! And what can I do? I'm a
Stewart, ye see, and must fend for my clan and family. Then
no later by than yesterday there was one of our Stewart lads
carried to the Castle. What for? I ken fine: Act of 1736:
recruiting for King Lewie.* And you'll see, he'll whistle me
in to be his lawyer, and there'll be another black mark on my
chara'ter! I tell you fair: if I but kent the heid of a Hebrew
word from the hurdies of it, be damned but I would fling the
whole thing up and turn minister!'

'It's rather a hard position,' said I.

'Dooms hard!' cries he. 'And that's what makes me think
so much of ye—you that's no Stewart—to stick your head so
deep in Stewart business. And for what, I do not know:
unless it was the sense of duty.'

'I hope it will be that,' said I.

'Well,' says he, 'it's a grand quality. But here is my clerk
back; and, by your leave, we'll pick a bit of dinner, all the
three of us. When that's done, I'll give you the direction of a
very decent man, that'll be very fain to have you for a lodger.
And I'll fill your pockets to ye, forbye, out of your ain bag.
For this business 'll not be near as dear as ye suppose—not
even the ship part of it.'

I made him a sign that his clerk was within hearing.

'Hoot, ye neednae mind for Robbie,' cries he. 'A Stewart,
too, puir deevil! and has smuggled out more French recruits
and trafficking Papists than what he has hairs upon his face.
Why it's Robin that manages that branch of my affairs. Who
will we have now, Rob, for across the water?'

'There'll be Andie Scougal, in the *Thristle*,' replied Rob.
'I saw Hoseason the other day, but it seems he's wanting the
ship. Then there'll be Tam Stobo; but I'm none so sure of
Tam. I've seen him colloguing with some gey queer acquaintances; and if was anybody important, I would give Tam the
go-by.'

'The head's worth two hundred pounds, Robin,' said
Stewart.

'Gosh, that'll no be Alan Breck?' cried the clerk.

'Just Alan,' said his master.

'Weary winds! that's sayrious,' cried Robin. 'I'll try Andie, then; Andie 'll be the best.'

'It seems it's quite a big business,' I observed.

'Mr. Balfour, there's no end to it,' said Stewart.

'There was a name your clerk mentioned,' I went on: 'Hoseason. That must be my man, I think: Hoseason, of the brig *Covenant*. Would you set your trust on him?'

'He didnae behave very well to you and Alan,' said Mr. Stewart; 'but my mind of the man in general is rather otherwise. If he had taken Alan on board his ship on an agreement, it's my notion he would have proved a just dealer. How say ye, Rob?'

'No more honest skipper in the trade than Eli,' said the clerk. 'I would lippen to[1] Eli's word—ay, if it was the Chevalier, or Appin himsel',' he added.

'And it was him that brought the doctor, wasnae't?' asked the master.

'He was the very man,' said the clerk.

'And I think he took the doctor back?' says Stewart.

'Ay, with his sporran full!' cried Robin. 'And Eli kent of that!'[2]

'Well, it seems it's hard to ken folk rightly,' said I.

'That was just what I forgot when ye came in, Mr. Balfour!' says the Writer

CHAPTER III
I GO TO PILRIG

THE next morning, I was no sooner awake in my new lodging than I was up and into my new clothes; and no sooner the breakfast swallowed, than I was forth on my adventures. Alan, I could hope, was fended for; James was

1 Trust to.

2 This must have reference to Dr. Cameron on the fiist visit.—D.B.

like to be a more difficult affair, and I could not but think
that enterprise might cost me dear, even as everybody said
to whom I had opened my opinion. It seemed I was come
to the top of the mountain only to cast myself down; that
I had clambered up, through so many and hard trials, to be
rich, to be recognised, to wear city clothes and a sword to my
side, all to commit mere suicide at the last end of it, and the
worst kind of suicide besides, which is to get hanged at the
King's charges.

What was I doing it for? I asked, as I went down the High
Street and out north by Leith Wynd. First I said it was to save
James Stewart; and no doubt the memory of his distress, and
his wife's cries, and a word or so I had let drop on that occasion worked upon me strongly. At the same time I reflected
that it was (or ought to be) the most indifferent matter to my
father's son, whether James died in his bed or from a scaffold.
He was Alan's cousin, to be sure; but so far as regarded Alan,
the best thing would be to lie low, and let the King, and his
Grace of Argyll, and the corbie crows, pick the bones of his
kinsman their own way. Nor could I forget that, while
we were all in the pot together, James had shown no such
particular anxiety whether for Alan or me.

Next it came upon me I was acting for the sake of justice:
and I thought that a fine word, and reasoned it out that (since
we dwelt in polities, at some discomfort to each one of us) the
main thing of all must still be justice, and the death of any
innocent man a wound upon the whole community. Next,
again, it was the Accuser of the Brethren that gave me a turn
of his argument; bade me think shame for pretending myself
concerned in these high matters, and told me I was but a
prating vain child, who had spoken big words to Rankeillor
and to Stewart, and held myself bound upon my vanity to
make good that boastfulness. Nay, and he hit me with the
other end of the stick; for he accused me of a kind of artful
cowardice, going about at the expense of a little risk to purchase greater safety. No doubt, until I had declared and
cleared myself, I might any day encounter Mungo Campbell
or the sheriff's officer, and be recognised, and dragged into

the Appin murder by the heels; and, no doubt, in case I could manage my declaration with success, I should breathe more free for ever after. But when I looked this argument full in the face I could see nothing to be ashamed of. As for the rest, 'Here are the two roads,' I thought, 'and both go to the same place. It's unjust that James should hang if I can save him; and it would be ridiculous in me to have talked so much and then do nothing. It's lucky for James of the Glens that I have boasted beforehand; and none so unlucky for myself, because now I'm committed to do right. I have the name of a gentleman and the means of one; it would be a poor discovery that I was wanting in the essence.' And then I thought this was a Pagan spirit, and said a prayer in to myself, asking for what courage I might lack, and that I might go straight to my duty like a soldier to battle, and come off again scatheless as so many do.

This train of reasoning brought me to a more resolved complexion; though it was far from closing up my sense of the dangers that surrounded me, nor of how very apt I was (if I went on) to stumble on the ladder of the gallows. It was a plain, fair morning, but the wind in the east. The little chill of it sang in my blood, and gave me a feeling of the autumn, and the dead leaves, and dead folks' bodies in their graves. It seemed the devil was in it, if I was to die in that tide of my fortunes and for other folks' affairs. On the top of the Calton Hill, though it was not the customary time of year for that diversion, some children were crying and running with their kites. These toys appeared very plain against the sky; I remarked a great one soar on the wind to a high altitude and then plump among the whins; and I thought to myself at sight of it, 'There goes Davie.'

My way lay over Mouter's Hill, and through an end of a clachan on the braeside among fields. There was a whir of looms in it went from house to house; bees bummed in the gardens! the neighbours that I saw at the doorsteps talked in a strange tongue; and I found out later that this was Picardy, a village where the French weavers wrought for the Linen Company. Here I got a fresh direction for Pilrig, my destination; and a little beyond, on the wayside, came by a gibbet and two men hanged in chains. They were dipped in tar, as the manner is; the wind span them, the chains clattered, and the birds hung about the uncanny jumping-jacks and cried. The sight coming on me suddenly, like an illustration of my fears, I could scarce be done with examining it and drinking in discomfort. And as I thus turned and turned about the gibbet, what should I strike on, but a weird old wife, that sat behind a leg of it, and nodded, and talked aloud to herself with becks and courtesies.

'Who are these two, mother?' I asked, and pointed to the corpses.

'A blessing on your precious face!' she cried. 'Twa joes[1] o' mine: just twa o' my old joes, my hinny dear.'

'What did they suffer for?' I asked.

'Ou, just for the guid cause,' said she. 'Aften I spaed to them the way that it would end. Twa shillin' Scots: no pickle mair; and there are twa bonny callants hingin' for 't! They took it frae a wean[2] belanged to Broughton.'

'Ay!' said I to myself, and not to the daft limmer, 'and did they come to such a figure for so poor a business? This is to lose all indeed.'

'Gie's your loof,[3] hinny,' says she, 'and let me spae your weird to ye.'

'No, mother,' said I, 'I see far enough the way I am. It's an unco thing to see too far in front.'

'I read it in your bree,' she said. 'There's a bonnie lassie that has bricht een, and there's a wee man in a braw coat, and a big man in a pouthered wig, and there's the shadow of the wuddy,[4] joe, that lies braid across your path. Gie's your loof, hinny, and let Auld Merren spae it to ye bonny.'*

The two chance shots that seemed to point at Alan and the daughter of James More struck me hard; and I fled from the eldritch creature, casting her a baubee, which she continued to sit and play with under the moving shadows of the hanged.

1 Sweethearts.   2 Child.   3 Palm.   4 Gallows.

My way down the causeway of Leith Walk would have been more pleasant to me but for this encounter. The old rampart ran among fields, the like of them I had never seen for artfulness of agriculture; I was pleased, besides, to be so far in the still countryside; but the shackles of the gibbet clattered in my head; and the mops and mows of the old witch, and the thought of the dead men, hag-rode my spirits. To hang on a gallows, that seemed a hard case; and whether a man came to hang there for two shillings Scots, or (as Mr. Stewart had it) from the sense of duty, once he was tarred and shackled and hung up, the difference seemed small. There might David Balfour hang, and other lads pass on their errands and think light of him; and old daft limmers sit at a leg-foot and spae their fortunes; and the clean genty maids go by, and look to the other side, and hold a nose. I saw them plain, and they had grey eyes, and their screens upon their heads were of the Drummond colours.

I was thus in the poorest of spirits, though still pretty resolved, when I came in view of Pilrig, a pleasant gabled house set by the walk-side among some brave young woods. The laird's horse was standing saddled at the door as I came up, but himself was in the study, where he received me in the midst of learned works and musical instruments, for he was not only a deep philosopher but much of a musician. He greeted me at first pretty well, and when he had read Rankeillor's letter, placed himself obligingly at my disposal.

'And what is it, cousin David?' said he—'since it appears that we are cousins—what is this that I can do for you? A word to Prestongrange? Doubtless that is easily given. But what should be the word?'

'Mr. Balfour,' said I, 'if I were to tell you my whole story the way it fell out, it's my opinion (and it was Rankeillor's before me) that you would be very little made up with it.'

'I am sorry to hear this of you, kinsman,' says he.

'I must not take that at your hands, Mr. Balfour,' said I; 'I have nothing to my charge to make me sorry, or you for me, but just the common infirmities of mankind. "The guilt of Adam's first sin, the want of original righteousness, and the corruption of my whole nature," so much I must answer for, and I hope I have been taught where to look for help,' I said; for I judged from the look of the man he would think the better of me if I knew my questions.[1] 'But in the way of worldly honour I have no great stumble to reproach myself with; and my difficulties have befallen me very much against my will and (by all that I can see) without my fault. My trouble is to have become dipped in a political complication, which it is judged you would be blithe to avoid a knowledge of.'

'Why, very well, Mr. David,' he replied. 'I am pleased to see you are all that Rankeillor represented. And for what you say of political complications, you do me no more than justice. It is my study to be beyond suspicion, and indeed outside the field of it. The question is,' says he, 'how, if I am to know nothing of the matter, I can very well assist you?'

'Why, sir,' said I, 'I propose you should write to his lordship, that I am a young man of reasonable good family and of good means: both of which I believe to be the case.'

'I have Rankeillor's word for it,' said Mr. Balfour, 'and I count that a warrandice against all deadly.'

'To which you might add (if you will take my word for so much) that I am a good churchman, loyal to King George, and so brought up,' I went on.

'None of which will do you any harm,' said Mr. Balfour.

'Then you might go on to say that I sought his lordship on a matter of great moment, connected with his Majesty's service and the administration of justice,' I suggested.

'As I am not to hear the matter,' says the laird, 'I will not take upon myself to qualify its weight. "Great moment" therefore falls, and "moment" along with it. For the rest I might express myself much as you propose.'

'And then, sir,' said I, and rubbed my neck a little with my thumb, 'then I would be very desirous if you could slip in a word that might perhaps tell for my protection.'

---

[1] My Catechism

'Protection?' says he, 'for your protection? Here is a phrase that somewhat dampens me. If the matter be so dangerous, I own I would be a little loath to move in it blind-fold.'

'I believe I could indicate in two words where the thing sticks,' said I.

'Perhaps that would be the best,' said he.

'Well, it's the Appin murder,' said I.

He held up both the hands. 'Sirs! sirs!' cried he.

I thought by the expression of his face and voice that I had lost my helper.

'Let me explain . . .' I began.

'I thank you kindly, I will hear no more of it,' says he. 'I decline *in toto* to hear more of it. For your name's sake and Rankeillor's, and perhaps a little for your own, I will do what I can to help you; but I will hear no more upon the facts. And it is my first clear duty to warn you. These are deep waters, Mr. David, and you are a young man. Be cautious and think twice.'

'It is to be supposed I will have thought oftener than that, Mr. Balfour,' said I, 'and I will direct your attention again to Rankeillor's letter, where (I hope and believe) he has regis-tered his approval of that which I design.'

'Well, well,' said he; and then again, 'Well, well! I will do what I can for you.' Therewith he took a pen and paper, sat awhile in thought, and began to write with much con-sideration. 'I understand that Rankeillor approves of what you have in mind?' he asked presently.

'After some discussion, sir, he bade me to go forward in God's name,' said I.

'That is the name to go in,' said Mr. Balfour, and resumed his writing. Presently, he signed, re-read what he had written, and addressed me again. 'Now here, Mr. David,' said he, 'is a letter of introduction, which I will seal without closing, and give into your hands open, as the form requires. But, since I am acting in the dark, I will just read it to you, so that you may see if it will secure your end—

' "PILRIG, *August 26th, 1751.*

' "MY LORD,— This is to bring to your notice my namesake and cousin, David Balfour Esquire of Shaws, a young gentleman of unblemished descent and good estate. He has enjoyed besides the more valuable advantages of a godly training, and his political principles are all that your lordship can desire. I am not in Mr. Balfour's confidence, but I understand him to have a matter to declare, touching his Majesty's service and the administration of justice: purposes for which your Lordship's zeal is known. I should add that the young gentleman's intention is known to and approved by some of his friends, who will watch with hopeful anxiety the event of his success or failure."

'Whereupon,' continued Mr. Balfour, 'I have subscribed myself with the usual compliments. You observe I have said "some of your friends"; I hope you can justify my plural?'

'Perfectly, sir; my purpose is known and approved by more than one,' said I. 'And your letter, which I take a pleasure to thank you for, is all I could have hoped.'

'It was all I could squeeze out,' said he; 'and from what I know of the matter you design to meddle in, I can only pray God that it may prove sufficient.'

CHAPTER IV

LORD ADVOCATE PRESTONGRANGE

MY kinsman kept me to a meal, 'for the honour of the roof,' he said; and I believe I made the better speed on my return. I had no thought but to be done with the next stage, and have myself fully committed; to a person circumstanced as I was, the appearance of closing a door on hesitation and temptation was itself extremely tempting; and I was the more disappointed, when I came to Prestongrange's house, to be informed he was abroad. I believe it was true at the moment, and for some hours after; and then I have no doubt the Advocate came home again, and enjoyed himself in a neighbouring chamber among friends, while perhaps the very fact of my arrival was forgotten. I would have gone away a dozen times, only for this strong drawing to have done with my declaration out of hand and be able to lay me down to sleep with a free conscience. At first I read, for the little cabinet where I was left contained a variety of books. But I fear I read with little profit; and the weather falling cloudy, the dusk coming up earlier than usual, and my cabinet being lighted with but a loophole of a window, I was at last obliged to desist from this diversion (such as it was), and pass the rest of my time of waiting in a very burthensome vacuity. The sound of people talking in a near chamber, the pleasant note of a harpsichord, and once the voice of a lady singing, bore me a kind of company.

I do not know the hour, but the darkness was long come, when the door of the cabinet opened, and I was aware, by the light behind him, of a tall figure of a man upon the threshold. I rose at once.

'Is anybody there?' he asked. 'Who is that?'

'I am bearer of a letter from the laird of Pilrig to the Lord Advocate,' said I.

'Have you been here long?' he asked.

'I would not like to hazard an estimate of how many hours,' said I.

'It is the first I hear of it,' he replied, with a chuckle. 'The lads must have forgotten you. But you are in the bit at last, for I am Prestongrange.'

So saying, he passed before me into the next room, whither (upon his sign) I followed him, and where he lit a candle and took his place before a business-table. It was a long room, of a good proportion, wholly lined with books. That small spark of light in a corner struck out the man's handsome person and strong face. He was flushed, his eye watered and sparkled, and before he sat down I observed him to sway back and forth. No doubt he had been supping liberally; but his mind and tongue were under full control.

'Well, sir, sit ye down,' said he, 'and let us see Pilrig's letter.'

He glanced it through in the beginning carelessly, looking

up and bowing when he came to my name; but at the last
words I thought I observed his attention to redouble, and
I made sure he read them twice. All this while you are to
suppose my heart was beating, for I had now crossed my
Rubicon and was come fairly on the field of battle.

'I am pleased to make your acquaintance, Mr. Balfour,' he
said, when he had done. 'Let me offer you a glass of claret.'

'Under your favour, my lord, I think it would scarce be
fair on me,' said I. 'I have come here, as the letter will have
mentioned, on a business of some gravity to myself; and as I
am little used with wine, I might be the sooner affected.'

'You shall be the judge,' said he. 'But if you will permit,
I believe I will even have the bottle in myself.'

He touched a bell, and a footman came, as at a signal,
bringing wine and glasses,

'You are sure you will not join me?' asked the Advocate.
'Well, here is to our better acquaintance! In what way can
I serve you?'

'I should perhaps, begin by telling you, my lord, that I am
here at your own pressing invitation,' said I.

'You have the advantage of me somewhere,' said he, 'for
I profess I think I never heard of you before this evening.'

'Right, my lord, the name is indeed new to you,' said I. 'And
yet you have been for some time extremely wishful to make
my acquaintance, and have declared the same in public.'

'I wish you would afford me a clue,' says he. 'I am no
Daniel.'

'It will perhaps serve for such,' said I, 'that if I was in a
jesting humour—which is far from the case—I believe I
might lay a claim on your lordship for two hundred pounds.'

'In what sense?' he inquired.

'In the sense of rewards offered for my person,' said I.

He thrust away his glass once and for all, and sat straight
up in the chair where he had been previously lolling. 'What
am I to understand?' said he.

'*A tall strong lad of about eighteen,*' I quoted, '*speaks like
a Lowlander, and has no beard.*'

'I recognise those words,' said he, 'which if you have come

here with any ill-judged intention of amusing yourself, are like to prove extremely prejudicial to your safety.'

'My purpose in this,' I replied, 'is just entirely as serious as life and death, and you have understood me perfectly. I am the boy who was speaking with Glenure when he was shot.'

'I can only suppose (seeing you here) that you claim to be innocent,' said he.

'The inference is clear,' I said. 'I am a very loyal subject to King George, but if I had anything to reproach myself with, I would have had more discretion than to walk into your den.'

'I am glad of that,' said he. 'This horrid crime, Mr. Balfour, is of a dye which cannot permit any clemency. Blood has been barbarously shed. It has been shed in direct opposition to his Majesty and our whole frame of laws, by those who are their known and public oppugnants. I take a very high sense of this. I will not deny that I consider the crime as directly personal to his Majesty.'

'And unfortunately, my lord,' I added, a little drily, 'directly personal to another great personage who may be nameless.'

'If you mean anything by those words, I must tell you I consider them unfit for a good subject; and were they spoken publicly, I should make it my business to take note of them,' said he. 'You do not appear to me to recognise the gravity of your situation, or you would be more careful not to pejorate the same by words which glance upon the purity of justice. Justice, in this country, and in my poor hands, is no respecter of persons.'

'You give me too great a share in my own speech, my lord,' said I. 'I did but repeat the common talk of the country, which I have heard everywhere, and from men of all opinions as I came along.'

'When you are come to more discretion you will understand such talk is not to be listened to, how much less repeated,' said the Advocate. 'But I acquit you of an ill-intention. That nobleman, whom we all honour, and who has indeed been wounded in a near place by the late barbarity, sits too high to be reached by these aspersions. The Duke of

Argyle—you see that I deal plainly with you—takes it to heart as I do, and as we are both bound to do by our judicial functions and the service of his Majesty; and I could wish that all hands, in this ill age, were equally clean of family rancour. But from the accident that this is a Campbell who has fallen martyr to his duty—as who else but the Campbells have ever put themselves foremost on that path?—I may say it, who am no Campbell—and that the chief of that great house happens (for all our advantages) to be the present head of the College of Justice, small minds and disaffected tongues are set agog in every change-house in the country; and I find a young gentleman like Mr. Balfour so ill-advised as to make himself their echo.' So much he spoke with a very oratorical delivery, as if in court, and then declined again upon the manner of a gentleman. 'All this apart,' said he. 'It now remains that I should learn what I am to do with you.'

'I had thought it was rather I that should learn the same from your lordship,' said I.

'Ay, true,' says the Advocate. 'But, you see, you come to me well recommended. There is a good honest Whig name to this letter,' says he, picking it up a moment from the table. 'And—extra-judicially, Mr. Balfour—there is always the possibility of some arrangement. I tell you, and I tell you beforehand that you may be the more upon your guard, your fate lies with me singly. In such a matter (be it said with reverence) I am more powerful than the King's Majesty; and should you please me—and of course satisfy my conscience—in what remains to be held of our interview, I tell you it may remain between ourselves.'

'Meaning how?' I asked.

'Why, I mean it thus, Mr. Balfour,' said he, 'that if you give satisfaction, no soul need know so much as that you visited my house; and you may observe that I do not even call my clerk.'

I saw what way he was driving. 'I suppose it is needless anyone should be informed upon my visit,' said I, 'though the precise nature of my gains by that I cannot see. I am not at all ashamed of coming here.'

'And have no cause to be,' says he, encouragingly. 'Nor yet (if you are careful) to fear the consequences.'

'My lord,' said I, 'speaking under your correction I am not very easy to be frightened '

'And I am sure I do not seek to frighten you,' says he. 'But to the interrogation; and let me warn you to volunteer nothing beyond the questions I shall ask you. It may consist very immediately with your safety. I have a great discretion, it is true, but there are bounds to it.'

'I shall try to follow your lordship's advice,' said I.

He spread a sheet of paper on the table and wrote a heading. 'It appears you were present, by the way, in the wood of Lettermore at the moment of the fatal shot,' he began. 'Was this by accident?'

'By accident,' said I.

'How came you in speech with Colin Campbell?' he asked.

'I was inquiring my way of him to Aucharn,' I replied.

I observed he did not write this answer down.

'H'm, true,' said he, 'I had forgotten that. And do you know, Mr. Balfour, I would dwell, if I were you, as little as might be on your relations with these Stewarts? It might be found to complicate our business. I am not yet inclined to regard these matters as essential.'

'I had thought, my lord, that all points of fact were equally material in such a case,' said I.

'You forget we are now trying these Stewarts,' he replied, with great significance. 'If we should ever come to be trying you, it will be very different; and I shall press these very questions that I am now willing to glide upon. But to resume: I have it here in Mr. Mungo Campbell's precognition that you ran immediately up the brae. How came that?'

'Not immediately, my lord, and the cause was my seeing of the murderer.'

'You saw him, then?'

'As plain as I see your lordship, though not so near hand.'

'You know him?'

'I should know him again.'

'In your pursuit you were not so fortunate, then, as to overtake him?'

'I was not.'

'Was he alone?'

'He was alone.'

'There was no one else in that neighbourhood?'

'Alan Breck Stewart was not far off, in a piece of a wood.'

The Advocate laid his pen down. 'I think we are playing at cross purposes,' said he, 'which you will find to prove a very ill amusement for yourself.'

'I content myself with following your lordship's advice, and answering what I am asked,' said I.

'Be so wise as to bethink yourself in time,' said he, 'I use you with the most anxious tenderness, which you scarce seem to appreciate, and which (unless you be more careful) may prove to be in vain.'

'I do appreciate your tenderness, but conceive it to be mistaken,' I replied, with something of a falter, for I saw we were come to grips at last. 'I am here to lay before you certain information, by which I shall convince you Alan had no hand whatever in the killing of Glenure.'

The Advocate appeared for a moment at a stick, sitting with pursed lips, and blinking his eyes upon me like an angry cat. 'Mr. Balfour,' he said at last, 'I tell you pointedly you go an ill way for your own interests.'

'My lord,' I said, 'I am as free of the charge of considering my own interests in this matter as your lordship. As God judges me, I have but the one design, and that is to see justice executed and the innocent go clear. If in pursuit of that I come to fall under your lordship's displeasure, I must bear it as I may.'

At this he rose from his chair, lit a second candle, and for a while gazed upon me steadily. I was surprised to see a great change of gravity fallen upon his face, and I could have almost thought he was a little pale.

'You are either very simple, or extremely the reverse, and I see that I must deal with you more confidentially,' says he. 'This is a political case—ah, yes, Mr. Balfour! whether we like it or no, the case is political—and I tremble when I think what issues may depend from it. To a political case, I need scarce tell a young man of your education, we approach with very different thoughts from one which is criminal only. *Salus populi suprema lex** is a maxim susceptible of great abuse, but it has that force which we find elsewhere only in the laws of nature: I mean it has the force of necessity. I will open this out to you, if you will allow me, at more length. You would have me believe——'

'Under your pardon, my lord, I would have you to believe nothing but that which I can prove,' said I.

'Tut! tut; young gentleman,' says he, 'be not so pragmatical, and suffer a man who might be your father* (if it was nothing more) to employ his own imperfect language, and express his own poor thoughts, even when they have the misfortune not to coincide with Mr. Balfour's. You would have me to believe Breck innocent. I would think this of little account, the more so as we cannot catch our man. But the matter of Breck's innocence shoots beyond itself. Once admitted, it would destroy the whole presumptions of our case against another and a very different criminal; a man grown old in treason, already twice in arms against his king and already twice forgiven; a fomenter of discontent, and (whoever may have fired the shot) the unmistakable original of the deed in question. I need not tell you that I mean James Stewart.'

'And I can just say plainly that the innocence of Alan and of James is what I am here to declare in private to your lordship, and what I am prepared to establish at the trial by my testimony,' said I.

'To which I can only answer by an equal plainness, Mr. Balfour,' said he, 'that (in that case) your testimony will not be called by me, and I desire you to withhold it altogether.'

'You are at the head of Justice in this country,' I cried, 'and you propose to me a crime!'

'I am a man nursing with both hands the interests of this country,' he replied, 'and I press on you a political necessity. Patriotism is not always moral in the formal sense. You might be glad of it I think: it is your own protection; the facts are heavy against you; and if I am still trying to except you from a very dangerous place, it is in part of course because I am not insensible to your honesty in coming here; in part because of Pilrig's letter; but in part, and in chief part, because I regard in this matter my political duty first and my judicial duty only second. For the same reason—I repeat it to you in the same frank words—I do not want your testimony.'

'I desire not to be thought to make a repartee, when I express only the plain sense of our position,' said I. 'But if your lordship has no need of my testimony, I believe the other side would be extremely blythe to get it.'

Prestongrange arose and began to pace to and fro in the room. 'You are not so young,' he said, 'but what you must remember very clearly the year '45 and the shock that went about the country. I read in Pilrig's letter that you are sound in Kirk and State. Who saved them in that fatal year? I do not refer to His Royal Highness and his ramrods, which were extremely useful in their day; but the country had been saved and the field won before ever Cumberland came upon Drummossie.* Who saved it? I repeat; who saved the Protestant religion and the whole frame of our civil institutions? The late Lord President Culloden,* for one; he played a man's part, and small thanks he got for it—even as I, whom you see before you, straining every nerve in the same service, look for no reward beyond the conscience of my duties done. After the President, who else? You know the answer as well as I do; 'tis partly a scandal, and you glanced at it yourself, and I reproved you for it, when you first came in. It was the Duke and the great clan of Campbell. Now here is a Campbell foully murdered, and that in the King's service. The Duke and I are Highlanders. But we are Highlanders civilised, and it is not so with the great mass of our clans and families. They have still savage virtues and defects. They are still barbarians, like these Stewarts; only the Campbells were barbarians on the right side, and the Stewarts were barbarians on the wrong. Now be you the judge. The Campbells expect vengeance. If they do not get it—if this man James escape—there will be trouble with the Campbells. That means disturbance in the Highlands, which are uneasy and very far from being disarmed: the disarming is a farce. . . .'

'I can bear you out in that,' said I.

'Disturbance in the Highlands makes the hour of our old watchful enemy,' pursued his lordship, holding out a finger as he paced; 'and I give you my word we may have a '45 again with the Campbells on the other side. To protect the life of this man Stewart—which is forfeit already on half-a-dozen different counts if not on this—do you propose to plunge your country in war, to jeopardise the faith of your fathers, and to expose the lives and fortunes of how many thousand innocent persons? . . . These are considerations that weigh with me, and that I hope will weigh no less with yourself, Mr. Balfour, as a lover of your country, good government, and religious truth.'

'You deal with me very frankly, and I thank you for it,' said I. 'I will try on my side to be no less honest. I believe your policy to be sound. I believe these deep duties may lie upon your lordship; I believe you may have laid them on your conscience when you took the oaths of the high office which you hold. But for me, who am just a plain man—or scarce a man yet—the plain duties must suffice. I can think but of two things, of a poor soul in the immediate and unjust danger of a shameful death, and of the cries and tears of his wife that still tingle in my head. I cannot see beyond, my lord. It's the way that I am made. If the country has to fall, it has to fall. And I pray God, if this be wilful blindness, that He may enlighten me before too late.'

He had heard me motionless, and stood so a while longer.

'This is an unexpected obstacle,' says he, aloud, but to himself.

'And how is your lordship to dispose of me?' I asked.

'If I wished,' said he, 'you know that you might sleep in gaol?'

'My lord,' said I, 'I have slept in worse places.'

'Well, my boy,' said he, 'there is one thing appears very plainly from our interview, that I may rely on your pledged word. Give me your honour that you will be wholly secret, not only on what has passed to-night, but in the matter of the Appin case, and I let you go free.'

'I will give it till to-morrow or any other near day that you may please to set,' said I. 'I would not be thought too wily; but if I gave the promise without qualification your lordship would have attained his end.'

'I had no thought to entrap you,' said he.

'I am sure of that,' said I.

'Let me see,' he continued. 'To-morrow is the Sabbath. Come to me on Monday by eight in the morning, and give me your promise until then.'

'Freely given, my lord,' said I. 'And with regard to what has fallen from yourself, I will give it for as long as it shall please God to spare your days.'

'You will observe,' he said next, 'that I have made no employment of menaces.'

'It was like your lordship's nobility,' said I. 'Yet I am not altogether so dull but what I can perceive the nature of those you have not uttered.'

'Well,' said he, 'good-night to you. May you sleep well, for I think it is more than I am like to do.'

With that he sighed, took up a candle, and gave me his conveyance as far as the street door.

CHAPTER V

IN THE ADVOCATE'S HOUSE

THE next day, Sabbath, August 27th, I had the occasion I had long looked forward to, to hear some of the famous Edinburgh preachers, all well known to me already by the report of Mr. Campbell. Alas! and I might just as well have been at Essendean, and sitting under Mr. Campbell's worthy self! the turmoil of my thoughts, which dwelt continually on the interview with Prestongrange, inhibiting me from all attention. I was indeed much less impressed by the reasoning

of the divines than by the spectacle of the thronged congregation in the churches, like what I imagined of a theatre or (in
my then disposition) of an assize of trial; above all at the
West Kirk, with its three tiers of galleries, where I went in
the vain hope that I might see Miss Drummond.

On the Monday I betook me for the first time to a barber's,
and was very well pleased with the result. Thence to the
Advocate's, where the red coats of the soldiers showed again
about his door, making a bright place in the close. I looked
about for the young lady and her gillies: there was never a
sign of them. But I was no sooner shown into the cabinet
or antechamber where I had spent so wearyful a time upon
the Saturday, than I was aware of the tall figure of James
More in a corner. He seemed a prey to a painful uneasiness,
reaching forth his feet and hands, and his eyes speeding here
and there without rest about the walls of the small chamber,
which recalled to me with a sense of pity the man's wretched
situation. I suppose it was partly this, and partly my strong
continuing interest in his daughter, that moved me to accost
him.

'Give you a good-morning, sir,' said I.

'And a good-morning to you, sir,' said he.

'You bide tryst with Prestongrange?' I asked.

'I do, sir, and I pray your business with that gentleman
be more agreeable than mine,' was his reply.

'I hope at least that yours will be brief, for I suppose you
pass before me,' said I.

'All pass before me,' he said, with a shrug and a gesture
upward of the open hands. 'It was not always so, sir, but
times change. It was not so when the sword was in the scale,
young gentleman, and the virtues of the soldier might sustain
themselves.'

There came a kind of Highland snuffle out of the man that
raised my dander strangely.

'Well, Mr. Macgregor,' said I, 'I understand the main
thing for a soldier is to be silent, and the first of his virtues
never to complain.'

'You have my name, I perceive'—he bowed to me with

his arms crossed—'though it's one I must not use myself. Well, there is a publicity—I have shown my face and told my name too often in the beards of my enemies. I must not wonder if both should be known to many that I know not.'

'That you know not in the least, sir,' said I, 'nor yet anybody else; but the name I am called, if you care to hear it, is Balfour.'

'It is a good name,' he replied, civilly; 'there are many decent folk that use it. And now that I call to mind, there was a young gentleman, your namesake, that marched surgeon in the year '45 with my battalion.'

'I believe that would be a brother to Balfour of Baith,' said I, for I was ready for the surgeon now.

'The same, sir,' said James More. 'And since I have been fellow-soldier with your kinsman, you must suffer me to grasp your hand.'

He shook hands with me long and tenderly, beaming on me the while as though he had found a brother.

'Ah!' says he, 'these are changed days since your cousin and I heard the balls whistle in our lugs.'

'I think he was a very far-away cousin,' said I, drily, 'and I ought to tell you that I never clapped eyes upon the man.'

'Well, well,' said he, 'it makes no change. And you—I do not think you were out yourself, sir—I have no clear mind of your face, which is one not probable to be forgotten.'

'In the year you refer to, Mr. Macgregor, I was getting skelped in the parish school,' said I.

'So young!' cries he. 'Ah, then, you will never be able to think what this meeting is to me. In the hour of my adversity, and here in the house of my enemy, to meet in with the blood of an old brother-in-arms—it heartens me, Mr. Balfour, like the skirling of the Highland pipes! Sir, this is a sad look-back that many of us have to make: some with falling tears. I have lived in my own country like a king; my sword, my mountains, and the faith of my friends and kinsmen sufficed for me. Now I lie in a stinking dungeon; and do you know, Mr. Balfour,' he went on, taking my arm and beginning to lead me about, 'do you know, sir, that I lack mere necessaries?

The malice of my foes has quite sequestered my resources. I lie, as you know, sir, on a trumped-up charge, of which I am as innocent as yourself. They dare not bring me to my trial, and in the meanwhile I am held naked in my prison. I could have wished it was your cousin I had met, or his brother Baith himself. Either would, I know, have been rejoiced to help me; while a comparative stranger like yourself——'

I would be ashamed to set down all he poured out to me in this beggarly vein, or the very short and grudging answers that I made to him. There were times when I was tempted to stop his mouth with some small change; but whether it was from shame or pride—whether it was for my own sake or Catriona's—whether it was because I thought him no fit father for his daughter, or because I resented that grossness of immediate falsity that clung about the man himself—the thing was clean beyond me. And I was still being wheedled and preached to, and still being marched to and fro, three steps and a turn, in that small chamber, and had already, by some very short replies, highly incensed, although not finally discouraged, my beggar, when Prestongrange appeared in the doorway and bade me eagerly into his big chamber.

'I have a moment's engagement,' said he; 'and that you may not sit empty-handed I am going to present you to my three braw daughters, of whom perhaps you may have heard, for I think they are more famous than papa. This way.'

He led me into another room above, where a dry old lady sat at a frame of embroidery, and the three handsomest young women (I suppose) in Scotland stood together by a window.

'This is my new friend, Mr. Balfour,' said he, presenting me by the arm. 'David, here is my sister, Miss Grant, who is so good as keep my house for me, and will be very pleased if she can help you. And here,' says he, turning to the three younger ladies, 'here are my *three braw dauchters*. A fair question to ye, Mr. Davie: which of the three is the best favoured? And I wager he will never have the impudence to propound honest Alan Ramsay's answer!'*

Hereupon all three, and the old Miss Grant as well, cried out against this sally, which (as I was acquainted with the verses he referred to) brought shame into my own cheek. It seemed to me a citation unpardonable in a father, and I was amazed that these ladies could laugh even while they reproved, or made believe to.

Under cover of this mirth, Prestongrange got forth of the chamber, and I was left, like a fish upon dry land, in that very unsuitable society. I could never deny, in looking back upon what followed, that I was eminently stockish; and I must say the ladies were well drilled to have so long a patience with me. The aunt indeed sat close at her embroidery, only looking now and again and smiling; but the misses, and especially the eldest, who was besides the most handsome, paid me a score of attentions which I was very ill able to repay. It was all in vain to tell myself I was a young fellow of some worth as well as a good estate, and had no call to feel abashed before these lasses, the eldest not so much older than myself, and no one of them by any probability half as learned. Reasoning would not change the fact; and there were times when the colour came into my face to think I was shaved that day for the first time.

The talk going, with all their endeavours, very heavily, the eldest took pity on my awkwardness, sat down to her instrument, of which she was a passed mistress, and entertained me for a while with playing and singing, both in the Scots and in the Italian manners; this put me more at my ease, and being reminded of Alan's air that he had taught me in the hole near Carriden, I made so bold as to whistle a bar or two, and ask if she knew that.

She shook her head. 'I never heard a note of it,' said she. 'Whistle it all through. And now once again,' she added after I had done so.

Then she picked it out upon the keyboard, and (to my surprise) instantly enriched the same with well-sounding chords, and sang, as she played, with a very droll expression and broad accent—

      'Haenae I got just the lilt of it?
      Isnae this the tune that ye whustled?'

'You see,' she says, 'I can do the poetry too, only it won't rhyme.' And then again:

> 'I am Miss Grant, sib to the Advocate;
> You, I believe, are Dauvit Balfour.'*

I told her how much astonished I was by her genius.

'And what do you call the name of it?' she asked.

'I do not know the real name,' said I. 'I just call it *Alan's air*.'

She looked at me directly in the face. 'I shall call it *David's air*,' said she; 'though if it's the least like what your name-sake of Israel played to Saul I would never wonder that the king got little good by it, for it's but melancholy music. Your other name I do not like; so if you was ever wishing to hear your tune again you are to ask for it by mine.'

This was said with a significance that gave my heart a jog. 'Why that, Miss Grant?' I asked.

'Why,' says she, 'if ever you should come to get hanged, I will set your last dying speech and confession to that tune and sing it.'

This put it beyond a doubt that she was partly informed of my story and peril. How, or just how much, it was more difficult to guess. It was plain she knew there was something of danger in the name of Alan, and thus warned me to leave it out of reference; and plain she knew that I stood under some criminal suspicion. I judged besides that the harshness of her last speech (which besides she had followed up im-mediately with a very noisy piece of music) was to put an end to the present conversation. I stood beside her, affecting to listen and admire, but truly whirled away by my own thoughts. I have always found this young lady to be a lover of the mysterious; and certainly this first interview made a mystery that was beyond my plummet. One thing I learned long after, the hours of the Sunday had been well employed, the bank porter had been found and examined, my visit to Charles Stewart was discovered, and the deduction made that I was pretty deep with James and Alan, and most likely in a continued correspondence with the last. Hence this broad hint that was given me across the harpsichord.

In the midst of the piece of music, one of the younger misses, who was at a window over the close, cried on her sisters to come quick, for there was 'Grey eyes again.' The whole family trooped there at once, and crowded one another for a look. The window whither they ran was in an odd corner of that room, gave above the entrance door, and flanked up the close.

'Come, Mr. Balfour,' they cried, 'come and see. She is the most beautiful creature! She hangs round the close-head these last days, always with some wretched-like gillies, and yet seems quite a lady.'

I had no need to look; neither did I look twice, or long. I was afraid she might have seen me there, looking down upon her from that chamber of music, and she without, and her father in the same house, perhaps begging for his life with tears, and myself come but newly from rejecting his petitions. But even that glance set me in a better conceit of myself, and much less awe of the young ladies. They were beautiful, that was beyond question, but Catriona was beautiful too, and had a kind of brightness in her like a coal of fire. As much as the others cast me down, she lifted me up. I remembered I had talked easily with her. If I could make no hand of it with these fine maids, it was perhaps something their own fault. My embarrassment began to be a little mingled and lightened with a sense of fun; and when the aunt smiled at me from her embroidery, and the three daughters unbent to me like a baby, all with 'papa's orders' written on their faces, there were times when I could have found it in my heart to smile myself.

Presently papa returned, the same kind, happy-like, pleasant-spoken man.

'Now, girls,' said he, 'I must take Mr. Balfour away again; but I hope you have been able to persuade him to return where I shall be always gratified to find him.'

So they each made me a little farthing compliment, and I was led away.

If this visit to the family had been meant to soften my resistance, it was the worst of failures. I was no such ass but what I understood how poor a figure I had made, and that the girls would be yawning their jaws off as soon as my stiff back was turned. I felt I had shown how little I had in me of what was soft and graceful; and I longed for a chance to prove that I had something of the other stuff, the stern and dangerous.

Well, I was to be served to my desire, for the scene to which he was conducting me was of a different character.

CHAPTER VI

UMQUHILE THE MASTER OF LOVAT

THERE was a man waiting us in Prestongrange's study, whom I distasted at the first look, as we distaste a ferret or an earwig. He was bitter ugly, but seemed very much of a gentleman; had still manners, but capable of sudden leaps and violences; and a small voice, which could ring out shrill and dangerous when he so desired.

The Advocate presented us in a familiar, friendly way.

'Here, Fraser,' said he, 'here is Mr. Balfour whom we talked about. Mr. David, this is Mr. Simon Fraser, whom we used to call by another title, but that is an old song. Mr. Fraser has an errand to you.'

With that he stepped aside to his book-shelves, and made believe to consult a quarto volume in the far end.

I was thus left (in a sense) alone with perhaps the last person in the world I had expected. There was no doubt upon the terms of introduction; this could be no other than the forfeited Master of Lovat and chief of the great clan Fraser.* I knew he had led his men in the rebellion; I knew his father's head—my old lord's, that grey fox of the mountains—to have fallen on the block for that offence, the lands of the family to have been seized, and their nobility attainted. I could not conceive what he should be doing in Grant's house; I could not conceive that he had been called to the bar, had eaten all his principles, and was now currying favour with the Government even to the extent of acting Advocate-Depute in the Appin murder.

'Well, Mr. Balfour,' said he, 'what is all this I hear of ye?'

'It would not become me to prejudge,' said I, 'but if the Advocate was your authority he is fully possessed of my opinions.'

'I may tell you I am engaged in the Appin case,' he went on; 'I am to appear under Prestongrange; and from my study of the precognitions I can assure you your opinions are erroneous. The guilt of Breck is manifest; and your testimony, in which you admit you saw him on the hill at the very moment, will certify his hanging.'

'It will be rather ill to hang him till you catch him,' I observed. 'And for other matters I very willingly leave you to your own impressions.'

'The Duke has been informed,' he went on. 'I have just come from his Grace, and he expressed himself before me with an honest freedom like the great nobleman he is. He spoke of you by name, Mr. Balfour, and declared his gratitude beforehand in case you would be led by those who understand your own interests and those of the country so much better than yourself. Gratitude is no empty expression in that mouth: *experto crede*.* I dare say you know something of my name and clan, and the damnable example and lamented end of my late father, to say nothing of my own errata. Well, I have made my peace with that good Duke; he has intervened for me with our friend Prestongrange; and here I am with my foot in the stirrup again and some of the responsibility shared into my hand of prosecuting King George's enemies and avenging the late daring and barefaced insult to his Majesty.'

'Doubtless a proud position for your father's son,' says I.

He wagged his bald eyebrows at me. 'You are pleased to make experiments in the ironical, I think,' said he. 'But I am here upon duty, I am here to discharge my errand in good faith, it is in vain you think to divert me. And let me tell you, for a young fellow of spirit and ambition like yourself, a good shove in the beginning will do more than ten years' drudgery. The shove is now at your command; choose what you will to be advanced in, the Duke will watch upon you with the affectionate disposition of a father.'

'I am thinking that I lack the docility of the son,' says I.

'And do you really suppose, sir, that the whole policy of this country is to be suffered to trip up and tumble down for an ill-mannered colt of a boy?' he cried. 'This has been made a test case, all who would prosper in the future must put a shoulder to the wheel. Look at me! Do you suppose it is for my pleasure that I put myself in the highly invidious position of prosecuting a man that I have drawn the sword alongside of? The choice is not left me.'

'But I think, sir, that you forfeited your choice when you mixed in with that unnatural rebellion,' I remarked. 'My case is happily otherwise; I am a true man, and can look either the Duke or King George in the face without concern.'

'Is it so the wind sits?' says he. 'I protest you are fallen in the worst sort of error. Prestongrange has been hitherto so civil (he tells me) as not to combat your allegations; but you must not think they are not looked upon with strong suspicion. You say you are innocent. My dear sir, the facts declare you guilty.'

'I was waiting for you there,' said I.

"The evidence of Mungo Campbell; your flight after the completion of the murder; your long course of secrecy—my good young man!' said Mr. Simon, 'here is enough evidence to hang a bullock, let be a David Balfour! I shall be upon that trial; my voice shall be raised; I shall then speak much otherwise from what I do to-day, and far less to your gratification, little as you like it now! Ah, you look white!' cries he. 'I have found the key of your impudent heart. You look pale, your eyes waver, Mr. David! You see the grave and the gallows nearer by than you had fancied.'

'I own to a natural weakness,' said I. 'I think no shame for that. Shame . . .' I was going on.

'Shame waits for you on the gibbet,' he broke in.

'Where I shall but be even'd with my lord your father,' said I.

'Aha, but not so!' he cried, 'and you do not yet see to the bottom of this business. My father suffered in a great cause, and for dealing in the affairs of kings. You are to hang for a dirty murder about boddle-pieces. Your personal part in it, the treacherous one of holding the poor wretch in talk, your accomplices a pack of ragged Highland gillies. And it can be shown, my great Mr. Balfour—it can be shown, and it will be shown, trust *me* that has a finger in the pie—it can be shown, and shall be shown, that you were paid to do it. I think I can see the looks go round the court when I adduce my evidence, and it shall appear that you, a young man of education, let yourself be corrupted to this shocking act for a suit of cast clothes, a bottle of Highland spirits, and three-and-fivepence-halfpenny in copper money.'

There was a touch of the truth in these words that knocked me like a blow: clothes, a bottle of *usquebaugh*, and three-and-fivepence-halfpenny in change made up, indeed, the most of what Alan and I had carried from Aucharn; and I saw that some of James's people had been blabbing in their dungeons.

'You see I know more than you fancied,' he resumed in triumph. 'And as for giving it this turn, great Mr. David, you must not suppose the Government of Great Britain and Ireland will ever be stuck for want of evidence. We have men here in prison who will swear out their lives as we direct them; as I direct, if you prefer the phrase. So now you are to guess your part of glory if you choose to die. On the one hand, life, wine, women, and a duke to be your hand-gun: on the other, a rope to your craig, and a gibbet to clatter your bones on, and the lousiest, lowest story to hand down to your namesakes in the future that was ever told about a hired assassin. And see here!' he cried, with a formidable shrill voice, 'see this paper that I pull out of my pocket. Look at the name there: it is the name of the great David, I believe, the ink scarce dry yet. Can you guess its nature? It is the warrant for your arrest, which I have but to touch this bell beside me to have executed on the spot. Once in the Tolbooth upon this paper, may God help you, for the die is cast!'

I must never deny that I was greatly horrified by so much baseness, and much unmanned by the immediacy and ugliness of my danger. Mr. Simon had already gloried in the changes of my hue; I make no doubt I was now no ruddier than my shirt; my speech besides trembled.

'There is a gentleman in this room,' cried I. 'I appeal to him. I put my life and credit in his hands.'

Prestongrange shut his book with a snap. 'I told you so, Simon,' said he; 'you have played your hand for all it was worth, and you have lost. Mr. David,' he went on, 'I wish you to believe it was by no choice of mine you were subjected to this proof. I wish you could understand how glad I am you should come forth from it with so much credit. You may not quite see how, but it is a little of a service to myself. For had our friend here been more successful than I was last night, it might have appeared that he was a better judge of men than I; it might have appeared we were altogether in the wrong situations, Mr. Simon and myself. And I know our friend Simon to be ambitious,' says he, striking lightly on Fraser's shoulder. 'As for this stage play, it is over; my sentiments are very much engaged in your behalf; and whatever issue we can find to this unfortunate affair, I shall make it my business to see it is adopted with tenderness to you.'

These were very good words, and I could see besides that there was little love, and perhaps a spice of genuine ill-will, between those two who were opposed to me. For all that, it was unmistakable this interview had been designed, perhaps rehearsed, with the consent of both; it was plain my adversaries were in earnest to try me by all methods; and now (persuasion, flattery, and menaces, having been tried in vain) I could not but wonder what would be their next expedient. My eyes besides were still troubled, and my knees loose under me, with the distress of the late ordeal; and I could do no more than stammer the same form of words: 'I put my life and credit in your hands.'

'Well, well,' says he, 'we must try to save them. And in

the meantime let us return to gentler methods. You must not bear any grudge upon my friend, Mr. Simon, who did but speak by his brief. And even if you did conceive some malice against myself, who stood by and seemed rather to hold a candle, I must not let that extend to innocent members of my family. These are greatly engaged to see more of you, and I cannot consent to have my young women-folk disappointed. To-morrow they will be going to Hope Park, where I think it very proper you should make your bow. Call for me first, when I may possibly have something for your private hearing; then you shall be turned abroad again under the conduct of my misses; and until that time repeat to me your promise of secrecy.'

I had done better to have instantly refused, but in truth I was beside the power of reasoning; did as I was bid; took my leave I know not how; and when I was forth again in the close, and the door had shut behind me, was glad to lean on a house wall and wipe my face. That horrid apparition (as I may call it) of Mr. Simon rang in my memory, as a sudden noise rings after it is over in the ear. Tales of the man's father, of his falseness, of his manifold perpetual treacheries, rose before me from all that I had heard and read, and joined on with what I had just experienced of himself. Each time it occurred to me, the ingenious foulness of that calumny he had proposed to nail upon my character startled me afresh. The case of the men upon the gibbet by Leith Walk appeared scarce distinguishable from that I was now to consider as my own. To rob a child of so little more than nothing was certainly a paltry enterprise for two grown men; but my own tale, as it was to be represented in a court by Simon Fraser, appeared a fair second in every possible point of view of sordidness and cowardice.

The voices of two of Prestongrange's liveried men upon his doorstep recalled me to myself.

'Ha'e,' said the one, 'this billet as fast as ye can link to the captain.'

'Is that for the cateran back again?' asked the other.

'It would seem sae,' returned the first. 'Him and Simon are seeking him.'

'I think Prestongrange is gane gyte,' says the second. 'He'll have James More in bed with him next.'

'Weel, it's neither your affair nor mine's,' says the first.

And they parted, the one upon his errand, and the other back into the house.

This looked as ill as possible. I was scarce gone and they were sending already for James More, to whom I thought Mr. Simon must have pointed when he spoke of men in prison and ready to redeem their lives by all extremities. My scalp curdled among my hair, and the next moment the blood leaped in me to remember Catriona. Poor lass! her father stood to be hanged for pretty indefensible misconduct. What was yet more unpalatable, it now seemed he was prepared to save his four quarters by the worst of shame and the most foul of cowardly murders—murder by the false oath; and to complete our misfortunes, it seemed myself was picked out to be the victim.

I began to walk swiftly and at random, conscious only of a desire for movement, air, and the open country.

CHAPTER VII

I MAKE A FAULT IN HONOUR

I CAME forth, I vow I know not how, on the *Lang Dykes*.[1] This is a rural road which runs on the north side over against the city. Thence I could see the whole black length of it tail down, from where the Castle stands upon its crags above the loch in a long line of spires and gable ends, and smoking chimneys, and at the sight my heart swelled in my bosom. My youth, as I have told you, was already inured to dangers; but such danger as I had seen the face of but that morning, in the midst of what they call the safety of a town, shook me

1 Now Prince's Street.

beyond experience. Peril of slavery, peril of shipwreck, peril of sword and shot. I had stood all of these without discredit; but the peril there was in the sharp voice and the fat face of Simon, properly Lord Lovat, daunted me wholly.

I sat by the lake side in a place where the rushes went down into the water, and there steeped my wrists and laved my temples. If I could have done so with any remains of self-esteem I would now have fled from my foolhardy enterprise. But (call it courage or cowardice, and I believe it was both the one and the other) I decided I was ventured out beyond the possibility of a retreat. I had out-faced these men, I would continue to out-face them; come what might, I would stand by the word spoken.

The sense of my own constancy somewhat uplifted my spirits, but not much. At the best of it there was an icy place about my heart, and life seemed a black business to be at all engaged in. For two souls in particular my pity flowed. The one was myself, to be so friendless and lost among dangers. The other was the girl, the daughter of James More. I had seen but little of her; yet my view was taken and my judgment made. I thought her a lass of a clean honour, like a man's; I thought her one to die of a disgrace; and now I believed her father to be at that moment bargaining his vile life for mine. It made a bond in my thoughts betwixt the girl and me. I had seen her before only as a wayside appearance, though one that pleased me strangely; I saw her now in a sudden nearness of relation, as the daughter of my blood foe, and I might say, my murderer. I reflected it was hard I should be so plagued and persecuted all my days for other folks' affairs, and have no manner of pleasure myself. I got meals and a bed to sleep in when my concerns would suffer it; beyond that my wealth was of no help to me. If I was to hang, my days were like to be short; if I was not to hang but to escape out of this trouble, they might yet seem long to me ere I was done with them. Of a sudden her face appeared in my memory, the way I had first seen it, with the parted lips; at that, weakness came in my bosom and strength into my legs; and I set resolutely forward on the way to Dean.

If I was to hang to-morrow, and it was sure enough I might very likely sleep that night in a dungeon, I determined I should hear and speak once more with Catriona.

The exercise of walking and the thought of my destination braced me yet more, so that I began to pluck up a kind of spirit. In the village of Dean, where it sits in the bottom of the glen beside the river, I inquired my way of a miller's man, who sent me up the hill upon the farther side by a plain path, and so to a decent-like small house in a garden of lawns and apple-trees. My heart beat high as I stepped inside the garden hedge, but it fell low indeed when I came face to face with a grim and fierce old lady, walking there in a white mutch with a man's hat strapped upon the top of it.

'What do ye come seeking here?' she asked.

I told her I was after Miss Drummond.

'And what may be your business with Miss Drummond?' says she.

I told her I had met her on Saturday last, had been so fortunate as to render her a trifling service, and was come now on the young lady's invitation.

'O, so you're Saxpence!' she cried, with a very sneering manner. 'A braw gift, a bonny gentleman. And hae ye ony ither name and designation, or were ye bapteesed Saxpence?' she asked.

I told my name.

'Preserve me!' she cried. 'Has Ebenezer gotten a son?'

'No, ma'am,' said I. 'I am a son of Alexander's. It's I that am the Laird of Shaws.'

'Ye'll find your work cut out for ye to establish that,' quoth she.

'I perceive you know my uncle,' said I; 'and I daresay you may be the better pleased to hear that business is arranged.'

'And what brings ye here after Miss Drummond?' she pursued.

'I'm come after my saxpence, mem,' said I. 'It's to be thought, being my uncle's nephew, I would be found a careful lad.'

'So ye have a spark of sleeness in ye?' observed the old lady, with some approval. 'I thought ye had just been a cuif—you and your saxpence, and your *lucky day* and your *sake of Balwhidder*'—from which I was gratified to learn that Catriona had not forgotten some of our talk. 'But all this is by the purpose,' she resumed. 'Am I to understand that ye come here keeping company?'

'This is surely rather an early question,' said I. 'The maid is young, so am I, worse fortune. I have but seen her the once. I'll not deny,' I added, making up my mind to try her with some frankness, 'I'll not deny but she has run in my head a good deal since I met in with her. That is one thing; but it would be quite another, and I think I would look very like a fool, to commit myself.'

'You can speak out of your mouth, I see,' said the old lady. 'Praise God, and so can I! I was fool enough to take charge of this rogue's daughter: a fine charge I have gotten; but it's mine, and I'll carry it the way I want to. Do ye mean to tell me, Mr. Balfour of Shaws, that would marry James More's daughter, and him hanged? Well, then, where there's no possible marriage there shall be no manner of carryings on, and take that for said. Lasses are bruckle things,' she added, with a nod; 'and though ye would never think it by my wrunkled chafts, I was a lassie mysel', and a bonny one.'

'Lady Allardyce,' said I, 'for that I suppose to be your name, you seem to do the two sides of the talking, which is a very poor manner to come to an agreement. You give me rather a home thrust when you ask if I would marry, at the gallows' foot, a young lady whom I have seen but the once. I have told you already I would never be so untenty as to commit myself. And yet I'll go some way with you. If I continue to like the lass as well as I have reason to expect, it will be something more than her father, or the gallows either, that keeps the two of us apart. As for my family, I found it by the wayside like a lost bawbee! I owe less than nothing to my uncle; and if ever I marry, it will be to please one person: that's myself.'

'I have heard this kind of talk before ye were born,' said Mrs. Ogilvy, 'which is perhaps the reason that I think of it so little. There's much to be considered. This James More is a kinsman of mine, to my shame be it spoken. But the better the family, the mair men hanged or heided, that's always been poor Scotland's story. And if it was just the hanging! For my part, I think I would be best pleased with James upon the gallows, which would be at least an end to him. Catrine's a good lass enough, and a good-hearted, and lets herself be deaved all day with a runt of an auld wife like me. But, ye see, there's the weak bit. She's daft about that long, false, fleeching beggar of a father of hers, and red-mad about the Gregara, and proscribed names, and King James, and a wheen blethers. And you might think ye could guide her, ye would find yourself sore mista'en. Ye say ye've seen her but the once. . . .'

'Spoke with her but the once, I should have said,' I interrupted. 'I saw her again this morning from a window at Prestongrange's.'

This I dare say I put in because it sounded well; but I was properly paid for my ostentation on the return.

'What's this of it?' cries the old lady, with a sudden pucker of her face. 'I think it was at the Advocate's doorcheek that ye met her first.'

I told her that was so.

'H'm,' she said; and then suddenly, upon rather a scolding tone, 'I have your bare word for it,' she cries, 'as to who and what you are. By your way of it, you're Balfour of the Shaws; but for what I ken you may be Balfour of the Deevil's oxter. It's possible ye may come here for what ye say, and it's equally possible ye may come here for deil care what! I'm good enough Whig to sit quiet, and to have keepit all my men-folks' heads upon their shoulders. But I'm not just a good enough Whig to be made a fool of neither. And I tell you fairly, there's too much Advocate's door and Advocate's window here for a man that comes taigling after Macgregor's daughter. Ye can tell that to the Advocate that sent ye, with my fond love. And I kiss my loof to ye, Mr. Balfour,' says she, suiting the action to the word; 'and a braw journey to ye back to where ye cam frae.'

'If you think me a spy,' I broke out, and speech stuck in my throat. I stood and looked murder at the old lady for a space, then bowed and turned away.

'Here! Hoots! The callant's in a creel!' she cried. 'Think ye a spy? What else should I think ye—me that kens naething by ye? But I see that I was wrong; and as I cannot fight, I'll have to apologise. A bonny figure I would be with a broadsword. Ay! Ay!' she went on, 'you're none such a bad lad in your way; I think ye'll have some redeeming vices. But, O! Davit Balfour, ye're damned countryfeed. Ye'll have to win over that, lad; ye'll have to soople your back-bone, and think a wee pickle less of your dainty self; and ye'll have to try to find out that women-folk are nae grenadiers. But that can never be. To your last day you'll ken no more of women-folk than what I do of sow-gelding.'

I had never been used with such expressions from a lady's tongue, the only two ladies I had known, Mrs. Campbell and my mother, being most devout and most particular women; and I suppose my amazement must have been depicted in my countenance, for Mrs. Ogilvy burst forth suddenly in a fit of laughter.

'Keep me!' she cried, struggling with her mirth, 'you have the finest timber face—and you to marry the daughter of a Hieland cateran! Davie, my dear, I think we'll have to make a match of it—if it was just to see the weans. And now,' she went on, 'there's no manner of service in your daidling here, for the young woman is from home, and it's my fear that the old woman is no suitable companion for your father's son. Forbye that I have nobody but myself to look after my reputation, and have been long enough alone with a sedooctive youth. And come back another day for your saxpence!' she cried after me as I left.

My skirmish with this disconcerting lady gave my thoughts a boldness they had otherwise wanted. For two days the image of Catriona had mixed in all my meditations; she made their background, so that I scarce enjoyed my own company without a glint of her in a corner of my mind. But now she came immediately near; I seemed to touch her, whom I had never touched but the once; I let myself flow out to her in a happy weakness, and looking all about, and before and behind, saw the world like an undesirable desert, where men go as soldiers on a march, following their duty with what constancy they have, and Catriona alone there to offer me some pleasure of my days. I wondered at myself that I could dwell on such considerations in that time of my peril and disgrace; and when I remembered my youth I was ashamed. I had my studies to complete; I had to be called into some useful business; I had yet to take my part of service in a place where all must serve; I had yet to learn, and know, and prove myself a man; and I had so much sense as blush that I should be already tempted with these further-on and holier delights and duties. My education spoke home to me sharply; I was never brought up on sugar biscuits but on the hard food of the truth. I knew that he was quite unfit to be a husband who was not prepared to be a father also; and for a boy like me to play the father was a mere derision.

When I was in the midst of these thoughts and about half-way back to town I saw a figure coming to meet me, and the trouble of my heart was heightened. It seemed I had everything in the world to say to her, but nothing to say first; and remembering how tongue-tied I had been that morning at the Advocate's I made sure that I would find myself struck dumb. But when she came up my fears fled away; not even the consciousness of what I had been privately thinking disconcerted me the least; and I found I could talk with her as easily and rationally as I might with Alan.

'Oh!' she cried, 'you have been seeking your sixpence: did you get it?'

I told her no; but now I had met with her my walk was not in vain. 'Though I have seen you to-day already,' said I, and told her where and when.

'I did not see you,' she said. 'My eyes are big, but there are better than mine at seeing far. Only I heard singing in the house.'

'That was Miss Grant,' said I, 'the eldest and the bonniest.'

'They say they are all beautiful,' said she.

'They think the same of you, Miss Drummond,' I replied, 'and were all crowding to the window to observe you.'

'It is a pity about my being so blind,' said she, 'or I might have seen them too. And you were in the house? You must have been having the fine time with the fine music and the pretty ladies.'

'There is just where you are wrong,' said I; 'for I was as uncouth as a sea-fish upon the brae of a mountain. The truth is that I am better fitted to go about with rudas men than pretty ladies.'

'Well, I would think so too, at all events!' said she, at which we both of us laughed.

'It is a strange thing, now,' said I. 'I am not the least afraid with you, yet I could have run from the Miss Grants. And I was afraid of your cousin too.'

'O, I think any man will be afraid of her,' she cried. 'My father is afraid of her himself.'

The name of her father brought me to a stop. I looked at her as she walked by my side; I recalled the man, and the little I knew and the much I guessed of him; and comparing the one with the other, felt like a traitor to be silent.

'Speaking of which,' said I, 'I met your father no later than this morning.'

'Did you?' she cried, with a voice of joy that seemed to mock at me. 'You saw James More? You will have spoken with him, then?'

'I did even that,' said I.

Then I think things went the worst way for me that was humanly possible. She gave me a look of mere gratitude. 'Ah, thank you for that!' says she.

'You thank me for very little,' said I, and then stopped. But it seemed when I was holding back so much, something at least had come out. 'I spoke rather ill to him,' said I; 'I did not like him very much; I spoke him rather ill, and he was angry.'

'I think you had little to do then, and less to tell it to his daughter!' she cried out. 'But those that do not love and cherish him I will not know.'

'I will take the freedom of a word yet,' said I, beginning to tremble. 'Perhaps neither your father nor I are in the best of good spirits at Prestongrange's. I dare say we both have anxious business there, for it's a dangerous house. I was sorry for him too, and spoke to him the first, if I could but have spoken the wiser. And for one thing, in my opinion, you will soon find that his affairs are mending.'

'It will not be through your friendship, I am thinking,' said she; 'and he is much made up to you for your sorrow.'

'Miss Drummond,' cried I, 'I am alone in this world. . . .'

'And I am not wondering at that,' said she.

'O, let me speak!' said I. 'I will speak but the once, and then leave you, if you will, for ever. I came this day in the hopes of a kind word that I am sore in want of. I know that what I said must hurt you, and I knew it then. It would have been easy to have spoken smooth, easy to lie to you; can you not think how I was tempted to the same? Cannot you see the truth of my heart shine out?'

'I think here is a great deal of work, Mr. Balfour,' said she. 'I think we will have met but the once, and will can part like gentle-folk.'

'O, let me have one to believe in me!' I pleaded, 'I cannae bear it else.* The whole world is clanned against me. How am I to go through with my dreadful fate? If there's to be none to believe in me I cannot do it. The man must just die, for I cannot do it.'

She had still looked straight in front of her, head in air; but at my words or the tone of my voice she came to a stop. 'What is this you say?' she asked. 'What are you talking of?'

'It is my testimony which may save an innocent life,' said I, 'and they will not suffer me to bear it. What would you do yourself? You know what this is, whose father lies in danger. Would you desert the poor soul? They have tried all ways with me. They have sought to bribe me; they offered me hills and valleys. And to-day that sleuth-hound told me how I stood, and to what a length he would go to butcher and disgrace me. I am to be brought in a party to the murder; I am to have held Glenure in talk for money and old clothes; I am to be killed and shamed. If this is the way I am to fall, and me scarce a man—if this is the story to be told of me in all Scotland—if you are to believe it too, and my name is to be nothing but a by-word—Catriona, how can I go through with it? The thing's not possible; it's more than a man has in his heart.'

I poured my words out in a whirl, one upon the other; and when I stopped I found her gazing on me with a startled face.

'Glenure! It is the Appin murder,' she said softly, but with a very deep surprise.

I had turned back to bear her company, and we were now come near the head of the brae above Dean village. At this word I stepped in front of her like one suddenly distracted.

'For God's sake!' I cried, 'for God's sake, what is this that I have done?' and carried my fists to my temples. 'What made me do it? Sure, I am bewitched to say these things!'

'In the name of heaven, what ails you now?' she cried.

'I gave my honour,' I groaned, 'I gave my honour and now I have broke it. O, Catriona!'

'I am asking you what it is,' she said; 'was it these things you should not have spoken? And do you think I have no honour, then? or that I am one that would betray a friend? I hold up my right hand to you and swear.'

'O, I knew you would be true!' said I. 'It's me—it's here. I that stood but this morning and outfaced them, that risked rather to die disgraced upon the gallows than do wrong—and a few hours after I throw my honour away by the roadside in common talk! "There is one thing clear upon our interview," says he, "that I can rely on your pledged word." Where is my word now? Who could believe me now? *You* could not believe me. I am clean fallen down; I had best die!' All this I said with a weeping voice, but I had no tears in my body.

'My heart is sore for you,' said she, 'but be sure you are too nice. I would not believe you, do you say? I would trust you with anything. And these men? I would not be thinking of them! Men who go about to entrap and to destroy you! Fy! this is no time to crouch. Look up! Do you not think I will be admiring you like a great hero of the good—and you a boy not much older than myself? And because you said a word too much in a friend's ear, that would die ere she betrayed you—to make such a matter! It is one thing that we must both forget.'

'Catriona,' said I, looking at her, hang-dog, 'is this true of it? Would ye trust me yet?'

'Will you not believe the tears upon my face?' she cried. 'It is the world I am thinking of you, Mr. David Balfour. Let them hang you; I will never forget, I will grow old and still remember you. I think it is great to die so; I will envy you that gallows.'

'And maybe all this while I am but a child frighted with bogles,' said I. 'Maybe they but make a mock of me.'

'It is what I must know,' she said. 'I must hear the whole. The harm is done at all events, and I must hear the whole.'

I had sat down on the wayside, where she took a place beside me, and I told her all that matter much as I have written it, my thoughts about her father's dealing being alone omitted.

'Well,' she said, when I had finished, 'you are a hero, surely, and I never would have thought that same! And I think you are in peril, too. O, Simon Fraser! to think upon that man! For his life and the dirty money, to be dealing in such traffic!' And just then she called out aloud with a queer word that was common with her, and belongs, I believe, to her own language. 'My torture!' says she, 'look at the sun!'

Indeed, it was already dipping towards the mountains.

She bid me come again soon, gave me her hand, and left me in a turmoil of glad spirits. I delayed to go home to my lodging, for I had a terror of immediate arrest; but got some supper at a change-house, and the better part of that night walked by myself in the barley-fields, and had such a sense of Catriona's presence that I seemed to bear her in my arms.

CHAPTER VIII

THE BRAVO

THE next day, August 29th, I kept my appointment at the Advocate's in a coat that I had made to my own measure, and was but newly ready.

'Aha,' says Prestongrange, 'you are very fine to-day; my misses are to have a fine cavalier. Come, I take that kind of you. I take that kind of you, Mr. David. O, we shall do very well yet, and I believe your troubles are nearly at an end.'

'You have news for me?' cried I.

'Beyond anticipation,' he replied. 'Your testimony is after all to be received; and you may go, if you will, in my company to the trial, which is to be held at Inverary, Thursday, 21st *proximo*.'

I was too much amazed to find words.

'In the meanwhile,' he continued, 'though I will not ask you to renew your pledge, I must caution you strictly to be reticent. To-morrow your precognition must be taken; and outside of that, do you know, I think least said will be soonest mended.'

'I shall try to go discreetly,' said I. 'I believe it is yourself that I must thank for his crowning mercy, and I do thank you gratefully. After yesterday, my lord, this is like the doors of Heaven. I cannot find it in my heart to get the thing believed.'

'Ah, but you must try and manage, you must try and manage to believe it,' says he, soothing-like, 'and I am very glad to hear your acknowledgment of obligation, for I think you may be able to repay me very shortly'—he coughed—'or even now. The matter is much changed. Your testimony, which I shall not trouble you for to-day, will doubtless alter the complexion of the case for all concerned, and this makes it less delicate for me to enter with you on a side issue.'

'My lord,' I interrupted, 'excuse me for interrupting you,

but how has this been brought about? The obstacles you told me of on Saturday appeared even to me to be quite insurmountable; how has it been contrived?'

'My dear Mr. David,' said he, 'it would never do for me to divulge (even to you, as you say) the councils of the Government; and you must content yourself, if you please, with the gross fact.'

He smiled upon me like a father as he spoke, playing the while with a new pen; methought it was impossible there could be any shadow of deception in the man: yet when he drew to him a sheet of paper, dipped his pen among the ink, and began to address me, I was somehow not certain, and fell instinctively into an attitude of guard.

'There is a point I wish to touch upon,' he began. 'I purposely left it before upon one side, which need be now no longer necessary. This is not, of course, a part of your examination, which is to follow by another hand; this is a private interest of my own. You say you encountered Alan Breck upon the hill?'

'I did, my lord,' said I.

'This was immediately after the murder?'

'It was.'

'Did you speak to him?'

'I did.'

'You had known him before, I think?' says my lord, carelessly.

'I cannot guess your reason for so thinking, my lord,' I replied, 'but such is the fact.'

'And when did you part with him again?' said he.

'I reserve my answer,' said I. 'The question will be put to me at the assize.'

'Mr. Balfour,' said he, 'will you not understand that all this is without prejudice to yourself? I have promised you life and honour; and, believe me, I can keep my word. You are therefore clear of all anxiety. Alan, it appears, you suppose you can protect; and you talk to me of your gratitude, which I think (if you push me) is not ill-deserved. There are a great many different considerations all pointing the same way; and

I will never be persuaded that you could not help us (if you chose) to put salt on Alan's tail.'

'My lord,' said I, 'I give you my word I do not so much as guess where Alan is.'

He paused a breath. 'Nor how he might be found?' he asked.

I sat before him like a log of wood.

'And so much for your gratitude, Mr. David!' he observed. Again there was a piece of silence. 'Well,' said he, rising, 'I am not fortunate, and we are a couple at cross purposes. Let us speak of it no more; you will receive notice when, where, and by whom, we are to take your precognition. And in the meantime, my misses must be waiting you. They will never forgive me if I detain their cavalier.'

Into the hands of these Graces I was accordingly offered up, and found them dressed beyond what I had thought possible, and looking fair as a posy.

As we went forth from the doors a small circumstance occurred which came afterwards to look extremely big. I heard a whistle sound loud and brief like a signal, and looking all about, spied for one moment the red head of Neil of the Tom, the son of Duncan. The next moment he was gone again, nor could I see so much as the skirt-tail of Catriona, upon whom I naturally supposed him to be then attending.

My three keepers led me out by Bristo and the Bruntsfield Links; whence a path carried us to Hope Park, a beautiful pleasance, laid with gravel-walks, furnished with seats and summer-sheds, and warded by a keeper. The way there was a little longsome; the two younger misses affected an air of genteel weariness that damped me cruelly, the eldest considered me with something that at times appeared like mirth; and though I thought I did myself more justice than the day before, it was not without some effort. Upon our reaching the park I was launched on a bevy of eight or ten young gentlemen (some of them cockaded officers, the rest chiefly advocates) who crowded to attend upon these beauties; and though I was presented to all of them in very good words, it seemed I was by all immediately forgotten. Young folk in a company are like to savage animals: they fall upon or scorn a stranger without civility, or I may say, humanity; and I am sure, if I had been among baboons, they would have shown me quite as much of both. Some of the advocates set up to be wits, and some of the soldiers to be rattles; and I could not tell which of these extremes annoyed me most. All had a manner of handling their swords and coat-skirts, for the which (in mere black envy) I could have kicked them from that park. I dare say, upon their side, they grudged me extremely the fine company in which I had arrived; and altogether I had soon fallen behind, and stepped stiffly in the rear of all that merriment with my own thoughts.

From these I was recalled by one of the officers, Lieutenant Hector Duncansby, a gawky, leering Highland boy, asking if my name was not 'Palfour.'*

I told him it was, not very kindly, for his manner was scant civil.

'Ha, Palfour,' says he, and then, repeating it, 'Palfour, Palfour!'

'I am afraid you do not like my name, sir,' says I, annoyed with myself to be annoyed with such a rustical fellow.

'No,' says he, 'but I wass thinking.'

'I would not advise you to make a practice of that, sir,' says I. 'I feel sure you would not find it to agree with you.'

'Tit you effer hear where Alan Grigor fand the tangs?' said he.

I asked him what he could possibly mean, and he answered, with a heckling laugh, that he thought I must have found the poker in the same place and swallowed it.

There could be no mistake about this, and my cheek burned.

'Before I went about to put affronts on gentlemen,' said I, 'I think I would learn the English language first.'

He took me by the sleeve with a nod and a wink, and led me quietly outside Hope Park. But no sooner were we beyond the view of the promenaders, than the fashion of his countenance changed. 'You tam Lowland scoon'rel!' cries he, and hit me a buffet on the jaw with his closed fist

I paid him as good or better on the return; whereupon he stepped a little back and took off his hat to me decorously.

'Enough plows, I think,' says he. 'I will be the offended shentleman, for who effer heard of such suffeeciency as tell a shentlemans that is the King's officer he cannae speak Cot's English? We have swords at our hurdies, and here is the King's Park at hand. Will ye walk first, or let me show ye the way?'

I returned his bow, told him to go first, and followed him. As he went I heard him grumble to himself about *Cot's English* and the *King's coat*, so that I might have supposed him to be seriously offended. But his manner at the beginning of our interview was there to belie him. It was manifest he had come prepared to fasten a quarrel on me, right or wrong; manifest that I was taken in a fresh contrivance of my enemies; and to me (conscious as I was of my deficiencies) manifest enough that I should be the one to fall in our encounter.

As we came into that rough rocky desert of the King's Park I was tempted half-a-dozen times to take to my heels and run for it, so loath was I to show my ignorance in fencing, and so much averse to die or even to be wounded. But I considered if their malice went as far as this, it would likely stick at nothing; and that to fall by the sword, however ungracefully, was still an improvement on the gallows. I considered besides that by the unguarded pertness of my words and the quickness of my blow I had put myself quite out of court; and that even if I ran, my adversary would probably pursue and catch me, which would add disgrace to my misfortune. So that, taking all in all, I continued marching behind him, much as a man follows the hangman, and certainly with no more hope.

We went about the end of the long craigs, and came into the Hunter's Bog. Here, on a piece of fair turf, my adversary drew. There was nobody there to see us but some birds; and no resource for me but to follow his example, and stand on guard with the best face I could display. It seems it was not good enough for Mr. Duncansby, who spied some flaw in my manœuvres, paused, looked upon me sharply, and came off

and on, and menaced me with his blade in the air. As I had
seen no such proceedings from Alan, and was besides a good
deal affected with the proximity of death, I grew quite be-
wildered, stood helpless, and could have longed to run away.

'Fat deil ails her?' cries the lieutenant.

And suddenly engaging, he twitched the sword out of my
grasp and sent it flying far among the rushes.

Twice was this manœuvre repeated; and the third time
when I brought back my humiliated weapon, I found he had
returned his own to the scabbard, and stood awaiting me with
a face of some anger, and his hands clasped under his
skirt.

'Pe tamned if I touch you!' he cried, and asked me bitterly
what right I had to stand up before 'shentlemans' when I did
not know the back of a sword from the front of it.

I answered that was the fault of my upbringing; and would
he do me the justice to say I had given him all the satisfaction
it was unfortunately in my power to offer, and stood up like
a man?

'And that is the truth,' said he. 'I am fery prave myself,
and pold as a lions. But to stand up there—and you ken
naething of fence!—the way that you did, I declare it was
peyond me. And I am sorry for the plow; though I declare
I pelief your own was the elder brother, and my heid still
sings with it. And I declare if I had kent what way it wass,
I would not put a hand to such a piece of pusiness.'

'That is handsomely said,' I replied, 'and I am sure you
will not stand up a second time to be the actor for my private
enemies.'

'Indeed, no, Palfour,' said he; 'and I think I was used
extremely suffeeciently myself to be set up to fecht with an
auld wife, or all the same as a bairn whateffer! And I will
tell the Master so, and fecht him, by Cot, himself!'

'And if you knew the nature of Mr. Simon's quarrel with
me,' said I, 'you would be yet the more affronted to be mingled
up with such affairs.'

He swore he could well believe it; that all the Lovats were
made of the same meal and the devil was the miller that

ground that; when suddenly shaking me by the hand, he vowed I was a pretty enough fellow after all, that it was a thousand pities I had been neglected, and that if he could find the time, he would give an eye himself to have me educated.

'You can do me a better service than even what you propose,' said I; and when he had asked its nature—'Come with me to the house of one of my enemies, and testify how I have carried myself this day,' I told him. 'That will be the true service. For though he has sent me a gallant adversary for the first, the thought in Mr. Simon's mind is merely murder. There will be a second and then a third; and by what you have seen of my cleverness with the cold steel, you can judge for yourself what is like to be the upshot.'

'And I would not like it myself, if I was no more of a man that what you wass!' he cried. 'But I will do you right, Palfour. Lead on!'

If I had walked slowly on the way into that accursed park my heels were light enough on the way out. They kept time to a very good old air, that is as ancient as the Bible, and the words of it are: '*Surely the bitterness of death is past.*' I mind that I was extremely thirsty, and had a drink at Saint Margaret's well on the road down, and the sweetness of that water passed belief. We went through the sanctuary, up the Canongate, in by the Netherbow, and straight to Prestongrange's door, talking as we came and arranging the details of our affair. The footman owned his master was at home, but declared him engaged with other gentlemen on very private business, and his door forbidden.

'My business is but for three minutes, and it cannot wait,' said I. 'You may say it is by no means private, and I shall be even glad to have some witnesses.'

As the man departed unwillingly enough upon this errand, we made so bold as to follow him to the ante-chamber, whence I could hear for a while the murmuring of several voices in the room within. The truth is, they were three at the one table—Prestongrange, Simon Fraser, and Mr. Erskine, Sheriff of Perth; and as they were met in consultation on the very

business of the Appin murder, they were a little disturbed at
my appearance, but decided to receive me.

'Well, well, Mr. Balfour, and what brings you here again?
and who is this you bring with you?' says Prestongrange.

As for Fraser, he looked before him on the table.

'He is here to bear a little testimony in my favour, my lord,
which I think it very needful you should hear,' said I, and
turned to Duncansby.

'I have only to say this,' said the lieutenant, 'that I stood
up this day with Palfour in the Hunter's Pog, which I am
now fery sorry for, and he behaved himself as pretty as a
shentlemans could ask it. And I have creat respects for
Palfour,' he added.

'I thank you for your honest expressions,' said I.

Whereupon Duncansby made his bow to the company,
and left the chamber, as we had agreed upon before.

'What have I to do with this?' says Prestongrange.

'I will tell your lordship in two words,' said I. 'I have
brought this gentleman, a King's officer, to do me so much
justice. Now I think my character is covered, and until a
certain date, which your lordship can very well supply, it will
be quite in vain to despatch against me any more officers.
I will not consent to fight my way through the garrison of
the castle.'

The veins swelled on Prestongrange's brow, and he
regarded me with fury.

'I think the devil uncoupled this dog of a lad between my
legs!' he cried; and then, turning fiercely on his neighbour,
'This is some of your work, Simon,' he said. 'I spy your hand
in the business, and, let me tell you, I resent it. It is disloyal,
when we are agreed upon one expedient, to follow another
in the dark. You are disloyal to me. What! you let me send
this lad to the place with my very daughters! And because
I let drop a word to you. . . . Fy, sir, keep your dishonours
to yourself!'

Simon was deadly pale. 'I will be a kick-ball between you
and the Duke no longer,' he exclaimed. 'Either come to an
agreement, or come to a differ, and have it out among our-

selves. But I will no longer fetch and carry, and get your contrary instructions, and be blamed by both. For if I were to tell you what I think of all your Hanover business it would make your head sing.'

But Sheriff Erskine had preserved his temper, and now intervened smoothly, 'And in the meantime,' says he, 'I think we should tell Mr. Balfour that his character for valour is quite established. He may sleep in peace. Until the date he was so good as to refer to it shall be put to the proof no more.'

His coolness brought the others to their prudence; and they made haste, with a somewhat distracted civility, to pack me from the house.

CHAPTER IX

THE HEATHER ON FIRE

WHEN I left Prestongrange that afternoon I was for the first time angry. The Advocate had made a mock of me. He had pretended my testimony was to be received and myself respected; and in that very hour, not only was Simon practising against my life by the hands of the Highland soldier, but (as appeared from his own language) Prestongrange himself had some design in operation. I counted my enemies: Prestongrange with all the King's authority behind him; and the Duke with the power of the West Highlands; and the Lovat interest by their side to help them with so great a force in the north, and the whole clan of old Jacobite spies and traffickers. And when I remembered James More, and the red head of Neil the son of Duncan, I thought there was perhaps a fourth in the confederacy, and what remained of Rob Roy's* old desperate sept of caterans would be banded against me with the others. One thing was requisite—some strong friend or wise adviser. The country must be full of such, both able and eager to support me, or Lovat and the Duke and Prestongrange had not been nosing for expedients;

and it made me rage to think that I might brush against my champions in the street and be no wiser.

And just then (like an answer) a gentleman brushed against me going by, gave me a meaning look, and turned into a close. I knew him with the tail of my eye—it was Stewart the Writer; and, blessing my good fortune, turned in to follow him. As soon as I had entered the close I saw him standing in the mouth of a stair, where he made me a signal and immediately vanished. Seven storeys up, there he was again in a house-door, which he locked behind us after we had entered. The house was quite dismantled, with not a stick of furniture; indeed, it was one of which Stewart had the letting in his hands.

'We'll have to sit upon the floor,' said he; 'but we're safe here for the time being, and I've been wearying to see ye, Mr. Balfour.'

'How's it with Alan?' I asked.

'Brawly,' said he. 'Andie picks him up at Gillane sands to-morrow, Wednesday. He was keen to say good-bye to ye, but the way that things were going, I was feared the pair of ye was maybe best apart. And that brings me to the essential: how does your business speed?'

'Why,' said I, 'I was told only this morning that my testimony was accepted, and I was to travel to Inverary with the Advocate, no less.'

'Hout awa!' cried Stewart. 'I'll never believe that.'

'I have maybe a suspicion of my own,' says I, 'but I would like fine to hear your reasons.'

'Well, I tell ye fairly, I'm horn-mad,' cries Stewart. 'If my one hand could pull their Government down I would pluck it like a rotten apple. I'm doer for Appin and for James of the Glens; and, of course, it's my duty to defend my kinsman for his life. Hear how it goes with me, and I'll leave the judgment of it to yourself. The first thing they have to do is to get rid of Alan. They cannae bring in James as art and part until they've brought in Alan first as principal; that's sound law: they could never put the cart before the horse.'

'And how are they to bring in Alan till they can catch him?' says I.

'Ah, but there is a way to evite that arrestment,' said he. 'Sound law, too. It would be a bonny thing if, by the escape of one ill-doer another was to go scatheless, and the remeid is to summon the principal and put him to outlawry for the non-compearance. Now there's four places where a person can be summoned: at his dwelling-house; at a place where he has resided forty days; at the head burgh of the shire where he ordinarily resorts; or lastly (if there be ground to think him forth of Scotland) *at the cross of Edinburgh, and the pier and shore of Leith, for sixty days.* The purpose of which last provision is evident upon its face: being that outgoing ships may have time to carry news of the transaction, and the summonsing be something other than a form. Now take the case of Alan. He has no dwelling-house that ever I could hear of; I would be obliged if anyone would show me where he has lived forty days together since the '45; there is no shire where he resorts whether ordinarily or extraordinarily; if he has a domicile at all, which I misdoubt, it must be with his regiment in France; and if he is not yet forth of Scotland (as we happen to know and they happen to guess) it must be evident to the most dull it's what he's aiming for. Where, then, and what way should he be summoned? I ask it at yourself, a layman.'

'You have given the very words,' said I. 'Here at the cross, and at the pier and shore of Leith, for sixty days.'

'Ye're a sounder Scots lawyer than Prestongrange, then!' cries the Writer. 'He has had Alan summoned once; that was on the twenty-fifth, the day that we first met. Once, and done with it. And where? Where, but at the cross of Inverary, the head burgh of the Campbells? A word in your ear, Mr. Balfour—they're not seeking Alan.'

'What do you mean?' I cried. 'Not seeking him?'

'By the best that I can make of it,' said he. 'Not wanting to find him, in my poor thought. They think perhaps he might set up a fair defence, upon the back of which James, the man they're really after, might climb out. This is not a case, ye see, it's a conspiracy.'

'Yet I can tell you Prestongrange asked after Alan keenly,' said I; 'though, when I come to think of it, he was something of the easiest put by.'

'See that!' says he. 'But there! I may be right or wrong, that's guesswork at the best, and let me get to my facts again. It comes to my ears that James and the witnesses—the witnesses, Mr. Balfour!—lay in close dungeons, and shackled forbye, in the military prison at Fort William; none allowed in to them, nor they to write. The witnesses, Mr. Balfour; heard ye ever the match of that? I assure ye, no old, crooked Stewart of the gang ever outfaced the law more impudently. It's clean in the two eyes of the Act of Parliament of 1700,* anent wrongous imprisonment. No sooner did I get the news than I petitioned the Lord Justice-Clerk. I have his word to-day. There's law for ye! Here's justice!'

He put a paper in my hand, that same mealy-mouthed, false-faced paper that was printed since in the pamphlet 'by a bystander,' for behoof (as the title says) of James's 'poor widow and five children.'

'See,' said Stewart, 'he couldn't dare to refuse me access to my client, so he *recommends the commanding officer to let me in*. Recommends!—the Lord Justice-Clerk of Scotland recommends. Is not the purpose of such language plain? They hope the officer may be so dull, or so very much the reverse, as to refuse the recommendation. I would have to make the journey back again betwixt here and Fort William. Then would follow a fresh delay till I got fresh authority, and they had disavowed the officer—military man, notoriously ignorant of the law, and that—I ken the cant of it. Then the journey a third time; and there we should be on the immediate heels of the trial before I had received my first instruction. Am I not right to call this a conspiracy?'

'It will bear that colour,' said I.

'And I'll go on to prove it to you outright,' said he. 'They have the right to hold James in prison, yet they cannot deny me to visit him. They have no right to hold the witnesses;

but am I to get a sight of them, that should be as free as the Lord Justice-Clerk himself! See—read: *For the rest, refuses to give any orders to keepers of prisons who are not accused as having done anything contrary to the duties of their office.* Anything contrary! Sirs! And the Act of seventeen hunner? Mr. Balfour, this makes my heart to burst; the heather is on fire inside my wame.'

'And the plain English of that phrase,' said I, 'is that the witnesses are still to lie in prison and you are not to see them?'

'And I am not to see them until Inverary, when the court is set!' cries he, 'and then to hear Prestongrange upon *the anxious responsibilities of his office and the great facilities afforded the defence!* But I'll begowk them there, Mr. David. I have a plan to waylay the witnesses upon the road, and see if I cannae get a little harle of justice out of the *military man notoriously ignorant of the law* that shall command the party.'

It was actually so—it was actually on the wayside near Tynedrum, and by the connivance of a soldier officer, that Mr. Stewart first saw the witnesses upon the case.

'There is nothing that would surprise me in this business,' I remarked.

'I'll surprise you ere I'm done!' cries he. 'Do ye see this?'— producing a print still wet from the press. 'This is the libel: see, there's Prestongrange's name to the list of witnesses, and I find no word of any Balfour. But here is not the question. Who do ye think paid for the printing of this paper?'

'I suppose it would likely be King George,' said I.

'But it happens it was me!' he cried. 'Not but it was printed by and for themselves, for the Grants and the Erskines, and yon thief of the black midnight, Simon Fraser. But could I win to get a copy? No! I was to go blindfold to my defence; I was to hear the charges for the first time in court alongst the jury.'

'Is not this against the law?' I asked.

'I cannot say so much,' he replied. 'It was a favour so natural and so constantly rendered (till this nonesuch business) that the law has never looked to it. And now admire the hand of Providence! A stranger is in Fleming's printing house, spies a proof on the floor, picks it up, and carries it to me. Of all things, it was just this libel. Whereupon I had it set again—printed at the expense of the defence: *sumptibus moesti rei**; heard ever the man the like of it?—and here it is for anybody, the muckle secret out—all may see it now. But how do you think I would enjoy this, that has the life of my kinsman on my conscience?'

'Troth, I think you would enjoy it ill,' said I.

'And now you see how it is,' he concluded, 'and why, when you tell me your evidence is to be let in, I laugh aloud in your face.'

It was now my turn. I laid before him in brief Mr. Simon's threats and offers, and the whole incident of the bravo, with the subsequent scene at Prestongrange's. Of my first talk, according to promise, I said nothing, nor indeed was it necessary. All the time I was talking Stewart nodded his head like a mechanical figure; and no sooner had my voice ceased, than he opened his mouth and gave me his opinion in two words, dwelling strong on both of them.

'Disappear yourself,' said he.

'I do not take you,' said I.

'Then I'll carry you there,' said he. 'By my view of it you're to disappear whatever. O, that's outside debate. The Advocate, who is not without some spunks of a remainder decency, has wrung your life-safe out of Simon and the Duke. He has refused to put you on your trial, and refused to have you killed; and there is the clue to their ill words together, for Simon and the Duke can keep faith with neither friend nor enemy. Ye're not to be tried then, and ye're not to be murdered; but I'm in bitter error if ye're not to be kidnapped and carried away like the Lady Grange.* Bet me what ye please—there was their *expedient!*'

'You make me think,' said I, and told him of the whistle and the red-headed retainer, Neil.

'Wherever James More is there's one big rogue, never be deceived on that,' said he. 'His father was none so ill a man, though a kenning on the wrong side of the law, and no friend to my family, that I should waste my breath to be defending him! But as for James he's a brock and a blagyard. I like the appearance of this red-headed Neil as little as yourself. It looks uncanny: fiegh! it smells bad. It was old Lovat that managed the Lady Grange affair; if young Lovat is to handle yours, it'll be all in the family. What's James More in prison for? The same offence: abduction. His men have had practice in the business. He'll be to lend them to be Simon's instruments; and the next thing we'll be hearing, James will have made his peace, or else he'll have escaped; and you'll be in Benbecula or Applecross.'

'Ye make a strong case,' I admitted.

'And what I want,' he resumed, 'is that you should disappear yourself ere they can get their hands upon ye. Lie quiet until just before the trial, and spring upon them at the last of it when they'll be looking for you least. This is always supposing, Mr. Balfour, that your evidence is worth so very great a measure of both risk and fash.'

'I will tell ye one thing,' said I. 'I saw the murderer and it was not Alan.'

'Then, by God, my cousin's saved!' cried Stewart. 'You have his life upon your tongue; and there's neither time, risk, nor money to be spared to bring you to the trial.' He emptied his pockets on the floor. 'Here is all that I have by me,' he went on. 'Take it, ye'll want it ere ye're through. Go straight down this close, there's a way out by there to the Lang Dykes, and by my will of it! see no more of Edinburgh till the clash is over.'

'Where am I to go, then?' I inquired.

'And I wish that I could tell ye!' says he, 'but all the places that I could send ye to would be just the places they would seek. No, ye must fend for yourself, and God be your guiding! Five days before the trial, September the sixteen, get word to me at the *King's Arms* in Stirling; and if ye've managed for yourself as long as that, I'll see that ye reach Inverary.'

'One thing more,' said I. 'Can I no see Alan?'

He seemed boggled. 'Hech, I would rather you wouldnae,' said he. 'But I can never deny that Alan is extremely keen of it, and is to lie this night by Silvermills on purpose. If you're sure that you're not followed, Mr. Balfour—but make sure of that—lie in a good place and watch your road for a clear hour before ye risk it. It would be a dreadful business if both you and him was to miscarry!'

CHAPTER X

THE RED-HEADED MAN

IT was about half-past three when I came forth on the Lang Dykes. Dean was where I wanted to go. Since Catriona dwelled there, and her kinsfolk the Glengyle Macgregors appeared almost certainly to be employed against me, it was just one of the few places I should have kept away from; and being a very young man, and beginning to be very much in love, I turned my face in that direction without pause. As a salve to my conscience and common sense, however, I took a measure of precaution. Coming over the crown of a bit of a rise in the road, I clapped down suddenly among the barley and lay waiting. After a while, a man went by that looked to be a Highlandman, but I had never seen him till that hour. Presently after came Neil of the red head. The next to go past was a miller's cart, and after that nothing but manifest country people. Here was enough to have turned the most foolhardy from his purpose, but my inclination ran too strong the other way. I argued it out that if Neil was on that road, it was the right road to find him in, leading direct to his chief's daughter; as for the other Highlandman, if I was to be startled off by every Highlandman I saw, I would scarce reach anywhere. And having quite satisfied myself with this disingenuous debate, I made the better speed of it, and came a little after four to Mrs. Drummond-Ogilvy's.

Both ladies were within the house; and upon my perceiving them together by the open door, I plucked off my hat and said, 'Here was a lad come seeking saxpence,' which I thought might please the dowager.

Catriona ran out to greet me heartily, and, to my surprise, the old lady seemed scarce less forward than herself. I learned long afterwards that she had despatched a horseman by daylight to Rankeillor at the Queensferry, whom she knew to be the doer for Shaws, and had then in her pocket a letter from that good friend of mine, presenting, in the most favourable view, my character and prospects. But had I read it I could scarce have seen more clear in her designs. Maybe I was *countryfeed*; at least, I was not so much so as she thought; and it was plain enough, even to my homespun wits, that she was bent to hammer up a match between her cousin and a beardless boy that was something of a laird in Lothian.

'Saxpence had better take his broth with us, Catrine,' says she. 'Run and tell the lasses.'

And for the little while we were alone was at a good deal of pains to flatter me; always cleverly, always with the appearance of a banter, still calling me Saxpence, but with such a turn that should rather uplift me in my own opinion. When Catriona returned, the design became if possible more obvious; and she showed off the girl's advantages like a horse-couper with a horse. My face flamed that she should think me so obtuse. Now I would fancy the girl was being innocently made a show of, and then I could have beaten the old carline wife with a cudgel; and now, that perhaps these two had set their heads together to entrap me, and at that I sat and gloomed betwixt them like the very image of ill-will. At last the match-maker had a better device, which was to leave the pair of us alone. When my suspicions are anyway roused it is sometimes a little the wrong side of easy to allay them. But though I knew what breed she was of, and that was a breed of thieves, I could never look in Catriona's face and disbelieve her.

'I must not ask?' says she, eagerly, the same moment we were left alone.

'Ah, but to-day I can talk with a free conscience,' I replied. 'I am lightened of my pledge, and indeed (after what has come and gone since morning) I would not have renewed it were it asked.'

'Tell me,' she said. 'My cousin will not be so long.'

So I told her the tale of the lieutenant from the first step to the last of it, making it as mirthful as I could, and, indeed, there was a matter of mirth in that absurdity.

'And I think you will be as little fitted for the rudas men as for the pretty ladies, after all!' says she, when I had done. 'But what was your father that he could not learn you to draw the sword? It is most ungentle; I have not heard the match of that in anyone.'

"It is most misconvenient at least," said I; 'and I think my father (honest man!)) must have been wool-gathering to learn me Latin in the place of it. But you see I do the best I can, and just stand up like Lot's wife* and let them hammer at me.'

'Do you know what makes me smile?' said she. 'Well, it is this. I am made this way, that I should have been a man child. In my own thoughts it is so I am always; and I go on telling myself about this thing that is to befall and that. Then it comes to the place of the fighting, and it comes over me that I am only a girl at all events, and cannot hold a sword or give one good blow; and then I have to twist my story round about, so that the fighting is to stop, and yet me have the best of it, just like you and the lieutenant; and I am the boy that makes the fine speeches all through, like Mr. David Balfour.'

'You are a bloodthirsty maid,' said I.

'Well, I know it is good to sew and spin, and to make samplers,' she said, 'but if you were to do nothing else in the great world, I think you will say yourself it is a driech business; and it is not that I want to kill, I think. Did ever you kill anyone?'

'That I have, as it chances. Two, no less, and me still a lad that should be at the college,' said I. 'But yet, in the look-back, I take no shame for it.'

'But how did you feel, then—after it?' she asked.

"Deed, I sat down and grat like a bairn,' said I.

'I know that, too,' she cried. 'I feel where these tears should come from. And at any rate, I would not wish to kill, only to be Catherine Douglas,* that put her arm through the staples of the bolt, where it was broken. That is my chief hero. Would you not love to die so—for your king?' she asked.

'Troth,' said I, 'my affection for my king, God bless the puggy face of him, is under more control; and I thought I saw death so near to me this day already, that I am rather taken up with the notion of living.'

'Right,' she said, 'the right mind of a man! Only you must learn arms; I would not like to have a friend that cannot strike. But it will not have been with the sword that you killed these two?'

'Indeed, no,' said I, 'but with a pair of pistols. And a fortunate thing it was the men were so near-hand to me, for I am about as clever with the pistols as I am with the sword.'

So then she drew from me the story of our battle in the brig, which I had omitted in my first account of my affairs.

'Yes,' said she, 'you are brave. And your friend, I admire and love him.'

'Well, and I think anyone would!' said I. 'He has his faults like other folk; but he is brave and staunch and kind, God bless him! That will be a strange day when I forget Alan.' And the thought of him, and that it was within my choice to speak with him that night, had almost overcome me.

'And where will my head be gone that I have not told my news!' she cried, and spoke of a letter from her father, bearing that she might visit him to-morrow in the castle whither he was now transferred, and that his affairs were mending. 'You do not like to hear it,' said she. 'Will you judge my father and not know him?'

'I am a thousand miles from judging,' I replied. 'And I give you my word I do rejoice to know your heart is lightened. If my face fell at all, as I suppose it must, you will allow this is rather an ill day for compositions, and the people in power extremely ill persons to be compounding with. I have Simon Fraser extremely heavy on my stomach still.'

'Ah!' she cried, 'you will not be evening these two; and

you should bear in mind that Prestongrange and James More, my father, are of the one blood.'

'I never heard tell of that,' said I.

'It is rather singular how little you are acquainted with,' said she. 'One part may call themselves Grant, and one Macgregor, but they are still of the same clan. They are all sons of Alpin, from whom, I think, our country has its name.'

'What country is that?' I asked.

'My country and yours,' said she.

'This is my day for discoveries, I think,' said I, 'for I always thought the name of it was Scotland.'

'Scotland is the name of what you call Ireland,' she replied. 'But the old ancient true name of this place that we have our foot-soles on, and that our bones are made of, will be Alban. It was Alban they called it when our forefathers will be fighting for it against Rome and Alexander; and it is called so still in your own tongue that you forget.'

'Troth,' said I, 'and that I never learned!' For I lacked heart to take her up about the Macedonian.*

'But your fathers and mothers talked it, one generation with another,' said she. 'And it was sung about the cradles before you or me were ever dreamed of; and your name remembers it still. Ah, if you could talk that language you would find me another girl. The heart speaks in that tongue.'

I had a meal with the two ladies, all very good, served in fine old plate, and the wine excellent, for it seems that Mrs. Ogilvy was rich. Our talk, too, was pleasant enough; but as soon as I saw the sun decline sharply and the shadows to run out long, I rose to take my leave. For my mind was now made up to say farewell to Alan; and it was needful I should see the trysting wood, and reconnoitre it, by daylight. Catriona came with me as far as to the garden gate.

'It is long till I see you now?' she asked.

'It is beyond my judging,' I replied. 'It will be long, it may be never.'

'It may be so,' said she. 'And you are sorry?'

I bowed my head, looking upon her.

'So am I, at all events,' said she. 'I have seen you but a small time, but I put you very high. You are true, you are brave; in time I think you will be more of a man yet. I will be proud to hear of that. If you should speed worse, if it will come to fall as we are afraid—O well! think you have the one friend. Long after you are dead and me an old wife, I will be telling the bairns about David Balfour, and my tears running. I will be telling how we parted, and what I said to you, and did to you. *God go with you and guide you, prays your little friend:* so I said—I will be telling them—and here is what I did.'

She took up my hand and kissed it. This so surprised my spirits that I cried out like one hurt. The colour came strong in her face, and she looked at me and nodded.

'O yes, Mr. David,' said she, 'that is what I think of you. The heart goes with the lips.'

I could read in her face high spirit, and a chivalry like a brave child's; not anything besides. She kissed my hand, as she had kissed Prince Charlie's, with a higher passion than the common kind of clay has any sense of. Nothing before had taught me how deep I was her lover, nor how far I had yet to climb to make her think of me in such a character. Yet I could tell myself I had advanced some way, and that her heart had beat and her blood flowed at thoughts of me.

After that honour she had done me I could offer no more trivial civility. It was even hard for me to speak; a certain lifting in her voice had knocked directly at the door of my own tears.

'I praise God for your kindness, dear,' said I. 'Farewell, my little friend!' giving her that name which she had given to herself; with which I bowed and left her.

My way was down the glen of the Leith River, towards Stockbridge and Silvermills. A path led in the foot of it, the water bickered and sang in the midst; the sunbeams overhead struck out of the west among long shadows and (as the valley turned) made like a new scene and a new world of it at every corner. With Catriona behind and Alan before me, I was like one lifted up. The place besides, and the hour, and the talking of the water, infinitely pleased me; and I lingered in my steps and looked before and behind me as I went. This was the cause, under Providence, that I spied a little in my rear a red head among some bushes.

Anger sprang in my heart, and I turned straight about and walked at a stiff pace to where I came from. The path lay close by the bushes where I had remarked the head. The cover came to the wayside, and as I passed I was all strung up to meet and to resist an onfall. No such thing befell, I went by unmeddled with; and at that fear increased upon me. It was still day indeed, but the place exceeding solitary. If my haunters had let slip that fair occasion I could but judge they aimed at something more than David Balfour. The lives of Alan and James weighed upon my spirit with the weight of two grown bullocks.

Catriona was yet in the garden walking by herself.

'Catriona,' said I, 'you see me back again.'

'With a changed face,' said she.

'I carry two men's lives besides my own,' said I. 'It would be a sin and a shame not to walk carefully. I was doubtful whether I did right to come here. I would like it ill, if it was by that means we were brought to harm.'

'I could tell you one that would be liking it less, and will like little enough to hear you talking at this very same time,' she cried. 'What have I done, at all events?'

'O, you! you are not alone,' I replied. 'But since I went off I have been dogged again, and I can give you the name of him that follows me. It is Neil, son of Duncan, your man or your father's.'

'To be sure you are mistaken there,' she said, with a white face. 'Neil is in Edinburgh on errands from my father.'

'It is what I fear,' said I, 'the last of it. But for his being in Edinburgh I think I can show you another of that. For sure you have some signal, a signal of need, such as would bring him to your help, if he was anywhere within the reach of ears and legs?'

'Why, how will you know that?' says she.

'By means of a magical talisman God gave to me when I was born, and the name they call it by is Commonsense,' said I. 'Oblige me so far as make your signal, and I will show you the red head of Neil.'

No doubt but I spoke bitter and sharp. My heart was bitter. I blamed myself and the girl and hated both of us: her for the vile crew that she was come of, myself for my wanton folly to have stuck my head in such a byke of wasps.

Catriona set her fingers to her lips and whistled once, with an exceeding clear, strong, mounting note, as full as a ploughman's. A while we stood silent; and I was about to ask her to repeat the same, when I heard the sound of someone bursting through the bushes below on the braeside. I pointed in that direction with a smile, and presently Neil leaped into the garden. His eyes burned, and he had a black knife (as they call it on the Highland side) naked in his hand; but, seeing me beside his mistress, stood like a man struck.

'He has come to your call,' said I; 'judge how near he was to Edinburgh, or what was the nature of your father's errands. Ask himself. If I am to lose my life, or the lives of those that hang by me, through the means of your clan, let me go where I have to go with my eyes open.'

She addressed him tremulously in the Gaelic. Remembering Alan's anxious civility in that particular, I could have laughed out loud for bitterness; here, sure, in the midst of these suspicions, was the hour she should have stuck by English.

Twice or thrice they spoke together, and I could make out that Neil (for all his obsequiousness) was an angry man.

Then she turned to me. 'He swears it is not,' she said.

'Catriona,' said I, 'do you believe the man yourself?'

She made a gesture like wringing the hands.

'How will I can know?' she cried.

'But I must find some means to know,' said I. 'I cannot continue to go dovering round in the black night with two men's lives at my girdle! Catriona, try to put yourself in my place, as I vow to God I try hard to put myself in yours. This is no kind of talk that should ever have fallen between me and you; no kind of talk; my heart is sick with it. See, keep

of wood by east of Silvermills and by south the south mill-lade.' This I found easy enough, where it grew on a steep brae, with the mill-lade flowing swift and deep along the foot of it; and here I began to walk slower and to reflect more reasonably on my employment. I saw I had made but a fool's bargain with Catriona. It was not to be supposed that Neil was sent alone upon his errand, but perhaps he was the only man belonging to James More; in which case, I should have done all I could to hang Catriona's father, and nothing the least material to help myself. To tell the truth, I fancied neither one of these ideas. Suppose, by holding back Neil, the girl should have helped to hang her father, I thought she would never forgive herself this side of time. And suppose there were others pursuing me that moment, what kind of a gift was I come bringing to Alan? and how would I like that?

I was up with the west end of that wood when these two considerations struck me like a cudgel. My feet stopped of themselves and my heart along with them. 'What wild game is this that I have been playing?' thought I; and turned instantly upon my heels to go elsewhere.

This brought my face to Silvermills; the path came past the village with a crook, but all plainly visible; and, Highland or Lowland, there was nobody stirring. Here was my advantage, here was just such a conjuncture as Stewart had counselled me to profit by, and I ran by the side of the mill-lade, fetched about beyond the east corner of the wood, threaded through the midst of it, and returned to the west selvage, whence I could again command the path, and yet be myself unseen. Again it was all empty, and my heart began to rise.

For more than an hour I sat close in the border of the trees, and no hare or eagle could have kept a more particular watch. When that hour began the sun was already set, but the sky still all golden and the daylight clear; before the hour was done it had fallen to be half mirk, the images and distances of things were mingled, and observation began to be difficult. All that time not a foot of man had come east from Silvermills, and the few that had gone west were honest country-folk and their wives upon the road to bed. If I were tracked by the most cunning spies in Europe, I judged it was beyond the course of nature they could have any jealousy of where I was; and going a little further home into the wood I lay down to wait for Alan.

The strain of my attention had been great, for I had watched not the path only, but every bush and field within my vision. That was now at an end. The moon, which was in her first quarter, glinted a little in the wood; all round there was a stillness of the country; and as I lay there on my back, the next three or four hours, I had a fine occasion to review my conduct.

Two things became plain to me first: that I had had no right to go that day to Dean, and (having gone there) had now no right to be lying where I was. This (where Alan was to come) was just the one wood in all broad Scotland that was, by every proper feeling, closed against me; I admitted that, and yet stayed on, wondering at myself. I thought of the measure with which I had meted to Catriona that same night; how I had prated of the two lives I carried, and had thus forced her to enjeopardy her father's; and how I was here exposing them again, it seemed in wantonness. A good conscience is eight parts of courage. No sooner had I lost conceit of my behaviour, than I seemed to stand disarmed amidst a throng of terrors. Of a sudden I sat up. How if I went now to Prestongrange, caught him (as I still easily might) before he slept, and made a full submission? Who could blame me? Not Stewart the Writer; I had but to say that I was followed, despaired of getting clear, and so gave in. Not Catriona: here, too, I had my answer ready; that I could not bear she should expose her father. So, in a moment, I could lay all these troubles by, which were after all and truly none of mine; swim clear of the Appin murder; get forth out of hand-stroke of all the Stewarts and Campbells, all the Whigs and Tories, in the land; and live thenceforth to my own mind, and be able to enjoy and to improve my fortunes, and devote some hours of my youth to courting Catriona, which would be surely a more suitable occupation than to hide and run and be followed like a hunted thief, and begin over again the dreadful miseries of my escape with Alan.

At first I thought no shame of this capitulation; I was only amazed I had not thought upon the thing and done it earlier; and began to inquire into the causes of the change. These I traced to my lowness of spirits, that back to my late recklessness, and that again to the common, old, public, disconsidered sin of self-indulgence. Instantly the text came in my head, 'How can Satan cast out Satan?' What? (I thought) I had, by self-indulgence, and the following of pleasant paths, and the lure of a young maid, cast myself wholly out of conceit with my own character, and jeopardised the lives of James and Alan? And I was to seek the way out by the same road as I had entered in? No; the hurt that had been caused by self-indulgence must be cured by self-denial; the flesh I had pampered must be crucified. I looked about me for that course which I least liked to follow: this was to leave the wood without waiting to see Alan, and go forth again alone, in the dark and in the midst of my perplexed and dangerous fortunes.

I have been the more careful to narrate this passage of my reflections, because I think it is of some utility, and may serve as an example to young men. But there is reason (they say) in planting kale, and even in ethic and religion, room for common sense. It was already close on Alan's hour, and the moon was down. If I left (as I could not very decently whistle to my spies to follow me) they might miss me in the dark and tack themselves to Alan by mistake. If I stayed, I could at the least of it set my friend upon his guard which might prove his mere salvation. I had adventured other people's safety in a course of self-indulgence; to have endangered them again, and now on a mere design of penance, would have been scarce rational. Accordingly, I had scarce risen from my place ere I sat down again, but already in a different frame of spirits, and equally marvelling at my past weakness and rejoicing in my present composure.

Presently after came a crackling in the thicket. Putting my mouth near down to the ground, I whistled a note or two of Alan's air; an answer came, in the like guarded tone, and soon we had knocked together in the dark.

'Is this you at last, Davie?' he whispered.

'Just myself,' said I.

'God, man, but I've been wearying to see ye!' says he. 'I've had the longest kind of a time. A' day, I've had my dwelling into the inside of a stack of hay, where I couldnae see the nebs of my ten fingers; and then two hours of it waiting here for you, and you never coming! Dod, and ye're none too soon the way it is, with me to sail the morn! The morn? what am I saying?—the day, I mean.'

'Ay, Alan, man, the day, sure enough,' said I. 'It's past twelve now, surely, and ye sail the day. This'll be a long road you have before you.'

'We'll have a long crack of it first,' said he.

'Well, indeed, and I have a good deal it will be telling you to hear,' said I.

And I told him what behooved, making rather a jumble of it, but clear enough when done. He heard me out with very few questions, laughing here and there like a man delighted: and the sound of his laughing (above all there, in the dark, where neither one of us could see the other) was extraordinary friendly to my heart.

'Ay, Davie, ye're a queer character,' says he, when I had done: 'a queer bitch after a', and I have no mind of meeting with the like of ye. As for your story, Prestongrange is a Whig like yoursel', so I'll say the less of him; and, dod! I believe he was the best friend ye had, if ye could only trust him. But Simon Fraser and James More are my ain kind of cattle, and I'll give them the name that they deserve. The muckle black deil was father to the Frasers, a'body kens that; and as for the Gregara, I never could abye the reek of them since I could stotter on two feet. I bloodied the nose of one, I mind, when I was still so wambly on my legs that I cowped upon the top of him. A proud man was my father that day, God rest him! and I think he had the cause. I'll never can deny but what Robin was something of a piper,' he added; 'but as for James More, the deil guide him for me!'

'One thing we have to consider,' said I. 'Was Charles Stewart right or wrong? Is it only me they're after, or the pair of us?'

'And what's your ain opinion, you that's a man of so much experience?' said he.

'It passes me,' said I.

'And me too,' says Alan. 'Do ye think this lass would keep her word to ye?' he asked.

'I do that,' said I.

'Well, there's nae telling,' said he. 'And anyway, that's over and done: he'll be joined to the rest of them lang syne.'

'How many would ye think there would be of them?' I asked.

'That depends,' said Alan. 'If it was only you, they would likely send two-three lively, brisk young birkies, and if they thought that I was to appear in the employ, I dare say ten or twelve,' said he.

It was no use, I gave a little crack of laughter.

'And I think your own two eyes will have seen me drive that number, or the double of it, nearer hand!' cries he.

'It matters the less,' said I, 'because I am well rid of them for this time.'

'Nae doubt that's your opinion,' said he; 'but I wouldnae be the least surprised if they were hunkering this wood. Ye see, David man, they'll be Hieland folk. There'll be some Frasers, I'm thinking, and some of the Gregara; and I would never deny but what the both of them, and the Gregara in especial, were clever experienced persons. A man kens little till he's driven a spreagh of neat cattle (say) ten miles through a throng Lowland country and the black soldiers maybe at his tail. It's there that I learned a great part of my penetration. And ye need nae tell me: it's better than war; which is the next best, however, though generally rather a bauchle of a business. Now the Gregara have had grand practice.'

'No doubt that's a branch of education that was left out with me,' said I.

'And I can see the marks of it upon ye constantly,' said Alan. 'But that's the strange thing about you folk of the college learning: ye're ignorant, and ye cannae see 't. Wae's me for my Greek and Hebrew; but, man, I ken that I dinnae ken them—there's the differ of it. No, here's you. Ye lie on your wame a bittie in the bield of this wood, and ye tell me that ye've cuist off these Frasers and Macgregors. Why? *Because I couldnae see them*, says you. Ye blockhead, that's their livelihood.'

'Take the worst of it,' said I, 'and what are we to do?'

'I am thinking of that same,' said he. 'We might twine. It wouldnae be greatly to my taste; and forby that, I see reasons against it. First, it's now unco dark, and it's just humanly possible we might give them the clean slip. If we keep together, we make but the ae line of it; if we gang separate, we make twae of them: the more likelihood to stave in upon some of these gentry of yours. And then, second, if they keep the track of us, it may come to a fecht for it yet, Davie; and then, I'll confess I would be blythe to have you at my oxter, and I think you would be none the worse of having me at yours. So, by my way of it, we should creep out of this wood no further gone than just the inside of next minute, and hold away east for Gillane, where I'm to find my ship. It'll be like old days while it lasts, Davie; and (come the time) we'll have to think what you should be doing. I'm wae to leave ye here, wanting me.'

'Have with ye, then!' says I. 'Do ye gang back where you were stopping?'

'Deil a fear!' said Alan. 'They were good folks to me, but I think they would be a good deal disappointed if they saw my bonny face again. For (the way times go) I amnae just what ye could call a Welcome Guest. Which makes me the keener for your company, Mr. David Balfour of the Shaws, and set ye up! For, leave aside twa cracks here in the wood with Charlie Stewart, I have scarce said black or white since the day we parted at Corstorphine.'

With which he rose from his place, and we began to move quietly eastward through the wood.

CHAPTER XII

ON THE MARCH AGAIN WITH ALAN

IT was likely between one and two; the moon (as I have said) was down; a strongish wind, carrying a heavy wrack of cloud, had set in suddenly from the west; and we began our movement in as black a night as ever a fugitive or a murderer wanted. The whiteness of the path guided us into the sleeping town of Broughton, thence through Picardy, and beside my old acquaintance the gibbet of the two thieves. A little beyond we made a useful beacon, which was a light in an upper window of Lochend. Steering by this, but a good deal at random, and with some trampling of the harvest, and stumbling and falling down upon the bauks, we made our way across country, and won forth at last upon the linky, boggy muirland that they call the Figgate Whins. Here, under a bush of whin, we lay down the remainder of that night and slumbered.

The day called us about five. A beautiful morning it was, the high westerly wind still blowing strong, but the clouds all blown away to Europe. Alan was already sitting up and smiling to himself. It was my first sight of my friend since we were parted, and I looked upon him with enjoyment. He had still the same big great-coat on his back; but (what was new) he had now a pair of knitted boot-hose drawn above the knee. Doubtless these were intended for disguise; but, as the day promised to be warm, he made a most unseasonable figure.

'Well, Davie,' said he, 'is this no a bonny morning? Here is a day that looks the way that a day ought to. This is a great change of it from the belly of my haystack; and while you were there sottering and sleeping I have done a thing that maybe I do over seldom.'

'And what was that?' said I.

'O, just said my prayers,' said he.

'And where are my gentry, as ye call them?' I asked.

'Gude kens;' says he. 'And the short and the long of it is that we must take our chance of them. Up with your foot-soles, Davie! Forth, Fortune, once again of it! And a bonny walk we are like to have.'

So we went east by the beach of the sea, towards where the salt-pans were smoking in by the Esk mouth. No doubt there was a by-ordinary bonny blink of morning sun on Arthur's Seat and the Green Pentlands; and the pleasantness of the day appeared to set Alan among nettles.

'I feel like a gomeral,' says he, 'to be leaving Scotland on a day like this. It sticks in my head; I would maybe like it better to stay here and hing.'

'Ay, but ye wouldnae, Alan,' said I.

'No, but what France is a good place too,' he explained; 'but it's some way no the same. It's brawer, I believe, but it's no Scotland. I like it fine when I'm there, man; yet I kind of weary for Scots divots and the Scots peat-reek.'

'If that's all you have to complain of, Alan, it's no such great affair,' said I.

'And it sets me ill to be complaining, whatever,' said he, 'and me but new out of yon deil's haystack.'

'And so you were unco weary of your haystack?' I asked.

'Weary's nae word for it,' said he. 'I'm not just precisely a man that's easily cast down; but I do better with caller air and the lift above my head. I'm like the auld Black Douglas (wasnae't?) that likit better to hear the laverock sing than the mouse cheep. And yon place, ye see, Davie—whilk was a very suitable place to hide in, as I'm free to own—was pit mirk from dawn to gloaming. There were days (or nights, for how would I tell one from other?) that seemed to me as long as a long winter.'

'How did you know the hour to bide your tryst?' I asked.

'The goodman brought me my meat and a drop brandy, and a candle-dowp to eat it by, about eleeven,' said he. 'So, when I had swallowed a bit, it would be time to be getting to the wood. There I lay and wearied for ye sore, Davie,' says he, laying his hand on my shoulder, 'and guessed when the two hours would be about by—unless Charlie Stewart would come and tell me on his watch—and then back to the dooms haystack. Na, it was a driech employ, and praise the Lord that I have warstled through with it!'

'What did you do with yourself?' I asked.

'Faith,' said he, 'the best I could! Whiles I played at the knucklebones. I'm an extraordinar good hand at the knuckle-bones, but it's a poor piece of business playing with naebody to admire ye. And whiles I would make songs.'

'What were they about?' says I.

'O, about the deer and the heather,' says he, 'and about the ancient old chiefs that are all by with it lang syne, and just about what songs are about in general. And then whiles I would make believe I had a set of pipes and I was playing. I played some grand springs, and I thought I played them awful bonny; I vow whiles that I could hear the squeal of them! But the great affair is that it's done with.'

With that he carried me again to my adventures, which he heard all over again with more particularity, and extra-ordinary approval, swearing at intervals that I was 'a queer character of a callant.'

'So ye were frich'ened of Sim Fraser?' he asked once.

'In troth was I?' cried I.

'So would I have been, Davie,' said he. 'And that is indeed a dreidful man. But it is only proper to give the deil his due; and I can tell you he is a most respectable person on the field of war.'

'Is he so brave?' I asked.

'Brave!' said he. 'He is as brave as my steel sword.'

The story of my duel set him beside himself.

'To think of that!' he cried. 'I showed ye the trick in Corrynakiegh too. And three times—three times disarmed! It's a disgrace upon my character that learned ye! Here, stand up, out with your airn; ye shall walk no step beyond this place upon the road till ye can do yoursel' and me mair credit.'

'Alan,' said I, 'this is midsummer madness. Here is no time for fencing lessons.'

'I cannae well say no to that,' he admitted. 'But three

times, man! And you standing there like a straw bogle and rinning to fetch your ain sword like a doggie with a pocket-napkin! David, this man Duncansby must be something alto-gether by-ordinar! He maun be extraordinar skilly. If I had the time, I would gang straight back and try a turn at him mysel'. The man must be a provost.'

'You silly fellow,' said I, 'you forget it was just me.'

'Na,' said he, 'but three times!'

'When ye ken yourself that I am fair incompetent,' I cried.

'Well, I never heard tell the equal of it,' said he.

'I promise you the one thing, Alan,' said I. 'The next time that we forgather, I'll be better learned. You shall not con-tinue to bear the disgrace of a friend that cannot strike.'

'Ay, the next time!' says he. 'And when will that be, I would like to ken?'

'Well, Alan, I have had some thoughts of that, too,' said I; 'and my plan is this. It's my opinion to be called an advocate.'

'That's but a weary trade, Davie,' says Alan, 'and rather a blagyard one forby. Ye would be better in a king's coat than that.'

'And no doubt that would be the way to have us meet,' cried I. 'But as you'll be in King Lewie's coat, and I'll be in King Geordie's, we'll have a dainty meeting of it.'

'There's some sense in that,' he admitted.

'An advocate, then, it'll have to be,' I continued, 'and I think it a more suitable trade for a gentleman that was *three times* disarmed. But the beauty of the thing is this: that one of the best colleges for that kind of learning—and the one where my kinsman, Pilrig, made his studies—is the college of Leyden in Holland. Now, what say you, Alan? Could not a cadet of *Royal Ecossais* get a furlough, slip over the marches, and call in upon a Leyden student?'

'Well, and I would think he could!' cried he. 'Ye see, I stand well in with my colonel, Count Drummond-Melfort; and, what's mair to the purpose, I have a cousin of mine lieutenant-colonel in a regiment of the Scots-Dutch. Naething could be mair proper than what I would get a leave to see

Lieutenant-Colonel Stewart of Halkett's. And Lord Melfort, who is a very scienteefic kind of a man, and writes books like Caesar, would be doubtless very pleased to have the advantage of my observes.'

'Is Lord Melfort an author, then?' I asked, for much as Alan thought of soldiers, I thought more of the gentry that write books.

'The very same, Davie,' said he. 'One would think a colonel would have something better to attend to. But what can I say that make songs?'

'Well, then,' said I, 'it only remains you should give me an address to write you at in France; and as soon as I am got to Leyden I will send you mine.'

'The best will be to write me in the care of my chieftain,' said he, 'Charles Stewart, of Ardshiel, Esquire, at the town of Melons, in the Isle of France. It might take long, or it might take short, but it would aye get to my hands at the last of it.'

We had a haddock to our breakfast in Musselburgh, where it amused me vastly to hear Alan. His great-coat and boot-hose were extremely remarkable this warm morning, and perhaps some hint of an explanation had been wise; but Alan went into that matter like a business, or I should rather say, like a diversion. He engaged the goodwife of the house with some compliments upon the rizzoring of our haddocks; and the whole of the rest of our stay held her in talk about a cold he had taken on his stomach, gravely relating all manner of symptoms and sufferings, and hearing with a vast show of interest all the old wives' remedies she could supply him with in return.

We left Musselburgh before the first ninepenny coach was due from Edinburgh, for (as Alan said) that was a rencounter we might very well avoid. The wind, although still high, was very mild, the sun shone strong, and Alan began to suffer in proportion. From Prestonpans he had me aside to the fields of Gladsmuir, where he exerted himself a great deal more than needful to describe the stages of the battle. Thence, at his old round pace, we travelled to Cockenzie. Though they were building herring-busses there at Mrs. Cadell's, it seemed a desert-like, backgoing town, about half full of ruined houses; but the ale-house was clean, and Alan, who was now in a glowing heat, must indulge himself with a bottle of ale, and carry on to the new luckie with the old story of the cold upon his stomach, only now the symptoms were all different.

I sat listening; and it came in my mind that I had scarce ever heard him address three serious words to any woman, but he was always drolling and fleering and making a private mock of them, and yet brought to that business a remarkable degree of energy and interest. Something to this effect I remarked to him, when the good-wife (as chanced) was called away.

'What do ye want?' says he. 'A man should aye put his best foot forrit with the womenkind; he should aye give them a bit of a story to divert them, the poor lambs! It's what ye should learn to attend to, David; ye should get the principles, it's like a trade. Now, if this had been a young lassie, or onyways bonnie, she would never have heard tell of my stomach, Davie. But since they're too old to be seeking joes, they a' set up to be apotecaries. Why? What do I ken? They'll be just the way God made them, I suppose. But I think a man would be a gomeral that didnae give his attention to the same.'

And here, the luckie coming back, he turned from me as if with impatience to renew their former conversation. The lady had branched some while before from Alan's stomach to the case of a goodbrother of her own in Aberlady, whose last sickness and demise she was describing at extraordinary length. Sometimes it was merely dull, sometimes both dull and awful, for she talked with unction. The upshot was that I fell in a deep muse, looking forth of the window on the road, and scarce marking what I saw. Presently had any been looking they might have seen me to start.

'We pit a fomentation to his feet,' the good-wife was saying, 'and a het stane to his wame, and we gied him hyssop and water of pennyroyal, and fine, clean balsam of sulphur for the hoast. . . .'

'Sir,' says I, cutting very quietly in, 'there's a friend of mine gone by the house.'

'Is that e'en sae?' replies Alan, as though it were a thing of small account. And then, 'Ye were saying, mem?' says he; and the wearyful wife went on.

Presently, however, he paid her with a half-crown piece, and she must go forth after the change.

'Was it him with the red head?' asked Alan.

'Ye have it,' said I.

'What did I tell you in the wood?' he cried. 'And yet it's strange he should be here too! Was he his lane?'

'His lee-lane for what I could see,' said I.

'Did he gang by?' he asked.

'Straight by,' said I, 'and looked neither to the right nor left.'

'And that's queerer yet,' said Alan. 'It sticks in my mind, Davie, that we should be stirring. But where to?—deil hae't! This is like old days fairly,' cries he.

'There is one big differ, though,' said I, 'that now we have money in our pockets.'

'And another big differ, Mr. Balfour,' says he, 'that now we have dogs at our tail. They're on the scent; they're in full cry, David. It's a bad business and be damned to it.' And he sat thinking hard with a look of his that I knew well.

'I'm saying, Luckie,' says he, when the good-wife returned, 'have ye a back road out of this change-house?'

She told him there was and where it led to.

'Then, sir,' says he to me, 'I think that will be the shortest road for us. And here's good-bye to ye, my braw woman; and I'll no forget thon of the cinnamon water.'

We went out by way of the woman's kale-yard, and up a lane among fields. Alan looked sharply to all sides, and seeing we were in a little hollow place of the country, out of view of men, sat down.

'Now for a council of war, Davie,' said he. 'But first of all, a bit lesson to ye. Suppose that I had been like you, what would yon old wife have minded of the pair of us? Just that we had gone out by the back gate. And what does she mind now? A fine, canty, friendly, cracky man, that suffered with the stomach, poor body! and was real ta'en up about the goodbrother. O man, David, try and learn to have some kind of intelligence!'

'I'll try, Alan,' said I.

'And now for him of the red head,' says he; 'was he gaun fast or slow?'

'Betwixt and between,' said I.

'No kind of hurry about the man?' he asked.

'Never a sign of it,' said I.

'Nhm!' said Alan, 'it looks queer. We saw nothing of them this morning on the Whins; he's passed us by, he doesnae seem to be looking, and yet here he is on our road! Dod, Davie, I begin to take a notion. I think it's no you they're seeking, I think it's me; and I think they ken fine where they're gaun.'

'They ken?' I asked.

'I think Andie Scougal's sold me—him or his mate wha kent some part of the affair—or else Chairlie's clerk callant, which would be a pity too,' says Alan; 'and if you askit me for just my inward private conviction, I think there'll be heads cracked on Gillane sands.'

'Alan,' I cried, 'if you're at all right there'll be folk there and to spare. It'll be small service to crack heads.'

'It would aye be a satisfaction though,' says Alan. 'But bide a bit, bide a bit; I'm thinking—and thanks to this bonny westland wind, I believe I've still a chance of it. It's this way, Davie. I'm no trysted with this man Scougal till the gloaming comes. "But," says he, "*if I can get a bit of a wind out of the west I'll be there long or that,*" he says, "*and lie-to for ye behind the Isle of Fidra.*" Now if your gentry kens the place, they ken the time forbye. Do ye see me coming, Davie? Thanks to Johnnie Cope and other red-coat gomerals, I should ken this country like the back of my hand; and if ye're ready for another bit run with Alan Breck, we'll can cast back inshore, and come down to the seaside again by Dirleton. If the ship's there, we'll try and get on board of her. If she's no there, I'll just have to get back to my weary haystack. But either way of it, I think we will leave your gentry whistling on their thumbs.'

'I believe there's some chance in it,' said I. 'Have on with ye, Alan!'

CHAPTER XIII

GILLANE SANDS

I DID not profit by Alan's pilotage as he had done by his marchings under General Cope; for I can scarce tell what way we went. It is my excuse that we travelled exceeding fast. Some part we ran, some trotted, and the rest walked at a vengeance of a pace. Twice, while we were at top speed, we ran against country-folk; but though we plumped into the first from round a corner, Alan was as ready as a loaded musket.

'Hae ye seen my horse?' he gasped.

'Na, man, I haenae seen nae horse the day,' replied the countryman.

And Alan spared the time to explain to him that we were travelling 'ride and tie'; that our charger had escaped, and it was feared he had gone home to Linton. Not only that, but he expended some breath (of which he had not very much left) to curse his own misfortune and my stupidity which was said to be its cause.

'Them that cannae tell the truth,' he observed to myself as we went on again, 'should be aye mindful to leave an honest, handy lee behind them. If folk dinnae ken what ye're doing, Davie, they're terrible taken up with it; but if they think they ken, they care nae mair for it than what I do for pease porridge.'

As we had first made inland, so our road came in the end to lie very due north; the old Kirk of Aberlady for a land-mark on the left; on the right, the top of the Berwick Law; and it was thus we struck the shore again, not far from Dirleton. From North Berwick west to Gillane Ness there runs a string of four small islets, Craigleith, the Lamb, Fidra, and Eyebrough, notable by their diversity of size and shape. Fidra is the most particular, being a strange grey islet of two humps, made the more conspicuous by a piece of ruin; and I mind that (as we drew closer to it) by some door or window of these ruins the sea peeped through like a man's eye. Under the lee of Fidra there is a good anchorage in westerly winds, and there, from a far way off, we could see the *Thistle* riding.

The shore in face of these islets is altogether waste. Here is no dwelling of man, and scarce any passage, or at most of vagabond children running at their play. Gillane is a small place on the far side of the Ness, the folk of Dirleton go to their business in the inland fields, and those of North Berwick straight to the sea-fishing from their haven; so that few parts of the coast are lonelier. But I mind, as we crawled upon our bellies into that multiplicity of heights and hollows, keeping a bright eye upon all sides, and our hearts hammering at our ribs, there was such a shining of the sun and the sea, such a stir of the wind in the bent grass, and such a bustle of down-popping rabbits and up-flying gulls, that the desert seemed to me like a place alive. No doubt it was in all ways well chosen for a secret embarcation, if the secret had been kept; and even now that it was out, and the place watched, we were able to creep unperceived to the front of the sand-hills, where they look down immediately on the beach and sea.

But here Alan came to a full stop.

'Davie,' said he, 'this is a kittle passage! As long as we lie here we're safe; but I'm nane sae muckle nearer to my ship or the coast of France. And as soon as we stand up and signal the brig, it's another matter. For where will your gentry be, think ye?'

'Maybe they're no come yet,' said I. 'And even if they are, there's one clear matter in our favour. They'll be all arranged to take us, that's true. But they'll have arranged for our coming from the east and here we are upon their west.'

'Ay,' says Alan, 'I wish we were in some force, and this

was a battle, we would have bonnily out-manœuvred them! But it isnae, Davit; and the way it is, is a wee thing less inspiring to Alan Breck. I swither, Davie.'

'Time flies, Alan,' said I.

'I ken that,' said Alan. 'I ken naething else, as the French folk say. But this is a dreidful case of heids or tails. O! if I could but ken where your gentry were!'

'Alan,' said I, 'this is no like you. It's got to be now or never.'

> 'This is no me, quo' he,'

sang Alan, with a queer face betwixt shame and drollery,

> 'Neither you nor me, quo' he, neither you nor me,
> Wow, na, Johnnie man! neither you nor me.'

And then of a sudden he stood straight up where he was, and with a handkerchief flying in his right hand, marched down upon the beach. I stood up myself, but lingered behind him, scanning the sandhills to the east. His appearance was at first unremarked: Scougal not expecting him so early, and *my gentry* watching on the other side. Then they awoke on board the *Thistle*, and it seemed they had all in readiness, for there was scarce a second's bustle on the deck before we saw a skiff put round her stern and begin to pull lively for the coast. Almost at the same moment of time, and perhaps half a mile away towards Gillane Ness, the figure of a man appeared for a blink upon a sandhill, waving with his arms; and though he was gone again in the same flash, the gulls in that part continued a little longer to fly wild.

Alan had not seen this, looking straight to seaward at the ship and skiff.

'It maun be as it will!' said he, when I had told him. 'Weel may yon boatie row, or my craig'll have to thole a raxing.'

That part of the beach was long and flat, and excellent walking when the tide was down; a little cressy burn flowed over it in one place to the sea; and the sandhills ran along the head of it like the rampart of a town. No eye of ours could spy what was passsing behind there in the bents, no hurry of ours could mend the speed of the boat's coming: time stood still with us through that uncanny period of waiting.

'There is one thing I would like to ken,' says Alan. 'I would like fine to ken these gentry's orders. We're worth four hunner pound the pair of us: how if they took the guns to us, Davie? They would get a bonny shot from the top of that lang sandy bauk.'

'Morally impossible,' said I. 'The point is that they can have no guns. This thing has been gone about too secret; pistols they may have, but never guns.'

'I believe ye'll be in the right,' says Alan. 'For all which I am wearying a good deal for yon boat.'

And he snapped his fingers and whistled to it like a dog.

It was now perhaps a third of the way in, and we ourselves already hard on the margin of the sea, so that the soft sand rose over my shoes. There was no more to do whatever but to wait, to look as much as we were able at the creeping nearer of the boat, and as little as we could manage at the long impenetrable front of the sandhills, over which the gulls twinkled and behind which our enemies were doubtless marshalling.

'This is a fine, bright, caller place to get shot in,' says Alan suddenly; 'and, man, I wish that I had your courage!'

'Alan!' I cried, 'what kind of talk is this of it? You're just made of courage; it's the character of the man, as I could prove myself if there was nobody else.'

'And you would be the more mistaken,' said he. 'What makes the differ with me is just my great penetration and knowledge of affairs. But for auld, cauld dour, deidly courage, I am not fit to hold a candle to yourself. Look at us two here upon the sands. Here am I, fair hotching to be off; here's you (for all that I ken) in two minds of it whether you'll no stop. Do you think that I could do that, or would? No me! Firstly, because ɪ havenae got the courage and wouldnae daur; and ꜱecondly, because I am a man of so much penetration and would see ye damned first.'

'It's there ye're coming, is it?' I cried. 'Ah, man Alan, you can wile your old wives, but you never can wile me.'

Remembrance of my temptation in the wood made me strong as iron.

'I have a tryst to keep,' I continued. 'I am trysted with your cousin Charlie; I have passed my word.'

'Braw trysts that you'll can keep,' said Alan. 'Ye'll just mistryst aince and for a' with the gentry in the bents. And what for?' he went on with an extreme threatening gravity. 'Just tell me that, my mannie! Are ye to be speerited away like Lady Grange?* Are they to drive a dirk in your inside and bury ye in the bents? Or is it to be the other way, and are they to bring ye in with James? Are they folk to be trustit? Would ye stick your head in the mouth of Sim Fraser and the ither Whigs?' he added with extraordinary bitterness.

'Alan,' cried I, 'they're all rogues and liars, and I'm with ye there. The more reason there should be one decent man in such a land of thieves! My word is passed, and I'll stick to it. I said long syne to your kinswoman that I would stumble at no risk. Do ye mind of that?—the night Red Colin fell, it was. No more I will, then. Here I stop. Prestongrange promised me my life; if he's to be mansworn, here I'll have to die.'

'Aweel, aweel,' said Alan.

All this time we had seen or heard no more of our pursuers. In truth we had caught them unawares; their whole party (as I was to learn afterwards) had not yet reached the scene; what there was of them was spread among the bents towards Gillane. It was quite an affair to call them in and bring them over, and the boat was making speed. They were besides but cowardly fellows: a mere leash of Highland cattle-thieves, of several clans, no gentleman there to be the captain: and the more they looked at Alan and me upon the beach, the less (I must suppose) they liked the looks of us.

Whoever had betrayed Alan it was not the captain: he was in the skiff himself, steering and stirring up his oarsmen, like a man with his heart in his employ. Already he was near in, and the boat scouring—already Alan's face had flamed crimson with the excitement of his deliverance, when our friends in the bents, either in despair to see their prey escape them or with some hope of scaring Andie, raised suddenly a shrill cry of several voices.

This sound, arising from what appeared to be a quite deserted coast, was really very daunting, and the men in the boat held water instantly.

'What's this of it?' sings out the captain, for he was come within an easy hail.

'Freens o' mine,' says Alan, and began immediately to wade forth in the shallow water towards the boat. 'Davie,' he said, pausing, 'Davie, are ye no coming? I am swier to leave ye.'

'Not a hair of me,' said I.

He stood part of a second where he was to his knees in the salt water, hesitating.

'He that will to Cupar, maun to Cupar,' said he, and swashing in deeper than his waist, was hauled into the skiff, which was immediately directed for the ship.

I stood where he had left me, with my hands behind my back; Alan sat with his head turned watching me; and the boat drew smoothly away. Of a sudden I came the nearest hand to shedding tears, and seemed to myself the most deserted, solitary lad in Scotland. With that I turned my back upon the sea and faced the sandhills. There was no sight or sound of man; the sun shone on the wet sand and the dry, the wind blew in the bents, the gulls made a dreary piping. As I passed higher up the beach, the sand-lice were hopping nimbly about the stranded tangles. The devil any other sight or sound in that unchancy place. And yet I knew there were folk there, observing me, upon some secret purpose. They were no soldiers, or they would have fallen on and taken us ere now; doubtless they were some common rogues hired for my undoing, perhaps to kidnap, perhaps to murder me outright. From the position of those engaged, the first was the more likely; from what I knew of their character and ardency in this business, I thought the second very possible; and the blood ran cold about my heart.

I had a mad idea to loosen my sword in the scabbard; for though I was very unfit to stand up like a gentleman blade

to blade, I thought I could do some scathe in a random
combat. But I perceived in time the folly of resistance. This
was no doubt the joint 'expedient' on which Prestongrange
and Fraser were agreed. The first, I was very sure, had done
something to secure my life; the second was pretty likely to
have slipped in some contrary hints into the ears of Neil and
his companions; and if I were to show bare steel I might play
straight into the hands of my worst enemy and seal my own
doom.

These thoughts brought me to the head of the beach. I cast
a look behind, the boat was nearing the brig, and Alan flew
his handkerchief for a farewell, which I replied to with the
waving of my hand. But Alan himself was shrunk to a small
thing in my view, alongside of this pass that lay in front of
me. I set my hat hard on my head, clenched my teeth, and
went right before me up the face of the sand-wreath. It made
a hard climb, being steep, and the sand like water underfoot.
But I caught hold at last by the long bent-grass on the brae-
top, and pulled myself to a good footing. The same moment
men stirred and stood up here and there, six or seven of them,
ragged-like knaves, each with a dagger in his hand. The fair
truth is, I shut my eyes and prayed. When I opened them
again, the rogues were crept the least thing nearer without
speech or hurry. Every eye was upon mine, which struck me
with a strange sensation of their brightness, and of the fear
with which they continued to approach me. I held out my
hands empty; whereupon one asked, with a strong Highland
brogue, if I surrendered.

'Under protest,' said I, 'if ye ken what that means, which
I misdoubt.'

At that word, they came all in upon me like a flight of birds
upon a carrion, seized me, took my sword, and all the money
from my pockets, bound me hand and foot with some strong
line, and cast me on a tussock of bent. There they sat about
their captive in a part of a circle and gazed upon him silently
like something dangerous, perhaps a lion or a tiger on the
spring. Presently this attention was relaxed. They drew nearer
together, fell to speech in the Gaelic, and very cynically

divided my property before my eyes. It was my diversion
in this time that I could watch from my place the progress
of my friend's escape. I saw the boat come to the brig and
be hoisted in, the sails fill, and the ship pass out seaward
behind the isles and by North Berwick.

In the course of two hours or so, more and more ragged
Highlandmen kept collecting, Neil among the first, until the
party must have numbered near a score. With each new
arrival there was a fresh bout of talk, that sounded like
complaints and explanations; but I observed one thing, none
of those that came late had any share in the division of my
spoils. The last discussion was very violent and eager, so that
once I thought they would have quarrelled; on the heels of
which their company parted, the bulk of them returning
westward in a troop, and only three, Neil and two others,
remaining sentries on the prisoner.

'I could name one who would be very ill pleased with
your day's work, Neil Duncanson,' said I, when the rest had
moved away.

He assured me in answer I should be tenderly used, for
he knew I was 'acquent wi' the leddy.'

This was all our talk, nor did any other son of man appear
upon that portion of the coast until the sun had gone down
among the Highland mountains, and the gloaming was beginning to grow dark. At which hour I was aware of a long,
lean, bony-like Lothian man of a very swarthy countenance,
that came towards us among the bents on a farm horse.

'Lads,' cried he, 'hae ye a paper like this?' and held up
one in his hand. Neil produced a second, which the newcomer
studied through a pair of horn spectacles, and saying all was
right and we were the folk he was seeking, immediately dismounted. I was then set in his place, my feet tied under the
horse's belly, and we set forth under the guidance of the
Lowlander. His path must have been very well chosen, for
we met but one pair—a pair of lovers—the whole way, and
these, perhaps taking us to be free-traders, fled on our
approach. We were at one time close at the foot of Berwick
Law on the south side; at another, as we passed over some

open hills, I spied the lights of a clachan and the old tower of a church among some trees not far off, but too far to cry for help, if I had dreamed of it. At last we came again within sound of the sea. There was moonlight, though not much; and by this I could see the three huge towers and broken battlements of Tantallon,* that old chief place of the Red Douglases. The horse was picketed in the bottom of the ditch to graze, and I was led within, and forth into the court, and thence into the tumble-down stone hall. Here my conductors built a brisk fire in the midst of the pavement, for there was a chill in the night. My hands were loosed. I was set by the wall in the inner end, and (the Lowlander having produced provisions) I was given oatmeal bread and a pitcher of French brandy. This done, I was left once more alone with my three Highlandmen. They sat close by the fire drinking and talking; the wind blew in by the breaches, cast about the smoke and flames, and sang in the tops of the towers; I could hear the sea under the cliffs, and my mind being reassured as to my life, and my body and spirits wearied with the day's employment, I turned upon one side and slumbered.

I had no means of guessing at what hour I was wakened, only the moon was down and the fire low. My feet were now loosed, and I as carried through the ruins and down the cliff-side by a precipitous path to where I found a fisher's boat in a haven of the rocks. This I was had on board of, and we began to put forth from the shore in a fine starlight.

CHAPTER XIV

THE BASS

I HAD no thought where they were taking me; only looked here and there for the appearance of a ship; and there ran the while in my head a word of Ransome's—the *twenty-pounders*. If I were to be exposed a second time to that same former danger of the plantations, I judged it must turn ill with me; there was no second Alan, and no second shipwreck and spare yard to be expected now; and I saw myself hoe tobacco under the whip's lash. The thought chilled me; the air was sharp upon the water, the stretchers of the boat drenched with a cold dew; and I shivered in my place beside the steersman. This was the dark man whom I have called hitherto the Lowlander; his name was Dale, ordinarily called Black Andie. Feeling the thrill of my shiver, he very kindly handed me a rough jacket full of fish-scales, with which I was glad to cover myself.

'I thank you for this kindness,' said I, 'and will make so free as to repay it with a warning. You take a high responsibility in this affair. You are not like these ignorant, barbarous Highlanders, but know what the law is and the risks of those that break it.'

'I am no just exactly what ye would ca' an extremist for the law,' says he, 'at the best of times; but in this business I act with a good warranty.'

'What are you going to do with me?' I asked.

'Nae harm,' said he, 'nae harm ava'. Ye'll hae strong freens, I'm thinking. Ye'll be richt eneuch yet.'

There began to fall a greyness on the face of the sea; little dabs of pink and red, like coals of slow fire, came in the east; and at the same time the geese awakened, and began crying about the top of the Bass. It is just the one crag of rock, as everybody knows, but great enough to carve a city from. The sea was extremely little, but there went a hollow plowter round the base of it. With the growing of the dawn I could see it clearer and clearer; the straight crags painted with sea-birds' droppings like a morning frost, the sloping top of it green with grass, the clan of white geese that cried about the sides, and the black, broken buildings of the prison sitting close on the sea's edge.

At the sight the truth came in upon me in a clap.

'It's there you're taking me!' I cried.

'Just to the Bass, mannie,'* said he: 'Whaur the auld sants were afore ye, and I misdoubt if ye have come so fairly by your preeson.'

'But none dwells there now,' I cried; 'the place is long a ruin.'

'It'll be the mair pleisand a change for the solan geese, then,' quoth Andie drily.

The day coming slowly brighter, I observed on the bilge, among the big stones with which fisherfolk ballast their boats, several kegs and baskets, and a provision of fuel. All these were discharged upon the crag. Andie, myself, and my three Highlanders (I call them mine, although it was the other way about), landed along with them. The sun was not yet up when the boat moved away again, the noise of the oars on the thole-pins echoing from the cliffs, and left us in our singular reclusion.

Andie Dale was the Prefect (as I would jocularly call him) of the Bass, being at once the shepherd and the gamekeeper of that small and rich estate. He had to mind the dozen or so of sheep that fed and fattened on the grass of the sloping part of it, like beasts grazing the roof of a cathedral. He had charge besides of the solan geese that roosted in the crags; and from these an extraordinary income is derived. The young are dainty eating, as much as two shillings a-piece being a common price, and paid willingly by epicures; even the grown birds are valuable for their oil and feathers; and a part of the minister's stipend of North Berwick is paid to this day in solan geese, which makes it (in some folks' eyes) a parish to be coveted. To perform these several businesses, as well as to protect the geese from poachers, Andie had frequent occasion to sleep and pass days together on the crag; and we found the man at home there like a farmer in his steading. Bidding us all shoulder some of the packages, a matter in which I made haste to bear a hand, he led us in by a locked gate, which was the only admission to the island, and through the ruins of the fortress, to the governor's house. There we saw, by the ashes in the chimney and a standing bed-place in one corner, that he made his usual occupation.

This bed he now offered me to use, saying he supposed I would set up to be gentry.

'My gentrice has nothing to do with where I lie,' said I. 'I bless God I have lain hard ere now, and can do the same again with thankfulness. While I am here, Mr. Andie, if that be your name, I will do my part and take my place beside the rest of you; and I ask you on the other hand to spare me your mockery, which I own I like ill.'

He grumbled a little at this speech, but seemed upon reflection to approve it. Indeed, he was a long-headed, sensible man, and a good Whig and Presbyterian; read daily in a pocket Bible, and was both able and eager to converse seriously on religion, leaning more than a little towards the Cameronian extremes. His morals were of a more doubtful colour. I found he was deep in the free trade, and used the ruins of Tantallon for a magazine of smuggled merchandise. As for a gauger, I do not believe he valued the life of one at half-a-farthing. But that part of the coast of Lothian is to this day as wild a place, and the commons there as rough a crew, as any in Scotland.

One incident of my imprisonment is made memorable by a consequence it had long after. There was a warship at this time stationed in the Firth, the *Seahorse*, Captain Palliser. It chanced she was cruising in the month of September, plying between Fife and Lothian, and sounding for sunk dangers. Early one fine morning she was seen about two miles to the east of us, where she lowered a boat, and seemed to examine the Wildfire Rocks and Satan's Bush, famous dangers of that coast. And presently after having got her boat again, she came before the wind and was headed directly for the Bass. This was very troublesome to Andie and the Highlanders; the whole business of my sequestration was designed for privacy, and here, with a navy captain perhaps blundering ashore, it looked to become public enough, if it were nothing worse. I was in a minority of one, I am no Alan to fall upon so many, and I was far from sure that a warship was the least likely to improve my condition. All which considered, I gave Andie my parole of good behaviour and obedience, and was had briskly to the summit of the rock, where we all lay down, at the cliff's edge, in different places of observation and concealment. The *Seahorse* came straight on till I thought she would have struck, and we (looking giddily down) could see the ship's company at their quarters and hear the leadsman singing at the lead. Then she suddenly wore and let fly a

volley of I know not how many great guns. The rock was
shaken with the thunder of the sound, the smoke flowed over
our heads, and the geese rose in number beyond computation
or belief. To hear their screaming and to see the twinkling of
their wings, made a most inimitable curiosity; and I suppose
it was after this somewhat childish pleasure that Captain
Palliser had come so near the Bass. He was to pay dear for
it in time. During his approach I had the opportunity to make
a remark upon the rigging of that ship by which I ever after
knew it miles away; and this was a means (under Providence)
of my averting from a friend a great calamity, and inflicting
on Captain Palliser himself a sensible disappointment.

All the time of my stay on the rock we lived well. We had
small ale and brandy, and oatmeal of which we made our
porridge night and morning. At times a boat came from the
Castleton and brought us a quarter of mutton, for the sheep
upon the rock we must not touch, these being specially fed
to market. The geese were unfortunately out of season, and
we let them be. We fished ourselves, and yet more often made
the geese to fish for us: observing one when he had made
a capture and scaring him from his prey ere he had
swallowed it.

The strange nature of this place, and the curiosities with
which it abounded, held me busy and amused. Escape being
impossible, I was allowed my entire liberty, and continually
explored the surface of the isle wherever it might support
the foot of man. The old garden of the prison was still to be
observed, with flowers and pot-herbs running wild, and some
ripe cherries on a bush. A little lower stood a chapel or a
hermit's cell; who built or dwelt in it, none may know, and
the thought of its age made a ground of many meditations.
The prison too, where I now bivouacked with Highland cattle-
thieves, was a place full of history, both human and divine.
I thought it strange so many saints and martyrs should have
gone by there so recently, and left not so much as a leaf out
of their Bibles, or a name carved upon the wall, while the
rough soldier lads that mounted guard upon the battlements
had filled the neighbourhood with their mementoes—broken

tobacco-pipes for the most part, and that in a surprising plenty, but also metal buttons from their coats. There were times when I thought I could have heard the pious sound of psalms out of the martyrs' dungeons, and seen the soldiers tramp the ramparts with their glinting pipes, and the dawn rising behind them out of the North Sea.

No doubt it was a good deal Andie and his tales that put these fancies in my head. He was extraordinary well acquainted with the story of the rock in all particulars, down to the names of private soldiers, his father having served there in that same capacity. He was gifted besides with a natural genius for narration, so that the people seemed to speak and the things to be done before your face. This gift of his and my assiduity to listen brought us the more close together. I could not honestly deny but what I liked him; I soon saw that he liked me; and indeed, from the first I had set myself out to capture his good-will. An odd circumstance (to be told presently) effected this beyond my expectation; but even in early days we made a friendly pair to be a prisoner and his gaoler.

I should trifle with my conscience if I pretended my stay upon the Bass was wholly disagreeable. It seemed to me a safe place, as though I was escaped there out of my troubles. No harm was to be offered me; a material impossibility, rock and the deep sea, prevented me from fresh attempts; I felt I had my life safe and my honour safe, and there were times when I allowed myself to gloat on them like stolen waters. At other times my thoughts were very different. I recalled how strong I had expressed myself both to Rankeillor and to Stewart; I reflected that my captivity upon the Bass, in view of a great part of the coasts of Fife and Lothian, was a thing I should be thought more likely to have invented than endured; and in the eyes of these two gentlemen, at least, I must pass for a boaster and a coward. Now I would take this lightly enough; tell myself that so long as I stood well with Catriona Drummond, the opinion of the rest of man was but moonshine and spilled water; and thence pass off into those meditations of a lover which are so delightful to himself and must always appear so surprisingly idle to a reader. But anon the fear would take me otherwise; I would be shaken with a perfect panic of self-esteem, and these supposed hard judgments appear an injustice impossible to be supported. With that another train of thought would be presented, and I had scarce begun to be concerned about men's judgments of myself, than I was haunted with the remembrance of James Stewart in his dungeon and the lamentations of his wife. Then, indeed, passion began to work in me; I could not forgive myself to sit there idle; it seemed (if I were a man at all) that I could fly or swim out of my place of safety; and it was in such humours and to amuse my self-reproaches that I would set the more particularly to win the good side of Andie Dale.

At last, when we two were alone on the summit of the rock on a bright morning, I put in some hint about a bribe. He looked at me, cast back his head, and laughed out loud.

'Ay, you're funny, Mr. Dale,' said I, 'but perhaps if you'll glance an eye upon that paper you may change your note.'

The stupid Highlanders had taken from me at the time of my seizure nothing but hard money, and the paper I now showed Andie was an acknowledgment from the British Linen Company for a considerable sum.

He read it. 'Troth, and ye're nane sae ill aff,' said he.

'I thought that would maybe vary your opinions,' said I.

'Hout!' said he. 'It shows me ye can bribe; but I'm no to be bribit.'

'We'll see about that yet awhile,' says I. 'And first, I'll show you that I know what I am talking. You have orders to detain me here till after Thursday, 21st September.'

'Ye're no a'thegether wrong either,' says Andie. 'I'm to let you gang, bar orders contrair, on Saturday, the 23rd.'

I could not but feel there was something extremely insidious in this arrangement. That I was to reappear precisely in time to be too late would cast the more discredit on my tale, if I were minded to tell one; and this screwed me to fighting point.

'Now then, Andie, you that kens the world, listen to me,

and think while ye listen,' said I. 'I know there are great folks
in the business, and I make no doubt you have their names
to go upon. I have seen some of them myself since this affair
began, and said my say into their faces too. But what kind of
a crime would this be that I had committed? or what kind
of a process is this that I am fallen under? To be apprehended
by some ragged John-Hielandmen on August 30th, carried
to a rickle of old stones that is now neither fort nor gaol
(whatever it once was) but just the game-keeper's lodge of
the Bass Rock, and set free again, September 23rd, as secretly
as I was first arrested—does that sound like law to you? or
does it sound like justice? or does it not sound honestly like
a piece of some low dirty intrigue, of which the very folk that
meddle with it are ashamed?'

'I canna gainsay ye, Shaws. It looks unco underhand,' says
Andie. 'And werenae the folk guid sound Whigs and true-
blue Presbyterians I would hae seen them ayont Jordan and
Jeroozlem or I would have set hand to it.'

'The Master of Lovat'll be a braw Whig,' says I, 'and a
grand Presbyterian.'

'I ken naething by him,' said he. 'I hae nae trokings wi'
Lovats.'

'No, it'll be Prestongrange that you'll be dealing with,'
said I.

'Ah, but I'll no tell ye that,' said Andie.

'Little need when I ken,' was my retort.

'There's just the ae thing ye can be fairly sure of, Shaws,'
says Andie. 'And that is that (try as ye please) I'm no dealing
wi' yoursel'; nor yet I amnae goin' to,' he added.

'Well, Andie, I see I'll have to be speak out plain with
you,' I replied. And I told him so much as I thought needful
of the facts.

He heard me out with some serious interest, and when
I had done, seemed to consider a little with himself.

'Shaws,' said he at last, 'I deal with the naked hand. It's
a queer tale, and no very creditable, the way you tell it; and
I'm far frae minting that is other than the way that ye believe
it. As for yoursel', ye seem to me rather a dacent-like young

man. But me, that's aulder and mair judeecious, see perhaps
a wee bit further forrit in the job than what ye can dae. And
here is the maitter clear and plain to ye. There'll be nae skaith
to yoursel' if I keep ye here; far frae that, I think ye'll be
a hantle better by it. There'll be nae skaith to the kintry—just
ae mair Hielantman hangit—Gude kens, a guid riddance! On
the ither hand, it would be considerable skaith to me if I
would let you free. Sae, speakin as a guid Whig, an honest
freen' to you, and an anxious freen' to my ainsel', the plain
fact is that I think ye'll just have to bide here wi' Andie an'
the solans.'

'Andie,' said I, 'laying my hand upon his knee, 'this
Hielantman's innocent.'

'Ay, it's a peety about that,' said he. 'But ye see, in this
warld, the way God made it, we cannae just get a'thing that
we want.'

CHAPTER XV

BLACK ANDIE'S TALE OF TOD LAPRAIK*

I HAVE yet said little of the Highlanders. They were all
three of the followers of James More, which bound the accusation very tight about their master's neck. All understood a
word or two of English; but Neil was the only one who
judged he had enough of it for general converse, in which
(when once he got embarked) his company was often tempted
to the contrary opinion. They were tractable, simple
creatures; showed much more courtesy than might have been
expected from their raggedness and their uncouth appearance,
and fell spontaneously to be like three servants for Andie
and myself.

Dwelling in that isolated place, in the old falling ruins
of a prison, and among endless strange sounds of the sea and
the sea-birds, I thought I perceived in them early the effects
of superstitious fear. When there was nothing doing they
would either lie and sleep, for which their appetite appeared

insatiable, or Neil would entertain the others with stories which seemed always of a terrifying strain. If neither of these delights were within reach—if perhaps two were sleeping and the third could find no means to follow their example—I would see him sit and listen and look about him in a progression of uneasiness, starting, his face blenching, his hands clutched, a man strung like a bow. The nature of these fears I had never an occasion to find out, but the sight of them was catching, and the nature of the place that we were in favourable to alarms. I can find no word for it in the English, but Andie had an expression for it in the Scots from which he never varied.

'Ay,' he would say, 'it's an unco place, the Bass.'

It is so I always think of it. It was an unco place by night, unco by day; and these were unco sounds, of the calling of the solans, and the plash of the sea and the rock echoes, that hung continually in our ears. It was chiefly so in moderate weather When the waves were anyway great they roared about the rock like thunder and the drums of armies, dreadful but merry to hear; and it was in the calm days that a man could daunt himself with listening—not a Highlandman only, as I several times experimented on myself, so many still, hollow noises haunted and reverberated in the porches of the rock.

This brings me to a story I heard, and a scene I took part in, which quite changed our terms of living, and had a great effect on my departure. It chanced one night I fell in a muse beside the fire and (that little air of Alan's coming back to my memory) began to whistle. A hand was laid upon my arm, and the voice of Neil bade me to stop, for it was not 'canny musics.'

'Not canny?' I asked. 'How can that be?'

'Na,' said he; 'it will be made by a bogle and her wanting ta heid upon his body.'[1]

---

[1] A learned folklorist of my acquaintance hereby identifies Alan's air. It has been printed (it seems) in Campbell's *Tales of the West Highlands*, Vol. II., p. 91. Upon examination it would really seem as if Miss Grant's unrhymed doggerel (see Chapter V.) would fit, with a little humouring, to the notes in question.—R. L. S.

'Well,' said I, 'there can be no bogles here, Neil; for it's not likely they would fash themselves to frighten solan geese.'

'Ay?' says Andie, 'is that what ye think of it? But I'll can tell ye there's been waur nor bogles here.'

'What's waur than bogles, Andie?' said I.

'Warlocks,' said he. 'Or a warlock at the least of it. And that's a queer tale, too,' he added. 'And if ye would like, I'll tell it ye.'

To be sure we were all of the one mind, and even the Highlander that had the least English of the three set himself to listen with all his might.

THE TALE OF TOD LAPRAIK

MY faither, Tam Dale, peace to his banes, was a wild, sploring lad in his young days, wi' little wisdom and less grace. He was fond of a lass and fond of a glass, and fond of a ran-dan; but I could never hear tell that he was muckle use for honest employment. Frae ae thing to anither, he listed at last for a sodger and was in the garrison of this fort, which was the first way that ony of the Dales cam to set foot upon the Bass. Sorrow upon that service! The governor brewed his ain ale; it seems it was the warst conceivable. The rock was proveesioned frae the shore with vivers, the thing was ill-guided, and there were whiles when they but to fish and shoot solans for their diet. To crown a', thir was the Days of the Persecution. The perishin' cauld chalmers were all occupeed wi' sants and martyrs, the saut of the yearth, of which it wasnae worthy. And though Tam Dale carried a firelock there, a single sodger, and liked a lass and a glass, as I was sayin', the mind of the man was mair just than set with his position. He had glints of the glory of the kirk; there were whiles when his dander rase to see the Lord's sants misguided, and shame covered him that he should be haulding a can'le (or carrying a firelock) in so black a business. There were nights of it when he was here on sentry, the place a' wheesht, the frosts o' winter maybe riving in the wa's, and he would hear ane o' the prisoners strike up a psalm, and the rest join in, and the blessed sounds rising from the different chalmers —or dungeons, I would raither say—so that this auld craig in the sea was like a pairt of Heev'n. Black shame was on his saul; his sins hove up before him muckle as the Bass, and above a', that chief sin, that he should have a hand in hagging and hashing at Christ's Kirk. But the truth is that he resisted the spirit. Day cam, there were the rousing companions, and his guid resolves depairtit.

In thir days, dwalled upon the Bass a man of God, Peden the Prophet was his name. Ye'll have heard tell of Prophet Peden.* There was never the wale of him sinsyne, and it's a question wi' mony if there ever was his like afore. He was wild 's a peat-hag, fearsome to look at, fearsome to hear, his face like the day of judgment. The voice of him was like a solan's and dinnle'd in folks' lugs, and the words of him like coals of fire.

Now there was a lass on the rock, and I think she had little to do, for it was nae place far dacent weemen; but it seems she was bonny, and her and Tam Dale were very well agreed. It befell that Peden was in the gairden his lane at the praying when Tam and the lass cam by; and what should the lassie do but mock with laughter at the sant's devotions? He rose and lookit at the twa o' them, and Tam's knees knoitered thegether at the look of him. But whan he spak, it was mair in sorrow than in anger. 'Poor thing, poor thing!' says he, and it was the lass he lookit at, 'I hear you skirl and laugh,' he says, 'but the Lord has a deid shot prepared for you, and at that surprising judgment ye shall skirl but the ae time!' Shortly thereafter she was daundering on the craigs wi' twa-three sodgers, and it was a blawy day. There cam a gowst of wind, claught her by the coats, and awa' wi' her bag and baggage. And it was remarked by the sodgers that she gied but the ae skirl.

Nae doubt this judgment had some weicht upon Tam Dale; but it passed again and him none the better. Ae day he was flyting wi' anither sodger-lad. 'Deil hae me!' quo' Tam, for he was a profane swearer. And there was Peden glowering at him, gash an' waefu'; Peden wi' his lang chafts an' luntin' een, the maud happed about his kist, and the hand of him held out wi' the black nails upon the finger-nebs—for he had nae care of the body. 'Fy, fy, poor man!' cries he, 'the poor fool man! *Deil hae me*, quo' he; an' I see the deil at his oxter.' The conviction of guilt and grace cam in on Tam like the deep sea; he flang doun the pike that was in his hands—'I will nae mair lift arms against the cause o' Christ!' says he, and was as gude 's word. There was a sair fyke in the beginning, but the governor, seeing him resolved, gied him his dischairge, and he went and dwallt and married in North Berwick, and had aye a gude name with honest folk frae that day on.

It was in the year seeventeen hunner and sax that the Bass cam in the hands o' the Da'rymples, and there was twa men soucht the chairge of it. Baith were weel qualified, for they had baith been sodgers in the garrison, and kent the gate to handle solans, and the seasons and values of them. Forby that they were baith—or they baith seemed—earnest professors and men of comely conversation. The first of them was just Tam Dale, my faither. The second was ane Lapraik, whom the folk ca'd Tod Lapraik maistly, but whether for his name or his nature I could never hear tell. Weel, Tam gaed to see Lapraik upon this business, and took me, that was a toddlin' laddie, by the hand. Tod had his dwallin' in the lang loan benorth the kirk-yaird. It's a dark uncanny loan, forby that the kirk has aye had an ill name since the days o' James the Saxt and the deevil's cantrips played therein when the Queen was on the seas; and as for Tod's house, it was in the mirkest end, and was little liked by some that kenned the best. The door was on the sneck that day, and me and my faither gaed straucht in. Tod was a wabster to his trade; his loom stood in the but. There he sat, a muckle fat, white hash of a man like creish, wi' a kind of a holy smile that gart me scunner. The hand of him aye cawed the shuttle, but his een was steeked. We cried to him by his name, we skirled in the deid lug of him, we shook him by the shou'ther. Nae mainner o' service! There he sat on his dowp, an' cawed the shuttle and smiled like creish.

'God be guid to us,' says Tam Dale, 'this is no canny!'

He had jimp said the word, when Tod Lapraik cam to himsel'.

'Is this you, Tam?' says he. 'Haith, man! I'm blythe to see ye. I whiles fa' into a bit dwam like this,' he says; 'it's frae the stamach.'

Weel, they began to crack about the Bass and which of them twa was to get the warding o't, and by little and little cam to very ill words, and twined in anger. I mind weel, that as my faither and me gaed hame again, he cam ower and ower the same expression, how little he likit Tod Lapraik and his dwams.

'Dwam!' says he. 'I think folk hae brunt far dwams like yon.'

Aweel, my faither got the Bass and Tod had to go wantin'. It was remembered sinsyne what way he had ta'en the thing. 'Tam,' says he, 'ye hae gotten the better o' me aince mair, and I hope,' says he, 'ye'll find at least a' that ye expeckit at the Bass.' Which have since been thought remarkable expressions. At last the time came for Tam Dale to take young solans. This was a business he was weel used wi', he had been a craigsman frae a laddie, and trustit nane but himsel'. So there was he hingin' by a line an' speldering on the craig face, whaur it's hieest and steighest. Fower tenty lads were on the tap, hauldin' the line and mindin' for his signals. But whaur Tam hung there was naething but the craig, and the sea belaw, and the solan's skirling and flying. It was a braw spring morn, and Tam whustled as he claught in the young geese. Mony's the time I heard him tell of this experience, and aye the swat ran upon the man.

It chanced, ye see, that Tam keeked up, and he was awaur of a muckle solan, and the solan pyking at the line. He thocht this by-ordinar and outside the creature's habits. He minded that ropes was unco saft things, and the solan's neb and the Bass Rock unco hard, and that twa hunner feet were raither mair than he would care to fa'.

'Shoo!' says Tam. 'Awa', bird! Shoo, awa' wi' ye!' says he. The solan keekit doon into Tam's face, and there was something unco in the creature's ee. Just the ae keek it gied, and back to the rope. But now it wroucht and warstl't like a thing dementit. There never was the solan made that wroucht as that solan wroucht; and it seemed to understand its employ brawly, birzing the saft rope between the neb of it and a crunkled jag o' stane.

There gaed a cauld stend o' fear into Tam's heart. 'This thing is nae bird,' thinks he. His een turnt backward in his heid and the day gaed black about him. 'If I get a dwam here,' he thoucht, 'it's by wi' Tam Dale.' And he signalled for the lads to pu' him up.

And it seemed the solan understood about signals. For nae sooner was the signal made than he let be the rope, spried his wings, squawked out loud, took a turn flying, and dashed straucht at Tam Dale's een. Tam had a knife, he gart the cauld steel glitter. And it seemed the solan understood about knives, for nae suner did the steel glint in the sun than he gied the ae squawk, but laigher, like a body disappointit, and flegged aff about the roundness of the craig, and Tam saw him nae mair. And as sune as that thing was gane, Tam's heid drapt upon his shouther, and they pu'd him up like a deid corp, dadding on the craig.

A dram of brandy (which he went never without) broucht him to his mind, or what was left of it. Up he sat.

'Rin, Geordie, rin to the boat, mak' sure of the boat, man— rin!' he cries, 'or yon solan 'll have it awa',' says he.

The fower lads stared at ither, an' tried to whilly-wha him to be quiet. But naething would satisfy Tam Dale, till ane o' them had startit on aheid to stand sentry on the boat. The ithers askit if he was for down again.

'Na,' says he, 'and neither you nor me,' says he, 'and as sune as I can win to stand on my twa feet we'll be aff frae this craig o' Sawtan.'

Sure eneuch, nae time was lost, and that was ower muckle; for before they won to North Berwick Tam was in a crying fever. He lay a' the simmer; and wha was sae kind as come speiring for him, but Tod Lapraik! Folk thocht afterwards that ilka time Tod cam near the house the fever had worsened.

I kenna for that; but what I ken the best, that was the end of it.

It was about this time o' the year; my grandfaither was out at the white fishing; and like a bairn, I but to gang wi' him. We had a grand take, I mind, and the way that the fish lay broucht us near in by the bass, whaur we foregaithered wi' anither boat that belanged to a man Sandie Fletcher in Castleton. He's no lang deid neither, or ye could speir at himsel'. Weel, Sandie hailed.

'What's yon on the Bass?' says he.

'On the Bass?' says grandfaither.

'Ay,' says Sandie, 'on the green side o't.'

'Whatten kind of a thing?' says grandfaither. 'There cannae be naething on the Bass but just the sheep.'

'It looks unco like a body,' quo' Sandie, who was nearer in.

'A body!' says we, and we none of us likit that. For there was nae boat that could have brought a man, and the key o' the prison yett hung ower my faither's heid at hame in the press bed.

We keept the twa boats closs for company, and crap in nearer hand. Grandfaither had a gless, for he had been a sailor, and the captain of a smack, and had lost her on the sands of Tay. And when we took the gless to it, sure eneuch there was a man. He was in a crunkle o' green brae, a wee below the chaipel, a' by his lee lane, and lowped and flang and danced like a daft quean at a waddin'.

'It's Tod,' says grandfaither, and passed the gless to Sandie.

'Ay, it's him,' says Sandie.

'Or ane in the likeness o' him,' says grandfaither.

'Sma' is the differ,' quo' Sandie. 'De'il or warlock, I'll try the gun at him,' quo' he, and broucht up a fowling-piece that he aye carried, for Sandie was a notable famous shot in all that country.

'Haud your hand, Sandie,' says grandfaither; 'we maun see clearer first,' says he, 'or this may be a dear day's wark to the baith of us.'

'Hout!' says Sandie, 'this is the Lord's judgments surely, and be damned to it!' says he.

'Maybe ay, and maybe no,' says my grandfaither, worthy man! 'But have you a mind of the Procurator Fiscal, that I think ye'll have foregaithered wi' before,' says he.

This was ower true, and Sandie was a wee thing set ajee. 'Aweel, Edie,' says he, 'and what would be your way of it?'

'Ou, just this,' says grandfaither. 'Let me that has the fastest boat gang back to North Berwick, and let you bide here and keep an eye on Thon. If I cannae find Lapraik, I'll join ye and the twa of us'll have a crack wi' him. But if Lapraik's at hame, I'll rin up the flag at the harbour, and ye can try Thon Thing wi' the gun.'

Aweel, so it was agreed between them twa. I was just a bairn. an' clum in Sandie's boat, whaur I thoucht I would see the best of the employ. My grandsire gied Sandie a siller tester to pit in his gun wi' the leid draps, bein mair deidly again bogles. And then the ae boat set aff for North Berwick, an' the tither lay whaur it was and watched the wanchancy thing on the braeside.

A' the time we lay there it lowped and flang and capered and span like a teetotum, and whiles we could hear it skelloch as it span. I hae seen lassies, the daft queans, that would lowp and dance a winter's nicht, and still be lowping and dancing when the winter's day cam in. But there would be folk there to hauld them company, and the lads to egg them on; and this thing was its lee-lane. And there would be a fiddler diddling his elbock in the chimney-side; and this thing had nae music but the skirling of the solans. And the lassies were bits o' young things wi' the reid life dinnling and stending in their members; and this was a muckle, fat, creishy man, and him fa'n in the vale o' years. Say what ye like, I maun say what I believe. It was joy was in the creature's heart; the joy o' hell, I daursay: joy whatever. Mony a time I have askit mysel', why witches and warlocks should sell their sauls (whilk are their maist dear possessions) and be auld, duddy, wrunkl't wives or auld, feckless, doddered men; and then I mind upon Tod Lapraik dancing a' they hours by his lane in the black glory of his heart. Nae doubt they burn for it in muckle hell, but they have a grand time here of it, whatever! —and the Lord forgie us!

Weel, at the hinder end, we saw the wee flag yirk up to the mast-heid upon the harbour rocks. That was a' Sandie waited for. He up wi' the gun, took a deleeberate aim, an' pu'd the trigger. There cam' a bang and then ae waefu' skirl frae the Bass. And there were we rubbin' our een and lookin' at ither like daft folk. For wi' the bang and the skirl the thing had clean disappeared. The sun glintit, the wund blew, and there was the bare yaird whaur the Wonder had been lowping and flinging but ae second syne.

The hale way hame I roared and grat wi' the terror of that dispensation. The grawn folk were nane sae muckle better; there was little said in Sandie's boat but just the name of God; and when we won in by the pier, the harbour rocks were fair black wi' the folk waitin' us. It seems they had fund Lapraik in ane of his dwams, cawing the shuttle and smiling. Ae lad they sent to hoist the flag, and the rest abode there in the wabster's house. You may be sure they liked it little; but it was a means of grace to severals that stood there praying in to themsel's (for nane cared to pray out loud) and looking on thon awesome thing as it cawed the shuttle. Syne, upon a suddenty, and wi' the ae dreidfu' skelloch, Tod sprang up frae his hinderlands and fell forrit on the wab, a bluidy corp.

When the corp was examined the leid draps hadnae played buff upon the warlock's body; sorrow a leid drap was to be fund; but there was grandfaither's siller tester in the puddock's heart of him.

Andie had scarce done when there befell a mighty silly affair that had its consequence. Neil, as I have said, was himself a great narrator. I have heard since that he knew all the stories in the Highlands; and thought much of himself, and was thought much of by others, on the strength of it. Now Andie's tale reminded him of one he had already heard. 'She would ken that story afore,' he said. 'She was the story of Uistean More M'Gillie Phadrig and the Gavar Vore.'

'It is no sic a thing,' cried Andie. 'It is the story of my faither (now wi' God) and Tod Lapraik. And the same in your beard,' says he; 'and keep the tongue of ye inside your Hielant chafts!'

In dealing with Highlanders it will be found, and has been shown in history, how well it goes with Lowland gentlefolk; but the thing appears scarce feasible for Lowland commons. I had already remarked that Andie was continually on the point of quarrelling with our three Macgregors, and now, sure enough, it was to come.

'Thir will be no words to use to shentlemans,' says Neil.

'Shentlemans!' cried Andie. 'Shentlemans, ye Hielant stot! If God would give ye the grace to see yoursel' the way that ithers see ye, ye would throw your denner up.'

There came some kind of a Gaelic oath from Neil, and the black knife was in his hand that moment.

There was no time to think; and I caught the Highlander by the leg, and had him down, and his armed hand pinned out, before I knew what I was doing. His comrades sprang to rescue him, Andie and I were without weapons, the Gregara three to two. It seemed we were beyond salvation, when Neil screamed in his own tongue, ordering the others back, and made his submission to myself in a manner the most abject, even giving me up his knife which (upon a repetition of his promises) I returned to him on the morrow.

Two things I saw plain: the first, that I must not build too high on Andie, who had shrunk against the wall and stood there, as pale as death, till the affair was over; the second, the strength of my own position with the Highlanders, who must have received extraordinary charges to be tender of my safety. But if I thought Andie came not very well out in courage, I had no fault to find with him upon the account of gratitude. It was not so much that he troubled me with thanks, as that his whole mind and manner appeared changed; and as he preserved ever after a great timidity of our companions, he and I were yet more constantly together.

CHAPTER XVI

THE MISSING WITNESS

ON the seventeenth, the day I was trysted with the Writer, I had much rebellion against fate. The thought of him waiting in the *King's Arms*, and of what he would think, and what he would say when next we met, tormented and oppressed me. The truth was unbelievable, so much I had to grant, and it seemed cruel hard I should be posted as a liar and a coward, and have never consciously omitted what it was possible that I should do. I repeated this form of words with a kind of bitter relish, and reexamined in that light the steps of my behaviour. It seemed I had behaved to James Stewart as a brother might; all the past was a picture that I could be proud of, and there was only the present to consider. I could not swim the sea, nor yet fly in the air, but there was always Andie. I had done him a service, he liked me; I had a lever there to work on; if it were just for decency, I must try once more with Andie.

It was late afternoon; there was no sound in all the Bass but the lap and bubble of a very quiet sea; and my four companions were all crept apart, the three Macgregors higher on the rock, and Andie with his Bible to a sunny place among the ruins; there I found him in deep sleep, and, as soon as he was awake, appealed to him with some fervour of manner and a good show of argument.

'If I thoucht it was to do guid to ye, Shaws!' said he, staring at me over his spectacles.

'It's to save another,' said I, 'and to redeem my word. What would be more good than that? Do ye no mind the scripture, Andie? And you with the Book upon your lap! *What shall it profit a man if he gain the whole world?*'

'Ay,' said he, 'that's grand for you. But where do I come in? I have my word to redeem the same's yoursel'. And what are ye asking me to do, but just to sell it ye for siller?'

'Andie! have I named the name of siller?' cried I.

'Ou, the name's naething,' said he; 'the thing is there, whatever. It just comes to this; if I am to service ye the way that you propose, I'll lose my lifelihood. Then it's clear ye'll have to make it up to me, and a pickle mair, for your ain credit like. And what's that but just a bribe? And if even I was certain of the bribe! But by a' that I can learn, it's far frae that; and if *you* were to hang, where would I be? Na: the thing's no possible. And just awa' wi' ye like a bonny lad! and let Andie read his chapter.'

I remember I was at bottom a good deal gratified with this result; and the next humour I fell into was one (I had near said) of gratitude to Prestongrange, who had saved me, in this violent, illegal manner, out of the midst of my dangers, temptations, and perplexities. But this was both too flimsy and too cowardly to last me long, and the remembrance of James began to succeed to the possession of my spirits. The 21st, the day set for the trial, I passed in such misery of mind as I can scarce recall to have endured, save perhaps upon Isle Earraid only.* Much of the time I lay on a brae-side betwixt sleep and waking, my body motionless, my mind full of violent thoughts. Sometimes I slept indeed; but the court-house of Inverary and the prisoner glancing on all sides to find his missing witness, followed me in slumber; and I would wake again with a start to darkness of spirit and distress of body. I thought Andie seemed to observe me, but I paid him little heed. Verily, my bread was bitter to me, and my days a burthen.

Early the next morning (Friday, 22nd) a boat came with provisions, and Andie placed a packet in my hand. The cover was without address but sealed with a Government seal. It enclosed two notes. 'Mr. Balfour can now see for himself it is too late to meddle. His conduct will be observed and his discretion rewarded.' So ran the first, which seemed to be laboriously writ with the left hand. There was certainly nothing in these expressions to compromise the writer, even if that person could be found; the seal, which formidably served instead of signature, was affixed to a separate sheet on which there was no scratch of writing; and I had to confess that (so far) my adversaries knew what they were doing, and to digest as well as I was able the threat that peeped under the promise.

But the second enclosure was by far the more surprising. It was in a lady's hand of writ. '*Maister Dauvit Balfour is informed a friend was speiring for him, and her eyes were of the grey*,' it ran—and seemed so extraordinary a piece to come to my hands at such a moment and under cover of a Government seal, that I stood stupid. Catriona's grey eyes shone in my remembrance. I thought, with a bound of pleasure, she must be the friend. But who should the writer be, to have her billet thus enclosed with Prestongrange's? And of all wonders, why was it thought needful to give me this pleasing but most inconsequential intelligence upon the Bass? For the writer, I could hit upon none possible except Miss Grant. Her family, I remembered, had remarked on Catriona's eyes and even named her for their colour; and she herself had been much in the habit to address me with a broad pronunciation, by way of a sniff, I supposed, at my rusticity. No doubt, besides, but she lived in the same house as this letter came from. So there remained but one step to be accounted for; and that was how Prestongrange should have permitted her at all in an affair so secret, or let her daft-like billet go in the same cover with his own. But even here I had a glimmering. For, first of all, there was something rather alarming about the young lady, and papa might be more under her domination than I knew. And second, there was the man's continual policy to be remembered, how his conduct had been continually mingled with caresses, and he had scarce ever, in the midst of so much contention, laid aside a mask of friendship. He must conceive that my imprisonment had incensed me. Perhaps this little jesting, friendly message was intended to disarm my rancour?

I will be honest—and I think it did. I felt a sudden warmth towards that beautiful Miss Grant, that she should stoop to so much interest in my affairs. The summoning up of Catriona moved me of itself to milder and more cowardly counsels. If the Advocate knew of her and our acquaintance—if I should please him by some of that 'discretion' at which his letter pointed—to what might not this lead? *In vain is the net spread in the sight of any fowl,** the scripture says. Well, fowls must be wiser than folk! For I thought I perceived the policy, and yet fell in with it.

I was in this frame, my heart beating, the grey eyes plain before me like two stars, when Andie broke in upon my musing.

'I see ye hae gotten guid news,' said he.

I found him looking curiously in my face; with that, there came before me like a vision of James Stewart and the court of Inverary; and my mind turned at once like a door upon its hinges. Trials, I reflected, sometimes draw out longer than is looked for. Even if I came to Inverary just too late, something might yet be attempted in the interests of James—and in those of my own character, the best would be accomplished. In a moment, it seemed without thought, I had a plan devised.

'Andie,' said I, 'is it still to be to-morrow?'

He told me nothing was changed.

'Was anything said about the hour?' I asked.

He told me it was to be two o'clock afternoon.

'And about the place?' I pursued.

'Whatten place?' says Andie.

'The place I am to be landed at,' said I.

He owned there was nothing as to that.

'Very well, then,' I said, 'this shall be mine to arrange. The wind is in the east, my road lies westward: keep your boat, I hire it; let us work up the Forth all day; and land me at two o'clock to-morrow at the westmost we'll can have reached.'

'Ye daft callant!' he cried, 'ye would try for Inverary after a'!'

'Just that, Andie,' says I.

'Weel, ye're ill to beat!' says he. 'And I was kind o' sorry for ye a' day yesterday,' he added. 'Ye see, I was never entirely sure till then, which way of it ye really wantit.'

Here was a spur to a lame horse!

'A word in your ear, Andie,' said I. 'This plan of mine

has another advantage yet. We can leave these Hielandmen behind us on the rock, and one of your boats from the Castleton can bring them off to-morrow. Yon Neil has a queer eye when he regards you; maybe, if I was once out of the gate there might be knives again; these red-shanks are unco grudgeful. And if there should come to be any question, here is your excuse. Our lives were in danger by these savages; being answerable for my safety, you chose the part to bring me from their neighbourhood and detain me the rest of the time on board your boat: and do you know, Andie?' says I, with a smile, 'I think it was very wisely chosen.'

'The truth is I have nae goo for Neil,' says Andie, 'nor he for me, I'm thinking; and I would like ill to come to my hands wi' the man. Tam Anster will make a better hand of it with the cattle onyway.' (For this man, Anster, came from Fife, where the Gaelic is still spoken.) 'Ay, ay!' says Andie, 'Tam'll can deal with them the best. And troth! the mair I think of it, the less I see we would be required. The place— ay, feggs! they had forgot the place. Eh, Shaws, ye're a lang-heided chield when ye like! Forby that I'm awing ye my life,' he added, with more solemnity, and offered me his hand upon the bargain.

Whereupon, with scarce more words, we stepped suddenly on board the boat, cast off, and set the lug. The Gregara were then busy upon breakfast, for the cookery was their usual part; but, one of them stepping to the battlements, our flight was observed before we were twenty fathoms from the rock; and the three of them ran about the ruins and the landing-shelf, for all the world like ants about a broken nest, hailing and crying on us to return. We were still in both the lee and the shadow of the rock, which last lay broad upon the waters, but presently came forth in almost the same moment into the wind and sunshine; the sail filled, the boat heeled to the gunwale, and we swept immediately beyond sound of the men's voices. To what terrors they endured upon the rock, where they were now deserted without the countenance of any civilised person or so much as the protection of a Bible, no limit can be set; nor had they any brandy left to be their consolation, for even in the haste and secrecy of our departure Andie had managed to remove it.

It was our first care to set Anster ashore in a cove by the Glenteithy Rocks, so that the deliverance of our maroons might be duly seen to the next day. Thence we kept away up Firth. The breeze, which was then so spirited, swiftly declined, but never wholly failed us. All day we kept moving, though often not much more; and it was after dark ere we were up with the Queensferry. To keep the letter of Andie's engagement (or what was left of it) I must remain on board, but I thought no harm to communicate with the shore in writing. On Prestongrange's cover, where the Government seal must have a good deal surprised my correspondent, I writ, by the boat's lantern, a few necessary words, and Andie carried them to Rankeillor. In about an hour he came aboard again, with a purse of money and the assurance that a good horse should be standing saddled for me by two to-morrow at Clackmannan Pool. This done, and the boat riding by her stone anchor, we lay down to sleep under the sail.

We were in the Pool the next day long ere two; and there was nothing left for me but to sit and wait. I felt little alacrity upon my errand. I would have been glad of any passable excuse to lay it down; but none being to be found, my uneasiness was no less great than if I had been running to some desired pleasure. By shortly after one the horse was at the waterside, and I could see a man walking it to and fro till I should land, which vastly swelled my impatience. Andie ran the moment of my liberation very fine, showing himself a man of his bare word, but scarce serving his employers with a heaped measure; and by about fifty seconds after two I was in the saddle and on the full stretch for Stirling. In a little more than an hour I had passed that town, and was already mounting Alan Water side, when the weather broke in a small tempest. The rain blinded me, the wind had nearly beat me from the saddle, and the first darkness of the night surprised me in a wilderness still some way east of Balwhidder, not very sure of my direction and mounted on a horse that began already to be weary.

In the press of my hurry, and to be spared the delay and annoyance of a guide, I had followed (so far as it was possible for any horseman) the line of my journey with Alan. This I did with open eyes, foreseeing a great risk in it, which the tempest had now brought to a reality. The last that I knew of where I was, I think it must have been about Uam Var; the hour perhaps six at night. I must still think it great good fortune that I got about eleven to my destination, the house of Duncan Dhu. Where I had wandered in the interval perhaps the horse could tell. I know we were twice down, and once over the saddle and for a moment carried away in a roaring burn. Steed and rider were bemired up to the eyes.

From Duncan I had news of the trial. It was followed in all these Highland regions with religious interest; news of it spread from Inverary as swift as men could travel; and I was rejoiced to learn that, up to a late hour that Saturday, it was not yet concluded; and all men began to suppose it must spread over to the Monday. Under the spur of this intelligence I would not sit to eat; but, Duncan having agreed to be my guide, took the road again on foot, with the piece in my hand and munching as I went. Duncan brought with him a flask of usquebaugh and a hand-lantern; which last enlightened us just so long as we could find houses where to rekindle it, for the thing leaked outrageously and blew out with every gust. The more part of the night we walked blindfold among sheets of rain, and day found us aimless on the mountains. Hard by we struck a hut on a burn-side, where we got a bite and a direction; and, a little before the end of the sermon, came to the kirk doors of Inverary.

The rain had somewhat washed the upper parts of me, but I was still bogged as high as to the knees; I streamed water; I was so weary I could hardly limp, and my face was like a ghost's. I stood certainly more in need of a change of raiment and a bed to lie on, than of all the benefits in Christianity. For all which (being persuaded the chief point for me was to make myself immediately public) I set the door open, entered the church with the dirty Duncan at my tails, and finding a vacant place hard by, sat down.

'Thirteenthly, my brethren, and in parenthesis, the law itself must be regarded as a means of grace,' the minister was saying, in the voice of one delighting to pursue an argument.

The sermon was in English on account of the assize. The judges were present with their armed attendants, the halberts glittered in a corner by the door, and the seats were thronged beyond custom with the array of lawyers. The text was in Romans 5th and 13th*—the minister a skilled hand; and the whole of that able churchful—from Argyle, and my Lords Elchies and Kilkerran, down to the halbert-men that came in their attendance—was sunk with gathered brows in a profound critical attention. The minister himself and a sprinkling of those about the door observed our entrance at the moment and immediately forgot the same; the rest either did not hear or would not heed; and I sat there amongst my friends and enemies unremarked.

The first that I singled out was Prestongrange. He sat well forward, like an eager horseman in the saddle, his lips moving with relish, his eyes glued on the minister: the doctrine was clearly to his mind. Charles Stewart, on the other hand, was half asleep, and looked harassed and pale. As for Simon Fraser, he appeared like a blot, and almost a scandal, in the midst of that attentive congregation, digging his hands in his pockets, shifting his legs, clearing his throat, rolling up his bald eyebrows and shooting out his eyes to right and left, now with a yawn, now with a secret smile. At times too, he would take the Bible in front of him, run it through, seem to read a bit, run it through again, and stop and yawn prodigiously: the whole as if for exercise.

In the course of this restlessness his eye alighted on myself. He sat a second stupefied, then tore a half-leaf out of the Bible, scrawled upon it with a pencil, and passed it with a whispered word to his next neighbour. The note came to Prestongrange, who gave me but the one look; thence it voyaged to the hands of Mr. Erskine; thence again to Argyle, where he sat between the other two lords of session, and his Grace turned and fixed me with an arrogant eye. The last of those interested to observe my presence was Charlie

Stewart, and he too began to pencil and hand about despatches, none of which I was able to trace to their destination in the crowd.

But the passage of these notes had aroused notice; all who were in the secret (or supposed themselves to be so) were whispering information—the rest questions; and the minister himself seemed quite discountenanced by the flutter in the church and sudden stir and whispering. His voice changed, he plainly faltered, nor did he again recover the easy conviction and full tones of his delivery. It would be a puzzle to him till his dying day, why a sermon that had gone with triumph through four parts, should thus miscarry in the fifth.

As for me, I continued to sit there, very wet and weary, and a good deal anxious as to what should happen next, but greatly exulting in my success.

CHAPTER XVII

THE MEMORIAL

THE last word of the blessing was scarce out of the minister's mouth before Stewart had me by the arm. We were the first to be forth of the church, and he made such extraordinary expedition that we were safe within the four walls of a house before the street had begun to be thronged with the home-going congregation.

'Am I yet in time?' I asked.

'Ay and no,' said he. 'The case is over; the jury is enclosed, and will be so kind as let us ken their view of it to-morrow in the morning, the same as I could have told it my own self three days ago before the play began. The thing has been public from the start. The panel kent it, "*Ye may do what ye will for me*," whispers he two days ago. "*I ken my fate by what the Duke of Argyle has just said to Mr. Macintosh.*" O, it's been a scandal!

"The great Argyle he gaed before,
     He gart the cannons and guns to roar,"

and the very macer cried "Cruachan!" But now that I have
got you again I'll never despair. The oak shall go over the
myrtle yet; we'll ding the Campbells yet in their own town.
Praise God that I should see the day!'

He was leaping with excitement, emptied out his mails
upon the floor that I might have a change of clothes, and
incommoded me with his assistance as I changed. What
remained to be done, or how I was to do it, was what he
never told me nor, I believe, so much as thought of. 'We'll
ding the Campbells yet!' that was still his overcome. And it
was forced home upon my mind how this, that had the
externals of a sober process of law, was in its essence a clan
battle between savage clans. I thought my friend the Writer
none of the least savage. Who, that had only seen him at a
counsel's back before the Lord Ordinary or following a golf
ball and laying down his clubs on Bruntsfield links, could
have recognised for the same person this voluble and violent
clansman?

James Stewart's counsel were four in number—Sheriffs
Brown of Colstoun and Miller, Mr. Robert Macintosh and
Mr. Stewart younger of Stewart Hall. These were covenanted
to dine with the Writer after sermon, and I was very
obligingly included of the party. No sooner the cloth lifted,
and the first bowl very artfully compounded by Sheriff Miller,
than we fell to the subject in hand. I made a short narration
of my seizure and captivity, and was then examined and reexamined upon the circumstances of the murder. It will be
remembered this was the first time I had had my say out,
or the matter at all handled, among lawyers; and the consequence was very dispiriting to the others and (I must own)
disappointing to myself.

'To sum up,' said Colstoun, 'you prove that Alan was
on the spot; you have heard him proffer menaces against
Glenure; and though you assure us he was not the man who
fired, you leave a strong impression that he was in league

with him, and consenting, perhaps immediately assisting, in the act. You show him besides, at the risk of his own liberty, actively furthering the criminal's escape. And the rest of your tesimony (so far as the least material) depends on the bare word of Alan or of James, the two accused. In short, you do not at all break, but only lengthen by one personage, the chain that binds our client to the murderer; and I need scarcely say that the introduction of a third accomplice rather aggravates that appearance of a conspiracy which has been our stumbling block from the beginning.'

'I am of the same opinion,' said Sheriff Miller. 'I think we may all be very much obliged to Prestongrange for taking a most uncomfortable witness out of our way. And chiefly, I think, Mr. Balfour himself might be obliged. For you talk of a third accomplice, but Mr. Balfour (in my view) has very much the appearance of a fourth.'

'Allow me, sirs!' interposed Stewart the Writer. 'There is another view. Here we have a witness—never fash whether material or not—a witness in this cause, kidnapped by that old, lawless, bandit crew of the Glengyle Macgregors, and sequestered for near upon a month in a bourock of the old cold ruins on the Bass. Move that and see what dirt you fling on the proceedings! Sirs, this is a tale to make the world ring with! It would be strange, with such a grip as this, if we couldnae squeeze out a pardon for my client.'

'And suppose we took up Mr. Balfour's cause to-morrow?' said Stewart Hall. 'I am much deceived or we should find so many impediments thrown in our path, as that James should have been hanged before we had found a court to hear us. This is a great scandal, but I suppose we have none of us forgot a greater still, I mean the matter of the Lady Grange.* The woman was still in durance; my friend Mr. Hope of Rankeillor did what was humanly possible; and how did he speed? He never got a warrant! Well, it'll be the same now; the same weapons will be used. This is a scene, gentlemen, of clan animosity. The hatred of the name which I have the honour to bear rages in high quarters. There is nothing here to be viewed but naked Campbell spite and scurvy Campbell intrigue.'

You may be sure this was to touch a welcome topic, and I sat for some time in the midst of my learned counsel, almost deaved with their talk but extremely little the wiser for its purport. The Writer was led into some hot expressions; Colstoun must take him up and set him right; the rest joined in on different sides, but all pretty noisy; the Duke of Argyle was beaten like a blanket; King George came in for a few digs in the by-going and a great deal of rather elaborate defence: and there was only one person that seemed to be forgotten, and that was James of the Glens.

Through all this Mr. Miller sat quiet. He was a slip of an oldish gentleman, ruddy and twinkling; he spoke in a smooth rich voice, with an infinite effect of pawkiness, dealing out each word the way an actor does, to give the most expression possible; and even now, when he was silent, and sat there with his wig laid aside, his glass in both hands, his mouth funnily pursed, and his chin out, he seemed the mere picture of a merry slyness. It was plain he had a word to say, and waited for the fit occasion.

It came presently. Colstoun had wound up one of his speeches with some expression of their duty to their client. His brother sheriff was pleased, I suppose, with the transition. He took the table in his confidence with a gesture and a look.

'That suggests to me a consideration which seems overlooked,' said he. 'The interest of our client goes certainly before all, but the world does not come to an end with James Stewart.' Whereat he cocked his eye. 'I might condescend, *exempli gratia*, upon a Mr. George Brown, a Mr. Thomas Miller, and a Mr. David Balfour. Mr. David Balfour has a very good ground of complaint, and I think, gentlemen—if his story was properly redd out—I think there would be a number of wigs on the green.'

The whole table turned to him with a common movement.

'Properly handled and carefully redd out, his is a story that could scarcely fail to have some consequence,' he continued. 'The whole administration of justice, from its highest officer downward, would be totally discredited; and it looks to me as if they would need to be replaced.' He seemed to shine with cunning as he said it. And I need not point out to ye that this of Mr. Balfour's would be a remarkable bonny cause to appear in,' he added.

Well, there they all were started on another hare; Mr. Balfour's cause, and what kind of speeches could be there delivered, and what officials could be thus turned out, and who would succeed to their positions. I shall give but the two specimens. It was proposed to approach Simon Fraser, whose testimony, if it could be obtained, would prove certainly fatal to Argyle and Prestongrange. Miller highly approved of the attempt. 'We have here before us a dreeping roast,' said he, 'here is cut-and-come-again for all.' And methought all licked their lips. The other was already near the end. Stewart the Writer was out of the body with delight, smelling vengeance on his chief enemy, the Duke.

'Gentlemen,' cried he, charging his glass, 'here is to Sheriff Miller. His legal abilities are known to all. His culinary, this bowl in front of us is here to speak for. But when it comes to the poleetical!'—cries he, and drains the glass.

'Ay, but it will hardly prove politics in your meaning, my friend.' said the gratified Miller. 'A revolution, if you like, and I think I can promise you that historical writers shall date from Mr. Balfour's cause. But properly guided, Mr. Stewart, tenderly guided, it shall prove a peaceful revolution.'

'And if the damned Campbells get their ears rubbed, what care I?' cries Stewart, smiting down his fist.

It will be thought I was not very well pleased with all this, though I could scarce forbear smiling at a kind of innocency in these old intriguers. But it was not my view to have undergone so many sorrows for the advancement of Sheriff Miller or to make a revolution in the Parliament House: and I interposed accordingly with as much simplicity of manner as I could assume.

'I have to thank you, gentlemen, for your advice,' said I. 'And now I would like, by your leave, to set you two or three questions. There is one thing that has fallen rather on one side, for instance: Will this cause do any good to our friend James of the Glens?'

They seemed all a hair set back, and gave various answers, but concurring practically in one point, that James had now no hope but in the King's mercy.

'To proceed, then,' said I, 'will it do any good to Scotland? We have a saying that it is an ill bird that fouls his own nest. I remember hearing we had a riot in Edinburgh when I was an infant child, which gave occasion to the late Queen to call this country barbarous;* and I always understood that we had rather lost than gained by that. Then came the year 'Forty-five, which made Scotland to be talked of everywhere; but I never heard it said we had anyway gained by the 'Forty-five. And now we come to this cause of Mr. Balfour's, as you call it. Sheriff Miller tells us historical writers are to date from it, and I would not wonder. It is only my fear they would date from it as a period of calamity and public reproach.'

The nimble-witted Miller had already smelt where I was travelling to, and made haste to get on the same road. 'Forcibly put, Mr. Balfour,' says he. 'A weighty observe, sir.'

'We have next to ask ourselves if it will be good for King George,' I pursued. 'Sheriff Miller appears pretty easy upon this; but I doubt you will scarce be able to pull down the house from under him, without his Majesty coming by a knock or two, one of which might easily prove fatal.'

I gave them a chance to answer, but none volunteered.

'Of those for whom the case was to be profitable,' I went on, 'Sheriff Miller gave us the names of several, among the which he was good enough to mention mine. I hope he will pardon me if I think otherwise. I believe I hung not the least back in this affair while there was life to be saved; but I own I thought myself extremely hazarded, and I own I think it would be a pity for a young man, with some idea of coming to the Bar, to ingrain upon himself the character of a turbulent, factious fellow before he was yet twenty. As for James, it seems—at this date of the proceedings, with the sentence as good as pronounced—he has no hope but in the King's mercy. May not his Majesty, then, be more pointedly addressed, the characters of these high officers sheltered from the public, and myself kept out of a position which I think spells ruin for me?'

They all sat and gazed into their glasses and I could see they found my attitude on the affair unpalatable. But Miller was ready at all events.

'If I may be allowed to put our young friend's notion in more formal shape,' says he, 'I understand him to propose that we should embody the fact of his sequestration, and perhaps some heads of the testimony he was prepared to offer, in a memorial to the Crown. This plan has elements of success. It is as likely as any other (and perhaps likelier) to help our client. Perhaps his Majesty would have the goodness to feel a certain gratitude to all concerned in such a memorial, which might be construed into an expression of a very delicate loyalty; and I think, in the drafting of the same, this view might be brought forward.'

They all nodded to each other, not without sighs, for the former alternative was doubtless more after their inclination.

'Paper then, Mr. Stewart, if you please,' pursued Miller; 'and I think it might very fittingly be signed by the five of us here present, as procurators for the "condemned man."'

'It can do none of us any harm at least,' says Colstoun, heaving another sigh, for he had seen himself Lord Advocate the last ten minutes.

Thereupon they set themselves, not very enthusiastically, to draft the memorial—a process in the course of which they soon caught fire; and I had no more ado but to sit looking on and answer an occasional question. The paper was very well expressed; beginning with a recitation of the facts about myself, the reward offered for my apprehension, my surrender, the pressure brought to bear upon me; my sequestration; and my arrival at Inverary in time to be too late; going on to explain the reasons of loyalty and public interest for which it was agreed to waive any right of action; and winding

up with a forcible appeal to the King's mercy on behalf of
James.

Methought I was a good deal sacrificed, and rather represented in the light of a firebrand of a fellow whom my crowd
of lawyers had restrained with difficulty from extremes. But
I let it pass, and made but the one suggestion, that I should
be described as ready to deliver my own evidence and adduce
that of others before any commission of inquiry—and the one
demand, that I should be immediately furnished with a copy.

Colstoun hummed and hawed. 'This is a very confidential
document,' said he.

'And my position towards Prestongrange is highly peculiar,' I replied. 'No question but I must have touched his heart
at our first interview, so that he has since stood my friend
consistently. But for him, gentlemen, I must now be lying
dead or awaiting my sentence alongside poor James. For
which reason I choose to communicate to him the fact of this
memorial as soon as it is copied. You are to consider also that
this step will make for my protection. I have enemies here
accustomed to drive hard; his Grace is in his own country,
Lovat by his side; and if there should hang any ambiguity
over our proceedings I think I might very well awake in gaol.'

Not finding any very ready answer to these considerations,
my company of advisers were at the last persuaded to consent,
and made only this condition, that I was to lay the paper
before Prestongrange with the express compliments of all
concerned.

The Advocate was at the castle dining with his Grace. By
the hand of one of Colstoun's servants I sent him a billet
asking for an interview, and received a summons to meet him
at once in a private house of the town. Here I found him alone
in a chamber; from his face there was nothing to be gleaned;
yet I was not so unobservant but what I spied some halberts
in the hall, and not so stupid but what I could gather he was
prepared to arrest me there and then, should it appear
advisable.

'So, Mr. David, this is you?' said he.

'Where I fear I am not overly welcome, my lord,' said I.

'And I would like before I go further to express my sense of your lordship's continued good offices, even should they now cease.'

'I have heard of your gratitude before,' he replied drily, 'and I think this can scarce be the matter you called me from my wine to listen to. I would remember also, if I were you, that you still stand on a very boggy foundation.'

'Not now, my lord, I think,' said I; 'and if your lordship will but glance an eye along this, you will perhaps think as I do.'

He read it sedulously through, frowning heavily; then turned back to one part and another which he seemed to weigh and compare the effect of. His face a little lightened.

'This is not so bad but what it might be worse,' said he; 'though I am still likely to pay dear for my acquaintance with Mr. David Balfour.'

'Rather for your indulgence to that unlucky young man, my lord,' said I.

He still skimmed the paper, and all the while his spirits seemed to mend.

'And to whom am I indebted for this?' he asked presently. 'Other counsels must have been discussed, I think. Who was it proposed this private method? Was it Miller?'

'My lord, it was myself,' said I. 'These gentlemen have shown me no such consideration, as that I should deny myself any credit I can fairly claim, or spare them any responsibility they should properly bear. And the mere truth is, that they were all in favour of a process which should have remarkable consequences in the Parliament House, and prove for them (in one of their own expressions) a dripping roast. Before I intervened, I think they were on the point of sharing out the different law appointments. Our friend Mr. Simon was to be taken in upon some composition.'

Prestongrange smiled. 'These are our friends!' said he. 'And what were your reasons for dissenting, Mr. David?'

I told them without concealment, expressing, however, with more force and volume those which regarded Prestongrange himself.

'You do me no more than justice,' said he. 'I have fought as hard in your interest as you have fought against mine. And how came you here to-day?' he asked. 'As the case drew out, I began to grow uneasy that I had clipped the period so fine, and I was even expecting you to-morrow. But to-day—I never dreamed of it.'

I was not, of course, going to betray Andie.

'I suspect there is some very weary cattle by the road,' said I.

'If I had known you were such a moss-trooper you should have tasted longer of the Bass,' says he.

'Speaking of which, my lord, I return your letter.' And I gave him the enclosure in the counterfeit hand.

'There was the cover also with the seal,' said he.

'I have it not,' said I. 'It bore nought but the address, and could not compromise a cat. The second enclosure I have, and with your permission, I desire to keep it.'

I thought he winced a little, but he said nothing to the point. 'To-morrow,' he resumed, 'our business here is to be finished, and I proceed by Glasgow. I would be very glad to have you of my party, Mr. David.'

'My lord . . .' I began.

'I do not deny it will be of service to me,' he interrupted. 'I desire even that, when we shall come to Edinburgh you should alight at my house. You have very warm friends in the Miss Grants, who will be overjoyed to have you to themselves. If you think I have been of use to you, you can thus easily repay me, and so far from losing, may reap some advantage by the way. It is not every strange young man who is presented in society by the King's Advocate.'

Often enough already (in our brief relations) this gentleman had caused my head to spin; no doubt but what for a moment he did so again now. Here was the old fiction still maintained of my particular favour with his daughters, one of whom had been so good as to laugh at me, while the other two had scarce deigned to remark the fact of my existence. And now I was to ride with my lord to Glasgow; I was to dwell with him in Edinburgh; I was to be brought into society

under his protection! That he should have so much good-
nature as to forgive me was surprising enough; that he could
wish to take me up and serve me seemed impossible; and
I began to seek for some ulterior meaning. One was plain.
If I became his guest, repentance was excluded; I could never
think better of my present design and bring any action. And
besides, would not my presence in his house draw out the
whole pungency of the memorial? For that complaint could
not be very seriously regarded, if the person chiefly injured
was the guest of the official most incriminated. As I thought
upon this, I could not quite refrain from smiling.

'This is in the nature of a countercheck to the memorial?'
said I.

'You are cunning, Mr. David,' said he, 'and you do not
wholly guess wrong; the fact will be of use to me in my
defence. Perhaps, however, you underrate my friendly sentiments, which are perfectly genuine. I have a respect for you,
Mr. David, mingled with awe,' says he, smiling.

'I am more than willing, I am earnestly desirous to meet
your wishes,' said I. 'It is my design to be called to the Bar,
where your lordship's countenance would be invaluable; and
I am besides sincerely grateful to yourself and family for
different marks of interest and of indulgence. The difficulty
is here. There is one point in which we pull two ways. You
are trying to hang James Stewart, I am trying to save him.
In so far as my riding with you would better your lordship's
defence, I am at your lordship's orders; but in so far as it
would help to hang James Stewart, you see me at a stick.'

I thought he swore to himself. 'You should certainly be
called; the Bar is the true scene for your talents,' says he,
bitterly, and then fell a while silent. 'I will tell you,' he
presently resumed, 'there is no question of James Stewart,
for or against. James is a dead man; his life is given and
taken—bought (if you like it better) and sold; no memorial
can help—no defalcation of a faithful Mr. David hurt him.
Blow high, blow low, there will be no pardon for James
Stewart: and take that for said! The question is now of myself:
am I to stand or fall? and I do not deny to you that I am in

some danger. But will Mr. David Balfour consider why? It is not because I have pushed the case unduly against James; for that, I am sure of condonation. And it is not because I have sequestered Mr. David on a rock, though it will pass under that colour; but because I did not take the ready and plain path, to which I was pressed repeatedly, and send Mr. David to his grave or to the gallows. Hence the scandal—hence this damned memorial,' striking the paper on his leg. 'My tenderness for you has brought me in this difficulty. I wish to know if your tenderness to your own conscience is too great to let you help me out of it?'

No doubt but there was much of the truth in what he said; if James was past helping, whom was it more natural that I should turn to help than just the man before me, who had helped myself so often, and was even now setting me a pattern of patience? I was besides not only weary, but beginning to be ashamed of my perpetual attitude of suspicion and refusal.

'If you will name the time and place, I will be punctually ready to attend your lordship,' said I.

He shook hands with me. 'And I think my misses have some news for you,' says he, dismissing me.

I came away, vastly pleased to have my peace made, yet a little concerned in conscience; nor could I help wondering, as I went back, whether, perhaps, I had not been a scruple too good-natured. But there was the fact, that this was a man that might have been my father, an able man, a great dignitary, and one that, in the hour of my need, had reached a hand to my assistance. I was in the better humour to enjoy the remainder of that evening, which I passed with the Advocates, in excellent company no doubt, but perhaps with rather more than a sufficiency of punch: for though I went early to bed I have no clear mind of how I got there.

CHAPTER XVIII

THE TEE'D BALL

ON the morrow, from the justices' private room, where none could see me, I heard the verdict given in and judgment rendered upon James. The Duke's words I am quite sure I have correctly; and since that famous passage has been made a subject of dispute, I may as well commemorate my version. Having referred to the year '45, the chief of the Campbells, sitting as Justice-General upon the bench, thus addressed the unfortunate Stewart before him: 'If you had been successful in that rebellion, you might have been giving the law where you have now received the judgment of it; we, who are this day your judges, might have been tried before one of your mock courts of judicature; and then you might have been satiated with the blood of any name or clan to which you had an aversion.'

'This is to let the cat out of the bag, indeed,' thought I. And that was the general impression. It was extraordinary how the young advocate lads took hold and made a mock of this speech, and how scarce a meal passed but what someone would get in the words: 'And then you might have been satiated.' Many songs were made in that time for the hour's diversion, and are near all forgot. I remember one began:

'What do ye want the bluid of, bluid of?
    Is it a name, or is it a clan,
        Or is it an aefauld Hielandman,
That ye want the bluid of, bluid of?'

Another went to my old favourite air, *The House of Airlie,* and began thus:

'It fell on a day when Argyle was on the bench,
    That they served him a Stewart for his denner.'

And one of the verses ran:

> 'Then up and spak the Duke, and flyted on his cook,
>   I regaird it as a sensible aspersion,
> That I would sup ava', an' satiate my maw,
>   With the bluid of ony clan of my aversion.'

James was as fairly murdered as though the Duke had got a fowling-piece and stalked him. So much of course I knew: but others knew not so much, and were more affected by the items of scandal that came to light in the progress of the cause. One of the chief was certainly this sally of the justice's. It was run hard by another of a juryman, who had struck into the midst of Coulston's speech for the defence with a 'Pray, sir, cut it short, we are quite weary,' which seemed the very excess of impudence and simplicity. But some of my new lawyer friends were still more staggered with an innovation that had disgraced and even vitiated the proceedings. One witness was never called. His name, indeed, was printed, where it may still be seen on the fourth page of the list: 'James Drummond, *alias* Macgregor, *alias* James More, late tenant in Inveronachile'; and his precognition had been taken, as the manner is, in writing. He had remembered or invented (God help him) matter which was lead in James Stewart's shoes, and I saw was like to prove wings to his own. This testimony it was highly desirable to bring to the notice of the jury, without exposing the man himself to the perils of cross-examination; and the way it was brought about was a matter of surprise to all. For the paper was handed round (like a curiosity) in court; passed through the jury-box, where it did its work; and disappeared again (as though by accident) before it reached the counsel for the prisoner. This was counted a most insidious device; and that the name of James More should be mingled up with it filled me with shame for Catriona and concern for myself.

The following day, Prestongrange and I, with a considerable company, set out for Glasgow, where (to my impatience) we continued to linger some time in a mixture of pleasure and affairs. I lodged with my lord, with whom I was encouraged to familiarity; had my place at entertainments; was presented to the chief guests; and altogether made more of than I thought accorded either with my parts or station; so that, on strangers being present, I would often blush for Prestongrange. It must be owned the view I had taken of the world in these last months was fit to cast a gloom upon my character. I had met many men, some of them leaders in Israel whether by their birth or talents; and who among them all had shown clean hands? As for the Browns and Millers, I had seen their self-seeking, I could never again respect them. Prestongrange was the best yet; he had saved me, had spared me rather, when others had it in their minds to murder me outright; but the blood of James lay at his door; and I thought his present dissimulation with myself a thing below pardon. That he should affect to find pleasure in my discourse almost surprised me out of my patience. I would sit and watch him with a kind of a slow fire of anger in my bowels, 'Ah, friend, friend,' I would think to myself, 'if you were but through with this affair of the memorial, would you not kick me in the streets?' Here I did him, as events have proved, the most grave injustice; and I think he was at once far more sincere, and a far more artful performer than I supposed.

But I had some warrant for my incredulity in the behaviour of that court of young advocates that hung about him in the hope of patronage. The sudden favour of a lad not previously heard of troubled them at first out of measure; but two days were not gone by before I found myself surrounded with flattery and attention. I was the same young man, and neither better nor bonnier, that they had rejected a month before; and now there was no civility too fine for me! The same, do I say? It was not so; and the by-name by which I went behind my back confirmed it. Seeing me so firm with the Advocate, and persuaded that I was to fly high and far, they had taken a word from the golfing green, and called me *the Tee'd Ball*.[1] I was told I was now 'one of themselves'; I was to taste of their soft lining, who had already made my own experience

1 A ball placed upon a little mound for convenience of striking.

of the roughness of the outer husk; and one, to whom I had been presented in Hope Park, was so assured as even to remind me of that meeting. I told him I had not the pleasure of remembering it.

'Why,' says he, 'it was Miss Grant herself presented me! My name is so-and-so.'

'It may very well be, sir,' said I; 'but I have kept no mind of it.'

At which he desisted; and in the midst of the disgust that commonly overflowed my spirits I had a glisk of pleasure.

But I have not patience to dwell upon that time at length. When I was in company with these young politics I was borne down with shame for myself and my own plain ways, and scorn for them and their duplicity. Of the two evils, I thought Prestongrange to be the least; and while I was always as stiff as buckram to the young bloods, I made rather a dissimulation of my hard feelings towards the Advocate, and was (in old Mr. Campbell's word) 'soople to the laird.' Himself commented on the difference, and bid me be more of my age, and make friends with my young comrades.

I told him I was slow of making friends.

'I will take the word back,' said he. 'But there is such a thing as *Fair gude e'en and fair gude day*, Mr. David. These are the same young men with whom you are to pass your days and get through life: your backwardness has a look of arrogance; and unless you can assume a little more lightness of manner, I fear you will meet difficulties in the path.'

'It will be an ill job to make a silk purse of a sow's ear,' said I.

On the morning of October 1st I was awakened by the clattering in of an express; and getting to my window almost before he had dismounted, I saw the messenger had ridden hard. Somewhile after I was called to Prestongrange, where he was sitting in his bedgown and nightcap, with his letters round him.

'Mr. David,' said he, 'I have a piece of news for you. It concerns some friends of yours, of whom I sometimes think you are a little ashamed, for you have never referred to their existence.'

I suppose I blushed.

'I see you understand, since you make the answering signal,' said he. 'And I must compliment you on your excellent taste in beauty. But do you know, Mr. David, this seems to me a very enterprising lass? She crops up from every side. The Government of Scotland appears unable to proceed for Mistress Katrine Drummond, which was somewhat the case (no great while back) with a certain Mr. David Balfour. Should not these make a good match? Her first intromission in politics—but I must not tell you that story, the authorities have decided you are to hear it otherwise and from a livelier narrator. This new example is more serious, however; and I am afraid I must alarm you with the intelligence that she is now in prison.'

I cried out.

'Yes,' said he, 'the little lady is in prison. But I would not have you to despair. Unless you (with your friends and memorials) shall procure my downfall, she is to suffer nothing.'

'But what has she done? What is her offence?' I cried.

'It might be almost construed a high treason,' he returned, 'for she has broke the King's Castle of Edinburgh.'

'The lady is much my friend,' I said. 'I know you would not mock me if the thing were serious.'

'And yet it is serious in a sense,' said he; 'for this rogue of a Katrine—or Cateran, as we may call her—has set adrift again upon the world that very doubtful character, her papa.'

Here was one of my previsions justified: James More was once again at liberty. He had lent his men to keep me a prisoner; he had volunteered his testimony in the Appin case, and the same (no matter by what subterfuge) had been employed to influence the jury. Now came his reward, and he was free. It might please the authorities to give to it the colour of an escape; but I knew better—I knew it must be the fulfilment of a bargain. The same course of thought relieved me of the least alarm for Catriona. She might be thought to have broke prison for her father; she might have believed so herself. But the chief hand in the whole business was that of Prestongrange; and I was sure, so far from letting her come to punishment, he would not suffer her to be even tried. Whereupon thus came out of me the not very politic ejaculation:

'Ah! I was expecting that!'

'You have at times a great deal of discretion, too!' says Prestongrange.

'And what is my lord pleased to mean by that?' I asked.

'I was just marvelling,' he replied, 'that being so clever as to draw these inferences, you should not be clever enough to keep them to yourself. But I think you would like to hear the details of the affair. I have received two versions: and the least official is the more full and far the more entertaining, being from the lively pen of my eldest daughter. "Here is all the town bizzing with a fine piece of work," she writes, "and what would make the thing more noted (if it were only known) the malefactor is a *protégé* of his lordship my papa. I am sure your heart is too much in your duty (if it were nothing else) to have forgotten Grey Eyes. What does she do, but get a broad hat with the flaps open, a long hairy-like man's greatcoat, and a big gravatt; kilt her coats up to *Gude kens whaur*, clap two pair of boot-hose upon her legs, take a pair of *clouted brogues*[1] in her hand, and off to the Castle! Here she gives herself out to be a soutar[2] in the employ of James More, and gets admitted to his cell, the lieutenant (who seems to have been full of pleasantry) making sport among his soldiers of the soutar's greatcoat. Presently they hear disputation and the sound of blows inside. Out flies the cobbler, his coat flying, the flaps of his hat beat about his face, and the lieutenant and his soldiers mock at him as he runs off.* They laughed not so hearty the next time they had occasion to visit the cell and found nobody but a tall, pretty, grey-eyed lass in the female habit! As for the cobbler, he was 'over the hills ayont Dumblane,' and it's thought that poor Scotland will

---

1 Patched shoes.   2 Shoemaker.

have to console herself without him. I drank Catriona's health this night in public. Indeed, the whole town admires her; and I think the beaux would wear bits of her garters in their button-holes if they could only get them. I would have gone to visit her in prison too, only I remembered in time I was papa's daughter; so I wrote her a billet instead, which I entrusted to the faithful Doig, and I hope you will admit I can be political when I please. The same faithful gomeral is to despatch this letter by the express along with those of the wiseacres, so that you may hear Tom Fool in company with Solomon. Talking of *gomerals*, do tell *Dauvit Balfour*. I would I could see the face of him at the thought of a long-legged lass in such a predicament! to say nothing of the levities of your affectionate daughter, and his respectful friend." So my rascal signs herself!' continued Prestongrange. 'And you see, Mr. David, it is quite true what I tell you, that my daughters regard you with the most affectionate playfulness.'

'The gomeral is much obliged,' said I.

'And was not this prettily done?' he went on. 'Is not this Highland maid a piece of a heroine?'

'I was always sure she had a great heart,' said I. 'And I wager she guessed nothing . . . But I beg your pardon, this is to tread upon forbidden subjects.'

'I will go bail she did not,' he returned, quite openly. 'I will go bail she thought she was flying straight into King George's face.'

Remembrance of Catriona, and the thought of her lying in captivity, moved me strangely. I could see that even Prestongrange admired, and could not withhold his lips from smiling when he considered her behaviour. As for Miss Grant, for all her ill habit of mockery, her admiration shone out plain. A kind of a heat came on me.

'I am not your lordship's daughter . . .' I began.

'That I know of!' he put in smiling.

'I speak like a fool,' said I; 'or rather I began wrong. It would doubtless be unwise in Mistress Grant to go to her in prison; but for me, I think I would look like a half-hearted friend if I did not fly there instantly.'

'So-ho, Mr. David,' says he; 'I thought that you and I were in a bargain?'

'My lord, I said, 'when I made that bargain I was a good deal affected by your goodness, but I'll never can deny that I was moved besides by my own interest. There was self-seeking in my heart, and I think shame of it now. It may be for your lordship's safety to say this fashious Davie Balfour is your friend and housemate. Say it then; I'll never contradict you. But as for your patronage, I give it all back. I ask but the one thing—let me go, and give me a pass to set her in her prison.'

He looked at me with a hard eye. 'You put the cart before the horse, I think,' says he. 'That which I had given was a portion of my liking, which your thankless nature does not seem to have remarked. But for my patronage, it is not given, nor (to be exact) is it yet offered.' He paused a bit. 'And I warn you, you do not know yourself,' he added. 'Youth is a hasty season; you will think better of all this before a year.'

'Well, and I would like to be that kind of youth!' I cried. 'I have seen too much of the other party in these young advocates that fawn upon your lordship and are even at the pains to fawn on me. And I have seen it in the old ones also. They are all for by-ends, the whole clan of them! It's this that makes me seem to misdoubt your lordship's liking. Why would I think that you would like me? But ye told me yourself ye had an interest!'

I stopped at this, confounded that I had run so far; he was observing me with an unfathomable face.

'My lord, I ask your pardon,' I resumed. 'I have nothing in my chafts but a rough country tongue. I think it would be only decent-like if I would go to see my friend in her captivity; but I'm owing you my life—I'll never forget that; and if it's for your lordship's good, here I'll stay. That's barely gratitude.'

'This might have been reached in fewer words,' says Prestongrange grimly. 'It is easy, and it is at times gracious, to say a plain Scots "ay."'

'Ah, but, my lord, I think ye take me not yet entirely!'

cried I. 'For *your* sake, for my life-safe, and the kindness that ye say ye bear to me—for these, I'll consent; but not for any good that might be coming to myself. If I stand aside when this young maid is in her trial, it's a thing I will be noways advantaged by; I will lose by it, I will never gain. I would rather make a shipwreck wholly than to build on that foundation.'

He was a minute serious, then smiled. 'You mind me of the man with the long nose,' said he; 'was you to look at the moon by a telescope you would see David Balfour there! But you shall have your way of it. I will ask at you one service, and then set you free. My clerks are over-driven; be so good as copy me these few pages,' says he, visibly swithering among some huge rolls of manuscripts, 'and when that is done, I shall bid you God speed! I would never charge myself with Mr. David's conscience; and if you could cast some part of it (as you went by) in a moss hag, you would find yourself to ride much easier without it.'

'Perhaps not just entirely in the same direction though, my lord!' says I.

'And you shall have the last word, too!' cries he gaily.

Indeed he had some cause for gaiety, having now found the means to gain his purpose. To lessen the weight of the memorial, or to have a readier answer at his hand, he desired I should appear publicly in the character of his intimate. But if I were to appear with the same publicity as a visitor to Catriona in her prison the world would scarce stint to draw conclusions, and the true nature of James More's escape must become evident to all. This was the little problem I had set him of a sudden, and to which he had so briskly found an answer. I was to be tethered in Glasgow by that job of copying, which in mere outward decency I could not well refuse; and during these hours of my employment Catriona was privately got rid of. I think shame to write of this man that loaded me with so many goodnesses. He was kind to me as any father, yet I ever thought him as false as a cracked bell.

CHAPTER XIX

I AM MUCH IN THE HANDS OF THE LADIES

THE copying was a weary business, the more so as I perceived very early there was no sort of urgency in the matters treated, and began very early to consider my employment a pretext. I had no sooner finished, than I got to horse, used what remained of daylight to the best purpose, and being at last fairly benighted, slept in a house by Almond-Water side. I was in the saddle again before the day, and the Edinburgh booths were just opening when I clattered in by the West Bow and drew up a smoking horse at my lord Advocate's door. I had a written word for Doig, my lord's private hand that was thought to be in all his secrets—a worthy, little plain man, all fat and snuff and self-sufficiency. Him I found already at his desk and already bedabbled with maccabaw, in the same ante-room where I rencountered with James More. He read the notes scrupulously through like a chapter in his Bible.

'H'm,' says he; 'ye come a wee thing ahinthand, Mr. Balfour. The bird's flaen—we hae letten her out.'

'Miss Drummond is set free?' I cried.

'Achy!' said he. 'What would we keep her for, ye ken? To hae made a steer about the bairn would hae pleased naebody.'

'And where'll she be now?' says I.

'Gude kens!' says Doig, with a shrug.

'She'll have gone home to Lady Allardyce, I'm thinking,' said I.

'That'll be it,' said he.

'Then I'll gang there straight,' says I.

'But ye'll be for a bite or ye go?' said he.

'Neither bite nor sup,' said I. 'I had a good wauch of milk in by Ratho.'

'Aweel, aweel,' says Doig. 'But ye'll can leave your horse here and your bags, for it seems we're to have your up-put.'

'Na, na,' said I. 'Tamson's mear[1] would never be the thing for me this day of all days.'

Doig speaking somewhat broad, I had been led by imitation into an accent much more countrified than I was usually careful to affect*—a good deal broader indeed than I have written it down; and I was the more ashamed when another voice joined in behind me with a scrap of a ballad:

> 'Gae saddle me the bonny black,
>   Gae saddle sune and mak' him ready,
> Far I will down the Gatehope-slack,
>   And a' to see my bonny leddy.'

The young lady, when I turned to her, stood in a morning gown, and her hands muffled in the same, as if to hold me at a distance. Yet I could not but think there was kindness in the eye with which she saw me.

'My best respects to you, Mistress Grant,' said I, bowing.

'The like to yourself, Mr. David,' she replied, with a deep curtsy. 'And I beg to remind you of an old musty saw, that meat and mass never hindered man. The mass I cannot afford you, for we are all good Protestants. But the meat I press on your attention. And I would not wonder but I could find something for your private ear that would be the worth the stopping for.'

'Mistress Grant,' said I, 'I believe I am already your debtor for some merry words—and I think they were kind too—on a piece of unsigned paper.'

'Unsigned paper?' says she, and made a droll face, which was likewise wondrous beautiful, as of one trying to remember.

'Or else I am the more deceived,' I went on. 'But to be sure, we shall have the time to speak of these, since your father is so good as to make me for a while your inmate; and the *gomeral* begs you at this time only for the favour of his liberty.'

1 Tamson's mare—to go afoot.

'You give yourself hard names,' said she.

'Mr. Doig and I would be blythe to take harder at your clever pen,' says I.

'Once more I have to admire the discretion of all men-folk,' she replied. 'But if you will not eat, off with you at once; you will be back the sooner, for you go on a fool's errand. Off with you, Mr. David,' she continued, opening the door.

> 'He has lowpen on his bonny grey,
>   He rade the richt gate and the ready;
> I trow he would neither stint nor stay,
>   Far he was seeking his bonny leddy.'

I did not wait to be twice bidden, and did justice to Miss Grant's citation on the way to Dean.

Old Lady Allardyce walked there alone in the garden, in her hat and mutch, and having a silver-mounted staff of some black wood to lean upon. As I alighted from my horse, and drew near to her with *congees*, I could see the blood come in her face, and her head fling into the air like what I had conceived of empresses.

'What brings you to my poor door?' she cried, speaking high through her nose. 'I cannot bar it. The males of my house are dead and buried; I have neither son nor husband to stand in the gate for me; any beggar can pluck me by the baird[1]—and a baird there is, and that's the worst of it yet!' she added, partly to herself.

I was extremely put out at this reception, and the last remark, which seemed like a daft wife's, left me near hand speechless.

'I see I have fallen under your displeasure, ma'am,' said I. 'Yet I will still be so bold as ask after Mistress Drummond.'

She considered me with a burning eye, her lips pressed close together into twenty creases, her hand shaking on her staff. 'This cows all!' she cried. 'Ye come to me to speir for her? Would God I knew!'

'She is not here?' I cried.

----

[1] Beard.

She threw up her chin and made a step and a cry at me, so that I fell back incontinent.

'Out upon your leeing throat!' she cried. 'What! ye come and speir at me! She's in jyle, whaur ye took her to—that's all there is to it. And of a' the beings ever I beheld in breeks, to think it should be to you! Ye timmer scoun'rel, if I had a male left to my name I would have your jaicket dustit till ye raired.'

I thought it not good to delay longer in that place, because I remarked her passion to be rising. As I turned to the horse-post she even followed me; and I make no shame to confess that I rode away with the one stirrup on and scrambling for the other.

As I knew no other quarter where I could push my inquiries, there was nothing left me but to return to the Advocate's. I was well received by the four ladies, who were now in company together, and must give the news of Preston-grange and what word went in the west country, at the most inordinate length and with great weariness to myself; while all the time that young lady, with whom I so much desired to be alone again, observed me quizzically and seemed to find pleasure in the sight of my impatience. At last, after I had endured a meal with them, and was come very near the point of appealing for an interview before her aunt, she went and stood by the music-case, and picking out a tune, sang to it on a high key—'He that will not when he may, When he will he shall have nay.' But this was the end of her rigours, and presently, after making some excuse of which I have no mind, she carried me away in private to her father's library. I should not fail to say that she was dressed to the nines, and appeared extraordinary handsome.

'Now, Mr. David, sit ye down here and let us have a two-handed crack,' said she. 'For I have much to tell you, and it appears besides that I have been grossly unjust to your good taste.'

'In what manner, Mistress Grant?' I asked. 'I trust I have never seemed to fail in due respect.'

'I will be your surety, Mr. David,' said she. 'Your respect, whether to yourself or your poor neighbours, has been always and most fortunately beyond imitation. But that is by the question. You got a note from me?' she asked.

'I was so bold as to suppose so upon inference,' said I, 'and it was kindly thought upon.'

'It must have prodigiously surprised you,' said she. 'But let us begin with the beginning. You have not perhaps forgot a day when you were so kind as to escort three very tedious misses to Hope Park? I have the less cause to forget it myself, because you was so particular obliging as to introduce me to some of the principles of the Latin grammar, a thing which wrote itself profoundly on my gratitude.'

'I fear I was sadly pedantical,' said I, overcome with confusion at the memory. 'You are only to consider I am quite unused with the society of ladies.'

'I will say the less about the grammar then,' she replied. 'But how came you to desert your charge? "He has thrown her out, overboard his ain, dear Annie!"' she hummed; 'and his ain dear Annie and her two sisters had to taigle home by theirselves like a string of green geese! It seems you returned to my papa's, where you showed yourself excessively martial, and then on to realms unknown, with an eye (it appears) to the Bass Rock; solan geese being perhaps more to your mind than bonny lasses.'

Through all this raillery there was something indulgent in the lady's eye which made me suppose there might be better coming.

'You take a pleasure to torment me,' said I, 'and I make a very feckless plaything; but let me ask you to be more merciful. At this time there is but the one thing that I care to hear of, and that will be news of Catriona.'

'Do you call her by that name to her face, Mr. Balfour?' she asked.

'In troth, and I am not very sure,' I stammered.

'I would not do so in any case to strangers,' said Miss Grant. 'And why are you so much immersed in the affairs of this young lady?'

'I heard she was in prison,' said I.

'Well, and now you hear that she is out of it,' she replied, 'and what more would you have? She has no need of any further champion.'

'I may have the greater need of her, ma'am,' said I.

'Come, this is better!' says Miss Grant. 'But look me fairly in the face; am I not bonnier than she?'

'I would be the last to be denying it,' said I. 'There is not your marrow in all Scotland.'

'Well, here you have the pick of the two at your hand, and must needs speak of the other,' said she. 'This is never the way to please the ladies, Mr. Balfour.'

'But, mistress,' said I, 'there are surely other things besides mere beauty.'

'By which I am to understand that I am not better than I should be, perhaps?' she asked.

'By which you will please understand that I am like the cock in the midden in the fable book,' said I. 'I see the braw jewel—and I like fine to see it too—but I have more need of the pickle corn.'

'Bravissimo!' she cried. 'There is a word well said at last, and I will reward you for it with my story. That same night of your desertion I came late from a friend's house—where I was excessively admired, whatever you may think of it— and what should I hear but that a lass in a tartan screen desired to speak with me? She had been there an hour or better, said the servant-lass, and she grat in to herself as she sat waiting. I went to her direct; she rose as I came in, and I knew her at a look. "Grey Eyes!" says I to myself, but was more wise than to let on. *You will be Miss Grant at last?* she says, rising and looking at me hard and pitiful. *Ay, it was true he said, you are bonny at all events.—The way God made me, my dear,* I said, *but I would be gey and obliged if ye could tell me what brought you here at such a time of the night.—Lady,* she said, *we are kinsfolk, we are both come of the blood of the sons of Alpin.—My dear,* I replied, *I think no more of Alpin or his sons than what I do of a kalestock. You have a better argument in these tears upon your bonny face.* And at that I was so weak-minded as to kiss her, which

is what you would like to do dearly, and I wager will never
find the courage of. I say it was weak-minded of me, for I
knew no more of her than the outside; but it was the wisest
stroke I could have hit upon. She is a very staunch, brave
nature, but I think she has been little used with tenderness;
and at that caress (though to say the truth, it was but lightly
given) her heart went out to me. I will never betray the
secrets of my sex, Mr. Davie; I will never tell you the way
she turned me round her thumb, because it is the same she
will use to twist yourself. Ay, it is a fine lass! She is as clean
as hill well-water.'

'She is e'en't!' I cried.

'Well, then, she told me her concerns,' pursued Miss Grant,
'and in what a swither she was in about her papa, and what
a taking about yourself, with very little cause, and in what
a perplexity she had found herself after you was gone away.
And then I minded at long last, says she, *that we were kins-
women, and that Mr. David should have given you the name
of the bonniest of the bonny, and I was thinking to myself
"If she is so bonny she will be good at all events"; and I took
up my foot soles out of that.* That was when I forgave yourself, Mr. Davie. When you was in my society, you seemed
upon hot iron: by all marks, if ever I saw a young man that
wanted to be gone, it was yourself, and I and my two sisters
were the ladies you were so desirous to be gone from; and now
it appeared you had given me some notice in the by-going,
and was so kind as to comment on my attractions! From that
hour you may date our friendship, and I began to think with
tenderness upon the Latin grammar.'

'You will have many hours to rally me in,' said I; 'and I
think besides you do yourself injustice. I think it was
Catriona turned your heart in my direction. She is too simple
to perceive as you do the stiffness of her friend.'

'I would not like to wager upon that, Mr. David,' said she.
'The lasses have clear eyes. But at least she is your friend
entirely, as I was to see. I carried her in to his lordship my
papa; and his Advocacy, being in a favourable stage of claret,
was so good as to receive the pair of us. *Here is Grey Eyes*

that you have been deaved with these days past, said I, *she is come to prove that we spoke true, and I lay the prettiest lass in the three Lothians at your feet*—making a papistical reservation of myself. She suited her action to my words: down she went upon her knees to him—I would not like to swear but he saw two of her, which doubtless made her appeal the more irresistible, for you are all a pack of Mahomedans—told him what had passed that night, and how she had withheld her father's man from following of you, and what a case she was in about her father, and what a flutter for yourself; and begged with weeping for the lives of both of you (neither of which was in the slightest danger), till I vow I was proud of my sex because it was done so pretty, and ashamed for it because of the smallness of the occasion. She had not gone far, I assure you, before the Advocate was wholly sober, to see his inmost politics ravelled out by a young lass and discovered to the most unruly of his daughters. But we took him in hand, the pair of us, and brought that matter straight. Properly managed—and that means managed by me—there is no one to compare with my papa.'

'He has been a good man to me,' said I.

'Well, he was a good man to Katrine, and I was there to see to it,' said she.

'And she pled for me!' say I.

'She did that, and very movingly,' said Miss Grant. 'I would not like to tell you what she said—I find you vain enough already.'

'God reward her for it!' cried I.

'With Mr. David Balfour, I suppose?' says she.

'You do me too much injustice at the last!' I cried. 'I would tremble to think of her in such hard hands. Do you think I would presume, because she begged my life? She would do that for a new whelped puppy! I have had more than that to set me up, if you but ken'd. She kissed that hand of mine. Ay, but she did. And why? because she thought I was playing a brave part and might be going to my death. It was not for my sake—but I need not be telling that to you, that cannot look at me without laughter. It was for the love of what she

thought was bravery. I believe there is none but me and poor
Prince Charlie had that honour done them. Was this not to
make a god of me? and do you not think my heart would
quake when I remember it?'

'I do laugh at you a good deal, and a good deal more than
is quite civil,' said she; 'but I will tell you one thing: if you
speak to her like that, you have some glimmerings of a
chance.'

'Me?' I cried, 'I would never dare. I can speak to you, Miss
Grant, because it's a matter of indifference what ye think of
me. But her? no fear!' said I.

'I think you have the largest feet in all broad Scotland,'
says she.

'Troth they are no very small,' said I, looking down.

'Ah, poor Catriona,' cries Miss Grant.

And I could but stare upon her; for though I now see very
well what she was driving at (and perhaps some justification
for the same) I was never swift at the uptake in such flimsy
talk.

'Ah well, Mr. David,' she said, 'it goes sore against my
conscience, but I see I shall have to be your speaking board.
She shall know you came to her straight upon the news of her
imprisonment; she shall know you would not pause to eat;
and of our conversation she shall hear just so much as I think
convenient for a maid of her age and inexperience. Believe
me, you will be in that way much better served than you
could serve yourself, for I will keep the big feet out of the
platter.'

'You know where she is, then?' I exclaimed.

'That I do, Mr. David, and will never tell,' said
she.

'Why that?' I asked.

'Well,' she said, 'I am a good friend, as you will soon dis-
cover; and the chief of those that I am friend to is my papa.
I assure you, you will never heat nor melt me out of that,
so you may spare me your sheep's eyes; and adieu to your
David-Balfour-ship for the now.'

'But there is yet one thing more,' I cried. 'There is one

thing that must be stopped, being mere ruin to herself, and to me too.'

'Well,' she said, 'be brief; I have spent half the day on you already.'

'My Lady Allardyce believes,' I began—'she supposes—she thinks that I abducted her.'

The colour came into Miss Grant's face, so that at first I was quite abashed to find her ear so delicate, till I bethought she was struggling rather with mirth, a notion in which I was altogether confirmed by the shaking of her voice as she replied—

'I will take up the defence of your reputation,' said she. 'You may leave it in my hands.'

And with that she withdrew out of the library.

CHAPTER XX

I CONTINUE TO MOVE IN GOOD SOCIETY

FOR about exactly two months I remained a guest in Prestongrange's family, where I bettered my acquaintance with the bench, the bar, and the flower of Edinburgh company. You are not to suppose my education was neglected; on the contrary, I was kept extremely busy. I studied the French, so as to be more prepared to go to Leyden; I set myself to the fencing, and wrought hard, sometimes three hours in the day, with notable advancement; at the suggestion of my cousin, Pilrig, who was an apt musician, I was put to a singing class; and by the orders of my Miss Grant, to one for the dancing, at which I must say I proved far from ornamental. However, all were good enough to say it gave me an address a little more genteel; and there is no question but I learned to manage my coat skirts and sword with more dexterity, and to stand in a room as though the same belonged to me. My clothes themselves were all earnestly re-ordered; and the most trifling circumstances, such as where I should tie my hair, or the colour of my ribbon debated among the three misses like a thing of weight. One way with another, no doubt I was a good deal improved to look at, and acquired a bit of modish air that would have surprised the good folks at Essendean.

The two younger misses were very willing to discuss a point of my habiliment, because that was in the line of their chief thoughts. I cannot say that they appeared any other way conscious of my presence; and though always more than civil, with a kind of heartless cordiality, could not hide how much I wearied them. As for the aunt, she was a wonderful still woman; and I think she gave me much the same attention as she gave the rest of the family, which was little enough. The eldest daughter and the Advocate himself were thus my principal friends, and our familiarity was much increased by a pleasure that we took in common. Before the court met we spent a day or two at the house of Grange, living very nobly with an open table, and here it was that we three began to ride out together in the fields, a practice afterwards maintained in Edinburgh, so far as the Advocate's continual affairs permitted. When we were put in a good frame by the briskness of the exercise, the difficulties of the way, or the accidents of bad weather, my shyness wore entirely off; we forgot that we were strangers, and speech not being required, it flowed the more naturally on. Then it was that they had my story from me, bit by bit, from the time that I left Essendean, with my voyage and battle in the *Covenant*, wanderings in the heather, etc.; and from the interest they found in my adventures sprung the circumstance of a jaunt we made a little later on, on a day when the courts were not sitting, and of which I will tell a trifle more at length.

We took horse early, and passed first by the house of Shaws, where it stood smokeless in a great field of white frost, for it was yet early in the day. Here Prestongrange alighted down, gave me his horse, and proceeded alone to visit my uncle. My heart, I remember, swelled up bitter within me at the sight of that bare house and the thought of the old miser sitting chittering within the cold kitchen!

'There is my home,' said I; 'and my family.

'Poor David Balfour!' said Miss Grant.

What passed during the visit I have never heard; but it would doubtless not be very agreeable to Ebenezer, for when the Advocate came forth again his face was dark.

'I think you will soon be the laird indeed, Mr. Davie,' says he, turning half about with the one foot in the stirrup.

'I will never pretend sorrow,' said I; and, to say the truth, during his absence Miss Grant and I had been embellishing the place in fancy with plantations, parterres, and a terrace —much as I have since carried out in fact.*

Thence we pushed to the Queensferry, where Rankeillor gave us a good welcome, being indeed out of the body to receive so great a visitor. Here the Advocate was so unaffectedly good as to go quite fully over my affairs, sitting perhaps two hours with the Writer in his study, and expressing (I was told) a great esteem for myself and concern for my fortunes. To while this time, Miss Grant and I and young Rankeillor took boat and passed the Hope to Limekilns. Rankeillor made himself very ridiculous (and, I thought, offensive) with his admiration for the young lady, and to my wonder (only it is so common a weakness of her sex) she seemed, if anything, to be a little gratified. One use it had: for when we were come to the other side, she laid her commands on him to mind the boat, while she and I passed a little further to the alehouse. This was her own thought, for she had been taken with my account of Alison Hastie, and desired to see the lass herself. We found her once more alone—indeed, I believe her father wrought all day in the fields—and she curtsied dutifully to the gentry-folk and the beautiful young lady in the riding-coat.

'Is this all the welcome I am to get?' said I, holding out my hand. 'And have you no more memory of old friends?'

'Keep me! wha's this of it?' she cried, and then, 'God's truth, it's the tautit[1] laddie!'

'The very same,' says I.

'Mony's the time I've thocht upon you and your freen, and blythe am I to see you in your braws,'[2] she cried. 'Though

---

[1] Ragged.   [2] Fine things.

I kent ye were come to your ain folk by the grand present that ye sent me and that I thank ye for with a' my heart.'

'There,' said Miss Grant to me, 'run out by with ye, like a good bairn. I didnae come here to stand and haud a candle; it's her and me that are to crack.'

I suppose she stayed ten minutes in the house, but when she came forth I observed two things—that her eyes were reddened, and a silver brooch was gone out of her bosom. This very much affected me.

'I never saw you so well adorned,' said I.

'O Davie man, dinna be a pompous gowk!' said she, and was more than usually sharp to me the remainder of the day.

About candlelight we came home from this excursion.

For a good while I heard nothing further of Catriona—my Miss Grant remaining quite impenetrable, and stopping my mouth with pleasantries. At last, one day that she returned from walking and found me alone in the parlour over my French, I thought there was something unusual in her looks; the colour heightened, the eyes sparkling high, and a bit of a smile continually bitten in as she regarded me. She seemed indeed like the very spirit of mischief, and, walking briskly in the room, had soon involved me in a kind of quarrel over nothing and (at the least) with nothing intended on my side. I was like Christian in the slough—the more I tried to clamber out upon the side, the deeper I became involved; until at last I heard her declare, with a great deal of passion, that she would take that answer at the hands of none, and I must down upon my knees for pardon.

The causelessness of all this fuff stirred my own bile. 'I have said nothing you can properly object to,' said I, 'and as for my knees, that is an attitude I keep for God.'

'And as a goddess I am to be served!' she cried, shaking her brown locks at me and with a bright colour. 'Every man that comes within waft of my petticoats shall use me so!'

'I will go so far as ask your pardon for the fashion's sake, although I vow I know not why,' I replied. 'But for these play-acting postures, you can go to others.'

'O Davie!' she said. 'Not if I was to beg you?'

I bethought me I was fighting with a woman, which is the same as to say a child, and that upon a point entirely formal.

'I think it a bairnly thing,' I said, 'not worthy in you to ask, or me to render. Yet I will not refuse you, neither,' said I; 'and the stain, if there be any, rests with yourself.' And at that I kneeled fairly down.

'There!' she cried. 'There is the proper station, there is where I have been manœuvring to bring you.' And then, suddenly, 'Kep,'[1] said she, flung me a folded billet, and ran from the apartment laughing.

The billet had neither place nor date. 'Dear Mr. David,' it began, 'I get your news continually by my cousin, Miss Grant, and it is a pleisand hearing. I am very well, in a good place, among good folk, but necessitated to be quite private, though I am hoping that at long last we may meet again. All your friendships have been told me by my loving cousin, who loves us both. She bids me to send you this writing, and oversees the same. I will be asking you to do all her commands, and rest your affectionate friend, Catriona Macgregor-Drummond. P.S.—Will you not see my cousin, Allardyce?'

I think it not the least brave of my campaigns (as the soldiers say) that I should have done as I was here bidden and gone forthright to the house by Dean. But the old lady was now entirely changed and supple as a glove. By what means Miss Grant had brought this round I could never guess; I am sure, at least, she dared not to appear openly in the affair, for her papa was compromised in it pretty deep. It was he, indeed, who had persuaded Catriona to leave, or rather, not to return, to her cousin's, placing her instead with a family of Gregorys—decent people, quite at the Advocate's disposition, and in whom she might have the more confidence because they were of her own clan and family. These kept her private till all was ripe, heated and helped her to attempt her father's rescue, and after she was discharged from prison received her again into the same secrecy. Thus Prestongrange

1 Catch.

obtained and used his instrument; nor did there leak out the smallest word of his acquaintance with the daughter of James More. There was some whispering, of course, upon the escape of that discredited person; but the Government replied by a show of rigour, one of the cell porters was flogged, the lieutenant of the guard (my poor friend, Duncansby) was broken of his rank, and as for Catriona, all men were well enough pleased that her fault should be passed by in silence.

I could never induce Miss Grant to carry back an answer. 'No,' she would say, when I persisted, 'I am going to keep the big feet out of the platter.' This was the more hard to bear, as I was aware she saw my little friend many times in the week, and carried her my news whenever (as she said) I 'had behaved myself.' At last she treated me to what she called an indulgence, and I thought rather more of a banter. She was certainly a strong, almost a violent, friend to all she liked, chief among whom was a certain frail old gentlewoman, very blind and very witty, who dwelt on the top of a tall land on a strait close, with a nest of linnets in a cage, and thronged all day with visitors. Miss Grant was very fond to carry me there and put me to entertain her friend with the narrative of my misfortunes; and Miss Tibbie Ramsay (that was her name) was particular kind, and told me a great deal that was worth knowledge of old folks and past affairs in Scotland. I should say that from her chamber window, and not three feet away, such is the straitness of that close, it was possible to look into a barred loophole lighting the stairway of the opposite house.

Here, upon some pretext, Miss Grant left me one day alone with Miss Ramsay. I mind I thought that lady inattentive and like one preoccupied. I was besides very uncomfortable, for the window, contrary to custom, was left open and the day was cold. All at once the voice of Miss Grant sounded in my ears as from a distance.

'Here, Shaws!' she cried, 'keek out of the window and see what I have broughten you.'

I think it was the prettiest sight that ever I beheld. The well of the close was all in clear shadow where a man could see distinctly, the walls very black and dingy; and there from the barred loophole I saw two faces smiling across at me—Miss Grant's and Catriona's.

'There!' says Miss Grant, 'I wanted her to see you in your braws like the lass of Limekilns. I wanted her to see what I could make of you, when I buckled to the job in earnest!'

It came in my mind she had been more than common particular that day upon my dress; and I think that some of the same care had been bestowed upon Catriona. For so merry and sensible a lady, Miss Grant was certainly wonderful taken up with duds.

'Catriona!' was all I could get out.

As for her, she said nothing in the world, but only waved her hand and smiled to me, and was suddenly carried away again from before the loophole.

That vision was no sooner lost than I ran to the house door, where I found I was locked in; thence back to Miss Ramsay, crying for the key, but might as well have cried upon the castle rock. She had passed her word, she said, and I must be a good lad. It was impossible to burst the door, even if it had been mannerly; it was impossible I should leap from the window, being seven storeys above ground. All I could do was to crane over the close and watch for their reappearance from the stair. It was little to see, being no more than the tops of their two heads each on a ridiculous bobbin of skirts, like to a pair of pincushions. Nor did Catriona so much as look up for a farewell; being prevented (as I heard afterwards) by Miss Grant, who told her folk were never seen to less advantage than from above downward.

On the way home, as soon as I was set free, I upbraided Miss Grant with her cruelty.

'I am sorry you was disappointed,' says she demurely. 'For my part I was very pleased. You looked better than I dreaded; you looked—if it will not make you vain—a mighty pretty young man when you appeared in the window. You are to remember that she could not see your feet,' says she, with the manner of one reassuring me.

'O!' cried I, 'leave my feet be—they are no bigger than my neighbours'.'

'They are even smaller than some,' said she, 'but I speak in parables like a Hebrew prophet.'

'I marvel little they were sometimes stoned!' says I. 'But, you miserable girl, how could you do it? Why should you care to tantalise me with a moment?'

'Love is like folk,' says she; 'it needs some kind of vivers.'[1]

'Oh, Barbara, let me see her properly!' I pleaded. 'You can —you see her when you please; let me have half an hour.'

'Who is it that is managing this love affair? You? Or me?' she asked, and as I continued to press her with my instances, fell back upon a deadly expedient: that of imitating the tones of my voice when I called on Catriona by name; with which, indeed, she held me in subjection for some days to follow.

There was never the least word heard of the memorial, or none by me. Prestongrange and his grace the Lord President may have heard of it (for what I know) on the deafest sides of their heads; they kept it to themselves, at least—the public was none the wiser; and in course of time, on November 8th, and in the midst of a prodigious storm of wind and rain, poor James of the Glens was duly hanged at Lettermore by Ballachulish.

So there was the final upshot of my politics! Innocent men have perished before James, and are like to keep on perishing (in spite of all our wisdom) till the end of time. And till the end of time young folk (who are not yet used with the duplicity of life and men) will struggle as I did, and make heroical resolves, and take long risks; and the course of events will push them upon the one side and go on like a marching army. James was hanged; and here was I dwelling in the house of Prestongrange, and grateful to him for his fatherly attention. He was hanged; and behold! when I met Mr. Simon in the causeway, I was fain to pull off my beaver to him like a good little boy before his dominie. He had been hanged by fraud and violence, and the world wagged along, and there was not a pennyweight of difference; and the villains of that

1 Victuals.

horrid plot were decent, kind, respectable fathers of families, who went to kirk and took the sacrament!

But I had had my view of that detestable business they call politics—I had seen it from behind, when it is all bones and blackness; and I was cured for life of any temptations to take part in it again. A plain, quiet, private path was that which I was ambitious to walk in, when I might keep my head out of the way of dangers and my conscience out of the road of temptation. For, upon a retrospect, it appeared I had not done so grandly, after all; but with the greatest possible amount of big speech and preparation, had accomplished nothing.

The 25th of the same month a ship was advertised to sail from Leith; and I was suddenly recommended to make up my mails for Leyden. To Prestongrange I could, of course, say nothing; for I had already been a long while sorning on his house and table. But with his daughter I was more open, bewailing my fate that I should be sent out of the country, and assuring her, unless she should bring me to farewell with Catriona, I would refuse at the last hour.

'Have I not given you my advice?' she asked.

'I know you have,' said I, 'and I know how much I am beholden to you already, and that I am bidden to obey your orders. But you must confess you are something too merry a lass at times to lippen[1] to entirely.'

'I will tell you, then,' said she. 'Be you on board by nine o'clock forenoon; the ship does not sail before one; keep your boat alongside; and if you are not pleased with my farewells when I shall send them, you can come ashore again and seek Katrine for yourself.'

Since I could make no more of her, I was fain to be content with this.

The day came round at last when she and I were to separate. We had been extremely intimate and familiar; I was much in her debt; and what way we were to part was a thing that put me from my sleep, like the vails I was to give to the

---

[1] Trust.

domestic servants. I knew she considered me too backward, and rather desired to rise in her opinion on that head. Besides which, after so much affection shown and (I believe) felt upon both sides, it would have looked cold-like to be anyways stiff. Accordingly, I got my courage up and my words ready, and the last chance we were like to be alone, asked pretty boldly to be allowed to salute her in farewell.

'You forget yourself strangely, Mr. Balfour,' said she. 'I cannot call to mind that I have given you any right to presume on our acquaintancy.'

I stood before her like a stopped clock, and knew not what to think, far less to say, when of a sudden she cast her arms about my neck and kissed me with the best will in the world.

'You inimitable bairn!' she cried. 'Did you think that I would let us part like strangers? Because I can never keep my gravity at you five minutes on end, you must not dream I do not love you very well: I am all love and laughter, every time I cast an eye on you! And now I will give you an advice to conclude your education, which you will have need of before it's very long. Never *ask* womenfolk. They're bound to answer "No"; God never made the lass that could resist the temptation. It's supposed by divines to be the curse of Eve: because she did not say it when the devil offered her the apple, her daughters can say nothing else.'

'Since I am so soon to lose my bonny professor,' I began.

'This is gallant, indeed,' says she curtseying.

'—I would put the one question,' I went on: 'May I ask a lass to marry me?'

'You think you could not marry her without?' she asked. 'Or else get her to offer?'

'You see you cannot be serious,' said I.

'I shall be very serious in one thing, David,' said she: 'I shall always be your friend.'

As I got to my horse the next morning, the four ladies were all at that same window whence we had once looked down on Catriona, and all cried farewell and waved their pocket napkins as I rode away. One out of the four I knew was truly sorry; and at the thought of that, and how I had come to the door three months ago for the first time, sorrow and gratitude made a confusion in my mind.

PART II
FATHER AND DAUGHTER

CHAPTER XXI
THE VOYAGE INTO HOLLAND

THE ship lay at a single anchor, well outside the pier of
Leith, so that all we passengers must come to it by the means
of skiffs. This was very little troublesome, for the reason that
the day was a flat calm, very frosty and cloudy, and with a
low shifting fog upon the water. The body of the vessel was
thus quite hid as I drew near, but the tall spars of her stood
high and bright in a sunshine like the flickering of a fire. She
proved to be a very roomy, commodious merchant, but somewhat blunt in the bows, and loaden extraordinary deep with
salt, salted salmon, and fine white linen stockings for the
Dutch. Upon my coming on board, the captain welcomed me
—one Sang (out of Lesmahago, I believe), a very hearty,
friendly tarpaulin of a man, but at the moment in rather
of a bustle. There had no other of the passengers yet appeared,
so that I was left to walk about upon the deck, viewing the
prospect and wondering a good deal what these farewells
should be which I was promised.

All Edinburgh and the Pentland Hills glinted above me in
a kind of smuisty brightness, now and again overcome with
blots of cloud; of Leith there was no more than the tops of
chimneys visible, and on the face of the water, where the
haar[1] lay, nothing at all. Out of this I was presently aware
of a sound of oars pulling, and a little after (as if out of the
smoke of a fire) a boat issued. There sat a grave man in
the stern sheets, well muffled from the cold, and by his side
a tall, pretty, tender figure of a maid that brought my heart
to a stand. I had scarce the time to catch my breath in, and

1 Sea fog.

be ready to meet her, as she stepped upon the deck, smiling, and making my best bow, which was now vastly finer than some months before, when first I made it to her ladyship. No doubt we were both a good deal changed: she seemed to have shot up taller, like a young, comely tree. She had now a kind of pretty backwardness that became her well, as of one that regarded herself more highly and was fairly woman; and for another thing, the hand of the same magician had been at work upon the pair of us, and Miss Grant had made us both *braw*, if she could make but the one *bonny*.

The same cry, in words not very different, came from both of us, that the other was come in compliment to say farewell, and then we perceived in a flash we were to ship together.

'O, why will not Baby have been telling me!' she cried; and then remembered a letter she had been given, on the condition of not opening it till she was well on board. Within was an enclosure for myself, and ran thus:

'DEAR DAVIE,—What do you think of my farewell? and what do you say to your fellow-passenger? Did you kiss, or did you ask? I was about to have signed here, but that would leave the purport of my question doubtful; and in my own case *I ken the answer*. So fill up here with good advice. Do not be too blate,[1] and for God's sake do not try to be too forward; nothing sets you worse. I am

'Your affectionate friend and governess,
'BARBARA GRANT.'*

I wrote a word of answer and compliment on a leaf out of my pocket-book, put it in with another scratch from Catriona, sealed the whole with my new signet of the Balfour arms, and despatched it by the hand of Prestongrange's servant that still waited in my boat.

Then we had time to look upon each more at leisure, which we had not done for a piece of a minute before (upon a common impulse) we shook hands again.

'Catriona!' said I. It seemed that was the first and last word of my eloquence.

1 Bashful.

'You will be glad to see me again?' says she.

'And I think that is an idle word,' said I. 'We are too deep friends to make speech upon such trifles.'

'Is she not the girl of all the world?' she cried again. 'I was never knowing such a girl, so honest and so beautiful.'

'And yet she cared no more for Alpin than what she did for a kalestock,' said I.

'Ah, she will say so indeed!' cries Catriona. 'Yet it was for the name and the gentle kind blood that she took me up and was so good to me.'

'Well, I will tell you why it was,' said I. 'There are all sorts of people's faces in this world. There is Barbara's face, that everyone must look at and admire, and think her a fine, brave, merry girl. And then there is your face, which is quite different—I never knew how different till to-day. You cannot see yourself, and that is why you do not understand; but it was for the love of your face that she took you up and was so good to you. And everybody in the world would do the same.'

'Everybody?' says she.

'Every living soul!' said I.

'Ah, then, that will be why the soldiers at the castle took me up!' she cried.

'Barbara has been teaching you to catch me,' said I.

'She will have taught me more than that at all events. She will have taught me a great deal about Mr. David—all the ill of him, and a little that was not so ill either, now and then,' she said, smiling. 'She will have told me all there was of Mr. David, only just that he would sail upon this very same ship. And why it is you go?'

I told her.

'Ah, well,' said she, 'we will be some days in company and then (I suppose) good-bye for altogether! I go to meet my father at a place of the name of Helvoetsluys, and from there to France, to be exiles by the side of our chieftain.'

I could say no more than just 'O!' the name of James More always drying up my very voice.

She was quick to perceive it, and to guess some portion of my thought.

'There is one thing I must be saying first of all, Mr. David,' said she. 'I think two of my kinsfolk have not behaved to you altogether very well. And the one of them two is James More, my father, and the other is the Laird of Prestongrange. Prestongrange will have spoken by himself, or his daughter in the place of him. But for James More, my father, I have this much to say: he lay shackled in a prison; he is a plain honest soldier and a plain Highland gentleman; what they would be after he would never be guessing; but if he had understood it was to be some prejudice to a young gentleman like yourself, he would have died first. And for the sake of all your friendships, I will be asking you to pardon my father and family for that same mistake.'

'Catriona,' said I, 'what that mistake was I do not care to know. I know but the one thing—that you went to Prestongrange and begged my life upon your knees. O, I ken well it was for your father that you went, but when you were there you pleaded for me also. It is a thing I cannot speak of. There are two things I cannot think of into myself: and the one is your good words when you called yourself my little friend, and the other that you pleaded for my life. Let us never speak more, we two, of pardon or offence.'

We stood after that silent, Catriona looking on the deck and I on her; and before there was more speech, a little wind having sprung up in the nor'-west, they began to shake out the sails and heave in upon the anchor.

There were six passengers besides our two selves, which made of it a full cabin. Three were solid merchants out of Leith, Kirkcaldy, and Dundee, all engaged in the same adventure into High Germany. One was a Hollander returning; the rest worthy merchants' wives, to the charge of one of whom Catriona was recommended. Mrs. Gebbie (for that was her name) was by great good fortune heavily incommoded by the sea, and lay day and night on the broad of her back. We were besides the only creatures at all young on board the *Rose*, except a white-faced boy that did my old duty to attend upon the table; and it came about that Catriona and I were left almost entirely to ourselves. We had the next seats together at the table, where I waited on her with extraordinary pleasure. On deck, I made her a soft place with my cloak; and the weather being singularly fine for that season, with bright frosty days and nights, a steady, gentle wind, and scarce a sheet started all the way through the North Sea, we sat there (only now and again walking to and fro for warmth) from the first blink of the sun till eight or nine at night under the clear stars. The merchants or Captain Sang would sometimes glance and smile upon us, or pass a merry word or two and give us the go-by again; but the most part of the time they were deep in herring and chintzes and linen, or in computations of the slowness of the passage, and left us to our own concerns, which were very little important to any but ourselves.

At the first, we had a great deal to say, and thought ourselves pretty witty; and I was at a little pains to be the *beau*, and she (I believe) to play the young lady of experience. But soon we grew plainer with each other. I laid aside my high, clipped English (what little there was of it) and forgot to make my Edinburgh bows and scrapes; she, upon her side, fell into a sort of kind familiarity; and we dwelt together like those of the same household, only (upon my side) with a more deep emotion. About the same time, the bottom seemed to fall out of our conversation, and neither one of us the less pleased. Whiles she would tell me old wives' tales, of which she had a wonderful variety, many of them from my friend red-headed Neil. She told them very pretty, and they were pretty enough childish tales; but the pleasure to myself was in the sound of her voice, and the thought that she was telling and I listening. Whiles, again, we would sit entirely silent, not communicating even with a look, and tasting pleasure enough in the sweetness of that neighbourhood. I speak here only for myself. Of what was in the maid's mind, I am not very sure that I ever asked myself; and what was in my own, I was afraid to consider. I need make no secret of it now, either to myself or to the reader: I was fallen totally in love.

She came between me and the sun. She had grown suddenly taller, as I say, but with a wholesome growth; she seemed all health, and lightness, and brave spirits; and I thought she walked like a young deer, and stood like a birch upon the mountains. It was enough for me to sit near by her on the deck; and I declare I scarce spent two thoughts upon the future, and was so well content with what I then enjoyed that I was never at the pains to imagine any further step; unless perhaps that I would be sometimes tempted to take her hand in mine and hold it there. But I was too like a miser of what joys I had, and would venture nothing on a hazard.

What we spoke was usually of ourselves or of each other, so that if anyone had been at so much pains as overhear us, he must have supposed us the most egotistical persons in the world. It befell one day when we were at this practice, that we came on a discourse of friends and friendship, and I think now that we were sailing near the wind. We said what a fine thing friendship was, and how little we had guessed of it, and how it made life a new thing, and a thousand covered things of the same kind that will have been said, since the foundation of the world, by young folk in the same predicament. Then we remarked upon the strangeness of that circumstance, that friends came together in the beginning as if they were there for the first time, and yet each had been alive a good while, losing time with other people.

'It is not much that I have done,' said she, 'and I could be telling you the five-fifths of it in two-three words. It is only a girl I am, and what can befall a girl, at all events? But I went with the clan in the year '45. The men marched with swords and fire-locks, and some of them in brigades in the same set of tartan; they were not backward at the marching, I can tell you. And there were gentlemen from the Low Country, with their tenants mounted and trumpets to sound, and there was a grand skirling of war-pipes. I rode on a little Highland horse on the right hand of my father, James More, and of Glengyle himself. And here is one fine thing that I remember, that Glengyle kissed me in the face, because (says he) "my kinswoman, you are the only lady of the clan that has come out," and me a little maid of maybe twelve years old! I saw Prince Charlie too, and the blue eyes of him; he was pretty indeed! I had his hand to kiss in the front of the army. O, well, these were the good days, but it is all like a dream that I have seen and then awakened. It went what way you very well know; and these were the worst days of all, when the red-coat soldiers were out, and my father and my uncles lay in the hill, and I was to be carrying them their meat in the middle night, or at the short side of day when the cocks crow. Yes, I have walked in the night, many's the time, and my heart great in me for terror of the darkness. It is a strange thing I will never have been meddled with by a bogle; but they say a maid goes safe. Next there was my uncle's marriage, and that was a dreadful affair beyond all. Jean Kay was that woman's name; and she had me in the room with her that night at Inversnaid, the night we took her from her friends in the old, ancient manner. She would and she wouldn't; she was for marrying Rob the one minute, and the next she would be for none of him. I will never have seen such a feckless creature of a woman; surely all there was of her would tell her ay or no. Well, she was a widow, and I can never be thinking a widow a good woman.'

'Catriona!' says I, 'how do you make out that?'

'I do not know,' said she; 'I am only telling you the seeming in my heart. And then to marry a new man! Fy! But that was her; and she was married again upon my Uncle Robin, and went with him awhile to kirk and market; and then wearied, or else her friends got claught of her and talked her round, or maybe she turned ashamed; at the least of it, she ran away, and went back to her own folk, and said we had held her in the lake, and I will never tell you all what. I have never thought much of any females since that day. And so in the end my father, James More, came to be cast in prison, and you know the rest of it as well as me.'

'And through all you had no friends?' said I.

'No,' said she; ' I have been pretty chief with two-three lasses on the braes, but not to call it friends.'

'Well, mine is a plain tale,' said I. 'I never had a friend to my name till I met in with you.'

'And that brave Mr. Stewart?' she asked.

'O, yes, I was forgetting him,' I said. 'But he is a man, and that is very different.'

'I would think so,' said she. 'O, yes, it is quite different.'

'And then there was one other,' said I. 'I once thought I had a friend, but it proved a disappointment.'

She asked me who she was?

'It was a he, then,' said I. 'We were the two best lads at my father's school, and we thought we loved each other dearly. Well, the time came when he went to Glasgow to a merchant's house, that was his second cousin once removed; and wrote me two-three times by the carrier; and then he found new friends, and I might write till I was tired, he took no notice. Eh, Catriona, it took me a long while to forgive the world. There is not anything more bitter than to lose a fancied friend.'

Then she began to question me close upon his looks and character, for we were each a great deal concerned in all that touched the other; till at last, in a very evil hour, I minded of his letters and went and fetched the bundle from the cabin.

'Here are his letters,' said I, 'and all the letters that ever I got. That will be the last I'll can tell of myself; ye know the lave[1] as well as I do.'

'Will you let me read them, then?' says she.

I told her, *if she would be at the pains*; and she bade me go away and she would read them from the one end to the other. Now, in this bundle that I gave her, there were packed together not only all the letters of my false friend, but one or two of Mr. Campbell's when he was in town at the Assembly, and to make a complete roll of all that ever was written to me, Catriona's little word, and the two I had received from Miss Grant, one when I was on the Bass and one on board that ship. But of these last I had no particular mind at the moment.

---

1 Rest.

I was in that state of subjection to the thought of my friend that it mattered not what I did, nor scarce whether I was in her presence or out of it; I had caught her like some kind of a noble fever that lived continually in my bosom, by night and by day, and whether I was waking or asleep. So it befell that after I was come into the fore-part of the ship where the broad bows splashed into the billows, I was in no such hurry to return as you might fancy; rather prolonged my absence like a variety in pleasure. I do not think I am by nature much of an Epicurean; and there had come till then so small a share of pleasure in my way that I might be excused perhaps to dwell on it unduly.

When I returned to her again, I had a faint, painful impression as of a buckle slipped, so coldly she returned the packet.

'You have read them?' said I; and I thought my voice sounded not wholly natural, for I was turning in my mind for what could ail her.

'Did you mean me to read all?' she asked.

I told her 'Yes,' with a drooping voice.

'The last of them as well?' said she.

I knew where we were now; yet I would not lie to her either. 'I gave them all without afterthought,' I said, 'as I supposed that you would read them. I see no harm in any.'

'I will be differently made,' said she. 'I thank God I am differently made. It was not a fit letter to be shown me. It was not fit to be written.'

'I think you are speaking of your own friend, Barbara Grant?' said I.

'There will not be anything as bitter as to lose a fancied friend,' said she, quoting my own expression.

'I think it is sometimes the friendship that was fancied!' I cried. 'What kind of justice do you call this, to blame me for some words that a tomfool of a madcap lass has written down upon a piece of paper? You know yourself with what respect I have behaved—and would do always.'

'Yet you would show me that same letter!' says she. 'I want no such friends. I can be doing very well, Mr. Balfour, without her—or you.'

'This is your fine gratitude!' says I.

'I am very much obliged to you,' said she. 'I will be asking you to take away your—letters.' She seemed to choke upon the word, so that it sounded like an oath.

'You shall never ask twice,' said I; picked up that bundle, walked a little way forward and cast them as far as possible into the sea. For a very little more I could have cast myself after them.

The rest of the day I walked up and down raging. There were few names so ill but what I gave her them in my own mind before the sun went down. All that I had ever heard of Highland pride seemed quite outdone; that a girl (scarce grown) should resent so trifling an allusion, and that from her next friend, that she had near wearied me with praising of! I had bitter, sharp, hard thoughts of her, like an angry boy's. If I had kissed her indeed (I thought), perhaps she would have taken it pretty well; and only because it had been written down, and with a spice of jocularity, up she must fuff in this ridiculous passion. It seemed to me there was a want of penetration in the female sex, to make angels weep over the case of the poor men.

We were side by side again at supper, and what a change was there! She was like curdled milk to me; her face was like a wooden doll's; I could have indifferently smitten her or grovelled at her feet, but she gave me not the least occasion to do either. No sooner the meal done than she betook herself to attend on Mrs. Gebbie, which I think she had a little neglected heretofore. But she was to make up for lost time, and in what remained of the passage was extraordinary assiduous with the old lady, and on deck began to make a great deal more than I thought wise of Captain Sang. Not but what the Captain seemed a worthy, fatherly man; but I hated to behold her in the least familiarity with anyone except myself.

Altogether, she was so quick to avoid me, and so constant to keep herself surrounded with others, that I must watch a long while before I could find my opportunity; and after it was found, I made not much of it, as you are now to hear.

'I have no guess how I have offended,' said I; 'it should scarce be beyond pardon, then. O, try if you can pardon me.'

'I have no pardon to give,' said she; and the words seemed to come out of her throat like marbles. 'I will be very much obliged for all your friendships.' And she made an eighth part of a curtsey.

But I had schooled myself beforehand to say more, and I was going to say it too.

'There is one thing,' said I. 'If I have shocked your particularity by the showing of that letter, it cannot touch Miss Grant. She wrote not to you, but to a poor, common, ordinary lad, who might have had more sense than show it. If you are to blame me——'

'I will advise you to say no more about that girl, at all events!' said Catriona. 'It is her I will never look the road of, not if she lay dying.' She turned away from me, and suddenly back. 'Will you swear you will have no more to deal with her?' she cried.

'Indeed, and I will never be so unjust then,' said I; 'nor yet so ungrateful.'

And now it was I that turned away.

CHAPTER XXII

HELVOETSLUYS

THE weather in the end considerably worsened; the wind sang in the shrouds, the sea swelled higher, and the ship began to labour and cry out among the billows. The song of the leadsman in the chains was now scarce ceasing, for we thrid all the way among shoals. About nine in the morning, in a burst of wintry sun between two squalls of hail, I had my first look of Holland—a line of windmills birling in the breeze. It was besides my first knowledge of these daft-like contrivances, which gave me a near sense of foreign travel and a new world and life. We came to an anchor about half-past eleven, outside the harbour of Helvoetsluys, in a place

where the sea sometimes broke and the ship pitched outrageously. You may be sure we were all on deck save Mrs.
Gebbie, some of us in cloaks, others mantled in the ship's
tarpaulins, all clinging on by ropes, and jesting the most
like old sailor-folk that we could imitate.

Presently a boat, that was backed like a partan-crab, came
gingerly alongside, and the skipper of it hailed our master
in the Dutch. Thence Captain Sang turned, very troubled-
like, to Catriona; and the rest of us crowding about, the
nature of the difficulty was made plain to all. The *Rose* was
bound to the port of Rotterdam, whither the other passengers
were in a great impatience to arrive, in view of a conveyance
due to leave that very evening in the direction of the Upper
Germany. This, with the present half-gale of wind, the
captain (if not time were lost) declared himself still capable
to save. Now James More had trysted in Helvoet with his
daughter, and the captain had engaged to call before the port
and place her (according to the custom) in a shore boat. There
was the boat, to be sure, and here was Catriona ready: but
both our master and the patroon of the boat scrupled at the
risk, and the first was in no humour to delay.

'Your father,' said he, 'would be gey an little pleased if we
was to break a leg to ye, Miss Drummond, let-a-be drowning
of you. Take my way of it,' says he, 'and come on-by with
the rest of us here to Rotterdam. Ye can get a passage down
the Maes in a sailing scoot as far as to the Brill, and thence
on again, by a place in a rattel-waggon, back to Helvoet.'

But Catriona would hear of no change. She looked white-
like as she beheld the bursting of the sprays, the green seas
that sometimes poured upon the forecastle, and the perpetual
bounding and swooping of the boat among the billows; but
she stood firmly by her father's orders. 'My father, James
More, will have arranged it so,' was her first word and her
last. I thought it very idle and indeed wanton in the girl
to be so literal and stand opposite to so much kind advice;
but the fact is she had a very good reason, if she would have
told us. Sailing scoots and rattel-waggons are excellent things;
only the use of them must first be paid for, and all she was

possessed of in the world was just two shillings and a penny halfpenny sterling. So it fell out that captain and passengers, not knowing of her destitution—and she being too proud to tell them—spoke in vain.

'But you ken nae French and nae Dutch neither,' said one.

'It is very true,' says she, 'but since the year '46 there are so many of the honest Scots abroad that I will be doing very well, I thank you.'

There was a pretty country simplicity in this that made some laugh, others looked the more sorry, and Mr. Gebbie fall outright in a passion. I believe he knew it was his duty (his wife having accepted charge of the girl) to have gone ashore with her and seen her safe: nothing would have induced him to have done so, since it must have involved the loss of his conveyance; and I think he made it up to his conscience by the loudness of his voice. At least he broke out upon Captain Sang, raging and saying the thing was a disgrace; that it was mere death to try to leave the ship, and at any event we could not cast down an innocent maid in a boatful of nasty Holland fishers, and leave her to her fate. I was thinking something of the same; took the mate upon one side, arranged with him to send on my chests by track-scoot to an address I had in Leyden, and stood up and signalled to the fishers.

'I will go ashore with the young lady, Captain Sang,' said I. 'It is all one what way I go to Leyden;' and leaped at the same time into the boat, which I managed not so elegantly but what I fell with two of the fishers in the bilge.

From the boat the business appeared yet more precarious than from the ship, she stood so high over us, swung down so swift, and menaced us so perpetually with her plunging and passaging upon the anchor cable. I began to think I had made a fool's bargain, that it was merely impossible Catriona should be got on board to me, and that I stood to be set ashore at Helvoet all by myself and with no hope of any reward but the pleasure of embracing James More, if I should want to. But this was to reckon without the lass's courage. She had seen me leap with very little appearance (however much reality) of hesitation; to be sure, she was not to be beat by her discarded friend. Up she stood on the bulwarks and held by a stay, the wind blowing in her petticoats, which made the enterprise more dangerous, and gave us rather more of a view of her stockings than would be thought genteel in cities. There was no minutes lost, and scarce time given for any to interfere if they had wished the same. I stood up on the other side and spread my arms; the ship swung down on us, the patroon humoured his boat nearer in than was perhaps wholly safe, and Catriona leaped into the air. I was so happy as to catch her, and the fishers readily supporting us, escaped a fall. She held to me a moment very tight, breathing quick and deep; thence (she still clinging to me with both hands) we were passed aft to our places by the steersman; and Captain Sang and all the crew and passengers cheering and crying farewell, the boat was put about for shore.

As soon as Catriona came a little to herself she unhanded me suddenly but said no word. No more did I; and indeed the whistling of the wind and the breaching of the sprays made it no time for speech; and our crew not only toiled excessively but made extremely little way, so that the *Rose* had got her anchor and was off again before we had approached the harbour mouth.

We were no sooner in smooth water than the patroon, according to their beastly Hollands custom, stopped his boat and required of us our fares. Two guilders was the man's demand—between three and four shillings English money— for each passenger. But at this Catriona began to cry out with a vast deal of agitation. She had asked of Captain Sang, she said, and the fare was but an English shilling. 'Do you think I will have come on board and not ask first?' cries she. The patroon scolded back upon her in a lingo where the oaths were English and the rest right Hollands; till at last (seeing her near tears) I privately slipped in the rogue's hand six shillings, whereupon he was obliging enough to receive from her the other shilling without more complaint. No doubt I was a good deal nettled and ashamed. I like to see folk thrifty, but not with so much passion; and I dare say it would be rather coldly that I asked her, as the boat moved on again for shore, where it was that she was trysted with her father.

'He is to be inquired of at the house of one Sprott, an honest Scotch merchant,' says she; and then with the same breath, 'I am wishing to thank you very much—you are a brave friend to me.'

'It will be time enough when I get you to your father,' said I, little thinking that I spoke so true. 'I can tell him a fine tale of a loyal daughter.'

'O, I do not think I will be a loyal girl, at all events,' she cried, with a great deal of painfulness in the expression. 'I do not think my heart is true.'

'Yet there are very few that would have made that leap, and all to obey a father's orders,' I observed.

'I cannot have you to be thinking of me so,' she cried again. 'When you had done that same, how would I stop behind? And at all events that was not all the reasons.' Whereupon, with a burning face, she told me the plain truth upon her poverty.

'Good guide us!' cried I, 'what kind of daft-like proceeding is this, to let yourself be launched on the continent of Europe with an empty purse—I count it hardly decent—scant decent!' I cried.

'You forget James More, my father, is a poor gentleman,' said she. 'He is a hunted exile.'

'But I think not all your friends are hunted exiles,' I exclaimed. 'And was this fair to them that care for you? Was it fair to me? Was it fair to Miss Grant that counselled you to go, and would be driven fair horn-mad if she could hear of it? Was it even fair to these Gregory folk that you were living with, and used you lovingly? It's a blessing you have fallen in my hands! Suppose your father hindered by an accident, what would become of you here, and you your lee-lone in a strange place? The thought of the thing frightens me,' I said.

'I will have lied to all of them,' she replied. 'I will have told them all that I had plenty. I told *her* too. I could not be lowering James More to them.'

I found out later on that she must have lowered him in the very dust, for the lie was originally the father's, not the daughter's, and she thus obliged to persevere in it for the man's reputation. But at the time I was ignorant of this, and the mere thought of her destitution and the perils in which she must have fallen, had ruffled me almost beyond reason.

'Well, well, well,' said I, 'you will have to learn more sense.'

I left her mails for the moment in an inn upon the shore, where I got a direction for Sprott's house in my new French, and we walked there—it was some little way—beholding the place with wonder as we went. Indeed, there was much for Scots folk to admire: canals and trees being intermingled with the houses; the houses, each within itself, of a brave red brick, the colour of a rose, with steps and benches of blue marble at the cheek of every door, and the whole town so clean you might have dined upon the causeway. Sprott was within, upon his ledgers, in a low parlour, very neat and clean, and set out with china and pictures and a globe of the earth in a brass frame. He was a big-chafted, ruddy, lusty man, with a crooked hard look to him; and he made us not that much civility as offer us a seat.

'Is James More Macgregor now in Helvoet, sir?' says I.

'I ken nobody by such a name,' says he, impatient-like.

'Since you are so particular,' says I, 'I will amend my question, and ask you where we are to find in Helvoet one James Drummond, *alias* Macgregor, *alias* James More, late tenant in Inveronachile?'

'Sir,' says he, 'he may be in Hell for what I ken, and for my part I wish he was.'

'The young lady is that gentleman's daughter, sir,' said I, 'before whom, I think you will agree with me, it is not very becoming to discuss his character.'

'I have nothing to make either with him, or her, or you!' cries he in his gross voice.

'Under your favour, Mr. Sprott,' said I, 'this young lady

is come from Scotland seeking him, and by whatever mistake, was given the name of your house for a direction. An error it seems to have been, but I think this places both you and me—who am but her fellow-traveller by accident—under a strong obligation to help our country-woman.'

'Will you ding me daft?' he cries. 'I tell ye I ken naething and care less either for him or his breed. I tell ye the man owes me money.'

'That may very well be, sir,' said I, who was now rather more angry than himself. 'At least, I owe you nothing; the young lady is under my protection; and I am neither at all used with these manners, nor in the least content with them.'

As I said this, and without particularly thinking what I did, I drew a step or two nearer to his table; thus striking, by mere good fortune, on the only argument that could at all affect the man. The blood left his lusty countenance.

'For the Lord's sake dinna be hasty, sir!' he cried. 'I am truly wishfu' no to be offensive. But ye ken, sir, I'm like a wheen guid-natured, honest, canty auld fallows—my bark is waur nor my bite. To hear ye, ye micht whiles fancy I was a wee thing dour; but na, na! it's a kind auld fallow at heart, Sandie Sprott! And ye could never imagine the fyke and fash this man has been to me.'

'Very good, sir,' said I. 'Then I will make that much freedom with your kindness as trouble you for your last news of Mr. Drummond.'

'You're welcome, sir!' said he. 'As for the young leddy (my respec's to her!), he'll just have clean forgotten her. I ken the man, ye see; I have lost siller by him ere now. He thinks of naebody but just himsel'; clan, king, or dauchter, if he can get his wameful, he would give them a' the go-by! ay, or his correspondent either. For there is a sense in whilk I may be nearly almost said to be his correspondent. The fact is, we are employed thegether in a business affair, and I think it's like to turn out a dear affair for Sandie Sprott. The man's as guid's my pairtner, and I give ye my mere word I ken naething by where he is. He micht be coming here to Helvoet; he micht come here the morn, he michtnae come for a twalmonth; I would wonder at naething—or just at the ae thing, and that's if he was to pay me my siller. Ye see what way I stand with it; and it's clear I'm no very likely to meddle up with the young leddy, as ye ca' her. She cannae stop here, that's ae thing certain sure. Dod, sir, I'm a lone man! If I was to tak her in, it's highly possible the hellicat would try and gar me marry her when he turned up.'

'Enough of this talk,' said I. 'I will take the young lady among better friends. Give me pen, ink, and paper, and I will leave here for James More the address of my correspondent in Leyden. He can inquire from me where he is to seek his daughter.'

This word I wrote and sealed; which while I was doing, Sprott of his own motion made a welcome offer, to charge himself with Miss Drummond's mails, and even send a porter for them to the inn. I advanced him to that effect a dollar or two to be a cover, and he gave me an acknowledgment in writing of the sum.

Whereupon (I giving my arm to Catriona) we left the house of this unpalatable rascal. She had said no word throughout, leaving me to judge and speak in her place; I, upon my side, had been careful not to embarrass her by a glance; and even now, although my heart still glowed inside of me with shame and anger, I made it my affair to seem quite easy.

'Now,' said I, 'let us get back to yon same inn where they can speak the French, and have a piece of dinner, and inquire for conveyances to Rotterdam. I will never be easy till I have you safe again in the hands of Mrs. Gebbie.'

'I suppose it will have to be,' said Catriona, 'though who-ever will be pleased, I do not think it will be her. And I will remind you this once again that I have but one shilling, and three baubees.'

'And just this once again,' said I, 'I will remind you it was a blessing that I came alongst with you.'

'What else would I be thinking all this time?' says she, and I thought weighed a little on my arm. 'It is you that are the good friend to me.'

CHAPTER XXIII

TRAVELS IN HOLLAND

THE rattel-waggon, which is a kind of a long waggon set with benches, carried us in four hours of travel to the great city of Rotterdam. It was long past dark by then but the streets were pretty brightly lighted and thronged with wild-like, outlandish characters—bearded Hebrews, black men, and the hordes of courtesans, most indecently adorned with finery and stopping seamen by their very sleeves; the clash of talk about us made our heads to whirl; and what was the most unexpected of all, we appeared to be no more struck with all these foreigners than they with us. I made the best face I could, for the lass's sake, and my own credit; but the truth is I felt like a lost sheep, and my heart beat in my bosom with anxiety. Once or twice I inquired after the harbour or the berth of the ship *Rose*; but either fell on some who spoke only Hollands, or my own French failed me. Trying a street at a venture, I came upon a lane of lighted houses, the doors and windows thronged with wauf-like painted women; these jostled and mocked upon us as we passed, and I was thankful we had nothing of their language. A little after we issued forth upon an open place along the harbour.

'We shall be doing now,' cries I, as soon as I spied masts. 'Let us walk here by the harbour. We are sure to meet some that has the English, and at the best of it we may light upon that very ship.'

We did the next best, as happened; for, about nine of the evening, whom should we walk into the arms of but Captain Sang? He told us they had made their run in the most incredible brief time, the wind holding strong till they reached port; by which means his passengers were all gone already on their further travels. It was impossible to chase after the Gebbies into the High Germany, and we had no other acquaintance to fall back upon but Captain Sang himself. It was the more gratifying to find the man friendly and wishful to assist. He made it a small affair to find some good plain family of merchants, where Catriona might harbour till the *Rose* was loaden; declared he would then blithely carry her back to Leith for nothing and see her safe in the hands of Mr. Gregory; and in the meanwhile carried us to a late ordinary for the meal we stood in need of. He seemed extremely friendly, as I say, but what surprised me a good deal, rather boisterous in the bargain; and the cause of this was soon to appear. For at the ordinary, calling for Rhenish wine and drinking of it deep, he soon became unutterably tipsy. In this case, as too common with all men, but especially with those of his rough trade, what little sense or manners he possessed deserted him; and he behaved himself so scandalous to the young lady, jesting most ill-favouredly at the figure she had made on the ship's rail, that I had no resource but carry her suddenly away.

She came out of that ordinary clinging to me close. 'Take me away, David,' she said. 'You keep me. I am not afraid with you.'

'And have no cause, my little friend!' cried I, and could have found it in my heart to weep.

'Where will you be taking me?' she said again. 'Don't leave me at all events—never leave me.'

'Where am I taking you indeed?'* says I, stopping, for I had been staving on ahead in mere blindness. 'I must stop and think. But I'll not leave you, Catriona; the Lord do so to me, and more also, if I should fail or fash you.'

She crept close into me by way of a reply.

'Here,' I said, 'is the stillest place that we have hit on yet in this busy byke of a city. Let us sit down here under yon tree and consider of our course.'

That tree (which I am little like to forget) stood hard by the harbour side. It was a black night, but lights were in the houses, and nearer hand in the quiet ships; there was a shining of the city on the one hand, and a buzz hung over it of many thousands walking and talking; on the other, it was dark and the water bubbled on the sides. I spread my cloak upon a builder's stone, and made her sit there; she would have kept her hold upon me, for she still shook with the late affronts; but I wanted to think clear, disengaged myself, and paced to and fro before her, in the manner of what we call a smuggler's walk, belabouring my brains for any remedy. By the course of these scattering thoughts I was brought suddenly face to face with a remembrance that, in the heat and haste of our departure, I had left Captain Sang to pay the ordinary. At this I began to laugh out loud, for I thought the man well served; and at the same time, by an instinctive movement, carried my hand to the pocket where my money was. I suppose it was in the lane where the women jostled us; but there is only the one thing certain, that my purse was gone.

'You will have thought of something good,' said she, observing me to pause.

At the pinch we were in, my mind became suddenly clear as a perspective glass, and I saw there was no choice of methods. I had not one doit of coin, but in my pocket book I had still my letter on the Leyden merchant; and there was now but the one way to get to Leyden, and that was to walk on our two feet.

'Catriona,' said I, 'I know you're brave and I believe you're strong—do you think you could walk thirty miles on a plain road?' We found it, I believe, scarce the two-thirds of that, but such was my notion of the distance.

'David,' she said, 'if you will just keep near, I will go anywhere and do anything. The courage of my heart, it is all broken. Do not be leaving me in this horrible country by myself, and I will do all else.'

'Can you start now and march all night?' said I.

'I will do all that you can ask of me,' she said, 'and never ask you why. I have been a bad ungrateful girl to you; and do what you please with me now! And I think Miss Barbara Grant is the best lady in the world,' she added, 'and I do not see what she would deny you for at all events.'

This was Greek and Hebrew to me; but I had other matters to consider, and the first of these was to get clear of that city on the Leyden road. It proved a cruel problem; and it may have been one or two at night ere we had solved it. Once beyond the houses, there was neither moon nor stars to guide us; only the whiteness of the way in the midst and a blackness of an alley on both hands. The walking was besides made most extraordinary difficult by a plain black frost that fell suddenly in the small hours and turned that highway into one long slide.

'Well, Catriona,' said I, 'here we are like the king's sons and the old wives' daughters in your daft-like Highland tales. Soon we'll be going over the "*seven Bens, the seven glens, and the seven mountain moors.*" ' Which was a common byword or overcome in those tales of hers that had stuck in my memory.

'Ah,' says she, 'but here are no glens or mountains! Though I will never be denying but what the trees and some of the plain places hereabouts are very pretty. But our country is the best yet.'

'I wish we could say as much for our own folk,' says I, recalling Sprott and Sang, and perhaps James More himself.

'I will never complain of the country of my friend,' said she, and spoke it out with an accent so particular that I seemed to see the look upon her face.

I caught in my breath sharp and came near falling (for my pains) on the black ice.

'I do not know what *you* think, Catriona,' said I, when I was a little recovered, 'but this has been the best day yet! I think shame to say it, when you have met in with such misfortunes and disfavours; but for me, it has been the best day yet.'

'It was a good day when you showed me so much love,' said she.

'And yet I think shame to be happy too,' I went on, 'and you here on the road in the black night.'

'Where in the great world would I be else?' she cried. 'I am thinking I am safest where I am with you.'

'I am quite forgiven, then?' I asked.

'Will you not forgive me that time so much as not to take it in your mouth again?' she cried. 'There is nothing in this heart to you but thanks. But I will be honest too,' she added, with a kind of suddenness, 'and I'll never can forgive that girl.'

'Is this Miss Grant again?' said I. 'You said yourself she was the best lady in the world.'

'So she will be, indeed!' says Catriona. 'But I will never forgive her for all that. I will never, never forgive her, and let me hear tell of her no more.'

'Well,' said I, 'this beats all that ever came to my knowledge; and I wonder that you can indulge yourself in such bairnly whims. Here is a young lady that was the best friend in the world to the both of us, that learned us how to dress ourselves, and in a great manner how to behave, as anyone can see that knew us both before and after.'

But Catriona stopped square in the midst of the highway.

'It is this way of it,' said she. 'Either you will go on to speak of her, and I will go back to yon town, and let come of it what God pleases! Or else you will do me that politeness to talk of other things.'

I was the most nonplussed person in this world; but I bethought me that she depended altogether on my help, that she was of the frail sex and not so much beyond a child, and it was for me to be wise for the pair of us.

'My dear girl,' said I, 'I can make neither head nor tails of this; but God forbid that I should do anything to set you on the jee. As for talking of Miss Grant, I have no such a mind to it, and I believe it was yourself began it. My only design (if I took you up at all) was for your own improvement, for I hate the very look of injustice. Not that I do not wish you to have a good pride and a nice female delicacy; they become you well; but here you show them to excess.'

'Well, then, have you done?' said she.

'I have done,' said I.

'A very good thing,' said she, and we went on again, but now in silence.

It was an eerie employment to walk in the gross night, beholding only shadows and hearing nought but our own steps. At first, I believe our hearts burned against each other with a deal of enmity; but the darkness and the cold, and the silence, which only the cocks sometimes interrupted, or sometimes the farmyard dogs, had pretty soon brought down our pride to the dust; and for my own particular, I would have jumped at any decent opening for speech.

Before the day peeped, came on a warmish rain, and the frost was all wiped away from among our feet. I took my cloak to her and sought to hap her in the same; she bade me, rather impatiently, to keep it.

'Indeed and I will do no such thing,' said I. 'Here am I, a great, ugly lad that has seen all kinds of weather, and here are you a tender, pretty maid! My dear, you would not put me to a shame?'

Without more words she let me cover her; which as I was doing in the darkness, I let my hand rest a moment on her shoulder, almost like an embrace.

'You must try to be more patient of your friend,' said I.

I thought she seemed to lean the least thing in the world against my bosom, or perhaps it was but fancy.

'There will be no end to your goodness,' said she.

And we went on again in silence; but now all was changed; and the happiness that was in my heart was like a fire in a great chimney.

The rain passed ere day; it was but a sloppy morning as we came into the town of Delft. The red gabled houses made a handsome show on either hand of a canal; the servant lassies were out slestering and scrubbing at the very stones upon the public highway; smoke rose from a hundred kitchens; and it came in upon me strongly it was time to break our fasts.

'Catriona,' said I, 'I believe you have yet a shilling and three baubees?'

'Are you wanting it?' said she, and passed me her purse. 'I am wishing it was five pounds! What will you want it for?'

'And what have we been walking for all night, like a pair

of waif Egyptians?' says I. 'Just because I was robbed of my purse and all I possessed in that unchancy town of Rotterdam. I will tell you of it now, because I think the worst is over, but we have still a good tramp before us till we get to where my money is, and if you would not buy me a piece of bread, I were like to go fasting.'

She looked at me with open eyes. By the light of the new day she was all black and pale for weariness, so that my heart smote me for her. But as for her, she broke out laughing.

'My torture! are we beggars then?' she cried. 'You too? O, I could have wished for this same thing! And I am glad to buy your breakfast to you. But it would be pleisand if I would have had to dance to get a meal to you! For I believe they are not very well acquainted with our manner of dancing over here, and might be paying for the curiosity of that sight.'

I could have kissed her for that word, not with a lover's mind, but in a heat of admiration. For it always warms a man to see a woman brave.

We got a drink of milk from a country wife but new come to the town, and in a baker's, a piece of excellent, hot, sweet-smelling bread, which we ate upon the road as we went on. That road from Delft to the Hague is just five miles of a fine avenue shaded with trees, a canal on the one hand, on the other excellent pastures of cattle. It was pleasant here indeed.

'And now, Davie,' said she, 'what will you do with me at all events?'

'It is what we have to speak of,' said I, 'and the sooner yet the better. I can come by money in Leyden; that will be all well. But the trouble is how to dispose of you until your father come. I thought last night you seemed a little sweir to part from me?'

'It will be more than seeming then,' said she.

'You are a very young maid,' said I, 'and I am but a very young callant. This is a great piece of difficulty. What way are we to manage? Unless indeed, you could pass to be my sister?'

'And what for no?' said she, 'if you would let me!'

'I wish you were so, indeed!' I cried. 'I would be a fine man if I had such a sister. But the rub is that you are Catriona Drummond.'

'And now I will be Catrine Balfour,' she said. 'And who is to ken? They are all strange folk here.'

'If you think that it would do,' says I. 'I own it troubles me. I would like it very ill, if I advised you at all wrong.'

'David, I have no friend here but you,' she said.

The mere truth is, I am too young to be your friend,' said I. 'I am too young to advise you, or you to be advised. I see not what else we are to do, and yet I ought to warn you.'

'I will have no choice left,' said she. 'My father James More has not used me very well, and it is not the first time. I am cast upon your hands like a sack of barley meal, and have nothing else to think of but your pleasure. If you will have me, good and well. If you will not'—she turned and touched her hand upon my arm—'David, I am afraid,' said she.

'No, but I ought to warn you,' I began; and then bethought me that I was the bearer of the purse, and it would never do to seem too churlish. 'Catriona,' said I, 'don't misunderstand me: I am just trying to do my duty by you, girl! Here am I going alone to this strange city, to be a solitary student there; and here is this chance arisen that you might dwell with me a bit, and be like my sister: you can surely understand this much, my dear, that I would just love to have you?'

'Well, and here I am,' said she. 'So that's soon settled.'

I know I was in duty bounden to have spoke more plain. I know this was a great blot on my character, for which I was lucky that I did not pay more dear. But I minded how easy her delicacy had been startled with a word of kissing her in Barbara's letter; now that she depended on me, how was I to be more bold? Besides, the truth is, I could see no other feasible method to dispose of her. And I dare say inclination pulled me very strong.

A little beyond the Hague she fell very lame and made the rest of the distance heavily enough. Twice she must rest by the wayside, which she did with pretty apologies, calling herself a shame to the Highlands and the race she came of, and nothing but a hindrance to myself. It was her excuse, she said, that she was not much used with walking shod. I would have had her strip off her shoes and stockings and go barefoot. But she pointed out to me that the women of that country, even in the landward roads, appeared to be all shod.

'I must not be disgracing my brother,' said she, and was very merry with it all, although her face told tales of her.

There is a garden in that city we were bound to, sanded below with clean sand, the trees meeting overhead, some of them trimmed, some pleached, and the whole place beautified with alleys and arbours. Here I left Catriona, and went forward by myself to find my correspondent. There I drew on my credit, and asked to be recommended to some decent, retired lodging. My baggage not being yet arrived, I told him I supposed I should require his caution with the people of the house; and explained that, my sister being come for a while to keep house with me, I should be wanting two chambers. This was all very well; but the trouble was that Mr. Balfour in his letter of recommendation had condescended on a great deal of particulars, and never a word of any sister in the case. I could see my Dutchman was extremely suspicious; and viewing me over the rims of a great pair of spectacles—he was a poor, frail body, and reminded me of an infirm rabbit—he began to question me close.

Here I fell in a panic. Suppose he accept my tale (thinks I), suppose he invite my sister to his house, and that I bring her. I shall have a fine ravelled pirn to unwind, and may end by disgracing both the lassie and myself. Thereupon I began hastily to expound to him my sister's character. She was of a bashful disposition, it appeared, and so extremely fearful of meeting strangers that I had left her at that moment sitting in a public place alone. And then, being launched upon the stream of falsehood, I must do like all the rest of the world in the same circumstance, and plunge in deeper than was any service; adding some altogether needless particulars of Miss Balfour's ill-health and retirement during childhood.

In the midst of which I awoke to a sense of my behaviour, and was turned to one blush.

The old gentleman was not so much deceived but what he discovered a willingness to be quit of me. But he was first of all a man of business; and knowing that my money was good enough, however it might be with my conduct, he was so far obliging as to send his son to be my guide and caution in the matter of a lodging. This implied my presenting of the young man to Catriona. The poor, pretty child was much recovered with resting, looked and behaved to perfection, and took my arm and gave me the name of brother more easily than I could answer her. But there was one misfortune: thinking to help, she was rather towardly than otherwise to my Dutchman. And I could not but reflect that Miss Balfour had rather suddenly outgrown her bashfulness. And there was another thing, the difference of our speech. I had the Low Country tongue and dwelled upon my words; she had a hill voice, spoke with something of an English accent, only far more delightful, and was scarce quite fit to be called a deacon in the craft of talking English grammar; so that, for a brother and sister, we made a most uneven pair. But the young Hollander was a heavy dog, without so much spirit in his belly as to remark her prettiness, for which I scorned him. And as soon as he had found a cover to our heads, he left us alone, which was the greater service of the two.

CHAPTER XXIV
FULL STORY OF A COPY OF HEINECCIUS*

THE place found was in the upper part of a house backed on a canal. We had two rooms, the second entering from the first, each had a chimney built out into the floor in the Dutch manner; and being alongside, each had the same prospect from the window of the top of a tree below us in a little court, of a piece of the canal, and of houses in the Hollands archi-

tecture and a church spire upon the further side. A full set
of bells hung in that spire and made delightful music; and
when there was any sun at all, it shone direct in our two
chambers. From a tavern hard by we had good meals sent
in.

The first night we were both pretty weary, and she
extremely so. There was little talk between us, and I packed
her off to her bed as soon as she had eaten. The first thing
in the morning I wrote word to Sprott to have her mails sent
on, together with a line to Alan at his chief's; and had the
same despatched, and her breakfast ready, ere I waked her.
I was a little abashed when she came forth in her one habit,
and the mud of the way upon her stockings. By what inquiries
I had made, it seemed a good few days must pass before her
mails could come to hand in Leyden, and it was plainly needful she must have a shift of things. She was unwilling at first
that I should go to that expense; but I reminded her she was
now a rich man's sister and must appear suitably in the part,
and we had not got to the second merchant's before she was
entirely charmed into the spirit of the thing, and her eyes
shining. It pleased me to see her so innocent and thorough
in this pleasure. What was more extraordinary was the
passion into which I fell on it myself; being never satisfied
that I had bought her enough or fine enough, and never
weary of beholding her in different attires. Indeed, I began
to understand some little of Miss Grant's immersion in that
interest of clothes; for the truth is, when you have the
ground of a beautiful person to adorn, the whole business
becomes beautiful. The Dutch chintzes I should say were
extraordinary cheap and fine; but I would be ashamed to set
down what I paid for stockings to her. Altogether I spent
so great a sum upon this pleasuring (as I may call it) that
I was ashamed for a great while to spend more; and by way
of a set-off, I left our chambers pretty bare. If we had beds,
if Catriona was a little braw, and I had light to see her by, we
were richly enough lodged for me.

By the end of this merchandising I was glad to leave her
at the door with all our purchases, and go for a long walk

alone in which to read myself a lecture. Here had I taken under my roof, and as good as to my bosom, a young lass extremely beautiful, and whose innocence was her peril. My talk with the old Dutchman, and the lies to which I was constrained, had already given me a sense of how my conduct must appear to others; and now, after the strong admiration I had just experienced and the immoderacy with which I had continued my vain purchases, I began to think of it myself as very hazarded. I bethought me, if I had a sister indeed, whether I would so expose her; then, judging the case too problematical, I varied my question into this, whether I would so trust Catriona in the hands of any other Christian being: the answer to which made my face to burn. The more cause, since I had been entrapped and had entrapped the girl into an undue situation, that I should behave in it with scrupulous nicety. She depended on me wholly for her bread and shelter; in case I should alarm her delicacy, she had no retreat. Besides, I was her host and her protector; and the more irregularly I had fallen in these positions, the less excuse for me if I should profit by the same to forward even the most honest suit; for with the opportunities that I enjoyed, and which no wise parent would have suffered for a moment, even the most honest suit would be unfair. I saw I must be extremely hold-off in my relations; and yet not too much so neither; for if I had no right to appear at all in the character of a suitor, I must yet appear continually, and if possible agreeably, in that of host. It was plain I should require a great deal of tact and conduct, perhaps more than my years afforded. But I had rushed in where angels might have feared to tread, and there was no way out of that position save by behaving right while I was in it. I made a set of rules for my guidance; prayed for strength to be enabled to observe them, and as a more human aid to the same end purchased a study-book in law. This being all I could think of, I relaxed from these grave considerations; whereupon my mind bubbled at once into an effervescency of pleasing spirits, and it was like one treading on air that I turned homeward. As I thought that name of home, and recalled the image of that figure awaiting me between four walls, my heart beat upon my bosom.

My troubles began with my return. She ran to greet me with an obvious and affecting pleasure. She was clad, besides, entirely in the new clothes that I had bought for her; looked in them beyond expression well; and must walk about and drop me curtseys to display them and to be admired. I am sure I did it with an ill-grace, for I thought to have choked upon the words.

'Well,' she said, 'if you will not be caring for my pretty clothes, see what I have done with our two chambers.' And she showed me the place all very finely swept and the fires glowing in the two chimneys.

I was glad of a chance to seem a little more severe than I quite felt. 'Catriona,' said I, 'I am very much displeased with you, and you must never again lay a hand upon my room. One of us two must have the rule while we are here together; it is most fit it should be I who am both the man and the elder; and I give you that for my command.'

She dropped me one of her curtseys, which were extraordinary taking. 'If you will be cross,' said she, 'I must be making pretty manners at you, Davie. I will be very obedient, as I should be when every stitch upon all there is of me belongs to you. But you will not be very cross either, because now I have not anyone else.'

This struck me hard, and I made haste, in a kind of penitence, to blot out all the good effect of my last speech. In this direction progress was more easy, being down hill; she led me forward, smiling; at the sight of her, in the brightness of the fire and with her pretty becks and looks, my heart was altogether melted. We made our meal with infinite mirth and tenderness; and the two seemed to be commingled into one, so that our very laughter sounded like a kindness.

In the midst of which I awoke to better recollections, made a lame word of excuse, and set myself boorishly to my studies. It was a substantial, instructive book that I had bought, by the late Dr. Heineccius, in which I was to do a great deal of reading these next days, and often very glad that I had no one to question me of what I read. Methought she bit her lip at me a little, and that cut me. Indeed it left her wholly solitary, the more as she was very little of a reader, and had never a book. But what was I to do?

So the rest of the evening flowed by almost without speech.

I could have beat myself. I could not lie in my bed that night for rage and repentance, but walked to and fro on my bare feet till I was nearly perished, for the chimney was gone out and the frost keen. The thought of her in the next room, the thought that she might even hear me as I walked, the remembrance of my churlishness and that I must continue to practise the same ungrateful course or be dishonoured, put me beside my reason. I stood like a man between Scylla and Charybdis: *What must she think of me?* was my one thought that softened me continually into weakness. *What is to become of us?* the other which steeled me again to resolution. This was my first night of wakefulness and divided counsels, of which I was now to pass many, pacing like a madman, sometimes weeping like a childish boy, sometimes praying (I would fain hope) like a Christian.

But prayer is not very difficult, and the hitch comes in practice. In her presence, and above all if I allowed any beginning of familiarity, I found I had very little command of what should follow. But to sit all day in the same room with her, and feign to be engaged upon Heineccius, surpassed my strength. So that I fell instead upon the expedient of absenting myself so much as I was able; taking out classes and sitting there regularly, often with small attention, the test of which I found the other day in a notebook of that period, where I had left off to follow an edifying lecture and actually scribbled in my book some very ill verses, though the Latinity is rather better than I thought that I could ever have compassed. The evil of this course was unhappily near as great as its advantage. I had the less time of trial, but I believe, while that time lasted, I was tried the more extremely. For she being so much left to solitude, she came to greet my return with an increasing fervour that came nigh to overmaster me. These friendly offers I must barbarously cast back; and my rejection sometimes wounded her so cruelly that I must unbend and seek to make it up to her in kindness. So that our time passed in ups and downs, tiffs and disappointments, upon the which I could almost say (if it may be said with reverence) that I was crucified.

The base of my trouble was Catriona's extraordinary innocence, at which I was not so much surprised as filled with pity and admiration. She seemed to have no thought of our position, no sense of my struggles; welcomed any mark of my weakness with responsive joy; and when I was drove again to my retrenchments, did not always dissemble her chagrin. There were times when I have thought to myself, 'If she were over head in love, and set her cap to catch me, she would scarce behave much otherwise'; and then I would fall again into wonder at the simplicity of woman, from whom I felt (in these moments) that I was not worthy to be descended.

There was one point in particular on which our warfare turned, and of all things, this was the question of her clothes. My baggage had soon followed me from Rotterdam, and hers from Helvoet. She had now, as it were, two wardrobes; and it grew to be understood between us (I could never tell how) that when she was friendly she would wear my clothes, and when otherwise her own. It was meant for a buffet, and (as it were) the renunciation of her gratitude; and I felt it so in my bosom, but was generally more wise than to appear to have observed the circumstance.

Once, indeed, I was betrayed into a childishness greater than her own; it fell in this way. On my return from classes, thinking upon her devoutly with a great deal of love and a good deal of annoyance in the bargain, the annoyance began to fade away out of my mind; and spying in a window one of those forced flowers, of which the Hollanders are so skilled in the artifice, I gave way to an impulse and bought it for Catriona. I do not know the name of that flower, but it was of the pink colour, and I thought she would admire the same, and carried it home to her with a wonderful soft heart. I had left her in my clothes, and when I returned to find her all changed and a face to match, I cast but the one look at her from head to foot, ground my teeth together, flung the window open, and my flower into the court, and then (between rage and prudence) myself out of that room again, of which I slammed the door as I went out.

On the steep stair I came near falling, and this brought me to myself, so that I began at once to see the folly of my conduct. I went, not into the street as I had purposed, but to the house court, which was always a solitary place, and where I saw my flower (that had cost me vastly more than it was worth) hanging in the leafless tree. I stood by the side of the canal, and looked upon the ice. Country people went by on their skates, and I envied them. I could see no way out of the pickle I was in: no way so much as to return to the room I had just left. No doubt was in my mind but I had now betrayed the secret of my feelings; and to make things worse, I had shown at the same time (and that with wretched boyishness) incivility to my helpless guest.

I suppose she must have seen me from the open window. It did not seem to me that I had stood there very long before I heard the crunching of footsteps on the frozen snow, and turning somewhat angrily (for I was in no spirit to be interrupted) saw Catriona drawing near. She was all changed again, to the clocked stockings.

'Are we not to have our walk to-day?' said she.

I was looking at her in a maze. 'Where is your brooch?' says I.

She carried her hand to her bosom and coloured high. 'I will have forgotten it,' said she. 'I will run upstairs for it quick, and then surely we'll can have our walk?'

There was a note of pleading in that last that staggered me; I had neither words nor voice to utter them; I could do no more than nod by way of answer; and the moment she had left me, climbed into the tree and recovered my flower, which on her return I offered her.

'I bought it for you, Catriona,' said I.

She fixed it in the midst of her bosom with the brooch, I could have thought tenderly.

'It is none the better of my handling,' said I again, and blushed.

'I will be liking it none the worse, you may be sure of that,' said she.

We did not speak so much that day; she seemed a thought on the reserve, though not unkindly. As for me, all the time of our walking, and after we came home, and I had seen her put my flower into a pot of water, I was thinking to myself what puzzles women were. I was thinking, the one moment, it was the most stupid thing on earth she should not have perceived my love; and the next, that she had certainly perceived it long ago, and (being a wise girl with the fine female instinct of propriety) concealed her knowledge.

We had our walk daily. Out in the streets I felt more safe; I relaxed a little in my guardedness; and for one thing, there was no Heineccius.. This made these periods not only a relief to myself, but a particular pleasure to my poor child. When I came back about the hour appointed, I would generally find her ready dressed and glowing with anticipation. She would prolong their duration to the extreme, seeming to dread (as I did myself) the hour of the return; and there is scarce a field or waterside near Leyden, scarce a street or lane there, where we have not lingered. Outside of these, I bade her confine herself entirely to our lodgings; this in the fear of her encountering any acquaintance, which would have rendered our position very difficult. From the same apprehension I would never suffer her to attend church, nor even go myself; but made some kind of shift to hold worship privately in our own chamber—I hope with an honest, but I am quite sure with a very much divided mind. Indeed, there was scarce anything that more affected me, than thus to kneel down alone with her before God like man and wife.

One day it was snowing downright hard. I had thought it not possible that we should venture forth, and was surprised to find her waiting for me ready dressed.

'I will not be doing without my walk,' she cried. 'You are never a good boy, Davie, in the house; I will never be caring for you only in the open air. I think we two will better turn Egyptian and dwell by the roadside.'

That was the best walk yet of all of them; she clung

near to me in the falling snow; it beat about and melted on us, and tbe drops stood upon her bright cheeks like tears and ran into her smiling mouth. Strength seemed to come upon me with the sight like a giant's; I thought I could have caught her up and run with her into the uttermost places in the earth; and we spoke together all that time beyond belief for freedom and sweetness.

It was the dark night when we came to the house door. She pressed my arm upon her bosom. 'Thank you kindly for these same good hours,' said she, on a deep note of her voice.

The concern in which I fell instantly on this address, put me with the same swiftness on my guard; and we were no sooner in the chamber, and the light made, than she beheld the old, dour, stubborn countenance of the student of Heineccius. Doubtless she was more than usually hurt; and I know for myself, I found it more than usually difficult to maintain my strangeness. Even at the meal, I durst scarce unbuckle and scarce lift my eyes to her; and it was no sooner over than I fell again to my civilian, with more seeming abstraction and less understanding than before. Methought, as I read, I could hear my heart strike like an eight-day clock. Hard as I feigned to study, there was still some of my eyesight that spilled beyond the book upon Catriona. She sat on the floor by the side of my great mail, and the chimney lighted her up, and shone and blinked upon her, and made her glow and darken through a wonder of fine hues. Now she would be gazing in the fire, and then again at me; and at that I would be plunged in a terror of myself, and turn the pages of Heineccius like a man looking for the text in church.

Suddenly she called out aloud. 'O, why does not my father come?' she cried, and fell at once into a storm of tears.

I leaped up, flung Heineccius fairly in the fire, ran to her side, and cast an arm around her sobbing body.

She put me from her sharply. 'You do not love your friend,' says she. 'I could be so happy too, if you would let me!' And then, 'O, what will I have done that you should hate me so?'

'Hate you!' cries I, and held her firm. 'You blind lass, can you not see a little in my wretched heart? Do you think when I sit there, reading in that fool-book that I have just burned and be damned to it, I take ever the least thought of any stricken thing but just yourself? Night after night I could have grat to see you sitting there your lone. And what was I to do? You are here under my honour; would you punish me for that? Is it for that that you would spurn a loving servant?'

At the word, with a small, sudden motion, she clung near to me. I raised her face to mine, I kissed it, and she bowed her brow upon my bosom, clasping me tight. I sat in a mere whirl like a man drunken. Then I heard her voice sound very small and muffled in my clothes.

'Did you kiss her truly?' she asked.

There went through me so great a heave of surprise that I was all shook with it.

'Miss Grant!' I cried, all in a disorder. 'Yes, I asked her to kiss me good-bye, the which she did.'

'Ah, well!' said she, 'you have kissed me too, at all events.'

At the strangeness and sweetness of that word, I saw where we had fallen; rose, and set her on her feet.

'This will never do,' said I. 'This will never, never do. O Catrine, Catrine!' Then there came a pause in which I was debarred from any speaking. And then, 'Go away to your bed,' said I. 'Go away to your bed and leave me.'

She turned to obey me like a little child, and the next I knew of it, had stopped in the very doorway.

'Good-night, Davie!' said she.

'And O, good night, my love!' I cried, with a great outbreak of my soul, and caught her to me again, so that it seemed I must have broken her. The next moment I had thrust her from the room, shut to the door even with violence, and stood alone.

The milk was spilt now, the word was out and the truth told. I had crept like an untrusty man into the poor maid's affections; she was in my hand like any frail, innocent thing to make or mar; and what weapon of defence was left me? It seemed like a symbol that Heineccius, my old protection, was now burned. I repented, yet could not find it in my heart to blame myself for that great failure. It seemed not possible to have resisted the boldness of her innocence or that last temptation of her weeping. And all that I had to excuse me did but make my sin appear the greater—it was upon a nature so defenceless, and with such advantages of the position, that I seemed to have practised.

What was to become of us now? It seemed we could no longer dwell in the one place. But where was I to go? or where she? Without either choice or fault of ours, life had conspired to wall us together in that narrow place. I had a wild thought of marrying out of hand; and the next moment put it from me with revolt. She was a child, she could not tell her own heart; I had surprised her weakness, I must never go on to build on that surprisal; I must keep her not only clear of reproach, but free as she had come to me.

Down I sat before the fire, and reflected, and repented, and beat my brains in vain for any means of escape. About two of the morning, there were three red embers left and the house and all the city was asleep, when I was aware of a small sound of weeping in the next room. She thought that I slept, the poor soul; she regretted her weakness—and what perhaps (God help her!) she called her forwardness—and in the dead of the night solaced herself with tears. Tender and bitter feelings, love and penitence and pity, struggled in my soul; it seemed I was under bond to heal that weeping.

'O, try to forgive me!' I cried out, 'try, try to forgive me. Let us forget it all, let us try if we'll no can forget it!'

There came no answer, but the sobbing ceased. I stood a long while with my hands still clasped as I had spoken; then the cold of the night laid hold upon me with a shudder, and I think my reason reawakened.

'You can make no hand of this, Davie,' thinks I. 'To bed with you like a wise lad, and try if you can sleep. To-morrow you may see your way.'

CHAPTER XXV

THE RETURN OF JAMES MORE

I WAS called on the morrow out of a late and troubled slumber by a knocking on my door, ran to open it, and had almost swooned with the contrariety of my feelings, mostly painful; for on the threshold, in a rough wrap-rascal and an extraordinary big laced hat, there stood James More.

I ought to have been glad perhaps without admixture, for there was a sense in which the man came like an answer to prayer. I had been saying till my head was weary that Catriona and I must separate, and looking till my head ached for any possible means of separation. Here were the means come to me upon two legs, and joy was the hindmost of my thoughts. It is to be considered, however, that even if the weight of the future were lifted off me by the man's arrival, the present heaved up the more black and menacing; so that, as I first stood before him in my shirt and breeches, I believe I took a leaping step backward like a person shot.

'Ah,' said he, 'I have found you, Mr. Balfour.' And offered me his large, fine hand, the which (recovering at the same time my post in the doorway, as if with some thought of resistance) I took him by doubtfully. 'It is a remarkable circumstance how our affairs appear to intermingle,' he continued. 'I am owing you an apology for an unfortunate intrusion upon yours, which I suffered myself to be entrapped into by my confidence in that false-face, Prestongrange; I think shame to own to you that I was ever trusting to a lawyer.' He shrugged his shoulders with a very French air. 'But indeed the man is very plausible,' says he. 'And now it seems that you have busied yourself handsomely in the matter of my daughter, for whose direction I was remitted to yourself.'

'I think, sir,' said I, with a very painful air, 'that it will be necessary we two should have an explanation.'

'There is nothing amiss?' he asked. 'My agent, Mr. Sprott——'

'For God's sake moderate your voice!' I cried. 'She must not hear till we have had an explanation.'

'She is in this place?' cries he.

'That is her chamber door,' said I.

'You are here with her alone?' he asked.

'And who else would I have got to stay with us?' cries I.

I will do him the justice to admit that he turned pale.

'This is very unusual,' said he. 'This is a very unusual circumstance. You are right, we must hold an explanation.'

So saying, he passed me by, and I must own the tall old rogue appeared at that moment extraordinary dignified. He had now, for the first time, the view of my chamber, which I scanned (I may say) with his eyes. A bit of morning sun glinted in by the window pane, and showed it off; my bed, my mails, and washing dish, with some disorder of my clothes, and the unlighted chimney, made the only plenishing; no mistake but it looked bare and cold, and the most unsuitable, beggarly place conceivable to harbour a young lady. At the same time came in on my mind the recollection of the clothes that I had bought for her; and I thought this contrast of poverty and prodigality bore an ill appearance.

He looked all about the chamber for a seat, and finding nothing else to his purpose except my bed, took a place upon the side of it; where, after I had closed the door, I could not very well avoid joining him. For however this extraordinary interview might end, it must pass if possible without waking Catriona; and the one thing needful was that we should sit close and talk low. But I can scarce picture what a pair we made; he in his great coat which the coldness of my chamber made extremely suitable; I shivering in my shirt and breeks; he with very much the air of a judge; and I (whatever I looked) with very much the feelings of a man who has heard the last trumpet.

'Well?' says he.

And 'Well,' I began, but found myself unable to go further.

'You tell me she is here?' said he again, but now with a spice of impatience that seemed to brace me up.

'She is in this house,' said I, 'and I knew the circumstance would be called unusual. But you are to consider how very unusual the whole business was from the beginning. Here is a young lady landed on the coast of Europe with two shillings and a penny halfpenny. She is directed to yon man Sprott in Helvoet. I hear you call him your agent. All I can say is he could do nothing but damn and swear at the mere mention of your name, and I must fee him out of my own pocket even to receive the custody of her effects. You speak of unusual circumstances, Mr. Drummond, if that be the name you prefer. Here was a circumstance, if you like, to which it was barbarity to have exposed her.'

'But this is what I cannot understand the least,' said James. 'My daughter was placed into the charge of some responsible persons, whose names I have forgot.'

'Gebbie was the name,' said I; 'and there is no doubt that Mr. Gebbie should have gone ashore with her at Helvoet. But he did not, Mr. Drummond; and I think you might praise God that I was there to offer in his place.'

'I shall have a word to say to Mr. Gebbie before long,' said he. 'As for yourself, I think it might have occurred that you were somewhat young for such a post.'

'But the choice was not between me and somebody else, it was between me and nobody,' I cried. 'Nobody offered in my place, and I must say I think you show a very small degree of gratitude to me that did.'

'I shall wait until I understand my obligation a little more in the particular,' says he.

'Indeed, and I think it stares you in the face, then,' said I. 'Your child was deserted, she was clean flung away in the midst of Europe, with scarce two shillings, and not two words of any language spoken there: I must say, a bonny business! I brought her to this place. I gave her the name and the tenderness due to a sister. All this has not gone without expense, but that I scarce need to hint at. They were services due to the young lady's character which I respect; and I think it would be a bonny business too, if I was to be singing her praises to her father.'

'You are a young man,' he began.

'So I hear you tell me,' said I, with a good deal of heat.

'You are a very young man,' he repeated, 'or you would have understood the significancy of the step.'

'I think you speak very much at your ease,' cried I. 'What else was I to do? It is a fact I might have hired some decent, poor woman to be a third to us, and I declare I never thought of it until this moment! But where was I to find her, that am a foreigner myself? And let me point out to your observation, Mr. Drummond, that it would have cost me money out of my pocket. For here is just what it comes to, that I had to pay through the nose for your neglect; and there is only the one story to it, just that you were so unloving and so careless as to have lost your daughter.'

'He that lives in a glass house should not be casting stones,' says he; 'and we will finish inquiring into the behaviour of Miss Drummond before we go on to sit in judgment on her father.'

'But I will be entrapped into no such attitude,' said I. 'The character of Miss Drummond is far above inquiry, as her father ought to know. So is mine, and I am telling you that. There are but the two ways of it open. The one is to express your thanks to me as one gentleman to another, and to say no more. The other (if you are so difficult as to be still dissatisfied) is to pay me that which I have expended and be done.'

He seemed to soothe me with a hand in the air. 'There, there,' said he. 'You go too fast, you go too fast, Mr. Balfour. It is a good thing that I have learned to be more patient. And I believe you forget that I have yet to see my daughter.'

I began to be a little relieved upon this speech and a change in the man's manner that I spied in him as soon as the name of money fell between us.

'I was thinking it would be more fit—if you will excuse the plainness of my dressing in your presence—that I should go forth and leave you to encounter her alone?' said I.

'What I would have looked for at your hands;' says he; and there was no mistake but what he said it civilly.

I thought this better and better still, and as I began to pull on my hose, recalling the man's impudent mendicancy at Prestongrange's, I determined to pursue what seemed to be my victory.

'If you have any mind to stay some while in Leyden,' said I, 'this room is very much at your disposal, and I can easy find another for myself: in which way we shall have the least amount of flitting possible, there being only one to change.'

'Why, sir,' said he, making his bosom big. 'I think no shame of a poverty I have come by in the service of my king; I make no secret that my affairs are quite involved; and for the moment, it would be even impossible for me to undertake a journey.'

'Until you have occasion to communicate with your friends,' said I, 'perhaps it might be convenient for you (as of course it would be honourable to myself) if you were to regard yourself in the light of my guest?'

'Sir,' said he, 'when an offer is frankly made, I think I honour myself most to imitate that frankness. Your hand, Mr. David; you have the character that I respect the most; you are one of those from whom a gentleman can take a favour and no more words about it. I am an old soldier,' he went on, looking rather disgusted-like around my chamber, 'and you need not fear I shall prove burthensome. I have ate too often at a dyke-side, drank of the ditch, and had no roof but the rain.'

'I should be telling you,' said I, 'that our breakfasts are sent customarily in about this time of morning. I propose I should go now to the tavern, and bid them add a cover for yourself and delay the meal the matter of an hour, which will give you an interval to meet your daughter in.'

Methought his nostrils wagged at this. 'O, an hour?' says he. 'That is perhaps superfluous. Half an hour, Mr. David, or say twenty minutes; I shall do very well in that. And by the way,' he adds, detaining me by the coat, 'what is it you drink in the morning, whether ale or wine?'

'To be frank with you, sir,' says I, 'I drink nothing else but spare, cold water.'

'Tut-tut,' says he, 'that is fair destruction to the stomach, take an old campaigner's word for it. Our country spirit at home is perhaps the most entirely wholesome; but as that is not come-at-able, Rhenish or a white wine of Burgundy will be next best.'

'I shall make it my business to see you are supplied,' said I.

'Why, very good,' said he, 'and we shall make a man of you, yet, Mr. David.'

By this time, I can hardly say that I was minding him at all, beyond an odd thought of the kind of father-in-law that he was like to prove; and all my cares centred about the lass his daughter, to whom I determined to convey some warning of her visitor. I stepped to the door accordingly, and cried through the panels, knocking thereon at the same time: 'Miss Drummond, here is your father come at last.'

With that I went forth upon my errand, having (by two words) extraordinarily damaged my affairs.

CHAPTER XXVI

THE THREESOME

WHETHER or not I was to be so much blamed, or rather perhaps pitied, I must leave others to judge. My shrewdness (of which I have a good deal, too) seems not so great with the ladies. No doubt, at the moment when I awaked her, I was thinking a good deal of the effect upon James More; and similarly when I returned and we were all sat down to breakfast, I continued to behave to the young lady with deference and distance; as I still think to have been most wise. Her father had cast doubts upon the innocence of my friendship; and these, it was my first business to allay. But there is a kind of an excuse for Catriona also. We had shared in a scene of some tenderness and passion, and given and received caresses; I had thrust her from me with violence; I had called aloud upon her in the night from the one room to the other; she had passed hours of wakefulness and weeping; and it is not to be supposed I had been absent from her pillow thoughts. Upon the back of this, to be awaked, with unaccustomed formality, under the name of Miss Drummond, and to be thenceforth used with a great deal of distance and respect, led her entirely in error on my private sentiments; and she was indeed so incredibly abused as to imagine me repentant and trying to draw off!

The trouble betwixt us seems to have been this: that whereas I (since I had first set eyes on his great hat) thought singly of James More, his return and suspicions, she made so little of these that I may say she scarce remarked them, and all her troubles and doings regarded what had passed between us in the night before. This is partly to be explained by the innocence and boldness of her character; and partly because James More, having sped so ill in his interview with me, or had his mouth closed by my invitation, said no word to her upon the subject. At the breakfast, accordingly, it soon appeared we were at cross purposes. I had looked to find her in clothes of her own: I found her (as if her father were forgotten) wearing some of the best that I had bought for her and which she knew (or thought) that I admired her in. I had looked to find her imitate my affectation of distance, and be most precise and formal; instead I found her flushed and wild-like, with eyes extraordinary bright, and a painful and varying expression, calling me by name with a sort of appeal of tenderness, and referring and deferring to my thoughts and wishes like an anxious or a suspected wife.

But this was not for long. As I beheld her so regardless of her own interests, which I had jeopardised and was now endeavouring to recover, I redoubled my own coldness in the manner of a lesson to the girl. The more she came forward, the further I drew back; the more she betrayed the closeness of our intimacy, the more pointedly civil I became, until even her father (if he had not been so engrossed with eating) might have observed the opposition. In the midst of which, of a sudden, she became wholly changed, and I told

myself, with a good deal of relief, that she had took the hint
at last.

All day I was at my classes or in quest of my new lodging;
and though the hour of our customary walk hung miserably
on my hands, I cannot say but I was happy on the whole to find
my way cleared, the girl again in proper keeping, the father
satisfied or at least acquiescent, and myself free to prosecute
my love with honour. At supper, as at all our meals, it was
James More that did the talking. No doubt but he talked well,
if anyone could have believed him. But I will speak of him
presently more at large. The meal at an end, he rose, got his
greatcoat, and looking (as I thought) at me, observed he had
affairs abroad. I took this for a hint that I was to be going
also, and got up; whereupon the girl, who had scarce given
me greeting at my entrance, turned her eyes upon me wide
open with a look that bade me stay. I stood between them
like a fish out of water, turning from one to the other; neither
seemed to observe me, she gazing on the floor, he buttoning
his coat: which vastly swelled my embarrassment. This
appearance of indifference argued, upon her side, a good deal
of anger very near to burst out. Upon his, I thought it horribly alarming; I made sure there was a tempest brewing
there; and considering that to be the chief peril, turned
towards him and put myself (so to speak) in the man's
hands.

'Can I do anything for you, Mr. Drummond?' says I.

He stifled a yawn, which again I thought to be duplicity.
'Why, Mr. David,' said he, 'since you are so obliging as to
propose it, you might show me the way to a certain tavern'
(of which he gave the name) 'where I hope to fall in with
some old companions in arms.'

There was no more to say, and I got my hat and cloak to
bear him company.

'And as for you,' says he to his daughter, 'you had best
go to your bed. I shall be late home, and *Early to bed and
early to rise, gars bonny lasses have bright eyes.*'

Whereupon he kissed her with a good deal of tenderness,
and ushered me before him from the door. This was so done

(I thought on purpose) that it was scarce possible there should be any parting salutation; but I observed she did not look at me, and set it down to terror of James More.

It was some distance to that tavern. He talked all the way of matters which did not interest me the smallest, and at the door dismissed me with empty manners. Thence I walked to my new lodging, where I had not so much as a chimney to hold me warm, and no society but my own thoughts. These were still bright enough; I did not so much as dream that Catriona was turned against me; I thought we were like folk pledged; I thought we had been too near and spoke too warmly to be severed, least of all by what were only steps in a most needful policy. And the chief of my concern was only the kind of father-in-law that I was getting, which was not at all the kind I would have chosen: and the matter of how soon I ought to speak to him, which was a delicate point on several sides. In the first place, when I thought how young I was, I blushed all over, and could almost have found it in my heart to have desisted; only that if once I let them go from Leyden without explanation, I might lose her altogether. And in the second place, there was our very irregular situation to be kept in view, and the rather scant measure of satisfaction I had given James More that morning. I concluded, on the whole, that delay would not hurt anything, yet I would not delay too long neither; and got to my cold bed with a full heart.

The next day, as James More seemed a little on the complaining hand in the matter of my chamber, I offered to have in more furniture; and coming in the afternoon, with porters bringing chairs and tables, found the girl once more left to herself. She greeted me on my admission civilly, but withdrew at once to her own room, of which she shut the door. I made my disposition, and paid and dismissed the men so that she might hear them go, when I supposed she would at once come forth again to speak to me. I waited yet awhile, then knocked upon her door.

'Catriona!' said I.

The door was opened so quickly, even before I had the word

out, that I thought she must have stood behind it listening. She remained there in the interval quite still; but she had a look that I cannot put a name on, as of one in a bitter trouble.

'Are we not to have our walk to-day either?' so I faltered.

'I am thanking you,' said she. 'I will not be caring much to walk, now that my father is come home.'

'But I think he has gone out himself and left you here alone,' said I.

'And do you think that was very kindly said?' she asked.

'It was not unkindly meant,' I replied. 'What ails you, Catriona? What have I done to you that you should turn from me like this?'

'I do not turn from you at all,' she said, speaking very carefully. 'I will ever be grateful to my friend that was good to me; I will ever be his friend in all that I am able. But now that my father James More is come again, there is a difference to be made, and I think there are some things said and done that would be better to be forgotten. But I will ever be your friend in all that I am able, and if that is not all that . . . if it is not so much . . . Not that you will be caring! But I would not have you think of me too hard. It was true what you said to me, that I was too young to be advised, and I am hoping you will remember I was just a child. I would not like to lose your friendship, at all events.'

She began this very pale; but before she was done, the blood was in her face like scarlet, so that not her words only, but her face and the trembling of her very hands, besought me to be gentle. I saw, for the first time, how very wrong I had done to place the child in that position, where she had been entrapped into a moment's weakness, and now stood before me like a person shamed.

'Miss Drummond,' I said, and stuck, and made the same beginning once again, 'I wish you could see into my heart,' I cried. 'You would read there that my respect is undiminished. If that were possible, I should say it was increased. This is but the result of the mistake we made; and had to come; and the less said of it now the better. Of all of our life here, I promise you it shall never pass my lips; I would like to promise you too that I would never think of it, but it's a memory that will be always dear to me. And as for a friend, you have one here that would die for you.'

'I am thanking you,' said she.

We stood awhile silent, and my sorrow for myself began to get the upper hand; for here were all my dreams come to a sad tumble, and my love lost, and myself alone again in the world as at the beginning.

'Well,' said I, 'we shall be friends always, that's a certain thing. But this is a kind of a farewell, too: it's a kind of a farewell after all; I shall always ken Miss Drummond, but this is a farewell to my Catriona.'

I looked at her; I could hardly say I saw her, but she seemed to grow great and brighten in my eyes; and with that I suppose I must have lost my head, for I called out her name again and made a step at her with my hands reached forth.

She shrank back like a person struck, her face flamed; but the blood sprang no faster up into her cheeks, than what it flowed back upon my own heart, at sight of it, with penitence and concern. I found no words to excuse myself, but bowed before her very deep, and went my ways out of the house with death in my bosom.

I think it was about five days that followed without any change. I saw her scarce ever but at meals, and then of course in the company of James More. If we were alone even for a moment, I made it my devoir to behave the more distantly and to multiply respectful attentions, having always in my mind's eye that picture of the girl shrinking and flaming in a blush, and in my heart more pity for her than I could depict in words. I was sorry enough for myself, I need not dwell on that, having fallen all my length and more than all my height in a few seconds; but, indeed, I was near as sorry for the girl, and sorry enough to be scarce angry with her save by fits and starts. Her plea was good: she was but a child; she had been placed in an unfair position; if she had deceived herself and me, it was no more than was to have been looked for.

And for another thing she was now very much alone. Her father, when he was by, was rather a caressing parent: but he was very easy led away by his affairs and pleasures, neglected her without compunction or remark, spent his nights in taverns when he had the money, which was more often than I could at all account for; and even in the course of these few days, failed once to come to a meal, which Catriona and I were at last compelled to partake of without him. It was the evening meal, and I left immediately that I had eaten, observing I supposed she would prefer to be alone; to which she agreed and (strange as it may seem) I quite believed her. Indeed, I thought myself but an eyesore to the girl, and a reminder of a moment's weakness that she now abhorred to think of. So she must sit alone in that room where she and I had been so merry, and in the blink of that chimney whose light had shone upon our many difficult and tender moments. There she must sit alone, and think of herself as of a maid who had most unmaidenly proffered her affections and had the same rejected. And in the meanwhile I would be alone in some other place, and reading myself (whenever I was tempted to be angry) lessons upon human frailty and female delicacy. And altogether I suppose there were never two poor fools made themselves more unhappy in a greater misconception.

As for James, he paid not so much heed to us, or to anything in nature but his pocket, and his belly, and his own prating talk. Before twelve hours were gone he had raised a small loan of me; before thirty, he had asked for a second and been refused. Money and refusal he took with the same kind of high good nature. Indeed, he had an outside air of magnanimity that was very well fitted to impose upon a daughter; and the light in which he was constantly presented in his talk, and the man's fine presence and great ways went together pretty harmoniously. So that a man that had no business with him, and either very little penetration or a furious deal of prejudice, might almost have been taken in. To me, after my first two interviews, he was as plain as print; I saw him to be perfectly selfish, with a perfect innocency in the same; and I would hearken to his swaggering talk (of arms, and 'an old soldier,' and 'a poor Highland gentleman,' and 'the strength of my country and my friends') as I might to the babbling of a parrot.

The odd thing was that I fancy he believed some part of it himself, or did at times; I think he was so false all through that he scarce knew when he was lying; and for one thing, his moments of dejection must have been wholly genuine. There were times when he would be the most silent, affectionate, clinging creature possible, holding Catriona's hand like a big baby, and begging of me not to leave if I had any love to him; of which, indeed, I had none, but all the more to his daughter. He would press and indeed beseech us to entertain him with our talk, a thing very difficult in the state of our relations; and again break forth in pitiable regrets for his own land and friends, or into Gaelic singing.

'This is one of the melancholy airs of my native land,' he would say. 'You may think it strange to see a soldier weep, and indeed it is to make a near friend of you,' says he. 'But the notes of this singing are in my blood, and the words come out of my heart. And when I mind upon my red mountains and the wild birds calling there, and the brave streams of water running down, I would scarce think shame to weep before my enemies.' Then he would sing again, and translate to me pieces of the song, with a great deal of boggling and much expressed contempt against the English language. 'It says here,' he would say, 'that the sun is gone down, and the battle is at an end, and the brave chiefs are defeated. And it tells here how the stars see them fleeing into strange countries or lying dead on the red mountain; and they will never more shout the call of battle or wash their feet in the streams of the valley. But if you had only some of this language, you would weep also because the words of it are beyond all expression, and it is mere mockery to tell you it in English.'

Well, I thought there was a good deal of mockery in the business, one way and another; and yet, there was some feeling too, for which I hated him, I think, the worst of all.

And it used to cut me to the quick to see Catriona so much concerned for the old rogue, and weeping herself to see him weep, when I was sure one half of his distress flowed from his last night's drinking in some tavern. There were times when I was tempted to lend him a round sum, and see the last of him for good; but this would have been to see the last of Catriona as well, for which I was scarcely so prepared; and besides, it went against my conscience to squander my good money on one who was so little of a husband.

CHAPTER XXVII

A TWOSOME

I BELIEVE it was about the fifth day, and I know at least that James was in one of his fits of gloom, when I received three letters. The first was from Alan, offering to visit me in Leyden; the other two were out of Scotland and prompted by the same affair, which was the death of my uncle and my own complete accession to my rights. Rankeillor's was, of course, wholly in the business view; Miss Grant's was like herself, a little more witty than wise, full of blame to me for not having written (though how was I to write with such intelligence?) and of rallying talk about Catriona, which it cut me to the quick to read in her very presence.

For it was of course in my own rooms that I found them, when I came to dinner, so that I was surprised out of my news in the very first moment of reading it. This made a welcome diversion for all three of us, nor could any have foreseen the ill consequences that ensued. It was accident that brought the three letters the same day, and that gave them into my hand in the same room with James More; and of all the events that flowed from that accident, and which I might have prevented if I had held my tongue, the truth is that they were preordained before Agricola came into Scotland or Abraham set out upon his travels.

The first that I opened was naturally Alan's; and what

more natural than that I should comment on his design to visit me? but I observed James to sit up with an air of immediate attention.

'Is that not Alan Breck that was suspected of the Appin accident?' he inquired.

I told him, 'Ay,' it was the same; and he withheld me some time from my other letters, asking of our acquaintance, of Alan's manner of life in France, of which I knew very little, and further of his visit as now proposed.

'All we forfeited folk hang a little together,' he explained, 'and besides I know the gentleman: and though his descent is not the thing, and indeed he has no true right to use the name of Stewart, he was very much admired in the day of Drummossie. He did there like a soldier; if some that need not be named had done as well, the upshot need not have been so melancholy to remember. There were two that did their best that day, and it makes a bond between the pair of us,' says he.

I could scarce refrain from shooting out my tongue at him, and could almost have wished that Alan had been there to have inquired a little further into that mention of his birth. Though, they tell me, the same was indeed not wholly regular.

Meanwhile, I had opened Miss Grant's, and could not withhold an exclamation.

'Catriona,' I cried, forgetting, the first time since her father was arrived, to address her by a handle, 'I am come into my kingdom fairly, I am the laird of Shaws indeed—my uncle is dead at last.'

She clapped her hands together leaping from her seat. The next moment it must have come over both of us at once what little cause of joy was left to either, and we stood opposite, staring on each other sadly.

But James showed himself a ready hypocrite. 'My daughter,' says he, 'is this how my cousin learned you to behave? Mr. David has lost a near friend,* and we should first condole with him on his bereavement.'

'Troth, sir,' said I, turning to him in a kind of anger, 'I can make no such faces. His death is as blithe news as ever I got.'

'It's a good soldier's philosophy,' says James. "Tis the way of flesh, we must all go, all go. And if the gentleman was so far from your favour, why, very well! But we may at least congratulate you on your accession to your estates.'

'Nor can I say that either,' I replied, with the same heat. 'It is a good estate; what matters that to a lone man that has enough already? I had a good revenue before in my frugality; and but for the man's death—which gratifies me, shame to me that must confess it!—I see not how anyone is to be bettered by this change.'

'Come, come,' said he, 'you are more affected than you let on, or you would never make yourself out so lonely. Here are three letters; that means three that wish you well; and I could name two more, here in this very chamber. I have known you not so very long, but Catriona, when we are alone, is never done with the singing of your praises.'

She looked up at him, a little wild at that; and he slid off at once into another matter, the extent of my estate, which (during the most of the dinner time) he continued to dwell upon with interest. But it was to no purpose he dissembled; he had touched the matter with too gross a hand: and I knew what to expect. Dinner was scarce ate when he plainly discovered his designs. He reminded Catriona of an errand, and bid her attend to it. 'I do not see you should be gone beyond the hour,' he added, 'and friend David will be good enough to bear me company till you return.' She made haste to obey him without words. I do not know if she understood, I believe not; but I was completely satisfied, and sat strengthening my mind for what should follow.

The door had scarce closed behind her departure, when the man leaned back in his chair and addressed me with a good affectation of easiness. Only the one thing betrayed him, and that was his face; which suddenly shone all over with fine points of sweat.

'I am rather glad to have a word alone with you,' says he, 'because in our first interview there were some expressions you misapprehended and I have long meant to set you right upon. My daughter stands beyond doubt. So do you, and I would make that good with my sword against all gainsayers. But, my dear David, this world is a censorious place—as who should know it better than myself, who have lived ever since the days of my late departed father, God sain him! in a perfect spate of calumnies? We have to face to that; you and me have to consider of that; we have to consider of that.' And he wagged his head like a minister in a pulpit.

'To what effect, Mr. Drummond?' said I. 'I would be obliged to you if you would approach your point.'

'Ay, ay,' says he, laughing, 'like your character indeed! and what I most admire in it. But the point, my worthy fellow, is sometimes in a kittle bit.' He filled a glass of wine. 'Though between you and me, that are such fast friends, it need not bother us long. The point, I need scarcely tell you, is my daughter. And the first thing is that I have no thought in my mind of blaming you. In the unfortunate circumstances, what could you do else? 'Deed, and I cannot tell.'

'I thank you for that,' said I, pretty close upon my guard.

'I have besides studied your character,' he went on; 'your talents are fair; you seem to have a moderate competence, which does no harm; and one thing with another, I am very happy to have to announce to you that I have decided on the latter of the two ways open.'

'I am afraid I am dull,' said I. 'What ways are these?'

He bent his brows upon me formidably and uncrossed his legs. 'Why, sir, says he, 'I think I need scarce describe them to a gentleman of your condition: either that I should cut your throat or that you should marry my daughter.'

'You are pleased to be quite plain at last,' said I.

'And I believe I have been plain from the beginning!' cries he robustiously. 'I am a careful parent, Mr. Balfour; but I thank God, a patient and deleeberate man. There is many a father, sir, that would have hirsled you at once either to the altar or the field. My esteem for your character——'

'Mr. Drummond,' I interrupted, 'if you have any esteem for me at all, I will beg of you to moderate your voice. It is

quite needless to rowt at a gentleman in the same chamber
with yourself and lending you his best attention.'

'Why, very true,' says he, with an immediate change. 'And
you must excuse the agitations of a parent.'

'I understand you then,' I continued—'for I will take no
note of your other alternative, which perhaps it was a pity
you let fall—I understand you rather to offer me encourage-
ment in case I should desire to apply for your daughter's
hand?'

'It is not possible to express my meaning better,' said he,
'and I see we shall do well together.'

'That remains to be yet seen,' said I. 'But so much I need
make no secret of, that I bear the lady you refer to the most
tender affection, and I could not fancy, even in a dream, a
better fortune than to get her.'

'I was sure of it, I felt certain of you, David,' he cried, and
reached out his hand to me.

I put it by. 'You go too fast, Mr. Drummond,' said I. 'There
are conditions to be made; and there is a difficulty in the path,
which I see not entirely how we shall come over. I have told
you that, upon my side, there is no objection to the marriage,
but I have good reason to believe there will be much on the
young lady's.'

'This is all beside the mark,' says he. 'I will engage for her
acceptance.'

'I think you forget, Mr. Drummond,' said I, 'that even in
dealing with myself you have been betrayed into two-three
unpalatable expressions. I will have none such employed to
the young lady. I am here to speak and think for the two
of us; and I give you to understand that I would no more let
a wife be forced upon myself, than what I would let a
husband be forced on the young lady.'

He sat and glowered at me like one in doubt and a good
deal of temper.

'So that this is to be the way of it,' I concluded. 'I will
marry Miss Drummond, and that blithely, if she is entirely
willing. But if there be the least unwillingness, as I have
reason to fear—marry her will I never.'

'Well, well,' said he, 'this is a small affair. As soon as she returns I will sound her a bit, and hope to reassure you——'

But I cut in again. 'Not a finger of you, Mr. Drummond, or I cry off, and you can seek a husband to your daughter somewhere else,' said I. 'It is that I am to be the only dealer and the only judge. I shall satisfy myself exactly; and none else shall anyways meddle—you the least of all.'

'Upon my word, sir!' he exclaimed, 'and who are you to be the judge?'

'The bridegroom, I believe,' said I.

'This is to quibble,' he cried. 'You turn your back upon the facts. The girl, my daughter, has no choice left to exercise. Her character is gone.'

'And I ask your pardon,' said I, 'but while this matter lies between her and you and me, that is not so.'

'What security have I!' he cried. 'Am I to let my daughter's reputation depend upon a chance?'

'You should have thought of all this long ago,' said I, 'before you were so misguided as to lose her; and not afterwards, when it is quite too late. I refuse to regard myself as any way accountable for your neglect, and I will be browbeat by no man living. My mind is quite made up, and come what may, I will not depart from it a hair's-breadth. You and me are to sit here in company till her return; upon which, without either word or look from you, she and I are to go forth again to hold our talk. If she can satisfy me that she is willing to this step, I will then make it; and if she cannot I will not.'

He leaped out of his seat like a man stung. 'I can spy your manœuvre,' he cried; 'you would work upon her to refuse!'

'Maybe ay, and maybe no,' said I. 'That is the way it is to be, whatever.'

'And if I refuse?' cries he.

'Then, Mr. Drummond, it will have to come to the throat-cutting,' said I.

What with the size of the man, his great length of arm in which he came near rivalling his father, and his reputed skill at weapons, I did not use this word without some trepidation, to say nothing at all of the circumstances that he was

Catriona's father. But I might have spared myself alarms.
From the poorness of my lodging—he does not seem to have
remarked his daughter's dresses, which were indeed all
equally new to him—and from the fact that I had shown
myself averse to lend, he had embraced a strong idea of my
poverty. The sudden news of my estate convinced him of his
error, and he had made but the one bound of it on this fresh
venture, to which he was now so wedded, that I believe he
would have suffered anything rather than fall to the alternative of fighting.

A little while longer he continued to dispute with me, until
I hit upon a word that silenced him.

'If I find you so averse to let me see the lady by herself,'
said I, 'I must suppose you have very good grounds to think
me in the right about her unwillingness.'

He gabbled some kind of an excuse.

'But all this is very exhausting to both of our tempers,'
I added, 'and I think we would do better to preserve a
judicious silence.'

The which we did until the girl returned, and I must
suppose would have cut a very ridiculous figure, had there
been any there to view us.

CHAPTER XXVIII

IN WHICH I AM LEFT ALONE

I OPENED the door to Catriona and stopped her on the
threshold.

'Your father wishes us to take our walk,' said I.

She looked to James More, who nodded, and at that, like
a trained soldier, she turned to go with me.

We took one of our old ways, where we had gone often
together, and been more happy than I can tell of in the past.
I came a half step behind, so that I could watch her un-
observed. The knocking of her little shoes upon the way
sounded extraordinary pretty and sad; and I thought it a

strange moment that I should be so near both ends of it at once, and walk in the midst between two destinies, and could not tell whether I was hearing these steps for the last time, or whether the sound of them was to go in and out with me till death should part us.

She avoided even to look at me, only walked before her, like one who had a guess of what was coming. I saw I must speak soon before my courage was run out, but where to begin I knew not. In this painful situation, when the girl was as good as forced into my arms and had already besought my forbearance, any excess of pressure must have seemed indecent; yet to avoid it wholly would have a very cold-like appearance. Between these extremes I stood helpless, and could have bit my fingers; so that, when at last I managed to speak at all, it may be said I spoke at random.

'Catriona,' said I, 'I am in a very painful situation; or rather, so we are both; and I would be a good deal obliged to you if you would promise to let me speak through first of all, and not to interrupt till I have done.'

She promised me that simply.

'Well,' said I, 'this that I have got to say is very difficult, and I know very well I have no right to be saying it. After what passed between the two of us last Friday, I have no manner of right. We have got so ravelled up (and all by my fault) that I know very well the least I could do is just to hold my tongue, which was what I intended fully, and there was nothing further from my thoughts than to have troubled you again. But, my dear, it has become merely necessary, and no way by it. You see, this estate of mine has fallen in, which makes of me rather a better match; and the—the business would not have quite the same ridiculous-like appearance that it would before. Besides which, it's supposed that our affairs have got so much ravelled up (as I was saying) that it would be better to let them be the way they are. In my view, this part of the thing is vastly exaggerate, and if I were you I would not ware two thoughts on it. Only it's right I should mention the same, because there's no doubt it has some influence on James More. Then I think we were none

so unhappy when we dwelt together in this town before.
I think we did pretty well together. If you would look back,
my dear——'

'I will look neither back nor forward,' she interrupted. 'Tell
me the one thing: this is my father's doing?'

'He approves of it,' said I. 'He approved that I should ask
your hand in marriage,' and was going on again with somewhat more of an appeal upon her feelings; but she marked
me not, and struck into the midst.

'He told you to!' she cried. 'It is no sense denying it, you
said yourself that there was nothing farther from your
thoughts. He told you to.'

'He spoke of it the first, if that is what you mean,' I began.

She was walking ever the faster, and looking fair in front
of her; but at this she made a little noise in her head, and
I thought she would have run.

'Without which,' I went on, 'after what you said last
Friday, I would never have been so troublesome as make the
offer. But when he as good as asked me, what was I to
do?'

She stopped and turned round upon me.

'Well, it is refused at all events,' she cried, 'and there will
be an end of that.'

And she began again to walk forward.

'I suppose I could expect no better,' said I, 'but I think
you might try to be a little kind to me for the last end of it.
I see not why you should be harsh. I have loved you very
well, Catriona—no harm that I should call you so for the last
time. I have done the best that I could manage, I am trying
the same still, and only vexed that I can do no better. It is
a strange thing to me that you can take any pleasure to be
hard to me.'

'I am not thinking of you,' she said, 'I am thinking of that
man, my father.'

'Well, and that way, too!' said I. 'I can be of use to you
that way, too; I will have to be. It is very needful, my dear,
that we should consult about your father; for the way this
talk has gone, an angry man will be James More.'

She stopped again. 'It is because I am disgraced?' she asked.

'That is what he is thinking,' I replied, 'but I have told you already to make nought of it.'

'It will be all one to me,' she cried. 'I prefer to be disgraced!'

I did not know very well what to answer, and stood silent.

There seemed to be something working in her bosom after that last cry; presently she broke out, 'And what is the meaning of all this? Why is this shame loundered on my head? How could you dare it, David Balfour?'

'My dear,' said I, 'what else was I to do?'

'I am not your dear,' she said, 'and I defy you to be calling me these words.'

'I am not thinking of my words,' said I. 'My heart bleeds for you, Miss Drummond. Whatever I may say, be sure you have my pity in your difficult position. But there is just the one thing that I wish you would bear in view, if it was only long enough to discuss it quietly; for there is going to be a collieshangie when we two get home. Take my word for it, it will need the two of us to make this matter end in peace.'

'Ay,' said she. There sprang a patch of red in either of her cheeks. 'Was he for fighting you?' said she.

'Well, he was that,' said I.

She gave a dreadful kind of laugh. 'At all events, it is complete!' she cried. And then turning on me: 'My father and I are a fine pair,' said she, 'but I am thanking the good God there will be somebody worse than what we are. I am thanking the good God that he has let me see you so. There will never be the girl made that would not scorn you.'

I had borne a good deal pretty patiently, but this was over the mark.

'You have no right to speak to me like that,' said I. 'What have I done but to be good to you, or try to be? And here is my repayment! O, it is too much.'

She kept looking at me with a hateful smile. 'Coward!' said she.

'The word in your throat and in your father's!' I cried. 'I

have dared him this day already in your interest. I will dare
him again, the nasty pole-cat; little I care which of us should
fall! Come,' said I, 'back to the house with us; let us be done
with it, let me be done with the whole Hieland crew of you!
You will see what you think when I am dead.'

She shook her head at me with that same smile I could have
struck her for.

'O, smile away!' I cried. 'I have seen your bonny father
smile on the wrong side this day. Not that I mean he was
afraid, of course,' I added hastily, 'but he preferred the other
way of it.'

'What is this?' she asked.

'When I offered to draw with him,' said I.

'You offered to draw upon James More?' she cried.

'And I did so,' said I, 'and found him backward enough,
or how would we be here?'

'There is a meaning upon this,' said she. 'What is it you
are meaning?'

'He was to make you take me,' I replied, 'and I would not
have it. I said you should be free, and I must speak with you
alone; little I supposed it would be such a speaking! "*And
what if I refuse?*" says he.—"*Then it must come to the throat-
cutting*," says I, "*for I will no more have a husband forced on
that young lady, than what I would have a wife forced upon
myself.*" These were my words, they were a friend's words;
bonnily have I been paid for them! Now you have refused me
of your own clear free will, and there lives no father in the
Highlands, or out of them, that can force on this marriage.
I will see that your wishes are respected; I will make the same
my business, as I have all through. But I think you might
have that decency as to affect some gratitude. 'Deed, and
I thought you knew me better! I have not behaved quite well
to you, but that was weakness. And to think me a coward,
and such a coward as that—O, my lass, there was a stab for
the last of it!'

'Davie, how would I guess?' she cried. 'O, this is a dreadful
business! Me and mine,'—she gave a kind of wretched cry
at the word—'me and mine are not fit to speak to you. O, I

could be kneeling down to you in the street, I could be kissing your hands for your forgiveness!'

'I will keep the kisses I have got from you already,' cried I. 'I will keep the ones I wanted and that were something worth; I will not be kissed in penitence.'

'What can you be thinking of this miserable girl?' says she.

'What I am trying to tell you all this while!' said I, 'that you had best leave me alone, whom you can make no more unhappy if you tried, and turn your attention to James More, your father, with whom you are like to have a queer pirn to wind.'

'Oh, that I must be going out into the world alone with such a man!' she cried, and seemed to catch herself in with a great effort. 'But trouble yourself no more for that,' said she. 'He does not know what kind of nature is in my heart. He will pay me dear for this day of it; dear, dear, will he pay.'

She turned, and began to go home and I to accompany her. At which she stopped.

'I will be going alone,' she said. 'It is alone I must be seeing him.'

Some little while I raged about the streets, and told myself I was the worst-used lad in Christendom. Anger choked me; it was all very well for me to breathe deep; it seemed there was not air enough about Leyden to supply me, and I thought I would have burst like a man at the bottom of the sea. I stopped and laughed at myself at a street corner a minute together, laughing out loud, so that a passenger looked at me, which brought me to myself.

'Well,' I thought, 'I have been a gull and a ninny and a soft Tommy long enough. Time it was done. Here is a good lesson to have nothing to do with that accursed sex, that was the ruin of the man in the beginning and will be so to the end. God knows I was happy enough before ever I saw her; God knows I can be happy enough again when I have seen the last of her.'

That seemed to me the chief affair: to see them go. I dwelled upon the idea fiercely; and presently slipped on, in a kind of malevolence, to consider how very poorly they were like to fare when Davie Balfour was no longer by to be their milk-cow; at which, to my own very great surprise, the disposition of my mind turned bottom up. I was still angry; I still hated her; and yet I thought I owed it to myself that she should suffer nothing.

This carried me home again at once, where I found the mails drawn out and ready fastened by the door, and the father and daughter with every mark upon them of a recent disagreement. Catriona was like a wooden doll; James More breathed hard, his face was dotted with white spots, and his nose upon one side. As soon as I came in, the girl looked at him with a steady, clear, dark look that might very well have been followed by a blow. It was a hint that was more contemptuous than a command, and I was surprised to see James More accept it. It was plain he had had a master talking-to; and I could see there must be more of the devil in the girl than I had guessed, and more good humour about the man than I had given him the credit of.

He began, at least, calling me Mr. Balfour, and plainly speaking from a lesson; but he got not very far, for at the first pompous swell of his voice, Catriona cut in.

'I will tell you what James More is meaning,' said she. 'He means we have come to you, beggar-folk, and have not behaved to you very well, and we are ashamed of our ingratitude and ill-behaviour. Now we are wanting to go away and be forgotten; and my father will have guided his gear so ill, that we cannot even do that unless you will give us some more alms. For that is what we are, at all events, beggar-folk and sorners.'

'By your leave, Miss Drummond,' said I, 'I must speak to your father by myself.'

She went into her own room and shut the door, without a word or a look.

'You must excuse her, Mr. Balfour,' says James More. 'She has no delicacy.'

'I am not here to discuss that with you,' said I, 'but to be quit of you. And to that end I must talk of your position. Now, Mr. Drummond, I have kept the run of your affairs more closely than you bargained for. I know you had money of your own when you were borrowing mine. I know you have had more since you were here in Leyden, though you concealed it even from your daughter.'

'I bid you beware. I will stand no more baiting,' he broke out. 'I am sick of her and you. What kind of a damned trade is this to be a parent! I have had expressions used to me——' There he broke off. 'Sir, this is the heart of a soldier and a parent,' he went on again, laying his hand on his bosom, 'outraged in both characters—-and I bid you beware.'

'If you would have let me finish,' says I, 'you would have found I spoke for your advantage.'

'My dear friend,' he cried, 'I know I might have relied upon the generosity of your character.'

'Man! will you let me speak?' said I. 'The fact is that I cannot win to find out if you are rich or poor. But it is my idea that your means, as they are mysterious in their source, so they are something insufficient in amount; and I do not choose your daughter to be lacking. If I durst speak to herself, you may be certain I would never dream of trusting it to you; because I know you like the back of my hand, and all your blustering talk is that much wind to me. However, I believe in your way you do still care something for your daughter after all; and I must just be doing with that ground of confidence, such as it is.'

Whereupon, I arranged with him that he was to communicate with me, as to his whereabouts and Catriona's welfare, in consideration of which I was to serve him a small stipend.

He heard the business out with a great deal of eagerness; and when it was done, 'My dear fellow, my dear son,' he cried out, 'this is more like yourself than any of it yet! I will serve you with a soldier's faithfulness——'

'Let me hear no more of it!' says I. 'You have got me to that pitch that the bare name of soldier rises on my stomach. Our traffic is settled; I am now going forth and will return in one half-hour, when I expect to find my chambers purged of you.'

I gave them good measure of time; it was my one fear that I might see Catriona again, because tears and weakness were ready in my heart, and I cherished my anger like a piece of dignity. Perhaps an hour went by; the sun had gone down, a little wisp of a new moon was following it across a scarlet sunset; already there were stars in the east, and in my chambers, when at last I entered them, the night lay blue. I lit a taper and reviewed the rooms; in the first there remained nothing so much as to awake a memory of those who were gone; but in the second, in a corner of the floor, I spied a little heap that brought my heart into my mouth. She had left behind at her departure all that she had ever had of me. It was the blow that I felt sorest, perhaps because it was the last; and I fell upon that pile of clothing and behaved myself more foolish than I care to tell of.

Late in the night, in a strict frost, and my teeth chattering, I came again by some portion of my manhood and considered with myself. The sight of these poor frocks and ribbons, and her shifts, and the clocked stockings, was not to be endured; and if I were to recover any constancy of mind, I saw I must be rid of them ere the morning. It was my first thought to have made a fire and burned them; but my disposition has always been opposed to wastery, for one thing; and for another, to have burned these things that she had worn so close upon her body seemed in the nature of a cruelty. There was a corner cupboard in that chamber; there I determined to bestow them. The which I did and made it a long business, folding them with very little skill indeed but the more care; and sometimes dropping them with my tears. All the heart was gone out of me, I was weary as though I had run miles, and sore like one beaten; when, as I was folding a kerchief that she wore often at her neck, I observed there was a corner neatly cut from it. It was a kerchief of a very pretty hue, on which I had frequently remarked; and once that she had it on, I remembered telling her (by way of a banter) that she wore my colours. There came a glow of hope and like a tide of sweetness in my bosom; and the next moment I was plunged back in a fresh despair. For there was the corner crumpled in a knot and cast down by itself in another part of the floor.

But when I argued with myself, I grew more hopeful. She had cut that corner off in some childish freak that was manifestly tender; that she had cast it away again was little to be wondered at; and I was inclined to dwell more upon the first than upon the second, and to be more pleased that she had ever conceived the idea of that keepsake, than concerned because she had flung it from her in an hour of natural resentment.

CHAPTER XXIX

WE MEET IN DUNKIRK

ALTOGETHER, then, I was scarce so miserable the next days but what I had many hopeful and happy snatches; threw myself with a good deal of constancy upon my studies; and made out to endure the time till Alan should arrive, or I might hear word of Catriona by the means of James More. I had altogether three letters in the time of our separation. One was to announce their arrival in the town of Dunkirk in France, from which place James shortly after started alone upon a private mission. This was to England and to see Lord Holderness;* and it has always been a bitter thought that my good money helped to pay the charges of the same. But he has need of a long spoon who sups with the deil, or James More either. During this absence, the time was to fall due for another letter; and as the letter was the condition of his stipend, he had been so careful as to prepare it beforehand and leave it with Catriona to be despatched. The fact of our correspondence aroused her suspicions, and he was no sooner gone than she had burst the seal. What I received began accordingly in the writing of James More:

'My dear Sir,— Your esteemed favour came to hand duly, and I have to acknowledge the inclosure according to agreement. It shall be all faithfully expended on my daughter, who is well, and desires to be remembered to her dear friend. I find her in rather a melancholy disposition, but trust in the mercy of God to see her re-established. Our manner of life is very much alone, but we solace ourselves with the melancholy tunes of our native mountains, and by walking upon the margin of the sea that lies next to Scotland. It was better days with me when I lay with five wounds upon my body on the field of Gladsmuir.* I have found employment here in the *haras* of a French nobleman, where my experience is valued. But, my dear Sir, the wages are so exceedingly unsuitable that I would be ashamed to mention them, which makes your remittances the more necessary to my daughter's comfort, though I daresay the sight of old friends would be still better.

> 'My dear Sir,
> "Your affectionate, obedient servant,
> 'JAMES MACGREGOR DRUMMOND.'

Below it began in the hand of Catriona:—

> 'Do not be believing him, it is all lies together.—C. M. D.'

Not only did she add this postscript, but I think she must have come near suppressing the letter; for it came long after date, and was closely followed by the third. In the time betwixt them, Alan had arrived, and made another life to me with his merry conversation; I had been presented to his cousin of the Scots-Dutch, a man that drank more than I could have thought possible and was not otherwise of interest; I had been entertained to many jovial dinners and given some myself, all with no great change upon my sorrow; and we two (by which I mean Alan and myself, and not at all the cousin) had discussed a good deal the nature of my relations with James More and his daughter. I was naturally diffident to give particulars; and this disposition was not anyway lessened by the nature of Alan's commentary upon those I gave.

'I cannae make heed nor tail of it,' he would say, 'but it sticks in my mind ye've made a gowk of yourself. There's few people that has had more experience than Alan Breck; and I can never call to mind to have heard tell of a lassie like this one of yours. The way that you tell it, the thing's fair impossible. Ye must have made a terrible hash of the business, David.'

'There are whiles that I am of the same mind,' said I.

'The strange thing is that ye seem to have a kind of a fancy for her too!' said Alan.

'The biggest kind, Alan,' said I, 'and I think I'll take it to my grave with me.'

'Well, ye beat me, whatever!' he would conclude.

I showed him the letter with Catriona's postscript. 'And here again!' he cried. 'Impossible to deny a kind of decency to this Catriona, and sense forby! As for James More, the man's as boss as a drum; he's just a wame and a wheen words; though I'll can never deny that he fought reasonably well at Gladsmuir, and it's true what he says here about the five wounds. But the loss of him is that the man's boss.'

'Ye see, Alan,' said I, 'it goes against the grain with me to leave the maid in such poor hands.'

'Ye couldnae weel find poorer,' he admitted. 'But what are ye to do with it? It's this way about a man and a woman, ye see, Davie: The weemenfolk have got no kind of reason to them. Either they like the man, and then a' goes fine; or else they just detest him, and ye may spare your breath—ye can do naething. There's just the two sets of them—them that would sell their coats for ye, and them that never look the road ye're on. That's a' that there is to women; and you seem to be such a gomeral that ye cannae tell the tane frae the tither.'

'Well, and I'm afraid that's true for me,' said I.

'And yet there's naething easier!' cried Alan. 'I could easy learn ye the science of the thing; but ye seem to me to be born blind, and there's where the deefficulty comes in!'

'And can you no help me?' I asked, 'you that's so clever at the trade?'

'Ye see, David, I wasnae here,' said he. 'I'm like a field officer that has naebody but blind men for scouts and éclaireurs; and what would he ken? But it sticks in my mind that ye'll have made some kind of bauchle; and if I was you, I would have a try at her again.'

'Would ye so, man Alan?' said I.

'I would e'en't,' says he.

The third letter came to my hand while we were deep in some such talk; and it will be seen how pat it fell to the occasion. James professed to be in some concern upon his daughter's health, which I believe was never better; abounded in kind expressions to myself; and finally proposed that I should visit them at Dunkirk.

'You will now be enjoying the society of my old comrade, Mr. Stewart,' he wrote. 'Why not accompany him so far in his return to France? I have something very particular for Mr. Stewart's ear; and, at any rate, I would be pleased to meet in with an old fellow-soldier and one so mettle as himself. As for you, my dear sir, my daughter and I would be proud to receive our benefactor, whom we regard as a brother and a son. The French nobleman has proved a person of the most filthy avarice of character, and I have been necessitate to leave the *haras*. You will find us in consequence a little poorly lodged in the *auberge* of a man Bazin on the dunes; but the situation is caller, and I make no doubt but we might spend some very pleasant days, when Mr. Stewart and I could recall our services, and you and my daughter divert yourselves in a manner more befitting your age. I beg at least that Mr. Stewart would come here; my business with him opens a very wide door.'

'What does the man want with me?' cried Alan, when he had read. 'What he wants with you is clear enough—it's siller. But what can he want with Alan Breck?'

'O, it'll be just an excuse,' said I. 'He is still after this marriage, which I wish from my heart that we could bring about. And he asks you because he thinks I would be less likely to come wanting you.'

'Well, I wish that I kent,' says Alan. 'Him and me were never onyways pack; we used to girn at ither like a pair of pipers. "Something for my ear," quo' he! I'll maybe have something for his hinder-end, before we're through with it. Dod, I'm thinking it would be a kind of divertisement to gang and see what he'll be after! Forbye that I could see your lassie then. What say ye, Davie? Will ye ride with Alan?'

You may be sure I was not backward, and Alan's furlough

running towards an end, we set forth presently upon this joint adventure.

It was near dark of a January day when we rode at last into the town of Dunkirk. We left our horses at the post, and found a guide to Bazin's inn, which lay beyond the walls. Night was quite fallen, so that we were the last to leave that fortress, and heard the doors of it close behind us as we passed the bridge. On the other side there lay a lighted suburb, which we thridded for a while, then turned into a dark lane, and presently found ourselves wading in the night among deep sand where we could hear a bullering of the sea. We travelled in this fashion for some while, following our conductor mostly by the sound of his voice; and I had begun to think he was perhaps misleading us, when we came to the top of a small brae, and there appeared out of the darkness a dim light in a window.

'Voilà l'auberge à Bazin,' says the guide.

Alan smacked his lips. 'An unco lonely bit,' said he, and I thought by his tone he was not wholly pleased.

A little after, and we stood in the lower storey of that house, which was all in the one apartment, with a stair leading to the chambers at the side, benches and tables by the wall, the cooking fire at the one end of it, and shelves of bottles and the cellar-trap at the other. Here Bazin, who was an ill-looking, big man, told us the Scottish gentleman was gone abroad he knew not where, but the young lady was above, and he would call her down to us.

I took from my breast that kerchief wanting the corner, and knotted it about my throat. I could hear my heart go; and Alan patting me on the shoulder with some of his laughable expressions, I could scarce refrain from a sharp word. But the time was not long to wait. I heard her step pass overhead, and saw her on the stair. This she descended very quietly, and greeted me with a pale face and a certain seeming of earnestness, or uneasiness, in her manner that extremely dashed me.

'My father, James More, will be here soon. He will be very pleased to see you,' she said. And then of a sudden her face flamed, her eyes lightened, the speech stopped upon her lips; and I made sure she had observed the kerchief. It was only for a breath that she was discomposed; but methought it was with a new animation that she turned to welcome Alan. 'And you will be his friend, Alan Breck?' she cried. 'Many is the dozen times I will have heard him tell of you; and I love you already for all your bravery and goodness.'

'Well, well,' says Alan, holding her hand in his and viewing her, 'and so this is the young lady at the last of it! David, ye're an awful poor hand of a description.'

I do not know that ever I heard him speak so straight to people's hearts; the sound of his voice was like song.

'What? will he have been describing me?' she cried.

'Little else of it since I ever came out of France!' says he, 'forbye a bit of a speciment one night in Scotland in a shaw of wood by Silvermills. But cheer up, my dear! ye're bonnier than what he said. And now there's one thing sure: you and me are to be a pair of friends. I'm a kind of a henchman to Davie here; I'm like a tyke at his heels: and whatever he cares for, I've got to care for too—and by the holy airn! they've got to care for me! So now you can see what way you stand with Alan Breck, and ye'll find ye'll hardly lose on the transaction. He's no very bonny, my dear, but he's leal to them he loves.'

'I thank you with my heart for your good words,' said she. 'I have that honour for a brave, honest man that I cannot find any to be answering with.'

Using travellers' freedom, we spared to wait for James More, and sat down to meat, we threesome. Alan had Catriona sit by him and wait upon his wants: he made her drink first out of his glass, he surrounded her with continual kind gallantries, and yet never gave me the most small occasion to be jealous; and he kept the talk so much in his own hand, and that in so merry a note, that neither she nor I remembered to be embarrassed. If any had seen us there, it must have been supposed that Alan was the old friend and I the stranger. Indeed, I had often cause to love and to admire the man, but I never loved or admired him better than that night; and I could not help remarking to myself (what I was sometimes rather in danger of forgetting) that he had not only much experience of life, but in his own way a great deal of natural ability besides. As for Catriona she seemed quite carried away; her laugh was like a peal of bells, her face gay as a May morning; and I own, although I was very well pleased, yet I was a little sad also, and thought myself a dull, stockish character in comparison of my friend, and very unfit to come into a young maid's life, and perhaps ding down her gaiety.

But if that was like to be my part, I found at least I was not alone in it; for, James More returning suddenly, the girl was changed into a piece of stone. Through the rest of that evening, until she made an excuse and slipped to bed, I kept an eye upon her without cease: and I can bear testimony that she never smiled, scarce spoke, and looked mostly on the board in front of her. So that I really marvelled to see so much devotion (as it used to be) changed into the very sickness of hate.

Of James More it is unnecessary to say much; you know the man already, what there was to know of him; and I am weary of writing out his lies. Enough that he drank a great deal, and told us very little that was to any possible purpose. As for the business with Alan, that was to be reserved for the morrow and his private hearing.

It was the more easy to be put off, because Alan and I were pretty weary with our day's ride, and sat not very late after Catriona.

We were soon alone in a chamber where we were to make shift with a single bed. Alan looked on me with a queer smile.

'Ye muckle ass!' said he.

'What do ye mean by that?' I cried.

'Mean? What do I mean? It's extraordinar, David man,' says he, 'that you should be so mortal stupit.'

Again I begged him to speak out.

'Well, it's this of it,' said he. 'I told ye there were the two kinds of women—them that would sell their shifts for ye, and the others. Just you try for yoursel, my bonny man! But what's that neepkin at your craig?'

I told him.

'I thocht it was something thereabout,' said he.

Nor would he say another word though I besieged him long with importunities.

CHAPTER XXX

THE LETTER FROM THE SHIP

DAYLIGHT showed us how solitary the inn stood. It was plainly hard upon the sea, yet out of all view of it, and beset on every side with scabbit hills of sand. There was, indeed, only one thing in the nature of a prospect, where there stood out over a brae the two sails of a windmill, like an ass's ears, but with the ass quite hidden. It was strange (after the wind rose, for at first it was dead calm) to see the turning and following of each other of these great sails behind the hillock. Scarce any road came by there; but a number of footways travelled among the bents in all directions up to Mr. Bazin's door. The truth is, he was a man of many trades, not any one of them honest, and the position of his inn was the best of his livelihood. Smugglers frequented it; political agents and forfeited persons bound across the water came there to await their passages; and I dare say there was worse behind, for a whole family might have been butchered in that house and nobody the wiser.

I slept little and ill. Long ere it was day, I had slipped from beside my bedfellow, and was warming myself at the fire or walking to and fro before the door. Dawn broke mighty sullen; but a little after, sprang up a wind out of the west, which burst the clouds, let through the sun, and set the mill to the turning. There was something of spring in the sunshine, or else it was in my heart; and the appearing of the great sails one after another from behind the hill, diverted me extremely. At times I could hear a creak of the machinery;

and by half-past eight of the day, Catriona began to sing in the house. At this I would have cast my hat in the air; and I thought this dreary, desert place was like a paradise.

For all which, as the day drew on and nobody came near, I began to be aware of an uneasiness that I could scarce explain. It seemed there was trouble afoot; the sails of the windmill, as they came up and went down over the hill, were like persons spying; and outside of all fancy, it was surely a strange neighbourhood and house for a young lady to be brought to dwell in.

At breakfast, which we took late, it was manifest that James More was in some danger or perplexity; manifest that Alan was alive to the same, and watched him close; and this appearance of duplicity upon the one side, and vigilance upon the other, held me on live coals. The meal was no sooner over than James seemed to come to a resolve, and began to make apologies. He had an appointment of a private nature in the town (it was with the French nobleman, he told me), and we would please excuse him till about noon. Meanwhile, he carried his daughter aside to the far end of the room, where he seemed to speak rather earnestly and she to listen with much inclination.

'I am caring less and less about this man James,' said Alan. 'There's something no right with the man James, and I wouldnae wonder but what Alan Breck would give an eye to him this day. I would like fine to see yon French nobleman, Davie; and I dare say you could find an employ to yoursel, and that would be to speir at the lassie for some news of your affair. Just tell it to her plainly—tell her ye're a muckle ass at the off-set; and then, if I were you, and ye could do it naitural, I would just mint to her I was in some kind of a danger; a' weemenfolk likes that.'

'I cannae lee, Alan, I cannae do it naitural,' says I, mocking him.

'The more fool you!' says he. 'Then ye'll can tell her that I recommended it; that'll set her to the laughing; and I wouldnae wonder but what that was the next best. But see to the pair of them! If I didnae feel just sure of the lassie, and that she was awful pleased and chief with Alan, I would think there was some kind of hocus-pocus about yon.'

'And is she so pleased with ye, then, Alan?' I asked.

'She thinks a heap of me,' says he. 'And I'm no like you: I'm one that can tell. That she does—she thinks a heap of Alan. And troth! I'm thinking a good deal of him mysel'; and with your permission, Shaws, I'll be getting a wee yont amang the bents, so that I can see what way James goes.'

One after another went, till I was left alone beside the breakfast table; James to Dunkirk, Alan dogging him, Catriona up the stairs to her own chamber. I could very well understand how she should avoid to be alone with me; yet was none the better pleased with it for that, and bent my mind to entrap her to an interview before the men returned. Upon the whole, the best appeared to me to do like Alan. If I was out of view among the sandhills, the fine morning would decoy her forth; and once I had her in the open, I could please myself.

No sooner said that done; nor was I long under the bield of a hillock before she appeared at the inn door, looked here and there, and (seeing nobody) set out by a path that led directly seaward, and by which I followed her. I was in no haste to make my presence known; the further she went I made sure of the longer hearing to my suit; and the ground being all sandy it was easy to follow her unheard. The path rose and came at last to the head of a knowe. Thence I had a picture for the first time of what a desolate wilderness that inn stood hidden in; where was no man to be seen, nor any house of man, except just Bazin's and the windmill. Only a little further on, the sea appeared and two or three ships upon it, pretty as a drawing. One of these was extremely close in to be so great a vessel; and I was aware of a shock of new suspicion, when I recognised the trim of the *Seahorse*. What should an English ship be doing so near in to France? Why was Alan brought into her neighbourhood, and that in a place so far from any hope of rescue? and was it by accident, or by design, that the daughter of James More should walk that day to the seaside?

Presently I came forth behind her in the front of the sand-hills and above the beach. It was here long and solitary; with a man-o'-war's boat drawn up about the middle of the prospect, and an officer in charge and pacing the sands like one who waited. I sat immediately down where the rough grass a good deal covered me, and looked for what should follow. Catriona went straight to the boat; the officer met her with civilities; they had ten words together; I saw a letter changing hands; and there was Catriona returning. At the same time, as if this were all her business on the Continent, the boat shoved off and was headed for the *Seahorse*. But I observed the officer to remain behind and disappear among the bents.

I liked the business little; and the more I considered of it, liked it less. Was it Alan the officer was seeking? or Catriona? She drew near with her head down, looking constantly on the sand, and made so tender a picture that I could not bear to doubt her innocence. The next, she raised her face and recognised me; seemed to hesitate, and then came on again, but more slowly, and I thought with a changed colour. And at that thought, all else that was upon my bosom—fears, suspicions, the care of my friend's life—was clean swallowed up; and I rose to my feet and stood waiting her in a drunkenness of hope.

I gave her 'good morning' as she came up, which she returned with a good deal of composure.

'Will you forgive my having followed you?' said I.

'I know you are always meaning kindly,' she replied; and then, with a little outburst, 'but why will you be sending money to that man? It must not be.'

'I never sent it for him,' said I, 'but for you, as you know well.'

'And you have no right to be sending it to either one of us,' said she. 'David, it is not right.'

'It is not, it is all wrong,' said I; 'and I pray God he will help this dull fellow (if it be at all possible) to make it better. Catriona, this is no kind of life for you to lead; and I ask your pardon for the word, but yon man is no fit father to take care of you.'

'Do not be speaking of him, even!' was her cry.

'And I need speak of him no more; it is not of him that I am thinking. O, be sure of that!' says I. 'I think of the one thing. I have been alone now this long time in Leyden; and when I was by way of at my studies, still I was thinking of that. Next Alan came, and I went among soldier-men to their big dinners; and still I had the same thought. And it was the same before, when I had her there beside me. Catriona, do you see this napkin at my throat? You cut a corner from it once and then cast it from you. They're *your* colours now; I wear them in my heart. My dear, I cannot be wanting you. O, try to put up with me!'

I stepped before her so as to intercept her walking on.

'Try to put up with me,' I was saying, 'try and bear with me a little.'

Still she had never the word, and a fear began to rise in me like a fear of death.

'Catriona,' I cried, gazing on her hard, 'is it a mistake again? Am I quite lost?'

She raised her face to me, breathless.

'Do you want me, Davie, truly?' said she, and I scarce could hear her say it.

'I do that,' said I. 'O, sure you know it—I do that.'

'I have nothing left to give or to keep back,' said she. 'I was all yours from the first day, if you would have had a gift of me!' she said.

This was on the summit of a brae; the place was windy and conspicuous, we were to be seen there even from the English ship; but I kneeled down before her in the sand, and embraced her knees, and burst into that storm of weeping that I thought it must have broken me. All thought was wholly beaten from my mind by the vehemency of my discomposure. I knew not where I was. I had forgot why I was happy; only I knew she stooped, and I felt her cherish me to her face and bosom, and heard her words out of a whirl.

'Davie,' she was saying, 'O, Davie, is that what you think of me? Is it so that you were caring for poor me? O, Davie, Davie!'

With that she wept also, and our tears were commingled in a perfect gladness.

It might have been ten in the day before I came to a clear sense of what a mercy had befallen me; and sitting over against her, with her hands in mine, gazed in her face, and laughed out loud for pleasure like a child, and called her foolish and kind names. I have never seen the place that looked so pretty as these bents by Dunkirk; and the windmill sails, as they bobbed over the knowe, were like a tune of music.

I know not how much longer we might have continued to forget all else besides ourselves, had I not chanced upon a reference to her father, which brought us to reality.

'My little friend,' I was calling her again and again, rejoicing to summon up the past by the sound of it, and to gaze across on her, and to be a little distant—'My little friend, now you are mine altogether; mine for good, my little friend; and that man's no longer at all.'

There came a sudden whiteness in her face, she plucked her hands from mine.

'Davie, take me away from him!' she cried. 'There's something wrong; he's not true. There will be something wrong; I have a dreadful terror here at my heart. What will he be wanting at all events with that King's ship? What will this word be saying?' And she held the letter forth. 'My mind misgives me, it will be some ill to Alan. Open it, Davie—open it and see.'

I took it, and looked at it, and shook my head.

'No,' said I, 'it goes against me, I cannot open a man's letter.'

'Not to save your friend?' she cried.

'I cannae tell,' said I. 'I think not. If I was only sure!'

'And you have but to break the seal!' said she.

'I know it,' said I, 'but the thing goes against me.'

'Give it here,' said she, 'and I will open it myself.'

'Nor you neither,' said I. 'You least of all. It concerns your father, and his honour, dear, which we are both misdoubting. No question but the place is dangerous-like, and the

English ship being here, and your father having word from it, and yon officer that stayed ashore! He would not be alone either; there must be more along with him; I dare say we are spied upon this minute. Ay, no doubt, the letter should be opened; but somehow, not by you nor me.'

I was about thus far with it, and my spirit very much overcome with a sense of danger and hidden enemies, when I spied Alan, come back again from following James and walking by himself among the sandhills. He was in his soldier's coat, of course, and mighty fine; but I could not avoid to shudder when I thought how little that jacket would avail him, if he were once caught and flung in a skiff, and carried on board of the *Seahorse*, a deserter, a rebel, and now a condemned murderer.

'There,' said I, 'there is the man that has the best right to open it: or not, as he thinks fit.'

With which I called upon his name, and we both stood up to be a mark for him.

'If it is so—if it be more disgrace—will you can bear it?' she asked, looking upon me with a burning eye.

'I was asked something of the same question when I had seen you but the once,' said I. 'What do you think I answered? That if I liked you as I thought I did—and O, but I like you better!—I would marry you at his gallows' foot.'

The blood rose in her face; she came close up and pressed upon me, holding my hand: and it was so that we awaited Alan.

He came with one of his queer smiles. 'What was I telling ye, David?' says he.

'There is a time for all things, Alan,' said I, 'and this time is serious. How have you sped? You can speak out plain before this friend of ours.'

'I have been upon a fool's errand,' said he.

'I doubt we have done better than you, then,' said I; 'and, at least, here is a great deal of matter that you must judge of. Do you see that?' I went on, pointing to the ship. 'That is the *Seahorse*, Captain Palliser.'

'I should ken her, too,' says Alan. 'I had fyke enough with

her when she was stationed in the Forth. But what ails the man to come so close?'

'I will tell you why he came there first,' said I. 'It was to bring this letter to James More. Why he stops here now that it's delivered, what it's likely to be about, why there's an officer hiding in the bents, and whether or not it's probable that he's alone—I would rather you considered for yourself.'

'A letter to James More?' said he.

'The same,' said I.

'Well, and I can tell ye more than that,' said Alan. 'For last night, when you were fast asleep, I heard the man colloguing with some one in the French, and then the door of that inn to be opened and shut.'

'Alan!' cried I, 'you slept all night, and I am here to prove it.'

'Ay, but I would never trust Alan whether he was asleep or waking!' says he. 'But the business looks bad. Let's see the letter.'

I gave it him.

'Catriona,' said he, 'ye'll have to excuse me, my dear; but there's nothing less than my fine bones upon the cast of it, and I'll have to break this seal.'

'It is my wish,' said Catriona.

He opened it, glanced it through, and flung his hand in the air.

'The stinking brock!' says he, and crammed the paper in his pocket. 'Here, let's get our things thegether. This place is fair death to me.' And he began to walk towards the inn.

It was Catriona that spoke the first. 'He has sold you?' she asked.

'Sold me, my dear,' said Alan. 'But thanks to you and Davie, I'll can jink him yet. Just let me win upon my horse!' he added.

'Catriona must come with us,' said I. 'She can have no more traffic with that man. She and I are to be married.' At which she pressed my hand to her side.

'Are ye there with it?' says Alan, looking back. 'The best

day's work that ever either of ye did yet! And I'm bound to say, my dawtie, ye make a real, bonny couple.'

The way that he was following brought us close in by the windmill, where I was aware of a man in seaman's trousers, who seemed to be spying from behind it. Only, of course, we took him in the rear.

'See, Alan!'

'Wheesht!' said he, 'this is my affairs.'

The man was, no doubt, a little deafened by the clattering of the mill, and we got up close before he noticed. Then he turned, and we saw he was a big fellow with a mahogany face.

'I think, sir,' says Alan, 'that you speak the English?'

'Non, *monsieur*,' says he, with an incredible bad accent.

'Non, *monsieur*,' cries Alan, mocking him. 'Is that how they learn you French on the *Seahorse*? Ye muckle gutsey hash, here's a Scots boot to your English hurdies!'

And bounding on him before he could escape, he dealt the man a kick that laid him on his nose. Then he stood, with a savage smile, and watched him scramble to his feet and scamper off into the sandhills.

'But it's high time I was clear of these empty bents!' said Alan; and continued his way at top speed and we still following, to the back door of Bazin's inn.

It chanced that as we entered by the one door we came face to face with James More entering by the other.

'Here!' said I to Catriona, 'quick! upstairs with you and make your packets; this is no fit scene for you.'

In the meanwhile James and Alan had met in the midst of the long room. She passed them close by to reach the stairs; and after she was some way up I saw her turn and glance at them again, though without pausing. Indeed, they were worth looking at. Alan wore as they met one of the best appearances of courtesy and friendliness, yet with something eminently warlike, so that James smelled danger off the man, as folk smell fire in a house, and stood prepared for accidents.

Time pressed. Alan's situation in that solitary place, and his enemies about him, might have daunted Cæsar. It made no change in him; and it was in his old spirit of mockery and daffing that he began the interview.

'A braw good day to ye again, Mr. Drummond,' said he. 'What'll yon business of yours be just about?'

'Why, the thing being private, and rather of a long story,' says James, 'I think it will keep very well till we have eaten.'

'I'm none so sure of that,' said Alan. 'It sticks in my mind it's either now or never; for the fact is me and Mr. Balfour here have gotten a line, and we're thinking of the road.'

I saw a little surprise in James's eye; but he held himself stoutly.

'I have but the one word to say to cure you of that,' said he, 'and that is the name of my business.'

'Say it then,' says Alan. 'Hout! wha minds for Davie?'

'It is a matter that would make us both rich men,' said James.

'Do ye tell me that?' cries Alan.

'I do sir,' said James. 'The plain fact is that it is Cluny's Treasure.'

'No!' cried Alan. 'Have ye got word of it?'

'I ken the place, Mr. Stewart, and can take you there,' said James.

'This crowns all!' says Alan. 'Well, and I'm glad I came to Dunkirk. And so this was your business, was it? Halvers, I'm thinking?'

'That is the business, sir,' said James.

'Well, well,' says Alan; and then in the same tone of child-like interest, 'it has naething to do with the *Seahorse*, then?' he asked.

'With what?' says James.

'Or the lad that I have just kicked the bottom of behind yon windmill?' pursued Alan. 'Hut, man! have done with your lees! I have Palliser's letter here in my pouch. You're by with it, James More. You can never show your face again with dacent folk.'

James was taken all aback with it. He stood a second, motionless and white, then swelled with the living anger.

'Do you talk to me, you bastard?' he roared out.

'Ye glee'd swine!' cried Alan, and hit him a sounding buffet on the mouth, and the next wink of time their blades clashed together.

At the first sound of the bare steel I instinctively leaped back from the collision. The next I saw, James parried a thrust so nearly that I thought him killed; and it lowed up in my mind that this was the girl's father, and in a manner almost my own, and I drew and ran in to sever them.

'Keep back, Davie! Are ye daft? Damn ye, keep back!' roared Alan. 'Your blood be on your ain heid then!'

I beat their blades down twice. I was knocked reeling against the wall; I was back again betwixt them. They took no heed of me, thrusting at each other like two furies. I can never think how I avoided being stabbed myself or stabbing one of these two Rodomonts, and the whole business turned about me like a piece of a dream; in the midst of which I heard a great cry from the stair, and Catriona sprang before her father. In the same moment the point of my sword encountered something yielding. It came back to me reddened. I saw the blood flow on the girl's kerchief, and stood sick.

'Will you be killing him before my eyes, and me his daughter after all?' she cried.

'My dear, I have done with him,' said Alan, and went and sat on a table, with his arms crossed and the sword naked in his hand.

Awhile she stood before the man, panting, with big eyes, then swung suddenly about and faced him.

'Begone!' was her word, 'take your shame out of my sight; leave me with clean folk. I am a daughter of Alpin! Shame of the sons of Alpin, begone!'

It was said with so much passion as awoke me from the horror of my own bloodied sword. The two stood facing, she with the red stain on her kerchief, he white as a rag. I knew him well enough—I knew it must have pierced him in the quick place of his soul; but he betook himself to a bravado air.

'Why,' says he, sheathing his sword, though still with a

bright eye on Alan, 'if this brawl is over I will but get my portmanteau——'

'There goes no pockmantie out of this place except with me,' says Alan.

'Sir!' cries James.

'James More,' says Alan, 'this lady daughter of yours is to marry my friend Davie, upon the which account I let you pack with a hale carcase. But take you my advice of it and get that carcase out of harm's way or ower late. Little as you suppose it, there are leemits to my temper.'

'Be damned, sir, but my money's there!' said James.

'I'm vexed about that, too,' says Alan, with his funny face, 'but now, ye see, it's mine's.' And then with more gravity, 'Be you advised, James More, you leave this house.'

James seemed to cast about for a moment in his mind; but it's to be thought he had enough of Alan's swordmanship, for he suddenly put off his hat to us and (with a face like one of the damned) bade us farewell in a series. With which he was gone.

At the same time a spell was lifted from me.

'Catriona,' I cried, 'it was me—it was my sword. O, are ye much hurt?'

'I know it, Davie, I am loving you for the pain of it; it was done defending that bad man, my father. See!' she said, and showed me a bleeding scratch, 'see, you have made a man of me now. I will carry a wound like an old soldier.'

Joy that she should be so little hurt, and the love of her brave nature, transported me. I embraced her, I kissed the wound.

'And am I to be out of the kissing, me that never lost a chance?' says Alan; and putting me aside and taking Catriona by either shoulder, 'My dear,' he said, 'you're a true daughter of Alpin. By all accounts, he was a very fine man, and he may weel be proud of you. If ever I was to get married, it's the marrow of you I would be seeking for a mother to my sons. And I bear a king's name and speak the truth.'

He said it with a serious heat of admiration that was honey to the girl, and through her, to me. It seemed to wipe us clean of all Jame's More's disgraces. And the next moment he was just himself again.

'And now by your leave, my dawties,' said he, 'this is a' very bonny; but Alan Breck'll be a wee thing nearer to the gallows than he's caring for; and Dod! I think this is a grand place to be leaving.'

The word recalled us to some wisdom. Alan ran upstairs and returned with our saddle-bags and James More's portmanteau; I picked up Catriona's bundle where she had dropped it on the stair; and we were setting forth out of that dangerous house, when Bazin stopped the way with cries and gesticulations. He had whipped under a table when the swords were drawn, but now he was as bold as a lion. There was his bill to be settled, there was a chair broken, Alan had sat among his dinner things, James More had fled.

'Here,' I cried, 'pay yourself,' and flung him down some Lewie d'ors; for I thought it was no time to be accounting.

He sprang upon that money, and we passed him by, and ran forth into the open. Upon three sides of the house were seamen hasting and closing in; a little nearer to us James More waved his hat as if to hurry them; and right behind him, like some foolish person holding up his hands, were the sails of the windmill turning.

Alan gave but the one glance, and laid himself down to run. He carried a great weight in James More's portmanteau; but I think he would as soon have lost his life as cast away that booty which was his revenge; and he ran so that I was distressed to follow him, and marvelled and exulted to see the girl bounding at my side.

As soon as we appeared, they cast off all disguise upon the other side; and the seamen pursued us with shouts and view-hullohs. We had a start of some two hundred yards, and they were but bandy-legged tarpaulins after all, that could not hope to better us at such an exercise. I suppose they were armed, but did not care to use their pistols on French ground. And as soon as I perceived that we not only held our advantage but drew a little away, I began to feel quite easy of the issue. For all which, it was a hot, brisk bit of work, so long as it lasted; Dunkirk was still far off; and when we popped over a knowe, and found a company of the garrison marching on the other side on some manœuvre, I could very well understand the word that Alan had.

He stopped running at once; and mopping at his brow. 'They're a real bonny folk, the French nation,' says he.

CONCLUSION

No sooner were we safe within the walls of Dunkirk than we held a very necessary council-of-war on our position. We had taken a daughter from her father at the sword's point; any judge would give her back to him at once, and by all likelihood clap me and Alan into jail; and though we had an argument upon our side in Captain Palliser's letter, neither Catriona nor I were very keen to be using it in public. Upon all accounts it seemed the most prudent to carry the girl to Paris to the hands of her own chieftain, Macgregor of Bohaldie, who would be very willing to help his kinswoman, on the one hand, and not at all anxious to dishonour James upon the other.

We made but a slow journey of it up, for Catriona was not so good at the riding as the running, and had scarce sat in the saddle since the 'Forty-five. But we made it out at last, reached Paris early of a Sabbath morning, and made all speed, under Alan's guidance, to find Bohaldie. He was finely lodged, and lived in a good style, having a pension on the Scots Fund, as well as private means; greeted Catriona like one of his own house, and seemed altogether very civil and discreet, but not particularly open. We asked of the news of James More. 'Poor James!' said he, and shook his head and smiled, so that I thought he knew further than he meant to tell. Then we showed him Palliser's letter, and he drew a long face at that.

'Poor James!' said he again. 'Well, there are worse folk than James More, too. But this is dreadful bad. Tut, tut, he must have forgot himself entirely! This is a most undesirable letter. But, for all that, gentlemen, I cannot see what we would want to make it public for. It's an ill bird that fouls his own nest, and we are all Scots folk and all Hieland.'

Upon this we were all agreed, save perhaps Alan; and still more upon the question of our marriage, which Bohaldie took in his own hands, as though there had been no such person as James More, and gave Catriona away with very pretty manners and agreeable compliments in French. It was not till all was over, and our healths drunk, that he told us James was in that city, whither he had preceded us some days, and where he now lay sick, and like to die. I thought I saw by my wife's face what way her inclination pointed.

'And let us go see him, then,' said I.

'If it is your pleasure,' said Catriona. These were early days.

He was lodged in the same quarter of the city with his chief, in a great house upon a corner; and we were guided up to the garret where he lay by the sound of Highland piping. It seemed he had just borrowed a set of them from Bohaldie to amuse his sickness; though he was no such hand as was his brother Rob, he made good music of the kind; and it was strange to observe the French folk crowding on the stairs, and some of them laughing. He lay propped in a pallet. The first look of him I saw he was upon his last business; and, doubtless, this was a strange place for him to die in. But even now I find I can scarce dwell upon his end with patience. Doubtless, Bohaldie had prepared him; he seemed to know we were married, complimented us on the event, and gave us a benediction like a patriarch.

'I have been never understood,' said he. 'I forgive you both without an afterthought'; after which he spoke for all the world in his old manner, was so obliging as to play us a tune or two upon his pipes, and borrowed a small sum before I left. I could not trace even a hint of shame in any part of his behaviour; but he was great upon forgiveness; it seemed always fresh to him. I think he forgave me every time we met; and when after some four days he passed away in a kind of odour of affectionate sanctity, I could have torn my hair out for exasperation. I had him buried; but what to put upon his tomb was quite beyond me, till at last I considered the date would look best alone.

I thought it wiser to resign all thoughts of Leyden, where we had appeared once as brother and sister, and it would certainly look strange to return in a new character. Scotland would be doing for us; and thither, after I had recovered that which I had left behind, we sailed in a Low Country ship.

And now, Miss Barbara Balfour (to set the ladies first), and Mr. Alan Balfour, younger of Shaws, here is the story brought fairly to an end. A great many of the folk that took a part in it, you will find (if you think well) that you have seen and spoken with. Alison Hastie in Limekilns was the lass that rocked your cradle when you were too small to know of it, and walked abroad with you in the policy when you were bigger. That very fine great lady that is Miss Barbara's name-mamma is no other than the same Miss Grant that made so much a fool of David Balfour in the house of the Lord Advocate. And I wonder whether you remember a little, lean, lively gentleman in a scratch wig and a wraprascal, that came to Shaws very late of a dark night, and whom you were awakened out of your beds and brought down to the dining-hall to be presented to, by the name of Mr. Jamieson? Or has Alan forgotten what he did at Mr. Jamieson's request—a most disloyal act—for which, by the letter of the law, he might be hanged—no less than drinking the king's health *across the water*? These were strange doings in a good Whig house! But Mr. Jamieson is a man privileged, and might set fire to my corn-barn; and the name they know him by now in France is the Chevalier Stewart.

As for Davie and Catriona, I shall watch you pretty close in the next days, and see if you are so bold as to be laughing at papa and mamma. It is true we were not so wise as we might have been, and made a great deal of sorrow out of nothing; but you will find as you grow up that even the artful Miss Barbara, and even the valiant Mr. Alan, will be not so very much wiser than their parents. For the life of man upon this world of ours is a funny business. They talk of the angels weeping; but I think they must more often be holding their sides, as they look on; and there was one thing I determined to do when I began this long story, and that was to tell out everything as it befell.

THE END

EXPLANATORY NOTES

Volume numbers of Stevenson's works and letters refer to *The Works of Robert Louis Stevenson*, Swanston Edition (1912).

EE: Edinburgh Edition (1894–8).

Hersey: F. W. C. Hersey (ed.), *Robert Louis Stevenson's 'Kidnapped'. Followed by 'Who Killed the Red Fox?'* (Boston, 1938).

Maixner: *Robert Louis Stevenson: The Critical Heritage*, ed. Paul Maixner (1981).

Swearingen: Roger G. Swearingen, *The Prose Writings of Robert Louis Stevenson: A Guide* (1981).

KIDNAPPED

title page: *David Balfour*: Stevenson employed his mother's maiden name (she was born Margaret Balfour) for his hero. He also, as he told J. M. Barrie, deliberately gave David 'a Gaelic name' (*Letters*, XXV, 155).

xli *in Alan's favour*: for further information about the Appin Murder and the mystery of who killed Colin Campbell of Glenure see Hersey, and also David N. Mackay, *The Trial of James Stewart* (Edinburgh, 1907).

xlii *the old Speculative*: a students' debating society at Edinburgh University, founded in 1764, of which R.L.S. was a noted member. He comments further on the society in 'A College Magazine', *Memories and Portraits* (1887), IX, 36–45.

Robert Emmet: an Irish patriot who led an insurrection in Ireland in 1803.

Macbean: William Macbean was the librarian of the Speculative 1840–1 and its secretary 1841–2.

L.J.R.: Sidney Colvin comments in a note to a letter of September 1872: 'The L.J.R. herein mentioned was a short-lived Essay Club of only six members; its meetings were held in a public-house in Advocate's Close; the meaning of its initials (as recently divulged by Mr. Baxter) was Liberty, Justice, Reverence; no doubt understood by the members in some fresh esoteric sense of their own' [*Letters*, XXIII, 46]. R.L.S.'s father strongly disapproved of this Club's doctrines and was especially concerned about his son's agnosticism.

5 *To Make Lilly of the Valley Water*: Fanny Stevenson had found this recipe in an old cookery book: see her account in 'Prefatory Note', Tusitala Edition, VI, x.

the city of Edinburgh smoking like a kiln: the city of Edinburgh fascinated R.L.S. throughout his life, and he wrote a series of essays about it in *Edinburgh: Picturesque Notes* (1879).

8 *black be their fall!*: Janet Clouston's speech and its effects, deriving in part from R.L.S.'s use of Scots, can be compared with Auld Merren's in *Catriona*, p. 234.

wonderfully ... store by: this passage is omitted in EE.

18 *Patrick Walker*: a well-known, seventeenth-century merchant and pedlar who wrote biographies of many of the great men of his day.

27 *For it's my delight ... of the year*: the lines come from 'The Lincolnshire Poacher'.

The Hawes Inn: this inn partly provided the inspiration for *Kidnapped*. Writing of the importance of places that 'speak distinctly' to the author, Stevenson commented:

The old 'Hawes Inn' at the Queen's Ferry makes a similar call upon my fancy. There it stands, apart from the town, beside the pier, in a climate of its own, half inland, half marine – in front, the ferry bubbling with the tide and the guardship swinging to her anchor; behind, the old garden with the trees. Americans seek it already for the sake of Lovel and Oldbuck, who dined there at the beginning of 'The Antiquary'. But you need not tell me – that is not all; there is some story, unrecorded or not yet complete, which must express the meaning of that inn more fully ['A Gossip on Romance', IX, 137].

34 *and if he but knew how to ride*: omitted in EE.

44 *twelve o'clock*: first impressions of the First Edition read 'nine o'clock', which R.L.S. amended later, in 1886, to 'twelve o'clock'; EE amends this again to 'eleven o'clock'.

50 *belted with a great sword*: the description of Alan Breck can be compared with the advertisement which appeared in the *Edinburgh Evening Courant* on 28 May 1752:

The person suspected of the murder is one Allan Breck Stewart, a French cadet, who was in Appin at the time. He is about 5 feet 10 inches high; his face much marked with the small Pox, black bushy hair put up in a bag, a little in-knee'd, round shouldered, has full black eyes, and is about 30 years of age. He is dressed much like a French cadet, shabby with an inclination to be genteel [Hersey, p. 418].

55 *Alan Breck*: foster brother of James of the Glens (see note to p. 68). Alan Breck travelled back and forth to France as rent collector for his chief Ardshiel, who had forfeited his estates after the 'Forty-five'.

57 *The Siege of the Roundhouse*: Henry James commented on this section: 'There could be no better instance of the author's talent for seeing the actual in the marvellous, and reducing the extravagant to plausible detail, than the description of Alan Breck's defence in the cabin of the ship' (*Henry James and Robert Louis Stevenson*, ed. J. Adam Smith (1948), p. 158). For further contemporary critical comments on the novel, see Maixner, pp. 232–48.

63 *as a very wise man once told me*: omitted in EE.

64 *biscuit*: EE reads 'bread'.

68 *The 'Red Fox'*: Colin Campbell of Glenure (1708–52). In 1748 he was appointed factor of the forfeited lands belonging to the Stewarts and the Camerons. These included Glenduror, the farm of which James Stewart (James of the Glens) was tenant. Following a quarrel with James, Glenure gave notice to quit to many of his Stewart tenants; on the way to carry out the evictions on 14 May 1752 he was shot. The identity of his killer remains uncertain, but see Hersey, p. 378f.

71 *Prestonpans*: Charles Edward, the Young Pretender, sailed for Scotland from France on 12 July 1745. He entered Edinburgh and defeated General Cope at Prestonpans on 21 September.

73 *Culloden*: the Jacobite forces were finally defeated at Culloden on 16 April 1746. See William Ferguson, *Scotland 1689 to the Present* (Edinburgh, 1968), pp. 152–3.

78 *Torran Rocks*: a very dangerous reef off the west coast of Scotland. See also R.L.S.'s short story, 'The Merry Men' (1882).

and two of these were hurt: omitted in EE.

82 *The Islet*: R.L.S. had visited this area and describes his youth-

ful experiences there in 'Memoirs of an Islet', IX, 61–7.

86 *his flight from Worcester*: Charles II was defeated by Cromwell at Worcester on 3 September 1651. He lived for six weeks as a fugitive and then sailed for France.

100 *'Lochaber no more'*: a Scots song attributed to Allan Ramsay (see note to p. 251).

101 *Henderland*: Thomas Stevenson had suggested the inclusion of such a character and scene. R.L.S. wrote to him on 25 January 1886:

> I quite agree with you, and had already planned a scene of religion in *Balfour*; the Society for the Propagation of Christian Knowledge furnishes me with a catechist whom I shall try to make the man. I have another catechist, the blind, pistol-carrying highway robber, whom I have transferred from the Long Island to Mull [*Letters*, XXIV, 179].

See also Swearingen, p. 104.

102 *the Disarming Act*: this was first passed in 1716 and imposed fines on those possessing arms, whilst a further act of 1725 made legal the search for a seizure of weapons.

106 *ferny howes*: the EE reading has been used here and not the First Edition's phrase 'ferny dells': on 17 July 1886, R.L.S. wrote in reply to a suggestion made by Edmund Gosse: 'You are right about "ferny dells" . . . damn, it's like Claribel's po'try. I shall change it to ferny howes, which would be unexceptionable' (Swearingen, p. 105).

120 *your ain French clothes*: EE adds 'We'll be to bury them, I believe.'

126 *Glencoe*: MacDonald of Glencoe failed to appear on 1 January 1692 to offer allegiance to King William. His clan was massacred at Glencoe on 13 February. See Ferguson, op. cit., pp. 23–4.

131 *nor yet altogether with the English grammar*: there are signs in the narrative passages, as well as in the dialogue, that David retains his Scots. For instance, he uses the following Scots words and Scotticisms in the narrative: *brae* (hill), *buckies* (periwinkles), *cushat-doves* (wood pigeons), *forenoon* (morning), *howe* (hollow), *lynn* (landing place), *my life in my hand*, *pitifullest*, *thole* (suffer), and *up the stair* (Standard English: *up the stairs*, cf. *my life in my hand*). For further

information on the grammatical differences between Scots and English see William Grant and James Main Dixon, *A Manual of Modern Scots* (Cambridge, 1921).

136 *crosstarrie*: the fiery cross. Walter Scott includes an interesting note on the Highlanders' 'Oath upon the Dirk' in this connection in *Waverley*. See *Waverley*, ed. Andrew Hook (1972), pp. 513–15.

147 *Cluny Macpherson*: Ewen Macpherson of Cluny (d. 1756), joined the Jacobites in 1745. He helped the Young Pretender to escape and later also went to France. His 'Cage' was a refuge made of trees and brushwood on the side of Ben Alder.

163 *Hey, Johnnie Cope, . . .*: a very popular Jacobite song, usually attributed to Adam Skirving (1719–1803). A version of the song is found in Burns's *Poems* (1790).

Do you know that you insult me? Mildred Wilsey points out that this is the only occasion in the MS on which Alan's speech is amended to become more anglicized (*ye* and *ye ken* are amended to *you* and *you know*). She comments: 'As a result the tension is greatly heightened, and the tone is sick with an unnatural formality' ('*Kidnapped* in Manuscript', *The American Scholar*, New York, XVII, 218 (Spring 1948)).

166 *clan of the Macgregors*: the most famous member of this clan was the noted Jacobite Rob Roy. In 1693 an Act made the name illegal (hence R.L.S.'s reference to the clan being 'nameless'), and Rob used his mother's name of Campbell. The family had a farm in Balquidder and Rob worked as a cattle dealer as well as involving himself in blackmail and a number of other illegal activities. He was arrested more than once and his escapes have become part of Scots historical tradition. In 1726 he was imprisoned in Newgate and just saved from transportation by a pardon.

Walter Scott made him the hero of his novel *Rob Roy* (1817), and an account of his life and clan appears in the 'Author's Introduction' to that novel (*Rob Roy*, Preface and Glossary by W. M. Parker (1962), p. 385f.).

168 *Robin Oig*: one of Rob Roy's sons; he abducted Jean Kay, a rich widow from Edinburgh, and married her. He was condemned to death for this, as was his brother James More (or Mhor). Robin was hanged in 1754 but James escaped from Edinburgh Castle. See *Catriona*, pp. 362–3, and note.

170 *a Macrimmon*: the Macrimmons were the hereditary pipers for MacLeod of Sky.

173 *the Highland Line*: the name for an imaginary boundary between the Highlands and Lowlands of Scotland and thus between the Gaelic-speaking clans and the Lowlanders. The line is drawn approximately from Dumbarton to Ballater and thence to Nairn (Mairi Robinson (ed.), *The Concise Scots Dictionary* (Aberdeen, 1985)).

It was the last . . . in a manner history: this paragraph was deleted in EE. At the time of Robin's death, according to *Catriona*, David was back in Scotland and not in Leyden.

179 *'Charlie is my darling'*: another famous Jacobite song (cf. note to p. 163). It is included in James Hogg, *The Jacobite Relics of Scotland* (Edinburgh, 1821), II, 93.

181 *only me and God*: Alan's Scots increases markedly here as he intensifies his pleas to Alison.

185 *Nec gemino bellum Trojanum orditur ab ovo*: Nor does the Trojan War begin from the twin eggs (Horace, *De Arte Poetica*, 147). The 'twin eggs' refer to the offspring of Leda from her union with Zeus: Helen, and Castor and Pollux. Mr. Rankeillor uses this quotation to encourage David to tell his story without unnecessary amplification, and without going back to the very beginning of his history.

186 *1734*: EE reads '1733'.

187 *Fui, non sum*: I was, but I am not now.

imberbis juvenis custode remoto: a beardless youth free from his guardian (Horace, *De Arte Poetica*, 161).

190 *quae regio in terris*: the full quotation is '*Quae regio in terris nostri non plena laboris?*' (What region of the world is not full of our labour?) (Virgil, *Aeneid*, I, 460).

190 *paribus curis vestigia figit*: the full quotation is '*Cui fidus Achates it comes, et paribus curis vestigia figit*' (Beside him the faithful Achates goes as a companion and sets his footsteps with equal care) (Virgil, *Aeneid*, VI, 158).

191 *Odi te, qui bellus es, Sabelle*: I hate you, O Sabellus, because you are good looking (Martial, XII, Epigram 39).

multum gementem: groaning much, loudly complaining.

majora canamus: let us sing of greater things (Virgil, *Eclogues*, V, 1).

192 *dignus vindice nodus*: the full quotation is '*Nec deus intersit, nisi dignus vindice nodus*' (A god should not interfere unless there is a situation worthy of his intervention) (Horace, *De Arte Poetica*, 191).

193 *Mr. Thomson*: in the First Edition this was misprinted 'Johnson': the EE reading is therefore used here.

195 *put out of countenance*: First Edition misprints this 'put of countenance'.

205 *timeo qui nocuere deos*: I fear the Gods who have harmed me (Ovid, *Tristia* I, 74).

206 *Mr. Balfour of Pilrig*: Stevenson's great-great grandfather on his mother's side of the family.

Lord Advocate Grant: refers to the Crown Prosecutor in Scotland; see also note to *Catriona*, p. 217.

208 *Just there . . . to themselves*: his passage, included in square brackets as in the First Edition, was deleted in EE. See also Introduction, p. ix.

CATRIONA

215 *The tall, black city*: Stevenson immediately introduces *Catriona* as a novel that is much more concerned with city experience than *Kidnapped*. See Introduction, p. xxi.

217 *William Grant Esquire of Prestongrange*: William Grant (?1701–64), appointed Lord Advocate in 1746 and Lord of Session in 1754.

220 *the name of the Macgregors*: see note to *Kidnapped*, p. 166.

221 *ta sneeshin*: Neil here speaks the kind of conventional Gaelic-ized English common in nineteenth-century Scots fiction. See note p. 275 and cf. p. 336.

230 *Act of 1736: recruiting for King Lewie*: Act forbidding the recruiting of men for the French Jacobite regiments. The Young Pretender later took refuge with Louis XV.

234 *spae it to ye bonny*: Auld Merren employs a broader variety of Scots speech than R.L.S.'s characters habitually use in this novel. Her language recalls Janet Clouston's in *Kidnapped*, pp. 7–8, and looks forward to the 'Tale of Tod Lapraik', pp. 328–35.

245 *Salus populi suprema lex*: The welfare of the people is the first great law (Cicero, *De Legibus*, III, 3, 8).

   a man who might be your father: R.L.S. insists on this link between David and Prestongrange (cf. pp. 273, 356, 365). The father–son relationship fascinated him throughout his literary career. Some biographical light is cast on this matter by the recently published *Edifying Letters of the Rutherford Family* (written in the 1870s) in *An Old Song and Edifying Letters of the Rutherford Family*, ed. Roger G. Swearingen (1982). One of the most interesting treatments of the theme is in *Weir of Hermiston* (posthumously published in 1896).

246 *Cumberland came upon Drummossie*: William Augustus, Duke of Cumberland (1721–65), third son of George II, commanded the army which defeated the Jacobites at Culloden. The site of this battle is on Drummossie Moor.

   Lord President Culloden: Duncan Forbes (1685–1747) was a lawyer and Laird of Culloden from 1734. In the period of the 'Forty-five he persuaded many members of the Northern clans not to join the Jacobites. Prestongrange here sees himself as dealing with a similarly delicate situation.

251 *Alan Ramsay's answer*: Allan Ramsay (1686–1758), a Scottish poet, who contributed poems to a Jacobite Association, the 'Easy Club' (1712–15). He is best known for *The Gentle Shepherd* (first part, 1720) and *The Tea Table Miscellany*. David here alludes to his poem, 'Spoken to Three Young Ladies, who would have me determine which of them was the bonniest'. The poet's 'answer' was:

   Shaw, a' your charms, and then ha'e wi' ye,
   Faith I shall be your Paris
   [*Poems* (Glasgow, 1797), I, 173].

253 *Dauvit Balfour*: Barbara Grant habitually uses Scots forms (and pronunciation features) when talking to or about David as a mark of her affectionate mockery of his lack of social ease, cf. pp. 339, 362–3.

255 *chief of the great clan Fraser*: son of Simon Fraser, 11th Lord Lovat, a noted Jacobite who was executed in 1747. *Catriona's* Simon Fraser (1726–82), Master of Lovat, led his clan in support of the Young Pretender in 1745 when he was taken prisoner. He was, however, pardoned in 1750 and in 1752 he acted as advocate for the widow of Colin Campbell of Glenure. His family's estates were restored in 1771.

256 *experto crede*: believe in him who has experience. Cf. *experto credite* (Virgil, *Aeneid*, 11, 283).

269 *I cannae bear it else*: here David intensifies his Scots in order to plead with Catriona, cf. his use of Scots forms in *Kidnapped*, at the end of his quarrel with Alan, pp. 164–6, and Alan's own pleading Scots used to Alison Hastie, pp. 180–1 and note.

275 *Palfour*: Lt. Duncansby has a number of Gaelicized-English features in his speech in this section, including *Cot* (God), *Palfour* (Balfour), *plows* (blows), *pog* (bog), *Tamn* (damn), *tit* (did) etc. For a discussion of this pseudo-dialect see Mairi Robinson, 'Modern Literary Scots: Ferguson and After', *Lowland Scots: Papers Presented to an Edinburgh Conference*, ed. A. J. Aitken (Edinburgh, 1973).

280 *Rob Roy*: see note to *Kidnapped*, p. 166.

283 *the Act of Parliament of 1700*: in Scotland the Act Anent Wrangous Imprisonment, the equivalent of the English Habeas Corpus, was passed in 1701.

285 *sumptibus moesti rei*: at the expense of the unhappy defendant.

Lady Grange: R.L.S. makes several references to her in his novel (cf. pp. 314, 347). Rachel Grange was the wife of James Erskine (1679–1754), brother of the Earl of Mar and Justice-Clerk from 1710. In order to prevent his wife from disclosing his Jacobite plotting, Erskine kept her imprisoned on the remote island of St. Kilda for seven years from 1732. In 1734 he became an MP, and he was also Secretary to Frederick, Prince of Wales.

Boswell comments:

The true story of this lady, which happened in this century, is as frightfully romantick as if it had been the fiction of a gloomy fancy . . . she was transported by sea to the remote rock of St. Kilda, where she remained, amongst its few wild inhabitants, a forlorn prisoner. . . No inquiry was made after her, till she at last found means to convey a letter to a confidential friend, by the daughter of a Catechist, who concealed it in a clue of yarn. Information being thus obtained at Edinburgh, a ship was sent to bring her off; but intelligence of this being received, she was conveyed to M'Leod's island of Herries, where she died [Johnson and Boswell, *A Journey to the Western Islands of Scotland* and *The Journal of A Tour to the Hebrides*, ed. R. W. Chapman (1924), p. 312].

289 *Lot's wife*: Genesis xix. She looked back at Sodom and Gomorrah and was turned into a pillar of salt.

290 *Catherine Douglas*: popular tradition remembers her for her brave efforts to defend James I from his murderers; she thrust her arm through the broken staples of the bolts securing the door to his room.

291 *the Macedonian*: Catriona's history is shaky here; she refers to their forefathers fighting against Rome and Alexander the Great ('the Macedonian'), whereas Alexander the Great had no connection with Rome or with any campaigns in Western Europe. David forbears to point out this error.

314 *like Lady Grange*: see note to p. 285. R.L.S. significantly places this reference shortly before David is removed to the Bass Rock, where like Lady Grange he waits either to be rescued or to escape.

318 *Tantallon*: a fourteenth-century castle in East Lothian, with later additions and alterations, associated with the first Earl of Douglas. It fell to the Earl of Angus, was beseiged by James IV in 1491, and again by James V in 1528. In 1639 it was occupied by the Covenanters.

319 *Just to the Bass, mannie*: the Bass is a rock at the entrance to the Firth of Forth. It has always been known as a bird sanctuary and especially as a breeding place for gannets. James I waited on the Bass for the ship that was to take him to France (cf. David's situation in *Catriona*, and see Introduction, pp. xxii–xxiii). The rock was also the site of the hermitage of St. Baldred. In the seventeenth century it was used as a prison for the Covenanters; in 1691, four Jacobites who were confined there overcame their guards and held the rock until 1694.

326 *Black Andie's Tale of Tod Lapraik*: this tale of possession, told in broad Scots, can be compared with 'Wandering Willie's Tale' in Walter Scott's *Redgauntlet* (1824).

   R.L.S. was particularly anxious to guard his Scots against editorial interference here; and he comments on this in a letter to Sidney Colvin from Vailima in 1893. He resists, in particular, the suggestion that he should include notes on the Scots words: 'I'd have to put a note to every word; and he who can't read Scots can *never* enjoy Tod Lapraik' (*Letters*, XXV, 294–6).

In view of R.L.S.'s dislike of extensive footnote glossing, meanings of the Scots words in this tale are included in the Glossary at the end of this edition.

329 *Prophet Peden*: Alexander Peden (1626–86), a minister who was deprived of his living during the Covenanting period in 1662. Thereafter he preached at conventicles; in 1673 he was imprisoned on the Bass.

338 *upon Isle Earraid only*: cf. *Kidnapped*, p. 82f., and note to p. 82.

340 *In vain is the net spread in the sight of any fowl*: Proverbs, I, 17.

344 *Romans 5th and 13th*: these texts deal with God's law; their presence at this point in the narrative makes an ironic comment on the conduct of man's law in the trial of James of the Glens.

347 *the matter of the Lady Grange*: again, the reference to Lady Grange is significantly placed just after David's confinement on the Bass Rock and emphasizes the anomalous way his evidence has been suppressed.

350 *occasion to the late Queen to call this country barbarous*: this refers to Caroline of Anspach, Queen Consort of George II, and the Porteous Riots of 1736. Walter Scott deals with these riots in the early chapters of *The Heart of Midlothian* (1818).

357 *The House of Airlie*, originally a well-known Scots ballad about the House of Airlie and its destruction by the Earl of Argyll in 1640. See Introduction, pp. xxiv–xxv, for a discussion of the ways songs intervene in the narrative at this point.

362 *as he runs off*: whilst his brother, Robin Oig, was hanged (for the abduction of Jean Kay), James More (or Mhor) escaped from Edinburgh Castle with the help of his daughter, who gained entrance to the castle disguised as a cobbler and gave these clothes to her father.

367 *an accent much more countrified . . . to affect*: David is here caught in an ungenteel linguistic posture (which he associates with his former, unrefined self). R.L.S. commented to Sidney Colvin that this is one instance on which David is 'attracted into a similar dialect' as Doig (*Letters*, XXV, 294).

377 *much as I have since carried out in fact*: David reveals himself here as an established eighteenth-century landowner.

'Mr. Betwixt and Between' of *Kidnapped* has, to some extent, settled for his Whiggish self. Further signs of this development in his character are seen in his legal ambitions when he is at Inverary (p. 350), and in his renouncing of dangerous political involvement (p. 383).

387 *Barbara Grant*: Barbara uses Scots in her letters here and on pp. 362–3 as a mark of her affection towards and gentle mockery of David. This is one written document that causes much trouble in the romantic plot of the novel, see Introduction, pp. xxv.

405 *Where am I taking you indeed?*: in this passage the language disparities differentiate the 'uneven pair': the heroine employs the pseudo-Highland English forms, asking 'Where will you be taking me?', whilst David corrects her in his Standard English reply.

   By 1893, the year that *Catriona* was published, reviewers had become a little tired of this picturesque Highland English: 'Her [Catriona's] forms of speech remind us, rather irritatingly, of those which Mr. Black has put into the mouth of so many young men and maidens that, pleasantly exotic at first, they have at last become wofully hackneyed' (*The Saturday Review*, LXXVI, 333, 16 September 1893).

413 *Heineccius*: Johann Gottlieb Heineccius (1681–1741) was a German jurist, appointed Professor of Philosophy at Halle University in 1713 and Professor of Jurisprudence in 1718. He belonged to the school of philosophical jurists who considered law as a rational science rather than an empirical art. His work is appropriate reading for David at this point in his personal history as he uses Heineccius's book as a means of trying, through reason, to control his passion for the heroine.

438 *a near friend*: 'friend' in the Scots sense is the equivalent of the Standard English 'relation'. James More is one of R.L.S.'s characters, comparable with James Durie, in *The Master of Ballantrae* (1889), who uses his Scots voice as part of his villainy and his efforts at dissembling, cf. p. 440.

452 *Lord Holderness*: a diplomat and politician (?1718–78), Holderness represented Britain at the Hague 1749–51 and was Secretary of State 1751–61. James More is presumably going

to see him to make his ignominious peace with the English Government.

455 *Gladsmuir*: the place where the battle of Prestonpans was fought in September 1745.

GLOSSARY

Note: this glossary has been compiled from the *Scottish National Dictionary* and the *Concise Scots Dictionary*, and includes words not glossed by R.L.S. in the text; it also includes words used more than once by R.L.S. but only glossed on a single occasion.

a', all
ae, one
aefauld, honest
aff, off
aheid, ahead
ahint, behind
ahinthand, late
ain, own
aince, ance, once
airn, iron
ajee, awry
amnae, am not
ane, one
anent, about, concerning
anither, another
argle-bargled, argued, wrangled
assoiled, decided in favour of, acquitted (Sc. law)
auld, old
aumry, cupboard
ava', at all
awa, away
awaur, aware
aweel, ah well
awing, owing
ay, aye, yes, always
ayont, beyond

bairn, child
baith, both
bane, bone

baubee, small coin, halfpenny
baubeejoes, street-walkers
bauchle, botch, muddle
bauks, ridges (often unploughed)
begowk, make a fool of
belanged, belonged
bents, sandy hillock
bield, shelter, house
birkies, lively fellows
birling, drinking
birstle, toast, roast, burn
birzing, fraying, putting a bristle on (e.g. a rope)
bitch, term of contempt, used of a man
bizz, bustle, commotion
blae, bluish grey, cold
bluid(y), blood(y)
bodle, small coin, two pence Scots
bogle, ghost, spirit, phantom
bottle, bundle (e.g. of hay)
bouman, tenant who takes stock from a landlord and shares profit with him; also man who has charge of cattle on a farm
bourock, mound
brae, hill
braw, brawly, good, fine, well
bree, brow, face, countenance
breeks, trousers

brock, contemptuous name for a person

broucht, brought

bruckle, brittle, delicate, fragile

brunt, burnt

buckie, perverse person

bullering, bubbling, gurgling

but, kitchen, or outer room

byke, bees', wasps' or ants' nest

by-ordinar, extraordinary

byre, cow-shed

ca'd, called

callant, youth

caller, fresh

candle-dowp, candle-end

canna, *cannae*, cannot

cannily, carefully

canny(ie), cautious, pleasant astute

cantrips, antics

canty, cheerful, pleasant

carline, like an old woman, witch-like

cateran, a Highland marauder or irregular fighting man

cauld, cold

cawed the shuttle, moved the shuttle to and fro

chafts, cheeks, mouth

chaipel, chapel

chapping, knocking

chield, young man, fellow

claes, clothes

clanjamfry, *clanjamphry*, rabble

clappermaclaw, scratched as if from fighting

claught, clutched, caught

claught of, hold of

cleikin, linking arms with

closs, close

clum, climbed

coble, small fishing boat

cold-rife, cold in temperament

collieshangie, uproar, disturbance

colloguing, chatting, scheming

collops, thickish slices of meat

corp, corpse

cowped, fell

cows, overtops, surpasses (this cows all: this beats everything)

crack(y), gossip, joke, friendly

craig, neck, throat; cliff

crap, crept

creel, in a, in confusion, perplexity

creish(y), fat, grease(y)

crunkle, wrinkle, small fold

cuif, idiot, simpleton

cushat-doves, wood pigeons, ring doves

cutty pipe, short pipe

dacent, decent

dadding, thudding, falling heavily

dae, do

daffing, playing the fool, play-acting

daft, mad

daidling, dallying, dawdling

dauchter, daughter

daunder, stroll

dauntons, scares, intimidates

daur, dare

dawtie, darling, dear

deave, deafen, plague someone about something

deid, dead

deil, *de'il*, devil

denner, dinner

diddling his elbock, moving his arm when playing the fiddle

didna(e), did not

ding, drive, beat

dinna(e), do not

dinnle, tremble, vibrate

dirl, ring, vibrate

distaste, dislike

divots, sods used for fuel, peat

doddered, withered

doer, agent

doit, small coin

donnered, dull, dazed, stupid

dowiest, dullest, most depressing

dowp, bottom, buttocks

drammach, mixture of raw oatmeal and water

draps, small shot, pellets

dreich, *dreigh*, dreary, slow, tedious

dreidfu', dreadful

dubs, pools of rainwater

duddy, ragged

duds, clothes

dunch, thump, bump

dwam, swoon, trance, daydream

een, eyes

eneuch, enough

evited, avoided, shunned

faither, father

fallows, fellows

fa'n, fallen

fand, found

farm-midden, dunghill

fash(ed), *trouble(d)*, bother

fecht, fight

feggs!, faith!

flaen, flown

fleeching, flattering

fleering, sneering

flegged, flew

flit, move, move house

fly up in the snuff, get into a rage

flyte, scold, chide, rail (at)

flyting, scolding, arguing match

forby, besides

forenoon, morning

forgie, forgive

forrit, forward

fowk, folk

frae, from

freen, friend

fu', full

fule, fool

fushionless, useless

fyke, fuss, commotion

fyle, foul

gaed, went

gang, go

gant, gasp, stutter

gar, make

gart me scunner, disgusted me

gash, ghastly

gauger, exciseman

gaun, gone

gey, *gey an*, very, rather

gie, give

girning, grimacing, grinning

glee'd, crooked

gless, glass, telescope

glisk, gleam, moment

gomeral, fool, idiot

goo, liking, relish

gowk, fool, idiot

gowl, howl, gust noisily (of wind)

gowst, gust

grat, wept

grue, shudder

guid, good

gutsey, greedy

gyte, mad

hadnae, had not

hae, have

hagging and hashing, hewing down and cutting up

hags, bogs, marshy ground

haith, a mild oath

hale, whole

halfling, adolescent (youth)

hame, home

hantle, considerable quantity

harle, small amount of something obtained with difficulty

hash, stupid, slovenly person; mess, muddle

haud, hold

hauldin, holding

havenae, have not

heid, head

hellicat, thoughtless young person, a good-for-nothing

het, hot

hingin', hanging

hirsled, dragged

hoast, cough

horn-mad, quite mad, thoroughly mad

hotching, fidgeting

howe, hill

hunkering, huddling

hunner, hundred

hurdies, buttocks

ilka, each

isnae, is not

ither, other

jaicket, jacket

jimp, just

jink, turn quickly to dodge someone or to escape notice

joes, sweethearts

jottering, fumbling

jyle, gaol

kale, cabbage

kale-stock, cabbage-stalk

keek, peep

keepit, kept

Kelpie, water demon, often in form of a horse

ken, know

kenna, not to know

kent, known

kist, chest

kitchen, condiment

kittle, delicate, subtle

knoiter, knock

knowe, knoll

kye, cows

kyte, belly, stomach

laigh, low, quietly

laigher, lower

land, tenement

lane, alone

lang, long

lang-heided, shrewd, wise

leddy, lady

lee, leeing, lie, lying

lee lane, all alone

lief, rather, prefer

yaird, yard
yearth, earth
yett, gate
yirk up, to move, raise jerkily
yon, that one, those over
    there, yonder
yont, further away

syne, then, since

tae, to, too
taigle, dally, drag the feet slowly
tane ... tither, the one ... the other
tangs, fand the, to find something where the Highlandman fand the tangs: to steal something, wrongly appropriate something
tass, cup
tauld, told
tenty, careful, prudent
thir, those
thocht, thought
thole, suffer, endure
thole-pins, rowlocks
thon, that, those
Thon Thing, That Thing (something not to be mentioned by name)
timmer, wooden, dull, stupid
tint, lost
tirl, rattle, beat
tod, fox
tow, rope
trokings, dealings
twa, two
twine, part, separate
tyke, dog, cur

uncanny, unnatural, strange
unchancy, unlucky, ill-fated
unco, onco, strange, weird, unfamiliar (also: very, extremely)
untenty, careless
usquebaugh, whisky (Gael.)

vivers, food, provisions

wab, web
wabster, weaver
wae, waefu', sad, sorrowful
waif word, single word, solitary word
waired, spent
wale, match, equal
wambly, shaky, unsteady
wame, belly, stomach
wanchancy, ill-omened, ill-fated
wark, work
warlock, ghost, possessed spirit
warstled, struggled, wrestled
wasna(e), was not
wauch, drink
wauf-like, disreputable
waur, whaur, worse
weicht, weight
well-kenned, well-known, reputable
wersh, insipid
wha, whae, who, whom
whaups, curlews
whatten, what kind of
wheen, few, small number
wheesht, silent
whilk, which
whilly-wha, flatter
whins, rocks, boulders
whin bush, gorse or furze
wi', with
wouldna(e), would not
writer, lawyer
wroucht, wrought
wrunkl't, wrinkled
wund, wind
wyte, blame

pyke, pick

quean, young woman (usually unmarried)

rade, rode
raired, roared
ran-dan, drinking match
raxing, stretching
redd out, arranged
redd up, organized, tidied
reid, red
richt, right
richt gate, right way
rickle, a pile, heap, tumbledown structure
rider, pedlar
rin, run
risp, knock
rive, tear, wrench, rend
rizzoring, drying in sun by way of curing (of fish)
rowt out, roar, bellow
rudas, wild, undisciplined

sae, so
saft, soft
sair, sore, sorely, greatly
sant, saint
sapless, spiritless
saul, soul
saut, salt
scabbit, infertile, bare
scrogs, stunted bushes
shouldnae, should not
shou'ther, shoulder
shune, soon
sib, related by blood
siller, silver
skaith, harm
skelloch, scream, shrill cry

skep, hive (for bees)
skirling, making a piercing sound
slestering, wetting, splashing
sma, small, little
smuisty, smoky (with thick, sulphurous smoke)
sneck, latch
sneck-draw, crafty, deceitful person
sneeshin, pinch of snuff (pseudo-Highland)
solan, soland goose, gannet
soople, astute, ingenious
sorners, beggars, spongers
sottering, making a burbling noise
soucht, sought
spae, foretell
spier, speer, ask
spledering, sprawling
sploring, wild in behaviour
spreagh, herd of cattle stolen and driven in a raid, esp. by Highlanders from the Lowlands
stane, stone
stave on, stagger, totter
steeked, closed (of eyes)
steer, stir, bustle
steighest, steepest
stend, sudden feeling
stot, bullock, clumsy person
stotter, stagger, totter
stotty, clumsy, stumbling
straucht, straight
stytering, faltering
sune, suner, soon, sooner
swat, sweat
swier, sweer, unwilling
swither, hesitate, be in doubt

limmer, old woman, hussy
loan, street, roadway
long syne, long ago
loof, palm of hand
loundered, aimed (at)
lout, bow, lower (the body)
lowped and flang, leaped and capered
lowpen, leaping, jumping
luckie, landlady
luntin', blazing

mails, travelling bags
mair, more
maist, most
maistly, mostly
maitter, matter
maun, must
micht (nae), might (not)
minting, suggesting, insinuating
mirkest, darkest
misdoubt, doubt, mistrust
mony, many
muckle, great, big, much
muirs, moors

na, nae, no
naething, nothing
nainsel, in pseudo-Highland speech the (male) speaker's way of referring to himself
nane, none
nebs, tips (of fingers)
neednae, need not
nicht, night
non-compearance, not appearing before a court (Sc. law)

o'. of
off-set, outset

ony, any
onyway, anyway
orra, odd, occasional, idle
ower, very, over
oxter, armpit

pack, friendly, intimate
panel, prisoner at the bar of the court, the accused
parritch, porridge
peat-hag, peat-bog
peat-reek, peat-smoke
pend, arch
philabeg, kilt
pibroch, classical or 'big' music of the bagpipes
pickle, a little
pickle corn, grain of corn
pirn, weaver's spool
pit, put
pit mirk, dark as the pit
plack, small coin, four pennies Scots
plaidneuk, small fold or flap in plaid used as pocket
pleisand, pleasant
plowter, pool
pock-puddens, steamed puddings, also derogatory term
precognitions, statements made by witness in initial investigation (Sc. law)
press bed, bed built into a recess with wooden doors
propone, advance or state in a court of law
pu'd, pulled
puddock, frog
puir, poor
pyats, magpies

THE WORLD'S CLASSICS

A Select List

JANE AUSTEN: Emma
Edited by James Kinsley and David Lodge

J. M. BARRIE: Peter Pan in Kensington Gardens & Peter and Wendy
Edited by Peter Hollindale

WILLIAM BECKFORD: Vathek
Edited by Roger Lonsdale

JOHN BUNYAN: The Pilgrim's Progress
Edited by N. H. Keeble

THOMAS CARLYLE: The French Revolution
Edited by K. J. Fielding and David Sorensen

GEOFFREY CHAUCER: The Canterbury Tales
Translated by David Wright

CHARLES DICKENS: Christmas Books
Edited by Ruth Glancy

MARIA EDGEWORTH: Castle Rackrent
Edited by George Watson

ELIZABETH GASKELL: Cousin Phillis and Other Tales
Edited by Angus Easson

THOMAS HARDY: A Pair of Blue Eyes
Edited by Alan Manford

HOMER: The Iliad
Translated by Robert Fitzgerald
Introduction by G. S. Kirk

HENRIK IBSEN: An Enemy of the People, The Wild Duck,
Rosmersholm
Edited and Translated by James McFarlane

HENRY JAMES: The Ambassadors
Edited by Christopher Butler

JOCELIN OF BRAKELOND:
Chronicle of the Abbey of Bury St. Edmunds
Translated by Diana Greenway and Jane Sayers

BEN JONSON: Five Plays
Edited by G. A. Wilkes

LEONARDO DA VINCI: Notebooks
Edited by Irma A. Richter

HERMAN MELVILLE: The Confidence-Man
Edited by Tony Tanner

PROSPER MÉRIMÉE: Carmen and Other Stories
Translated by Nicholas Jotcham

EDGAR ALLAN POE: Selected Tales
Edited by Julian Symons

MARY SHELLEY: Frankenstein
Edited by M. K. Joseph

BRAM STOKER: Dracula
Edited by A. N. Wilson

ANTHONY TROLLOPE: The American Senator
Edited by John Halperin

OSCAR WILDE: Complete Shorter Fiction
Edited by Isobel Murray

VIRGINIA WOOLF: Mrs Dalloway
Edited by Claire Tomalin

A complete list of Oxford Paperbacks, including The World's Classics, OPUS, Past Masters, Oxford Authors, Oxford Shakespeare, and Oxford Paperback Reference, is available in the UK from the Arts and Reference Publicity Department (BH), Oxford University Press, Walton Street, Oxford OX2 6DP.

In the USA, complete lists are available from the Paperbacks Marketing Manager, Oxford University Press, 200 Madison Avenue, New York, NY 10016.

Oxford Paperbacks are available from all good bookshops. In case of difficulty, customers in the UK can order direct from Oxford University Press Bookshop, Freepost, 116 High Street, Oxford, OX1 4BR, enclosing full payment. Please add 10 per cent of published price for postage and packing.